A Gallant Little Army

A Gallant Little Army

The Mexico City Campaign

Timothy D. Johnson

University Press of Kansas

Published by the University Press of Kansas (Lawrence, Kansas 66045), which was
organized by the Kansas Board of Regents and is operated and funded by Emporia State
University, Fort Hays State University, Kansas State University, Pittsburg State
University, the University of Kansas, and Wichita State University

ISBN 978-0-7006-1541-4

Printed in the United States of America

Book Club Edition

For Jayne

Contents

Acknowledgments   ix

Prologue   1

1. Veracruz: The Gibraltar of Mexico   9

2. Veracruz: The Slow, Scientific Process   30

3. The Army Advances: Olive Branch and Sword   52

4. Cerro Gordo: A Brilliant Affair   66

5. Cerro Gordo: Tomorrow Will Settle the Affair   84

6. Jalapa: Garden of Mexico   102

7. Puebla: Waiting All Summer   119

8. Puebla: Between the Devil and the Deep Sea   137

9. Into the Valley of Mexico: No Room for Error   151

10. The Battle of the Pedregal: Padierna and Churubusco   171

11. Mortification and Mistake: Armistice and Molino del Rey   194

12. God Is a Yankee: The Capture of Chapultepec   210

13. A Devil of a Time: Belén and San Cosme *Garitas*   227

14. The Preoccupations of the Occupation   242

Epilogue   266

Appendixes   273

Notes   297

Bibliography   345

Index   357

Acknowledgments

A project like this can not be completed without support, both technical and financial, and I have been fortunate enough to benefit from both. I am grateful to Yale University for a 2005 research fellowship that allowed me to mine the rich resources of the Beinecke Library. George Miles, Una Belau, and the rest of the Beinecke staff worked to ensure the success of my tenure there as a research fellow. In addition, I am indebted to the Virginia Historical Society for a 2002 research fellowship, and I especially wish to thank Charles Bryan, Nelson Lankford, Frances Pollard, and Greg Stoner for their valuable assistance. My home institution, Lipscomb University, also provided financial support and I am grateful for help with travel to distant repositories made possible by a David Laine Memorial Award. I especially wish to acknowledge the support of my college dean, Valery Prill.

Other individuals have rendered valuable assistance that warrants recognition and thanks. Kit Goodwin in the Special Collections Division of the University of Texas at Arlington Library, John White in the Manuscripts Division of the University of North Carolina Library, and Ann Lozano and Monica Rivera with the Benson Latin American Collection of the University of Texas at Austin Library made my work in those repositories pleasant and rewarding. To Carolyn Wilson and the following staff members at Lipscomb University's Beaman Library, I extent a heartfelt commendation and thanks: Judy Butler, Pam Eatherly, David Howard, Stacy Lusk, Susan Phifer, Rachel Pyle, Eunice Wells, and especially Marie Byers. The aforementioned Beaman staff members have often and graciously helped me locate resources and allowed me special privileges with noncirculating material. I also thank Robert Johannsen for his valuable role as an adjudicator in the early stages of this project. In addition, I am particularly indebted to Richard Bruce Winders for his careful reading of the entire manuscript and for his perceptive and constructive criticism. Few people know as much about the conflict with Mexico as Bruce, and his keen insights saved me from several pitfalls. Al Austelle rendered cordial and crucial aid in his capacity as Director of Instructional Technology at Lipscomb, and Jamie Johnson reproduced the maps and illustrations contained in this book. Maps are crucial to the reader of military history, and all of the maps in this book were reproduced from Donald S. Frazier's excellent encyclopedia *The United States and Mexico at War* (New

York: Macmillan, 1998), which were reprinted by permission of the Gale Group. Finally, for guiding me to places relevant to the Mexico City Campaign during a 1999 visit to Mexico, I thank David Brye, Andres Palacios Garcia, and Leopoldo Lagunes Figuera.

I also benefitted from the moral support of many people whose friendship I cherish. For their advice, encouragement, and in some cases for reading portions of this book in manuscript form, but most of all for the relationships we share, I thank the following people: Bill Collins, Jerry Gaw, Richard Goode, Bonnie Hooper, Robert Hooper, Glenn Johnson, Jennie Johnson, David Lawrence, Marc Schwerdt, Guy Swanson, Dwight Tays, Paul Turner, and Mark Williams. I continue to profit from the wise advice of my friend, Nathaniel Cheairs Hughes. During my periodic visits to Chattanooga, Nat is often gracious enough to sit with me over a cup of coffee and engage in discussions about our respective research projects. I am always the beneficiary of such meetings. Several students in my military history class read and commented on a portion of the manuscript, and I gratefully acknowledge their interest in this project: Finn Breland, Daniel Culbreath, Shaun Grubbs, Ben Ledger, Emily Nix, Gantt Pierce, and Robert Stevens. And thanks also to two more students, Grant Mullins and Reagan Thomas, whose enthusiastic interest in history is infectious.

There are also a host of individuals from my past who probably do not realize the formative influence they have had on me, and although all of their names cannot be mentioned here, their impact is remembered. I especially want to acknowledge four of my former professors and mentors who, despite the passage of two decades, continue to inspire. Howard Jones, Forrest McDonald, James Lee McDonough, and Grady McWhiney were and are scholars worthy of emulation. My parents, Hollis and Bea Johnson, and my sons, Garrett, Griffin, and Graham, have combined to be a great source of encouragement and inspiration. And once again it was a pleasure to work with Mike Briggs, Susan Schott, Larisa Martin, Susan McRory, and the rest of the staff at the University Press of Kansas. They are unfailingly cordial and professional, and especially sensitive to the peculiar quirks of authors—or at least to mine.

I have saved my deepest expression of gratitude for the person to whom I owe the greatest debt. Jayne is my friend, companion, confidant, and wife of twenty-eight years. I have benefitted from her insight, forethought, and wisdom, and I continue to be amazed at her unlimited capacity to love, nurture, understand, and forgive. Through her example, she exerts the kind of influence that makes those around her better. For her support and understanding and for her selfless sacrifices, I say an inadequate thank you. This book is the result of seven years and countless thousands of hours of work, and I dedicate it to her.

Let our people not altogether forget the ten thousand American soldiers who landed at Vera Cruz, the victorious and triumphant march to the capital of Mexico, and which never retreated an inch.
—J. Jacob Oswandel, First Pennsylvania
Infantry Regiment

Standing atop a hill called El Telégrafo, camera in hand, I scanned the countryside to the northeast. An adjoining hill, La Atalaya, rose directly in front of me, its rounded crest but a few hundred yards from where I stood. Behind it and as far as the eye could see were rows of hills and ridges, all of them green with vegetation. The panorama inspired awe and amazement—awe at the beauty of the landscape, and amazement in contemplating how 5,000 American soldiers with artillery in tow traversed that terrain to attack the left flank of the Mexican army. Some of the hills were so steep that the cannon had to be pulled up one side and let down the other by hand with ropes. I was standing at the critical point, the exact location of the Mexican flank on the Cerro Gordo battlefield, site of one of the most important engagements in the United States' war with Mexico. Here, on April 18, 1847, a desperate hand-to-hand struggle with muskets and bayonets drenched the crest of the hill with blood and sealed the American victory.

The small village of Cerro Gordo remains, but not much else. No signs designate it as the location where a Mexican army fought a bloody battle with the North Americans. A small stone marker sits on the southwest slope of El Telégrafo honoring Brigadier General Ciriaco Vásquez, who died there, but the vines and bushes that covered it hid even that memorial from public sight. The result of the battle probably explains why the locals choose not to honor the events that occurred in their backyards; nevertheless, the complete lack of commercialism on or around the battlefield surprised me. After all, as a Southerner who grew up in the shadow of Lookout Mountain and Missionary Ridge, and who has visited places like Shiloh and Stones River, I was accustomed to the losing side hallowing the locations of its greatest defeats.

Mexicans have not forgotten the battle or the disappointing results of the war; they simply prefer not to embrace such a national calamity. Most Americans, however, have forgotten this two-year war, or perhaps they have only a vague recollection of it, even though it resulted in the transfer of a sizable portion of the continent from Mexico to the United States. In forgetting the war, Americans also forget the sacrifice of approximately 13,000 American soldiers who died in it. One can go to places like Omaha Beach on the coast of France or to Bastogne, Belgium, and visit neatly manicured American cemeteries. There, thousands of white marble crosses and stars of David are routinely cleaned and respectfully maintained, as they should be. But what about men like Samuel Lauderdale from Tennessee, who died at Cerro Gordo and whose friends laid his body to rest on the bank of a nearby stream? Or William Eurick from Pennsylvania, who was killed during the Siege of Puebla and was buried in the city near the Plaza de San José? No one even knows the location of their final resting places.

This historical amnesia is unfortunate, for the Mexican War offers abundant intrigue and drama and produced its own anecdotes and heroes worth remembering. One of the most captivating stories from the war is a military campaign that, despite its relative obscurity, is one of the most brilliant operations in American history. It is typically called the Mexico City Campaign, and my interest in it is what compelled me to travel to Mexico in 1999 and retrace the route of the American army. During my journey across central Mexico, and through reading hundreds of pages of letters and diaries in manuscript repositories throughout the United States, I developed a fascination with this army. Following its path made me feel a certain bond with it, perhaps because of the knowledge that few others had visited the sites related to this great campaign. I wondered why no historian had ever written a book about it, and my visits to these locations created a growing sense of obligation to tell the army's story. Walking Collado Beach near Veracruz where it came ashore conjured images of a horizon cluttered with steam and sail naval vessels. I trudged up the hill to the Castle of Chapultepec with increased admiration for the soldiers who stormed the castle on September 13, 1847. On the morning of September 30, 1999, I experienced my first earthquake while sitting in an outdoor plaza in Puebla, and suddenly I could relate to the strange, disorienting feeling that many of the soldiers described in their letters after experiencing their first earthquake on October 2, 1847.

Numerous books that deal with this time period contain brief accounts or chapter overviews of the Mexico City Campaign. I first became interested in it in the 1990s while working on a biography of General Winfield Scott, who commanded the American army. In fact, that biography contains one of those "chapter overviews." However, the campaign and its participants deserve a book-length study. Many of the soldiers believed that they were participating in the greatest event of the nineteenth century and that their exploits would be forever remembered by their countrymen. But alas, they comprised an army whose conquest is largely forgotten. This is the story of that army and its quest.

In March 1847, an army of about 11,000 under Winfield Scott landed on the east coast of Mexico, and during the next six months, it marched over 250 miles, fought and won five major battles, inflicted enormous casualties on the Mexican army, captured that country's capital, pacified the country-side, and created favorable conditions for peace negotiations. It accomplished all of these things in the face of overwhelming odds. Unforeseen obstacles threatened the army's success, and some of them even emanated from the administration that sent it to war. The challenges included a president who distrusted his army commander and sought to replace him throughout the campaign, a constant lack of supplies and transportation, half the number of troops promised by the administration, an enemy army that at least doubled and sometimes tripled its numbers, and a potentially hostile foreign popula-tion on whom the army depended for its survival. Those factors were exter-nal, but the army also faced internal liabilities that had the potential to affect outcomes. They included animosity between regular army and volunteers, the termination of service for short-term enlistments two months into the campaign, disease that drained the life from thousands of soldiers and threat-ened to debilitate the army, and an ambitious officer corps competing with each other for glory and recognition.

The German chronicler of war, Carl von Clausewitz, called them the fric-tions of war—those unexpected obstacles that affect the course of a mili-tary campaign. In his famous study *On War,* he wrote about the difficulty of comprehending the problems associated with a military campaign for people who have never experienced war: "Everything looks simple; the knowledge required does not look remarkable, the strategic options are so obvious." Yet Clausewitz informs his reader that despite appearances, "the simplest thing is difficult" in war, and these "difficulties accumulate and end by producing a kind of friction" that ultimately reduces that army's level of performance.[1] In retrospect, the success of the Mexico City Campaign seems inevitable. It was not.

Scott's army encountered frictions in 1847, and one of the themes of this study is how he overcame them as he guided his small army deep into the enemy's country and all the way to its capital. It was a fascinating journey and a remarkable accomplishment. Despite the difficulties he encountered, some caused by his own men, Scott came to love his little band. Late in the cam-paign, after a particularly daring attack that routed the Mexican army, Scott, bursting with pride, exclaimed, "Glory to this gallant little army." Later, in a letter to Secretary of War William L. Marcy, he again referred to it as "this most gallant army." His affection for his men was obvious, and that affection was reciprocated.[2]

In January 1848, an American soldier named N. H. Clark arrived in Veracruz, Mexico. Ten months had passed since Scott's army landed and captured the coastal city. When Clark arrived, the United States Army occupied a line of posts from the coast stretching inland to Mexico City, and military action had ceased except for mounted troops that patrolled the roads in search of guerrilla bands. Although Clark was a latecomer to the theater of operations, his initial impression of the foreign country could easily have been written by any of the soldiers who arrived months earlier. "Every thing is new and novel to me, climate, people, habits, manners, customs, laws, religion, buildings, food etc.," thought Clark, "and to one who has never been out of his own country before, it fills him with curiosty and interest." It was indeed a new experience for all Americans who participated in this war far from home.[3]

However, the typical American soldier brought opinions with him to Mexico that were usually rooted in a belief in Anglo-Saxon superiority. Some of their opinions were preconceived, stereotypical, and prejudiced. They loved the beauty of the landscape and were intrigued with the differences that surrounded them, but they were often unimpressed with the people. "It is too good a country and too delightful a climate for so worthless a race," wrote Lt. William M. Gardner of the Second Infantry Regiment.[4] Many of the soldiers viewed their Mexican counterparts as ignorant, backward, and shiftless, a people kept in that state by the tyranny of a corrupt government and the oppression of a morally bankrupt Catholic church. To many American soldiers, the Catholic church in Mexico was but a manifestation of Old World corruption—a view that caused some to see the war as a redemptive crusade. They saw themselves as defenders of a better way of life, on a mission to expand the geographical boundaries of liberty and enlightenment.[5]

The war with Mexico was a turning point in American military history in at least two respects. One has to do with fighting a war outside the United States' borders. It was this country's first foreign war. There had been brief small-scale incursions into Tripoli in 1805 and British Canada during the Revolution and the War of 1812, but never before had U.S. forces attempted to operate at this level, distance, and duration in another country. All American wars since the one with Mexico, excluding the Civil War, have been expeditionary in nature. Some might contend that for the Union army, even the Civil War was expeditionary in nature. Waging war in a foreign country presented different and unprecedented challenges that American commanders had never before faced, and the questions that arose were manifold. How to maintain order and discipline in an army when the soldiers are beyond

the reach of civil law? How to treat civilians in occupied areas? How to provide for punishment not just of offending American soldiers but of Mexican
civilians as well? What rules will govern the gathering of supplies in a foreign land? Scott addressed all of the questions that tend to pose a dilemma
for an invading army, and the way he confronted them makes the Mexico
City Campaign unique. The army's ability to march through enemy country depended on discipline within its own ranks and the acquiescence of the
Mexican population. This study argues, as did my 1998 biography of Scott,
that the commanding general devised a sophisticated pacification plan that
was ahead of its time. Furthermore, this effort to placate the people, coupled
with Scott's willingness to stop military operations after major battles in the
hope that the enemy would seek to negotiate, indicates that Scott had adopted
a strategy of moderation. Although he ultimately captured Mexico City, he
repeatedly showed an inclination to halt his campaign short of the capital if
only the Mexicans would concede. In other words, his intention was not to
wage an unlimited war of destruction. Rather, it was to apply only as much
pressure as was necessary to end the war.

This war was also a turning point because of the level to which the army
utilized training and professionalism to accomplish its objective, and no other
army in the war better illustrates that than Scott's. The seeds of a professional American army had been sown years earlier, some of them by Scott
himself, and in this conflict the country witnessed the results. The war with
Mexico marks the first major conflict in which West Point graduates comprised a majority of the officer corps, and Scott relied heavily on their engineering and reconnaissance skills. Indeed, he credited his young engineer
officers with getting the army to Mexico City. Some of the army's crack regiments were led by young lieutenants and captains who were imbued with not
only practical knowledge but also with a sense of professionalism that had
never before been seen in American history. More than 130 officers in the
army later rose to the rank of general during the Civil War, and they carried
with them memories from Mexico that influenced their Civil War generalship. The proper role of a staff officer, the value of extensive reconnaissance,
the benefits that accrue from protecting civilian lives and property, the rapid
success that results from flank attacks, the need to occasionally resort to the
bloody bayonet assault in order to root out a stubborn opponent—these were
among the lessons learned in Mexico. In many respects, the Mexican War
served as a training ground.

Historians have produced excellent studies of the Mexican War over the
years. Justin Smith's old two-volume work, *The War with Mexico*, remains a
valuable but admittedly biased study. Another dated but still useful study is
Robert Selph Henry's *The Story of the Mexican War*. The most solid, scholarly

study that focuses on military aspects of the war remains K. Jack Bauer's *The Mexican War, 1846–1848*, while John S. D. Eisenhower wrote his account, *So Far from God: The U.S. War with Mexico, 1846–1848*, for a popular audience. Digging beneath the military events, other historians have produced important books that uncover additional layers of the conflict. Robert W. Johannsen's *To the Halls of the Montezumas* deals with how American society in the 1840s perceived the war. James M. McCaffrey in *Army of Manifest Destiny: The American Soldier in the Mexican War, 1846–1848*, and Richard Bruce Winders in *Mr. Polk's Army: The American Military Experience in the Mexican War*, provide two very different kinds of studies of the experience of the common soldier in Mexico. Winders is also the author of a book entitled *Crisis in the Southwest: The United States, Mexico, and the Struggle over Texas*, which is one of the best accounts of the events leading up to the war. Paul Foos's book, *A Short, Offhand, Killing Affair: Soldiers and Social Conflict during the Mexican-American War*, depicts a darker side of the conflict and often portrays American soldiers in an unfavorable light. In *Doniphan's Epic March: The 1st Missouri Volunteers in the Mexican War*, Joseph G. Dawson chronicles the invasion of northern Mexico by another American force. The following books take a closer look at the Mexican perspective: William A. DePalo's *The Mexican National Army, 1822–1852*, Irving W. Levinson's *Wars within War: Mexican Guerrillas, Domestic Elites, and the United States of America, 1846–1848*, and Robert L. Scheina's *Santa Anna: A Curse upon Mexico*. Finally, Donald S. Frazier edited what will likely remain for generations the best reference work on the conflict. *The United States and Mexico at War: Nineteenth-Century Expansionism and Conflict* is thorough, balanced, and authoritative. This is but a sampling, and one can readily see that a host of authors have covered various aspects of the war from different perspectives except, of course, Scott's Mexico City Campaign.

My intention was to write a book that would fill a long-existing void. In addition to dealing with leadership issues in the army's high command—the conduct of the campaign, the often shaky relationships among the generals, and civil-military relations—I have also tried to write from the perspective of the lower ranks. Wherever possible, I have allowed the soldiers who did the fighting to tell the story, and to that end I have incorporated many quotes from letters and diaries. This is the best way to provide a window through which the reader catches a glimpse of the ideas and attitudes of the participants. In weaving their words into this narrative, I opted to leave their passages just the way I found them in the primary sources, shunning the practice of indicating the obvious to the reader with the intrusive "[*sic*]." I have been especially attentive to reproduce the quotes exactly as they appear in the original texts so that when the reader encounters a misspelled word or incorrect punctuation, as in the misspelling of the word "curiosity" in the Clark quote above, he or she can safely assume that the soldier wrote it that way. The soldiers' own words provide rich insights into their opinions regarding battles, generals, friendships, and personal ambition as well as their biases concerning race and religion and their feelings of superiority.

The campaign began on March 9, when Scott's army landed at Veracruz and ended with the occupation of Mexico City on September 14. If one counts the four-day bombardment of Veracruz, two days of fighting at Cerro Gordo, a two-day battle around the Pedregal just south of Mexico City, and one day each for the battles at Molino del Rey and Chapultepec, that 190-day time period saw only 10 days of fighting. In the account that follows, I cover those battles in eight chapters, but I also devote a significant portion of the book to the issues that occupied the other 180 days of the campaign.

It might also be useful to the reader to know at the outset what this book is not. It is not an attempt to provide the Mexican side of the conflict, except where some context is necessary. Neither does it endeavor to provide an account of, or assign blame to, the causes of the conflict. I also chose not to provide detailed treatment of the months following the capture of Mexico City, which would involve a range of issues very different from the six-month military campaign. Tracking down guerrillas and setting up a system of taxation in Mexican towns and cities to help pay for the war are essential components of the occupation phase and worthy of an in-depth study. However, that aspect of the war in central Mexico, although no less important, was ancillary and almost anticlimactic to the march from Veracruz to Mexico City, and an entire book would be required to do it justice. I will leave that study for some other historian.

Also, a note about word usage is in order. The term *American* can be used to refer to South Americans and Central Americans as well as North Americans. However, because writing about the "Americans" is so much more convenient and less awkward than writing about the "United States soldiers" or "members of the North American army," I use the term *American* repeatedly in reference to those who are obvious to the reader, which is in keeping with the way others have used it when writing about the war. I also use the modern spelling *Monterey* and *Veracruz* rather than the old forms *Monterrey* and *Vera Cruz*.

The Mexico City Campaign, like all other military operations, provides an opportunity to observe the best and the worst of humanity. The individual soldiers brought to the army different attitudes and beliefs as dissimilar as the geographic regions from which they came. However, collectively, they gave the army the diversity to accommodate all of the following descriptive terms: brilliant, determined, sacrificial, heroic, benevolent, brave, incompetent, cruel, racist. The outward displays of personal conduct ranged from heroic and honorable to cowardly and unscrupulous, and the inward motivations that produced these acts also ran the gamut from patriotic and charitable to prejudiced and insubordinate. In war, some things never change.

There is a sense in which the Mexican War is like any other war, and that has to do with the evolution that often occurs in the mind of the soldier. When N. H. Clark arrived in occupied Veracruz, he was at the base of operations in central Mexico. It was the conduit through which all supplies flowed inland to the various elements of the army. It was also the beginning and ending point for every soldier's experience in Mexico as new recruits arrived and veterans left, and in both situations, soldiers painted a familiar picture. Those just arriving and preparing to march inland to join the army were excited and curious, anxious to make a name for themselves—according to Clark, "full of ambition, hope and chivalry." However, those who reached the coastal city on their way home, those who had tasted battle and who had had their thirst for excitement quenched, painted a different picture, and the contrast was striking to Clark. They arrived "broken down, out of health and despirited—many minus an arm or leg destined to be cripples all their life." It was an "unfortunate" type of glory, thought Clark, who concluded, "I would much prefer being killed."[6] Such is war, and such was the Mexico City Campaign.

CHAPTER ONE

Veracruz

The Gibraltar of Mexico

What a pity it is that Mexico wont succumb to the idea of our
power and thus render a demonstration of it unnecessary! It would
save a deal of trouble and expense.
—J. C. Phelps, American soldier

Major General Winfield Scott stood on the wooden deck of the steamer *Massachusetts* and watched as his men climbed from their large transport vessels into smaller landing craft. It was a warm afternoon, 85 degrees, with a gentle southeasterly breeze, barely strong enough to make a ripple on the water's smooth surface. Each soldier carried a three-day ration of bread and meat in his haversack and sixty rounds of ammunition for his .69 caliber smoothbore musket. The boats they climbed into were specially constructed beach landing craft made of white oak and white pine and constructed in Philadelphia at a cost of $795 per vessel. Each craft held about forty-five men, or half a company. These surfboats, identical on both ends, could be steered with a single oar in either direction to facilitate repeated trips from ship to shore. Although Scott had requested 141 of them, only 67 were completed in time to be used. After several hours of loading, the boats were sorted and tied off to the steamer *Princeton*.[1]

Soon after 5:00 P.M., as the sun sank in the western sky, the report of a signal gun marked the beginning of the largest amphibious assault in American history before World War II. Sailors cut the towlines releasing the surfboats for their first trip to the beach, and oarsmen began to row furiously as if in a race to cover the 450 yards to shore. Packed on the decks of the transports, other soldiers awaiting their turn to go ashore gave a shout, and bands began to play the "Star Spangled Banner" as the long line of boats plied their way toward the coast. Curious onlookers from British, French, and Spanish ships anchored nearby also watched the grand spectacle. The first wave of more than 2,500 men, one-fourth of the American army, affixed bayonets to their muskets in case they met resistance on the beach. Before reaching the surf, the shriek of artillery shells passed overhead from shallow draft steamers assigned to cover the landing. They were aimed at the scattered sand dunes

Major General Winfield Scott.
Courtesy of the author.

dotting the terrain 150 yards from the beach, where enemy cavalry had been spotted earlier in the afternoon.[2]

The date was March 9, 1847, and the war with Mexico was nearing the end of its first year. From his vantage point on the *Massachusetts*, Scott could see the entire stretch of coastline called Collado Beach, which he and Commodore David Conner had selected days earlier as the landing site. Collado Beach was located two miles south of the port city of Veracruz, and the Americans hoped to capture the city as the first step in establishing a firm foothold in central Mexico, and in so doing shift the focus of the war away from the north. For a year, American armies had been operating in the northern part of the country and had fought and won important battles, but they had been unable to bring the war to a close. To force the Mexicans to surrender, Scott, in his *Memoirs,* wrote that his army had "to strike, effectively, at the vitals of the nation."[3] Veracruz, if it could be captured, would serve as a base of operations for his army to march inland and threaten the enemy capital at Mexico City 260 miles away. Thus, the Mexico City Campaign represented a new strategy in the American effort to win the war.

Seizing the port city would be no easy feat because of its impressive defenses. A triangular wall fifteen feet high stretched around Veracruz, with a strong cannon-studded fort located at each angle. Fort Concepción stood at the northern end of the long waterfront wall, and on the angle at the southern end was Fort Santiago. At both of these forts, the wall turned inland and eventually met to form the third angle of the triangle at Fort Santa Barbara. Spaced between these large bastions were nine smaller forts, each mounting additional guns. Granite, coral, and bricks along with lime cement constituted the primary materials of the wall, and manning the fortifications were 3,360 men. The most impressive aspect of the city's defenses was the castle of San Juan de Ulúa standing a thousand yards offshore and dominating the water approach to the city. This quadrangle fortress rose sixty feet above a base that rested on Gallega Reef, and atop its stone walls rested 150 guns of various types. Within its walls were an additional 1,030 defenders. The city's intimidating defenses caused some soldiers, like Samuel Lauderdale, to refer to Veracruz as "the Gibraltar of Mexico." T. H. Towner predicted in a letter to his father that capturing San Juan de Ulúa will "certainly be the great fight of the war, indeed the greatest which has ever taken place on the American continents."[4] But the castle's strength is precisely what Scott sought to avoid by landing his army over two miles away. He would approach the city from the land side, thus negating the powerful seaward defenses.

For an old soldier like Scott, the scene was a sublime and majestic pageant. Surfboats stretched for hundreds of yards; naval gunfire whizzed overhead as they moved steadily toward land. From Scott's vantage point in the Gulf of Mexico, the snow-capped peak of Mount Orizaba, which reached an altitude of 17,400 feet, was sometimes visible late in the afternoon despite a distance of a hundred miles. It was late in the day, an hour before sunset, as the first boats touched sand. The landing at Veracruz set into motion a carefully planned operation that had been incubating since the previous fall. The masterful execution of the campaign would be the crowning achievement of Scott's career, and he hoped it might even win for him the prize he always had coveted: the presidency.

Like Orizaba, which towered above everything around it, Scott was the preeminent military giant of his day. A hero from the War of 1812, he had won fame fighting along the Niagara River where, in 1814, a British bullet had smashed into his left shoulder, scaring him for life. He did not fare well leading troops against the Seminole Indians in Florida in 1836, but he rejuvenated his reputation by demonstrating genuine diplomatic skill during the

Canadian border disputes of the 1830s and 1840s. However, periodically during his career, his ambition and temperamental disposition had caused him to become embroiled in bitter disputes with fellow officers and presidents. He had always envisioned himself as an aristocratic general out of the old European mold, which resulted in his condescending nature. Scott's strict enforcement of discipline and love of ornate uniforms had won him the soubriquet "Old Fuss and Feathers." He realized one of his life objectives in 1841 when he became the commanding general of the United States Army. He possessed both the image and the title to which younger officers aspired. He was a large man too, six feet, four inches tall, and had an ego to match. His legendary arrogance and penchant for indiscreet letter writing had resulted in a turbulent relationship with President James K. Polk, who had appointed Scott to field command in Mexico only as a last resort.

Their trouble began at the outset of the war ten months earlier, when Polk assigned Scott to take command of Brigadier General Zachary Taylor's army on the Rio Grande. The war was unpopular with the opposition Whig Party, and that made the prompt and vigorous prosecution of the conflict a political imperative. For Polk and the Democratic Party, the war was about land acquisition, but politics and an impatient public dictated that it be limited in both time and money. But Scott had a penchant for planning and for not moving until all of his plans were in place. A week after Scott's May 13 appointment, he was still in Washington, drafting orders, requisitioning supplies, and formulating strategy, all of which caused the president to conclude that Scott was too "scientific and visionary." The commanding general was all talk and no action, thought administration officials, and his delays were an embarrassment. Scott was not sympathetic to the president's political dilemma. But Polk had a knack for partisanship to go with his lack of understanding of the military prerequisites for waging war. Polk misinterpreted Scott's cautious planning for unnecessary lethargy, and this disconnect provided the bases for mutual misunderstandings from the outset. Furthermore, Scott's Whig affiliation and his presidential aspirations did not foster an atmosphere of cooperation between the two. So the president instructed Secretary of War William L. Marcy to prod the general into action. On May 21, Scott's arrogance took over, and he responded to the administration's push with a politically charged letter to Marcy. He informed the secretary that he was too smart a soldier to leave the capital without covering his back. "My explicit meaning is—that I do not desire to place myself in the most perilous of all positions:—*a fire upon my rear, from Washington and the fire, in front, from the Mexicans.*"[5]

The president exploded with anger. Now convinced that Scott's "foolish, & vindictive" letter proved his hostility toward the administration, Polk re-

President James K. Polk.
Courtesy Tennessee State
Library and Archives.

sponded in kind by rescinding Scott's appointment to field command. News of Taylor's victories earlier in the month at Palo Alto and Resaca de la Palma made Polk's decision possible. Previously, the president thought that Taylor lacked the capacity to prosecute the war effectively, but now he revised his opinion, decided to keep Taylor in command, and relegated Scott to a desk job in Washington. Although Scott remained Taylor's superior, he would serve essentially as a chief of staff, shuffling papers in the nation's capital. Scott was shocked by the decision, but Polk had demonstrated that he could be as obstinate as the general—and vindictive as well. Scott had gambled on his lofty position making him invulnerable, and he had lost.

Scott was out of his office on the evening that Marcy's message arrived informing him of the president's decision, and he quickly responded with another damaging letter. This one was not insubordinate, but awkward and silly. In an apologetic tone, he explained that he had just stepped out for "a hasty plate of soup" when the secretary's letter arrived—his way of assuring the administration that his hours were long and incessant. He explained that he intended no ill will toward the president in his May 21 letter, and that, while he preferred field command, he would dutifully accept whatever assignment the president gave him. His attempt to smooth things over failed, and as Polk wrote in his diary, Scott "now sees his error no doubt, but it is too late." All of the talk surrounding this incident prompted Congress to ask the administration to make public its correspondence with Scott, and the "hasty plate of soup" passage caused him considerable grief. It was the subject of many jokes around Washington and in the press. When Marcy hastily wrote a brief missive to a friend, he followed it the next day jokingly explaining, "I wrote you a 'hasty plate of soup' letter yesterday." "I have been exceedingly ridiculed" over it, Scott complained to a friend, and in his *Memoirs* two decades later, he remembered that his political opponents "maliciously" used the phrase against him with "much glee." Such humiliation had so defanged Scott that Marcy could boast in late June, "Scott is harmless."[6]

For the time being, Taylor remained in the spotlight as the principal field commander in Mexico. Secretary of State James Buchanan spent the summer in a fruitless effort to end the war through diplomacy, and Scott went about his duties in his assigned purgatory in Washington, diligently attending to the army's logistical needs. By October, three things had happened to rehabilitate his opportunity for field command. First, Taylor had won three battles and had occupied several towns in northern Mexico, and as a consequence of his growing hero status, he was being mentioned as a potential presidential candidate in 1848. The fact that this general, once thought to be apolitical, turned out to be a Whig caused the president to view him as a threat. Second, after his most recent victory at Monterey, Taylor had agreed to a two-month armistice and had granted to the defeated Mexican army generous terms that the administration believed to be too lenient and time consuming. These developments produced distrust and dismay in Washington. A third consideration completed the process of bringing Scott back into the president's orbit, if only reluctantly. The realization that battlefield victories and occupied territory in northern Mexico had done little to bring the opposing government to the peace table now made it obvious that the administration needed a new strategy.

That new strategy began to emerge in late summer but took clear shape in the last half of October. Although the administration had banished Scott from field command, it had not entirely ostracized him. In fact, Polk and Marcy had depended on him heavily in conducting the war and formulating plans. With Scott as the chief military advisor, if not the catalyst, the administration began to look for a way to strike at the heart of Mexico. Several ideas had surfaced over the weeks as they considered options, and gradually the blueprint for the Mexico City Campaign emerged. The general parameters of the plan called for the capture of the port city of Veracruz, which had a population of 15,000, and, using the good roads that emanated from there to the interior of the country, march on Mexico City 260 miles away.[7]

Scott gave the campaign plan definitive form on October 27, 1846, when, at the request of the president, he submitted to the War Department a five-page paper called "Vera Cruz & Its Castle." In it, he called for an invasion force of 10,000 men with appropriate cavalry and artillery. Aware of San Juan de Ulúa's strength, he insisted that the castle posed a significant threat and was the key to capturing the city. He went on to suggest a possible attack from the land side and a willingness to use siege tactics. However, despite the importance of capturing the city and the castle, both would be of limited value by themselves. "To conquer a peace, I am now persuaded that we must take the city of Mexico, or place it in imminent danger of capture." The plan called for an American army to march through three Mexican states, Veracruz, Puebla, and Mexico, with a combined population of over 2.3 million, or roughly a third of the country's total. Success, Scott argued, depended on augmenting the army to 20,000 and getting it away from the coast before the arrival of the deadly yellow fever season in the spring. He understood that the army could be ravaged and debilitated without firing a shot.[8]

The plan impressed Polk with its grasp of both military requirements and political considerations. Now that Taylor had fallen out of grace, the president needed a general, preferably a Democrat, who could execute the new strategy and bring the war to a successful conclusion. After considering a list of available candidates and finding none of them up to the task, the president and his cabinet began to gravitate back to the architect of the plan. Scott appeared to be not just the most logical choice but, in fact, the only viable one. Daily consultations with Scott during the three weeks after the submission of his "Vera Cruz & Its Castle" paper helped convince Polk of the obvious. On November 19, he called Scott to his office and offered him command of the new army that would be raised to invade central Mexico. He admonished Scott, however, to show support for the administration. The government and the army commander must share a common confidence in each other, Polk chided. Scott agreed and pledged his cooperation. Now willing to demonstrate a sensitivity to the president's political predicament, Scott consented to balance his officer corps with some prominent Democrats chosen by the president. Scott had worked tirelessly over the summer and fall to win the president's confidence. He believed that his appointment was evidence that he had succeeded, and with a grateful spirit, he acted in good faith.

Polk, however did not. Just the day before, he had told Democratic Senator Thomas Hart Benton that if he could get Congress to approve the creation of the rank of lieutenant general, he would appoint Benton to supersede Scott. The following month, Polk confided in his diary that appointing Scott was actually "a choice of evils"—or more precisely, a choice of Whig evils. Benton was a former militia officer and veteran of the War of 1812, but his primary qualification was political status. Polk apologized to fellow Democrats for the political makeup of the army's officer corps, and he lobbied key senators for weeks, but in the end, he lacked adequate support to make his scheme a reality.[9]

The campaign strategy that Scott had articulated resulted from an eighteenth-century mind-set. He possessed extensive knowledge of warfare from a time and place when wars were limited in nature and fought for limited objectives. The Polk administration's chief goal, the acquisition of land, was a limited objective, and Scott's approach to achieving it was limited as well. He nowhere mentioned or planned the destruction of the Mexican army, nor did he devise a strategy to overthrow the Mexican government. His plan was to apply steadily graduated levels of pressure until the enemy agreed to stipulated terms. Thus, he used terminology like "conquering a peace," not "conquering the enemy." And although his plan called for an invasion and a march on Mexico City, he left open the possibility of ending the war by merely placing the capital in "imminent danger of capture." Understanding Scott's war of moderation at the outset helps bring into clearer focus his motivation during the campaign to stop military operations after every battle. Winning on the battlefield and moving his army a step closer to Mexico City represented leverage, and Scott intended to apply just enough leverage to conquer a peace. Any more than that was militarily unnecessary and unnecessarily bloody. Evidence of Scott's moderate approach would become apparent as the campaign unfolded.

This aspect of the Mexico City Campaign was backward looking, but there was another facet that was forward looking. Scott was ahead of his time in contemplating how to deal with a potentially hostile citizenry as his army marched through Mexico. He understood the need to enforce strict discipline among soldiers in a foreign land for two reasons: to maintain the honor of the army and to pacify the inhabitants. Reports that came out of northern Mexico indicated that men in Taylor's army had engaged in all manner of atrocities, including rape and murder, and ample evidence indicated that volunteers were more frequent offenders than regulars. Such conduct could only create hostility among the Mexicans, who might then retaliate by rising up in a guerrilla war. The problem for Scott was that Congress had not anticipated an American army operating outside the borders of the United States. Therefore, it had never included in Articles of War provisions for punishing soldiers for crimes that were already punishable under civil law. But civil courts could not try Americans soldiers for offenses committed outside the United States. Scott had been contemplating this dilemma since summer, and his solution was to use martial law. Wherever his army went in Mexico, martial law would be in effect, outlawing assault, murder, rape, robbery, disruption of religious services, and destruction of property. Soldiers who violated these strictures would be tried in a military court and dealt with severely. Martial law was the centerpiece of a sophisticated pacification program, and it indicated his commitment to a strategy of moderation. The administration responded to Scott's unprecedented martial law proposal with a mixture of apprehension, skepticism, and, in the case of the attorney general, alarm, none of which deterred the general.[10]

Martial law was but one part of a dual approach to maintain order and pacify the Mexican countryside. The second, and complementary part, of Scott's plan was to purchase food and supplies from the Mexican people rather than resort to forced requisitions, which was common practice among invading armies. Taking what the army needed by force or allowing individual soldiers to freely forage on the general populace would constitute a dangerous practice that certainly, as Scott knew, would alienate the Mexican people. It would also foster the kind of reprisals that had already occurred in northern Mexico, where Taylor's men had not been held to the same standards that Scott envisioned for his army. The administration had encouraged Taylor to purchase his supplies in the early months of the war, but now the cost of the conflict presented a growing political problem in Washington. Scott, however, would not succumb to cost-cutting pressure from the administration. The erudite Scott conceived his two-part pacification strategy as a result of his study of the Napoleonic Wars. He was well aware of Napoleon's mistakes when France invaded Spain in 1808 and Russia in 1812, and he was determined not to repeat them.[11]

Scott needed an army to begin his campaign. He got it from two sources: newly authorized volunteer units and the transfer of a sizable portion of Taylor's army. The former caused delays and the latter caused animosity. Scott requisitioned from Taylor's command 4,000 regulars and 3,250 volunteers, ordering them to rendezvous at two locations on the coast, Brazos near the mouth of the Rio Grande and Tampico farther south. From those points, they would be transported to Lobos Island sixty-five miles below Tampico, where they would meet the new regiments and from which the entire army would make its descent on Veracruz. But losing the bulk of his command meant that Taylor would have to assume a defensive posture while the focus of the war (and of the public's attention) shifted to another theater of operations. He was not happy, nor were many of his men, to learn of the transfer of some of his best units. A junior officer in Taylor's army, Dabney Maury from

Virginia, was in Monterey when he heard that Scott intended to take many of Taylor's men away. "This caused much talk among us," he noted, "for Taylor had won the unbounded confidence and love of all of us, while Scott was sneered at as 'Old Fuss and Feathers.'" All of this naturally meant that Taylor was being relegated to a secondary role, which convinced him that Polk and Scott were conspiring against him.[12]

Despite Scott's efforts to soothe Taylor's ruffled ego, the latter avoided a meeting with the commanding general when he arrived on the Rio Grande in December. Without assistance from Taylor, Scott issued marching orders to the various units in Taylor's army, then waited for several weeks at Brazos for troops to arrive. During his extended stay along the Rio Grande, tension resurfaced with the administration as a result of two events. One had to do with a newspaper article wherein Polk's friend, Senator Benton, claimed to be the originator of the idea to seize Veracruz and march on Mexico City. After reading it, Scott wrote an angry letter to Marcy reminding the secretary that the plan "was derived from me!!" Then, perhaps because he was outside Washington and somehow felt beyond the president's grasp, he boldly lectured Marcy that "this is, from a *high quarter*, opening a fire upon my rear." Benton's actions, Scott continued, constitute "a crossfire, upon rear & front, with a vengence." This letter came only days after a conciliatory one to Marcy in which he had expressed his gratitude for the confidence the administration had shown in him. "It shall be justified in my public & private acts," he assured Marcy. "I laid down *whiggism*," he explained, and "I have felt very like a Polk-man." Whatever honeymoon might have existed between the general and the president, however, would soon end.[13]

The other source of friction concerned the commander of the Second Dragoons, Colonel William S. Harney. Scott had ordered him to send seven troops of cavalry to the coast and remain with his other three troops under Taylor's command. The high-spirited and brave Harney could also be vulgar and insubordinate. His cruelty was well known within the army, the result of his inhumane treatment of Indians during the Seminole War in Florida and from an incident in 1844 in which he beat an enlisted man almost to death for refusing to dig a latrine. For the latter, he was court-martialed and suspended from the army for four months. The previous summer, he had run afoul of one of his superiors for insubordination. Harney was anxious to distinguish himself in Mexico, so now he defied Scott's orders and proceeded to the coast with his troops. For this latest infraction, his division commander filed charges against him, and the court ordered him reprimanded. However, at this point, Scott magnanimously stepped in and changed his order to allow Harney to join him on the coast. The commanding general noted that Harney was "influenced by a laudable desire to lead his regiment into battle." Because

Harney was a Democrat, Polk, after hearing about the pending court-martial but before knowing the outcome of the case, ordered Marcy to send Scott a chastising letter demanding Harney's reinstatement to command. Polk charged that Scott had acted "arbitrarily" and in a way that revealed his political bias. It was Polk, however, who had acted with prejudice.[14]

Scott left some of his men at Brazos to await transports and proceeded on to Tampico, where he found a sizable number of volunteers and regulars preparing to sail for Lobos Island. Shops and grog houses of every description provided ample opportunities for party and vice. During his brief stay in Tampico, Lieutenant George McClellan reportedly enjoyed champagne dinners, parties, and fandangos attended by numerous officers like George G. Meade and John Magruder, both future Civil War generals but on opposite sides. At one such event, Meade informed his wife in a letter that he enjoyed dancing with English- and French-speaking ladies, but those who spoke Spanish held no attraction for him. He assured her that "to the Mexican girls, . . . I had but little to say. There was no beauty, and the prettiest girls would not have been noticed in one of our ball rooms." When Scott arrived, he found the guardhouse full of soldiers who had been arrested for intoxication, fighting, insubordination, and a host of other offenses. So, to maintain discipline, he issued General Order Number 20, which declared martial law.[15]

Scott had hoped to land his army at Veracruz by this time, but delays caused by a lack of supplies, horses, artillery, and shipping caused a daily revision of the invasion date. Now in mid-February he needed to bring his army together at Lobos as quickly as possible. Already volunteer regiments were arriving there. Consequently, after only a few days at Tampico, he prepared the troops for departure. On February 19, he drafted orders in typical Scott fashion—fastidious and with attention to every detail. On boarding the ships, equal numbers of troops were to be assigned to each side of the vessel, and no one was permitted "to loiter or sleep on the opposite side." His instructions included a demand for "frequent fumigations . . . between decks," using either brimstone with sawdust or nitre with vitriolic acid. In the event that one of the severe storms called *northers* arose, Scott also gave instructions, and in so doing gave meaning to his moniker "Old Fuss and Feathers." "In bad or heavy weather, the men . . . will remain steadily at their assigned quarters; nor are they, when the ship careens, to shift their position."[16]

Scott and the Tampico contingent arrived at Lobos on February 21. Several volunteer regiments were already there: the First and Second Pennsylvania, along with the Palmetto Regiment from South Carolina, were on hand. Parts of the Louisiana, New York, and Mississippi regiments had also arrived. The Isle of Lobos, which sat eight miles off the coast of Mexico, was about a mile long and a half mile wide, a beautiful tropical island with lush vegetation that, from a distance, looked like "a green speck or bubble, floating upon the blue." The earliest soldiers to arrive fought off lizards, sand crabs, and rats to clear space for the army that would soon be gathering there. Scott arrived to find the beach lined with tents and the camp already christened "Camp Winfield." He also found an outbreak of smallpox among the Pennsylvania troops and ordered them quarantined. While there, he informed Commodore David Conner that he was still waiting for troops and ships to arrive. In addition, he complained that many of his surfboats had not arrived, nor had over half of his supply wagons and two-thirds of his ordnance. Furthermore, the volunteer units suffered from a lack of food. However, bold leadership cannot wait for every detail to fall into place, and Scott knew that other expedients dictated that he forge ahead as quickly as possible—chief among them, the need to capture Veracruz and get away from the coast before the yellow fever season. Units continued to trickle in during the remaining days of February until the numbers reached about 10,000. He never received all of the supplies that he requested, but by March 2, he knew that he could wait no longer. Late that day Scott ordered their departure for Anton Lizardo, an anchorage several miles below the invasion site.[17]

Seven days later, on the thirty-third anniversary of his promotion to general, Scott watched as the first wave of his invasion army reached Collado Beach. As the boats reached the surf, the soldiers jumped overboard into waist-deep water and, holding their muskets over their heads, rushed up onto the sand. They "took the beach in beautiful style," with members of the Sixth Infantry first to plant their colors on shore. As they waded onto dry land, they formed under their regimental flags as officers sent skirmishers forward toward the sand hills. Moments later, all of them rushed to occupy the dunes and plant the American flag. From the fleet came a cheer. George W. Kendall, cofounder of and contributor to the pro-war New Orleans *Picayune*, traveled with Scott's army, and after watching the landing, thought that "It would take a page of our paper to give full effect to the description of the first landing of our troops . . . a more stirring spectacle has probably never been witnessed in America." Back on the transport steamers, soldiers who had feared a bloody fight on the beach and were happy not to be among the first to land now felt envy for those who were.[18]

An interesting lot comprised Scott's little army. A division of regulars belonging to Scott's old friend, William Worth, held the honor of landing first. Worth had served on Scott's staff during the War of 1812 and was a veteran of the Seminole War in Florida. A beaver cap covered his graying hair; he was average size and a good horseman. Soldiers had widely divergent views of Worth's abilities. A volunteer said that he was "a very great favorite" in the army, and that "his popularity [was due] to his great military talents and his well known regard for the comfort and lives of those under him." However, several professional officers had a different opinion. Lieutenant Colonel Ethan Allen Hitchcock thought that an entire volume would be required to list all of the "demerits" exhibited by this "prince of military humbugs." Lieutenant A. P. Hill called Worth "a weak headed, vain glorious, but brave man, perfectly reckless with the lives of his soldiers." Surgeon Madison Mills considered Worth "the most unpopular officer in the Army of Invasion." Lieutenants Daniel Harvey Hill and Ulysses S. Grant thought that the general pushed his men unnecessarily hard and was the nervous type who wore his men out without accomplishing much.[19]

Also in the first wave was the recently created Company "A" Corps of Engineers—a company made up of enlisted men who, by virtue of special training at West Point, were prepared for a variety of duties, including building roads, bridges, and gun emplacements. Officers of the unit, some of whom would distinguish themselves in the campaign, were all West Point graduates. The company occupied two of the surfboats, and in one of them sat the company commander, Captain Alexander J. Swift, son of Joseph G. Swift, who was the first graduate of the military academy. Company "A" was among the units transferred from Taylor's to Scott's army, but by the time it arrived at Anton Lizardo, Swift was critically ill with dysentery and so weak he could hardly stand. The next ranking officer, Lieutenant Gustavus W. Smith, along with Lieutenant George McClellan, tried to persuade Swift to stay on the ship and remain under medical care, but Swift insisted that he accompany his men to the beach. With great difficulty, he had climbed into the surfboat and positioned himself at the stern of the vessel. When they reached the shore, two of his men had to carry him through the surf, but once on the beach, he seemingly recovered some strength and proceeded to issue orders. After a few hours, however, he had spent all of his energy, and his men carried him by litter back to a surfboat, thence out to Scott's flagship. A few days later he was loaded on the first steamer back to New Orleans, where he died.[20]

As soon as the boats deposited their men on shore, the sailors rowed them back to the waiting fleet to load the second wave. Over the next few hours, first Major General Robert Patterson's volunteer division then the other division of regulars under Brigadier General David E. Twiggs boarded the small craft and made the brief voyage to shore. Patterson, although born in Ireland, had moved with his family to Pennsylvania when he was six years old. He served in the War of 1812, then became involved in business pursuits and Democratic politics. A kind gentleman in his mid-fifties, he accepted a commission as major general when the war started. Twiggs, the son of a Revolutionary War general, was two years older than Patterson and an impressive six feet, two inches tall. Nicknamed the "Bengal Tiger," he had a "head and mustache perfectly white." Twiggs began the war as a colonel but rose rapidly to become one of the three division commanders in Scott's army. He seemed to always be concerned lest one of his fellow officers get the best of him. The previous year, while in Taylor's army, he had become embroiled in a seniority dispute with Worth, and their rivalry would continue throughout the present campaign. Two months earlier, when transferred from Taylor's command and ordered to take his men to Tampico, Twiggs pushed his men incessantly to the coast, marching them thirty miles one day out of fear that Patterson might overtake him. If that had happened, Patterson's superior rank would have entitled him to command the whole.[21]

The landing continued after dark, and by 10 o'clock, three successive waves had deposited approximately 9,000 men on the beach without incident or casualties. The most vulnerable time for an invading army during an amphibious assault is in the initial phase when the first troops land. With insufficient strength to repel a counterattack, they must try to establish a beachhead and wait for their numbers to grow. General Juan Morales, commander of the Veracruz defenses, made a costly error in opting not to oppose the landing. His decision bewildered many of the invaders. "Why the Mexicans did not meet us on the beach when they might have annoyed and cut us up most unmercifully is most unaccountable," wrote Captain Robert Anderson. Lieutenant D. H. Hill of the Fourth Artillery, which belonged to Twiggs's division, recorded in his diary his opinion that "the Mexicans have made a fatal mistake in not opposing us on the beach with desperate determination. They will never again have so favorable an opportunity of cutting us to pieces."[22] For his part, Morales obviously decided that he could inflate the strength of his inferior numbers by keeping them inside the city's defenses in the hope that the Americans would suffer unbearable casualties in dashing themselves against the fortifications. However, it would turn out to be a fruitless gamble, because Scott had no intentions of playing into his opponents' hands.

In the days ahead, there would be occasional skirmishes with small parties of enemy troops, but no orchestrated attempt to repulse the invaders. Scattered elements of Mexican cavalry appeared occasionally. Called lancers, they generally were armed with long lances, *escopetas* (short-barreled shotguns), sabers, and lassos. Soldiers in Scott's invading army quickly learned that the lancers "cannot bear up against our heavily armed dragoon," which was their American counterpart. "Our Dragoon is probably among the best in the world," thought Moses Barnard. Armed with a pair of pistols, a carbine, and a saber, they also attached to their heavy saddles, bags containing extra horseshoes, a currycomb, and a brush to care for the mount. A canvas bag to water and feed the animal completed the dragoons' equipment, and their horses were generally large and strong.[23] In combat, they moved swiftly and, when possible, closed on an enemy force so as to use their sabers in a slashing fashion. Later, when the army marched inland, they conducted reconnaissance and served as the eyes and ears of the army. Combat and technology would soon go through significant changes that would make mounted troops obsolete, but in the coming campaign, they would play a vital role on numerous battlefields.

On the first night after the landing, the men pushed a short distance inland, then settled among the dunes and along the beach to sleep. Worth ordered the Second Artillery forward toward the city to deploy as skirmishers, half of the men being permitted to sleep at a time. A "cold heavy dew fell," however, making for a miserable night. They were already wet from wading ashore, and campfires were strictly forbidden. The few who carried a blanket with them were the lucky ones. Staff officers Colonel Joseph G. Totten, Major John L. Smith, and Captain Robert E. Lee landed with their overcoats, which served as their bedroll, but for the most part, the men shivered all night and slept little. Lieutenant McClellan remembered that "we slept in the sand—wet to the middle." There were false alarms during the night, and at 2:00 A.M., some enemy troops ventured close enough to the beach to engage in a brief and bloodless skirmish. There were no injuries, but it all made for a restless night.[24]

On Wednesday, Scott's plan for capturing the city began to take shape. Rather than batter his army against Veracruz's fortified walls, he would invest the city from the land side and bombard it into submission. His strategy was typical of what he would do in the upcoming campaign: avoid the enemy's strong points, and seek to use Napoleonic-style turning movements or flank attacks. His decision to besiege the city from the land side represented a turning movement by shifting the tactical front of the battle away from the strength of San Juan de Ulúa, and he further benefitted by isolating the city from the interior of Mexico from whence reinforcements might come. A siege had both positive and negative sides. On the favorable side, it would result in far fewer casualties than a frontal assault, and Scott felt the pressure to preserve his troops and protect his small army. He told one subordinate that if he lost more than a hundred men in taking Veracruz, he would "consider himself a murderer."[25] The unfavorable result of such a plan was simply the amount of time, and Scott knew that the Polk administration wanted haste. Also, the longer the army lingered on the coast, the more susceptible it would be to the approaching yellow fever season. Scott's decision to pursue the slower option, therefore, was a political and health gamble. So on March 10, instead of massing his troops for an attack, he began to extend his army north so as to occupy a line west of the city that stretched all the way to the coast on its northern side.

The day began with the *Spitfire,* a small side-wheel gunboat that mounted twelve 24-pounders, moving in close and opening fire on the city and on San Juan de Ulúa. The castle's guns returned fire in an exchange that lasted about half an hour. One American reported seeing a fire erupt inside the city as a result. Attention in Veracruz was focused on this diversionary duel, which Scott and Conner intended to cover the encirclement of the city. First Worth's division moved up to within two miles on the city's south side and nestled itself among the sand hills. Then General Patterson's division advanced to their assigned position. Brigadier General Gideon J. Pillow's brigade of Tennesseans and Pennsylvanians led the volunteers as they began to probe further inland.[26]

Pillow was a lawyer from Tennessee and a close friend of the president's, but he was not, as historians have often recorded, Polk's former law partner. He had no formal military training, was, in fact, one of Polk's political appointees, and as such was widely and correctly believed to be the president's eyes and ears in Mexico. Pillow had an inflated opinion of himself, which gave West Point officers incentive to ridicule him when he displayed military ineptitude. Some of his own men did not like him for a variety of reasons: either they disagreed with his politics or they simply did not trust him to lead competently. One Tennessee volunteer formed a negative impression of Pillow a few months earlier while still in northern Mexico. On Christmas Day past, while encamped next to a "black lake" from which not even the horses would drink, Pillow's men ate "hard crackers" or a "dirty piece of fat pork" and washed it down with brackish water. Meanwhile, they watched as their commanding officer seated nearby "regaled himself with some viands that his servant brought to him." Then he "raised a bottle to his lips," which the men assumed to contain "good old brandy." This impression of him did not wane. Colonel William B. Campbell, one of Pillow's regimental commanders and a future governor of Tennessee, thought Pillow to be "very agreeable" but in no way suited for the military.[27] Scott, knowing that he was a Polk man, treated Pillow cordially in an effort to win the president's favor, but he never fully trusted him.

The air was stagnant and the heat stifling as Pillow pushed his brigade inland. After about a mile, the volunteers approached the small village of Malibran, located among some hills and along the Alvarado Road that ran due south out of Veracruz. Several hundred Mexican lancers and infantry occupying one of the buildings and the surrounding high ground opened a harassing small arms fire on the Americans. Pillow unlimbered one of his batteries, fired several rounds at the building, then ordered Colonel Campbell's First Tennessee forward to dislodge them. Campbell's veteran regiment had been in the forefront of the fighting at Monterey the previous

September. With a shout, the Tennesseans rushed forward, and after a sharp skirmish that resulted in four American deaths, the Mexicans gave up the high ground and retreated to Veracruz. Upon investigation, Pillow discovered that the building he had just captured was being used as a magazine to store artillery rounds, indicating either a carelessness in not moving the ammunition to the safety of the city or an early intention to oppose the Americans outside the city walls. After the brief clash, Pillow left some troops to occupy the area around the Alvarado Road, then pressed the rest of his brigade forward in a northwesterly direction, gradually extending the investment line.[28]

Even as units worked to stretch the siege line north, the bulk of the army remained near Collado Beach in a precarious situation. Few had blankets, there were no tents, ammunition was limited, and the only water they had was what they carried in their canteens. Personnel from the ordnance and quartermaster departments were working to rectify the problem. Starting at 4:00 A.M., they began the cumbersome task of bringing cartridge cases, camp equipment, and other supplies ashore, but it would be a slow process that would take days. Meanwhile, that morning, a few additional troops landed, including volunteer regiments from New York and Alabama, as well as the Palmetto Regiment from South Carolina. Horses, however, remained on board the steamers and would have to get to shore by swimming. Troops that had been aboard ships for days were quickly exhausted walking in the deep sand, and with the unbearable heat, many began to discard what little equipment they had. All the while, Mexican artillery lobbed an occasional round toward the American position, although with little effect.[29]

General Scott also went ashore on March 10 and began to confer with his staff officers, or, as some referred to them, his "little cabinet." Scott relied heavily on these men—Totten, Lee, Lieutenant Colonel Ethan Allen Hitchcock, and other West Point–trained engineers like Lieutenants George McClellan and P. G. T. Beauregard—for reconnaissance, information, and recommendations throughout the campaign. In addition to Veracruz's hard defenses, the Mexicans had planted "thick clusters of prickly pear" around the outer walls. The ground closest to the city wall was relatively flat so that an attacking army would have to traverse 400 yards of open terrain, some of which was booby-trapped with concealed holes with sharpened stakes inside that pointed skyward. The Mexican defenders did not have the kind of defensive firepower that the rifled musket would afford to Civil War armies, but they held a superior position inside their fortified walls with a good field of fire. Their advantage did not go unnoticed among U.S. soldiers, many of whom recognized that a direct assault would carry with it heavy losses.[30] An American attack would give the Mexicans their best chance to inflict damage on the army, perhaps 2,000 casualties by Scott's estimation, but Old Fuss and Feathers was determined not to give his opponent that opportunity.

With these thoughts in mind, Scott met with his trusted staff and had a discussion that "could hardly have been more solemn." He explained to them that although a night attack would be successful, it would be "at the cost of an immense slaughter on both sides." Scott preferred the "slow, scientific process" of a siege even though he knew the president wanted rapid results, and although he felt "Mr. Polk's halter around my neck," he could not bring himself to order a headlong assault on the city. His staff concurred, and in the days immediately following the landing, they set out to identify the most favorable location for his artillery in preparation for bombarding the city. Scott hoped for a short siege and a quick march inland to a healthier climate; he would resort to a bloody assault only as a last option. He knew his use of time would be scrutinized by the impatient administration. A December 22 letter from Marcy suggesting that Scott take with him to Mexico volunteers who had been in the service longest indicated that the secretary probably did not expect the war to last into the summer, when the volunteers' one-year enlistments would expire.[31]

Scott discussed the options with his generals and other subordinate officers, and some of them were opposed to a siege. Upon learning of Scott's intentions, Worth expressed dismay over the amount of time that would be wasted with such a plan. "We took Monterey in three days, a stronger place than this," he told Hitchcock. Captain William Walker wrote home to his wife, stating, "I . . . feel that we could with very little loss batter down the walls and charge into the city." Then, with a tinge of sarcasm, he added, "*The Great Men* think not however. Old Zack in my opinion would have been sitting in the city to day. . . . He would have lost troops but that is to be expected in war." These expressions of sentiment for Old Zack and his army were reinforced by the news that had been circulating within the army of Taylor's victory at Buena Vista less than three weeks earlier. Although Old Rough and Ready, as he was sometimes called, lacked Scott's finesse, he was nevertheless a take-charge general, and his men knew that he got the job done on the battlefield. It would be inaccurate to characterize him as a commander who displayed recklessness with the lives of his men, however; he was more of a "feel-as-you-go leader," as one historian described him, not "a thinking man, a planner" like Scott.[32]

By March 11, Patterson's division was in place in the center of the American line of investment that ran southwest to west of the city. Pillow's brigade occupied the area closest to Malibran, where it had skirmished with Mexican troops the previous day. There he had posted men of the Second Pennsylvania along the Alvarado Road to guard this passageway into the city. However, his military inexperience revealed itself in that he positioned them on both sides of the road such that if enemy reinforcements tried to gain entry into the city, the Pennsylvanians would be compelled to fire in each other's direction. Realizing the potential danger, Pillow ordered everyone to get on the same side.[33] As elements of Twiggs's division passed by on their way to take their position on the northern end of the siege line, they came upon some of Pillow's men who occupied the captured magazine. The volunteers boasted of their valor during the skirmish of March 10, and they exhorted the regulars to do likewise. But Lieutenant Hill of the Fourth Artillery sardonically noted in his diary that they had not injured any of the Mexicans during the battle, while three of the volunteers had been wounded by their own men—an assertion that, if true, Patterson left out of his March 14 report to Scott.[34]

Extending the line north was a difficult affair. Walking through the sand proved unusually tiring, and thick patches of chaparral, prickly pear, and thorny mimosa had to be cleared and a path cut for soldiers and supplies. Occasional sand hills also provided little valleys where pools of stagnant water stood, not fit to drink but providing additional obstacles to the weary soldier. "More horrible ground I have never seen," thought Captain Lee. And while these activities went on, Mexican artillery continued its sporadic, unpredictable, but mostly ineffective fire at the Americans—except during the afternoon of March 11, when the pace of enemy fire increased and some of their rounds found targets. One cannonball struck within the lines of Twiggs's division and took off Captain William Alburtis's head. The captain was admired and respected by his men, and he had won promotion a few years earlier for gallantry in the Seminole War. Twenty-two-year-old Lieutenant Edmund Kirby Smith of Twiggs's Seventh Infantry "heard with fearful foreboding the heavy fall of shot in front," and when he reached the spot, he passed by Alburtis's body. Two others from Twiggs's division were wounded during the investment, one slightly and the other seriously. The seriously injured man was named Miller of the Mounted Rifles, and he was badly wounded in the leg when he and a few others slipped away from the main body to investigate a location where Mexican officers had been spotted. Thick chaparral and sand hills dominated the area. As they crept up a hill, the hidden enemy soldiers opened fire. A ball hit Miller in the leg, breaking the bone, and for a while, it appeared that he would lose the leg. Although other accounts, both primary and secondary, refer to the soldier's leg being amputated, doctors actually saved it.[35] Other casualties accrued that day. A drummer boy had his arm "carried off" by a round, and several volunteers, perhaps five, also were killed while standing on a hill.[36]

Meanwhile, army engineers ventured out in front of the lines, especially at night, to chart the topography and gather intelligence. Lee went out every day, sometimes "near enough to see their guns & batteries quite distinctly." During one such reconnaissance, Lee captured a young man, brought him back to camp, treated him well, and obtained from him "the most valuable information we have yet recd." Lieutenant McClellan brought back equally valuable news from one of his missions when he located an aqueduct. The pipes that he found ran from a lake several miles away and outside the American lines, and they carried water into the city. McClellan reported his discovery to the chief of engineers, Colonel Totten, who promptly issued orders for the destruction of this valuable conduit.[37]

On Friday, March 12, a norther blew in and lasted all day—actually, while the winds subsided in the evening, the weather remained bad for several days. The strong winds kicked up "clouds of sand," preventing Twiggs's division from completing the investment on the northern end of the line. The sand and dust were so thick that visibility was limited and it was difficult to walk. The men held handkerchiefs over their faces to try to keep the grit out of their mouths and noses, and if a soldier lay on the ground, he was soon covered with sediment. Hats and blankets caught in a gust sailed in the air as far as one could see without touching the ground. The cold wind made it impossible to perform the simplest of tasks, like setting up a tent and cooking food, and it blew sand not only into eyes, hair, and clothes, but also into equipment, provisions, and cooking gear. Before the storm subsided late in the day, it had beached dozens of vessels that were bringing supplies ashore and cut off communication between the army and navy.[38]

That evening, McClellan and fellow engineer Lieutenant Gustavus W. Smith went out and cut the aqueduct that McClellan had found the previous day. They broke the pipes near the lake and away from the American army so as not to flood its encampments. When they returned, Colonel Totten congratulated them, telling them that they were the only officers to provide such valuable service since landing. The two men celebrated late into the night as a result of such accolades.[39]

On March 13, Twiggs's men finally reached the coast at a small town called Vergara north of Veracruz, thus completing the encirclement. The division had skirmished with small bodies of enemy troops along the way, but at no time had its push north been seriously impeded. As they entered the village, the panicked inhabitants fled, and many of the hungry soldiers "dashed into the deserted ranchos" in search of food. The officers tried to restore order, but the scene was chaotic. Lieutenant Kirby Smith, sword drawn, confronted a soldier leaving one of the houses, and just as he was about to reprove him for his lack of discipline, the infantryman held up a bag of sugar and asked, "Will the Lieutenant take some?" It was an offer Smith could not refuse. He lowered his sword, relaxed his "ferocious look," and took some of the delectable treat. The lieutenant then instructed the boy to return to his unit, after which he divided the sugar with one of his superior officers. Here at the northern end of the line ran the National Road from the coast west to Jalapa, Perote, Puebla, and all the way to Mexico City. Upon arriving in position, Twiggs thought that his men were too close to the city, and he wished to pull them back. However, because of Mexican attempts to herd cattle and mules into Veracruz from the north, he was ordered to move in closer, close any gaps in his line, and extend all the way to the beach itself. One of Twiggs's artillery officers, the opinionated Lieutenant Hill, believed that his superiors had completely mismanaged the march and that the investment should have been completed two days earlier. Furthermore, Hill thought that his division commander was both a coward and incompetent.[40]

When completed, the siege line ran roughly in a northwesterly direction from Collado Beach below the city to Vergara six miles away and above the city. This shifting, zigzag line of trenches varied from about a mile to a mile and a half away from the city. Scott made his headquarters at the southern end, where Worth's division was encamped. The brigades of Lieutenant Colonel John Garland and Colonel Newman S. Clark constituted Worth's division. Patterson's volunteer division occupied the next place in line and was composed of the brigades of Colonel James Shields and Brigadier General Gideon J. Pillow. On the northern end, Brigadier General Persifor F. Smith and Colonel Bennet Riley commanded the brigades in Twiggs's division. Much more war matériel had to be brought ashore in the days ahead, but in four days, the Americans had successfully wrapped a noose around Veracruz, and in the days ahead, they would slowly tighten it.[41]

CHAPTER TWO

Veracruz

The Slow, Scientific Process

When we take this place, . . . the Mexicans will begin to think
matters are becoming serious.
—George G. Meade, Topographical Engineers

With his army now settled into position, Scott sent a message into Veracruz under a flag of truce addressed to the foreign consuls. He offered them safe passage out of the city before the fighting started, but none of them seized the opportunity. Some residents of the city, however, did leave before the shooting began. Eleven days after the American landing and two days before the bombardment started, Tennessee Colonel William Campbell informed a relative that many of the women and children had left the city. In addition to offering a protected evacuation of diplomats, Scott also considered the safety of his own troops once the conflict started in earnest. His primary objective was to force the surrender of the city as soon as was practical so he could start his inland march before the end of April.[1]

His correspondence with the War Department indicates that he antici-pated the battle of Veracruz to occur in two stages. He hoped that a bombard-ment would bring about a relatively quick surrender of the city's garrison, but Veracruz could not be immediately occupied because of the artillery lo-cated in San Juan de Ulúa. Lieutenant George Meade thought that the castle was such a source of pride to the Mexican people that they would capitulate quickly in order to prevent a fight that might destroy it. Scott did not think it would be quite that easy. He envisioned the capture of the castle as a second phase wherein he would constrict his line by half and move in closer while maintaining a safe distance from the enemy offshore batteries.[2] He knew that he could starve the castle garrison into submission, but doing so would likely protract his operations into the yellow fever season. To accomplish all that he needed to and then get his army off the coast before the disease hit would require perfect timing.

As soon as the encirclement was completed, Scott drafted specific orders to ensure the army's security. The day after Twiggs's division reached Ver-gara, he ordered each brigade to send one or two companies forward to drive

Castle of San Juan de Ulúa. Courtesy of the author.

all Mexican skirmishers, pickets, guards, and other scattered troops inside the city walls. These advance companies were to hold their advanced positions several hundred yards forward but in a safe location, usually behind sand dunes. Every twenty-four hours, they would rotate with other companies under cover of darkness. In addition to observing and sounding an early warning if danger approached, these units, by keeping the enemy at bay, deprived them from seeing what the Americans were doing. Being only about eight hundred yards from the city walls, soldiers on such duty were not only in range of the Mexican guns, but they were also close enough to "distinctly hear all of their noises, [and] challenging of sentinels." A line of sand hills, however, provided them with ample protection. As Captain James R. Smith of the Second Infantry Regiment recorded, "we lie so close behind the sand ridges that I do not believe they suspect an enemy so near them."[3]

Engineers already had been busily engaged both day and night reconnoitering to detect enemy strengths and, most importantly, to locate favorable positions for artillery emplacements. Night missions into no-man's-land were particularly perilous because of the possibility of being fired upon not only by enemy gunners, but also by nervous American sentries. Mexican scouts occasionally ventured outside the city walls at night conducting their own observations, and sometimes when they approached too close to the American lines, they drew fire. Thus, the greatest fear for an American officer when returning from such missions was that he might be mistaken for enemy scouts. And regular officers believed the chances of being shot at by friendly troops increased when they were engaged in reconnaissance in front of a volunteer unit. One night Lee and Beauregard slipped out into the darkness in front of the American lines, and upon their return, one of them stumbled and attracted the attention of a picket. The sentinel shouted a challenge, but without waiting for a response, he fired his musket at the shadowy figures. Both Lee and Beauregard were stunned and temporarily blinded by the muzzle flash that went off ten feet from their faces, but neither man was hit, and they were able to grab the soldier and disarm him.[4]

Only 20 percent of Scott's heavy guns and mortars had arrived by the time the investment had been completed, but this unexpected shortfall, this unfortunate friction of war, could not be allowed to delay the conduct of the campaign. Scott would make do with what he had. Colonel Totten, Captain Lee, and Captain Gustavus Smith were the principal engineers engaged in selecting locations for the artillery that was on hand. The sites chosen were south of Veracruz and within a half mile of the city wall—close enough to the Mexican guns to be dangerous. For more than a week after the siege line was established, engineers supervised the construction of trenches that zigzagged their way in advance of the American lines and toward the city. These trenches served as passageways to the front where the batteries were to be built, but the demanding work caused dissension. Lieutenant Isaac Stevens complained that it was only with great difficulty that the volunteers could be made to work in the trenches; they instead preferred to sleep or get drunk. Also a disagreement arose on about March 16 regarding the site chosen for the first battery. Colonel Totten ordered Beauregard to take a group of sappers forward and dig a trench, as specified by a profile previously laid out for the battery. When he arrived at the designated spot, he instantly felt reservations, so he climbed a tree and, with a glass, carefully surveyed the area and concluded that the location could be easily enfiladed by enemy artillery. With some trepidation, the young lieutenant refused to start work on the battery, and he returned to his superior officer and told him of his conclusion. After a brief clash, Totten agreed to go forward and reexamine the ground, and when he did so, he discovered that indeed Beauregard had been correct. The battery was moved to a safer location.[5]

This incident may have been a contributing factor to D. H. Hill's opinion that Totten "betrays imbecility every day." The young Hill viewed Totten as "a book man without practice and practical judgment"—hardly an attitude one would expect to encounter regarding a man with Totten's experience. He was the tenth graduate of West Point in 1805 and a veteran of the War of 1812. He became the army's chief engineer precisely because of his extensive and varied experience, and he fulfilled that role until his death in 1864. He was also one of the founding regents of the Smithsonian Institution. In Mexico,

Scott relied on him heavily and deferred to his many recommendations. Totten did not disappoint, and during the entire campaign, he sought to give to the corps of engineers high-profile assignments that met high expectations. Hill, on the other hand, was quick to pass judgment, and after only a few days at Veracruz, he had already grown frustrated, calling his superiors "old fogies" and condemning the operations as "most shameful."[6]

While Hill complained, the work continued. The day after Totten's and Beauregard's confrontation, Captain Smith found a new and much better place for Battery One only a few hundred yards away, near a cemetery. At the new site, "the conformation of the ground constituted almost a natural parapet for a six gun battery—requiring but little work to complete it for use. It afforded immediate shelter for men and guns." When the trenches were completed and the battery locations identified, work parties of twenty men each ventured forward every day to construct the gun emplacements. Armed with picks, shovels, and axes and laboring under the supervision of engineer officers, the work crews went about their tasks under orders to "observe profound silence" so as not to "attract the shot or Shells of the enemy." They did much of their work under cover of darkness. When practical, the batteries were cut into the sides of hills, and the men dug parallels to connect one battery to another and to allow for communication. They also had to dig earthen magazines so that the ordnance could be stored underground, where it would be relatively safe from enemy fire. As the work progressed, it became impossible to shield work parties from exposure to enemy fire. Mexican artillery continued to fire sporadically at the American lines, but even with the occasional exploding shell nearby, the labor continued with hardly a wince from the soldiers.[7]

Inside the American lines, soldiers had to grow accustomed to daily boredom punctuated by brief episodes of excitement. Companies took turns deploying forward among the sand hills, and their presence on the picket line resulted in occasional skirmishes with Mexican infantry and lancers. On the night of March 19, one large work party skirmished with about fifty lancers who were patrolling in front of the city walls. The intermittent enemy cannon fire prompted Captain Robert Anderson to conclude that the Mexicans "act very foolishly, throwing shot and shells at small bodies of men at distances so great as to make the chances almost nothing of their killing us." Nightly patrols continued, and during one of them, members of the Fourth Artillery captured a courier trying slip out of the city with dispatches. While working their way back into their own lines, startled guards shouted a challenge to them then fired into the group, wounding two men, one of them mortally. From the captured letters, Americans learned that supplies were beginning to run low in the city, and this after less than a week of siege. Lieutenant

Edmund Kirby Smith, in a letter home, referred to the intercepted letters and how they tell of "the great terror of the inhabitants and of their want of provisions." The Americans also learned of political turmoil in Mexico City and the fear that reinforcements would not be sent to relieve the city.[8]

The noose continued to tighten around the city with each passing day. When Scott heard reports that ships were sailing into nearby Antigua with supplies bound for Veracruz, he ordered the navy to cut off the entire coastline from outside contact. And the navy's efforts were effective. On March 20, two American ships captured a French vessel trying to run the blockade. This came after another French ship had successfully slipped through during a storm, anchored at the castle, and unloaded its cargo of black powder. The angry Americans thought it poetic justice that the vessel wrecked while trying to leave the harbor in the choppy waters. Also on March 20, some brave Mexicans came outside the city in an effort to gather cattle and drive them into the city, but Americans opened fire on them, wounding two and sending them scampering back to the safety of the walls. Already some Americans were beginning to hear stories coming out of the city about Mexican discontent over the war. Let those who made the war fight it, some were rumored to say.[9]

It was just the kind of attitude—disillusionment and discontent—that would bode well for relations between the American army and Mexican civilians when Scott put his pacification plan into action. Scott was as yet unaware of just how disgruntled the general population had become with their government's efforts to pay for the war. With financial difficulties mounting, acting president Valentín Gómez Farías devised a plan to use the extensive wealth of the Catholic church to help finance the country's defense. In January, he and his government in Mexico City issued a statement to the effect that it would mortgage 15 million pesos' worth of church property to serve as collateral for needed revenue. This confiscation of church property stirred opposition from both clergy and laity, and the resulting protest caused the government to enact strict regulations forbidding citizens from gathering in the streets of the capital. The growing animosity between soldiers and civilians peaked in late February, when Farías ordered four of Mexico City's national guard battalions to march to Veracruz to reinforce the army there. Members of these units were staunch defenders of the church, and because they generally came from upper-class elements of society that enjoyed polka dancing, they were often referred to as *polkos*. Most people suspected that the marching order was motivated more out of a wish to get these potentially disloyal troops out of the capital than by a desire to assist Veracruz. Thus, several days after Farías's order, several military units within the capital rose up against the government in what was called the "Polkos Rebellion." Santa

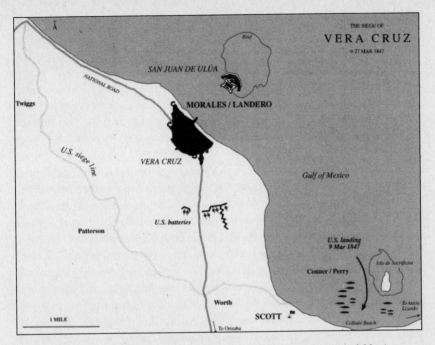

Siege of Veracruz. From Donald S. Frazier, ed., *The United States and Mexico at War* (New York: Macmillan, 1998). Reprinted by permission of The Gale Group.

Anna, still reeling from his Buena Vista defeat and trying to portray it as a victory, rushed to Mexico City in March to reassert his authority and bolster the crumbling power of the civil government.[10] It was this growing sense of anger and hopelessness among the Mexican people that would serve to complement Scott's pacification plan as his campaign progressed.

Not only was Scott unaware of all that was going on in the Mexican capital, he also was in the dark about events in his own capital. On March 21, he wrote to Secretary Marcy expressing his dismay at not having received any information from Washington regarding war measures that were before Congress or the shipment of his anticipated but still missing matériel. Thus far, Scott had not received resounding support from the administration. He expected to march into the interior of the country with 20,000 men, but he had only half that number. Surprisingly, the administration had not seen fit to inform him of the passage of the Ten Regiment Bill the previous month, which Congress hoped would ease the manpower shortage. Now Scott was in the theater of war with mounted troops who had no mounts and a shortage of artillery. Some of Scott's men blamed the well-known icy relationship between general and president for the inadequate transports, troops, and supplies that had plagued the campaign. Captain Anderson, a friend of Scott's and the future commander of the federal garrison at Fort Sumter, lamented that Scott's forethought and planning had been "cruelly . . . thwarted" by the administration's lack of support. Given the magnitude of his operation and all that had gone wrong, the general obviously thought it strange that the War Department had not communicated with him in two months, and he said as much to Marcy. Ultimately Scott found his own ways to cope with these frictions of war.[11]

While work parties constructed the gun emplacements, naval personnel continued to shuttle supplies from ship to shore. When weather permitted, they worked from 4:00 A.M. to 10:00 P.M., but after the norther hit on March 12, coming and going on the beach slowed considerably for several days as wind and rain continued. Soldiers just made do with what they had. Some of the regular troops became angry when volunteers plundered supplies as they landed on the beaches. The opinionated Lieutenant Hill not only expressed his resentment toward the volunteers' actions, but he also vented with an acrimonious passage concerning the officers of the Quartermaster Department. By this time, American vessels were steaming north of the city and offloading supplies near Vergara, where Twiggs's division occupied the trenches, and according to Hill, most of the quartermaster officers assigned to the area did little of their assigned tasks: "There are fifteen of the officers of this Department at this place all neat trim young men but only two of whom can be got to do anything." Apparently their own comfort concerned them more than bringing supplies ashore. "'Tis a fact," Hill continued, "that they had men employed in building *houses* for themselves before one fifth of the ordnance was landed and before a large portion of the troops had tents." Some soldiers went over a week without tents.[12]

For several days after the landing, units remained on half rations because so little had been brought ashore. "I came very near starving," remembered William Higgins. Consequently, many of the men took matters into their own hands. One day some Pennsylvania volunteers headed inland to search for cattle, and after going about a mile and a half, they ran across another group with the same objective. Together they killed a cow and divided the beef between the two parties before heading back to camp. One of the Pennsylvanians, Richard Coulter, built a fire when he got back, then cut himself a steak and proceeded to cook it, only to have it stolen by a stealthy comrade when he turned his back. He went to bed without dinner that night, but two days later, some of his companions went out, shot two cows, brought them back to camp, and made steaks and soup for the entire company. Evidently Coulter got his fill. A naval officer who had come ashore erected an awning, then treated himself and fellow officers to roasted chicken, no doubt obtained from a nearby home. Although such episodes violated Scott's orders, they were numerous enough to adequately supplement the soldiers' rations, as evidenced by Private William Johnson from South Carolina, who reported one week after the landing, "Beef plenty, nothing to do but cook and eat." Other items added some variety to the diet, whether it was cornbread purchased from local inhabitants or a more exotic meal like the one cooked by Lieutenant Thomas Ewell, brother of future Confederate General Richard Ewell. Fellow officer Thomas Claiborne came upon Ewell one day and found him boiling an iguana in a tin cup. It was a great delicacy in Jamaica, Ewell assured him, but upon tasting the dish, Claiborne's "stomach rejected it."[13]

Sometimes soldiers took more than food. On their first Sunday ashore (March 14), a group of soldiers spent the day "robbing the Ranchos of asses, horses, mules, chickens, etc." But because they needed most of the animals taken for hauling supplies, they thought that their actions were "justified by stern necessity." Unfortunately, the foraging sometimes led to looting. The members of one unit encamped close to a ranchero within days had "carried off everything that they could lay their hands upon." Some new recruits of the Second Artillery along with a few sailors journeyed several miles to the town of Medellin and "committed atrocities of every kind." Even General Twiggs engaged in such behavior. He took food and wine from a nearby ranchero, and after distributing the wine to his men, they became "noisy and turbulent." One regular officer, Lieutenant Hill, bemoaned such actions with the following diary entry: "Most deplorable are the evils of war. Plundering an enemy leads to carelessness and looseness in morals."[14]

Work on the batteries continued, and Scott believed that he would be ready to open his bombardment by March 22. Additional ordnance had arrived on March 19, but the continued shortage of heavy guns forced an improvisation. On March 21, Scott met with Commodores David Conner and Matthew Perry, who had just arrived with orders to relieve Conner of command, and the three discussed the need for additional firepower. The capable and ambitious Perry agreed to provide the army with six heavy guns that would be carried ashore and mounted as a new battery to add to those already under construction, but he stipulated that only naval personnel could man them. Scott acceded to the navy's desire to share in the military glory, and construction of the new battery began immediately under Captain Lee's supervision. The army called it Battery Five, but the navy referred to it as the Naval Battery, a name that more clearly defined ownership. It consisted of three 32-pounders that weighed three and a half tons each and fired a solid iron ball, and also of three 68-pound shell guns with a range 2,500 yards.[15]

Moving the guns ashore was a major project involving close to 1,500 men. The site chosen for the battery was seven hundred yards from the city (about a hundred yards closer than the other batteries) and just opposite Fort Santa Barbara on the southern side of the city's wall. The guns had to be hoisted out of the ships with tripods, then carried ashore and mounted on a large pair of wooden wheels for transportation to the designated spot. It took two hundred men with drag lines to pull the cannon, and Scott ordered this part of the task done after dark to maintain secrecy. Men of Pillow's brigade comprised the work parties for the Naval Battery, and all went well except for an episode involving an African American sailor who, while drunk, pulled a knife on a Tennessee volunteer. When a scuffle ensued over the infantryman's musket, the Tennessean shot him in the shoulder, inflicting a mortal wound. It would be two days after the beginning of the bombardment before the Naval Battery was ready to open on the city, but everyone believed that upon completion, it would be "the most important Battery we have from its proximity to the city and the commanding position it ocupies."[16]

While work continued on the land batteries, the navy played an important role. Vessels daily steamed in close to exchange fire with the city and castle batteries. One soldier reported that twice on March 21, the city appeared to be on fire, and on another day, gunboats approached to within six hundred yards and sparred with the castle guns for over an hour without losing a ship. Perry's goal was to project firepower and also to distract attention away from the ongoing work on the land batteries. He was partially successful, but not entirely. Mexican guns continued to hurl both shot and shell at the American line, firing over 170 rounds on March 19.[17]

While construction of the Naval Battery would continue until March 24, some of the other batteries were either finished or nearing completion on Monday, March 22. They comprised a variety of guns: 10-inch mortars, 8-inch cannon, 24-pounders, Paixhan guns. Roswell Ripley was certain that when "our bull dogs [are] at work . . . Shells will fall . . . thick & fast," and Hiram Yeager thought that when the bombardment started it would take "less than two hours . . . [to] destroy the city." At 2:00 P.M. on March 22, Scott sent a note into Veracruz addressed to General Juan Morales, the governor general of the city, calling on him to surrender to avoid a bombardment. Scott's message was courteous, but he demanded a response within two hours. Morales responded with an equally gracious note stating that it was his responsibility to defend the city and the castle.[18]

At the expiration of the two hours, Scott ordered his chief of artillery, Colonel James Bankhead, to open fire. Like Scott, Bankhead was a Virginian, and like Scott, he had entered the army in 1808 and fought in the War of 1812. As captains, he and Scott had become involved in a minor seniority dispute in

1809, but the issue did not have lasting consequences, which was not always the case with disagreements involving Scott. At Veracruz, the commanding general relied heavily on Bankhead and trusted his decisions and ability, and the colonel fulfilled the general's expectations, for he later would be promoted to brigadier general for gallantry and meritorious conduct during the siege.[19]

At 4 o'clock, the thundering boom of artillery filled the air as Bankhead opened with a battery of 10-inch mortars followed by guns of varying calibers. In all, three batteries and a total of seventeen guns unleashed their fire on the city from land, and they were joined by seven naval vessels from Perry's fleet that steamed in close enough to again lob shells into the city. One was the light-draft but well-armed *Spitfire* commanded by Lieutenant David D. Porter, a former midshipman in the Mexican navy and a future Union admiral. The *Spitfire* scored several direct hits in the heart of the city. Mexican batteries returned fire from their concealed positions in the city's fortifications, and the castle batteries opened on the naval vessels. The fire was continual on both sides for the next five hours, but, according to Lieutenant Kirby Smith, the enemy fired three rounds for every one fired by the Americans. The noise was deafening, and soon both the city and the American lines were enshrouded in smoke.[20]

"The battle now rages, the scene is grand," reported Stevens Mason. For most of the Americans, especially the young lower-grade officers, the bombardment offered a spectacular sight of fire and explosions. The sight of shells whizzing through the sky, crossing each other in midflight, and visible at night by their burning fuses, presented a fascinating scene for young soldiers. Those who had helped construct the gun emplacements were particularly interested in witnessing the effects of their handiwork. Lieutenant McClellan, who had worked on Batteries One and Three, crept up beyond the artillery to a position as close to the city as possible so as to observe the impact of the American fire. Later he remembered that "the effect was superb." Kirby Smith described it to his wife as "a sublime spectacle," and Hiram Yeager simply recorded, "God what a sight it was."[21]

Mingled with the roar of cannon and the blasts of explosions were screams from the citizens of Veracruz. Despite the distance, some of the soldiers claimed to "distinctly hear the wailing of human voices in the city" and likened the cries to defiant displays of "their bravery, and indifference." Perhaps some of what the soldiers heard actually came from Mexican inhabitants who lived in scattered houses and suburbs on the outskirts of the city and outside the walls. Some of these, erroneously believing that Santa Anna had defeated Taylor at Buena Vista, supposedly sang the praises of the Mexican general after the bombardment started. Some of the U.S. soldiers evidently were indifferent to the brilliant display or quickly tired of watching it, because one officer reported seeing some of the men going about their business, singing, and playing musical instruments.[22]

Neither civilian casualties nor collateral damage, as it is now called, evoked universal sympathy from the Americans. The primary objective of the bombardment was to destroy the fortifications ringed around Veracruz and knock holes in the wall to facilitate an assault, should one later be deemed necessary. However, Hill estimated that nine out of ten shells actually landed inside the city, doing unknown damage to nonmilitary targets. Most soldiers apparently did not care, or simply did not make the distinction that is possible now with precision-guided munitions. Indeed, Chauncey Sargent recorded in his journal on the second day of the bombardment that "every shot [from one battery] entered the city, and with good effect." In his *Memoirs,* Scott, displaying more sensitivity, asserted that in attempting to silence the enemy guns and breach the wall "a portion of our shots and shells . . . unavoidably penetrated the city and set fire to many houses." Although civilians were not intentionally targeted, the natural danger of war made them, as far as Scott was concerned, occasional, if unintentional, victims.[23]

The fire remained continuous on both sides until 9:00 P.M., when the gunboats retired and the castle guns ceased. After that, only the land batteries, both American and Mexican, continued all night, but at a slower rate of fire. On the first day of the bombardment, American casualties, according to Bankhead, amounted to a few wounded and one killed—a light toll except for the unfortunate death of Captain John R. Vinton. A native of Rhode Island and a West Point graduate with thirty years' experience, Vinton was universally respected and widely regarded as one of "the most accomplished officers in the army." He had been commanding Battery Three, and while rising up over the parapet to observe the accuracy of his guns, a shell struck him and killed him instantly. Accounts differ as to where he was hit because there was no visible wound or contusion on his body. Some of the soldiers thought he had been hit in the head, some said it was in the side, and one version even surmised that the shell had actually missed him, but, in a strange anomaly, killed him when it passed close by—killed by "the wind of a shell," it was said. A blow to the head was most likely. Ironically, Vinton had written a letter to his mother the previous month expressing concern that the Mexicans might not fight, thus depriving him of an opportunity for "exploits and honors." He further added that if it was his lot to die, he would do so "cheerfully." To honor his memory, fellow officers gathered that evening, and Scott gave a touching and "eloquent" eulogy—"every heart was full, every eye glistened." He was temporarily laid to rest among the sand dunes behind Veracruz, but the following year, friends sent his remains home. Today he is interred in the

Swan Point Cemetery in Providence, Rhode Island. Comrades recovered the unexploded shell that took his life, disarmed it, and sent it with his body, and it currently rests atop his grave.[24]

During the night, another norther blew in and continued through the next day, not only disrupting Vinton's burial but also damaging trenches and gun casements. The wind blew so hard that sand pricked the men's faces. Next morning, despite the ongoing storm, officers dispatched work parties to repair the trenches, but the sand blew back into them as fast as they could shovel it out. The bad weather also caused other, more serious problems. It halted the landing of artillery ordnance, which would have repercussions in the days ahead, and it delayed the completion of additional battery placements. The norther caused damage to Battery Four, a six-gun battery that was not yet operational, and impeded work on Battery Five, the Naval Battery. Construction on this battery, now entering its third day, had proceeded at an impressive pace, and it was scheduled for completion in one more day. As per Scott's order, the movement of the three-and-a-half-ton navy guns was to be done at night, but when the last gun was being pulled into place, General Gideon Pillow, who supervised the project, violated Scott's order and moved it the final distance in daylight. Everyone knew that Pillow was inexperienced when it came to military affairs, but this was simply a case of insubordination, something to which Pillow was prone. Because of his relationship with Polk, he took liberties that would in time create disharmony within the army.[25]

On the second day of the bombardment, March 23, Scott received intelligence that a Mexican force was a few miles away, probably probing for a point through which it could enter the lines and reinforce the city garrison. Accordingly, Twiggs ordered a company of regulars to reconnoiter in the direction of a bridge called Puente del Media. On their way, they spotted some Mexican sentries along the road, seemingly confirming that an enemy force was in the vicinity. As the unit approached the stream, the company commander, Lieutenant Roberts, halted his men in a safe place, sent ten of them into the chaparral along the right of the road, and took eight with him on toward the bridge.[26] When Roberts turned a bend in the road just as it descended down to the water, he discovered some enemy officers on the bridge. They immediately raised a white flag and asked to meet with him. The lieutenant approached alone and walked around a "strong abbatis" that was across the road and onto the bridge. Only then did he notice on the other side of the river what he estimated to be 250 Mexicans soldiers who had been concealed in a "strongly entrenched line," and he immediately suspected a trap. He boldly asserted that he commanded a strong force nearby and was there to demand their surrender, wherewith one of the Mexican officers instructed about thirty of his men to march onto the bridge. As they did, half of them filed down one side of Roberts and the other half down the other, then turned inward to face the American. Then as the lieutenant reached out to take a weapon from a Mexican soldier, a shout came up from the trenches: "No! No! Los Americanos rendes les Armes." Both sides obviously intended to be the captor.

At about that time, the ten-man detachment that had moved off to the right came out of the chaparral and, after crossing the stream, marched up to block the far end of the bridge between their lieutenant and the Mexican trenches. When one of the Mexican officers asked for an interpreter, Roberts and his men made their escape, telling the Mexicans that they would return with one soon. The lieutenant rejoined the main body of his company, which had been waiting several hundred yards away, formed them in a defensive position, and sent a runner back to camp to bring up reinforcements. General Persifor Smith immediately dispatched a portion of the Rifle Regiment, and when it arrived, a sharp skirmish ensued. Some of the Mexicans had crossed the stream and were ensconced among the chaparral to the right. Roberts wheeled his company to the right and plunged into the thickets to attack. For a half hour, these two forces exchanged musket fire, which gave way to hand-to-hand grappling. One American private successfully engaged three Mexicans but lost three fingers while holding up his weapon to fend off saber blows. Next the rifle companies opened on the trenches across the stream then charged the bridge, sending enemy soldiers in "every direction." In this skirmish, the Mexicans lost seven killed and forty wounded; American casualties consisted of four wounded.[27]

For several days, as engineers and work crews completed additional batteries, the American bombardment intensified. They fired at the city around the clock, but the rate of fire always increased in the daylight hours, with the Mexicans returning fire with their superior number of guns. On Wednesday, March 24, Batteries Four and Five opened, adding a dozen guns to the American arsenal and markedly increasing the magnitude of the artillery duel. The navy's big guns had a devastating effect as its heavy, solid shot smashed into the masonry and rock fortifications. During the course of the day, it disabled several enemy cannon. Manned by sailors from the *Potomac* and the *Saint Mary,* including Lee's brother, Lieutenant Sidney Smith Lee, who commanded one of the gun crews, the Naval Battery maintained an impressive rate of fire all day, and at one point, the crews had to stop to prevent the guns from overheating. By chance, one shot severed the flagpole over Fort Santa Barbara, and a second lucky shot scattered debris over the two Mexican soldiers who attempted to reattach it to the end of the broken staff. The Mexican defenders also accelerated their rate of fire on Wednesday, with results. They scored a direct hit on a mortar, throwing it twenty feet into the air and fifty feet to the rear. However, they concentrated their efforts on the navy guns. One shell from the castle landed just behind the battery, igniting casks of powder, and other rounds hit close enough to damage the battery's embrasures. During the course of the day, four sailors were killed.[28]

During this first day that the Naval Battery was in action, one of the openings through which the guns fired (embrasures) "became so badly choked that it could not be used." Officers concluded that the opening had been made too small and would have to be enlarged after nightfall. Apparently during construction of the battery site, a disagreement had arisen between engineers Lee and Gustavus Smith over the size of the embrasures, and when they called Totten in to settle the dispute, the chief of engineers sided with Lee and his recommendation for the smaller size. With one of the guns out of operation, Smith asked Lee what he now thought of the embrasures' dimensions, to which Lee responded, "They must be made greater."[29]

Also on this day, American rocketeers under Lieutenant George H. Talcott began to use frightening projectiles known as Congreve rockets. These missiles had a three-foot explosive charge wrapped in metal casing and a guide stick that added another thirteen feet to the rocket's length. They looked rather like a giant bottle rocket. The Congreve rocket, named for its inventor, an officer in the British army, William Congreve, had been around for decades. Their shrill, whistling sound and long tail of fire gave them an ominous appearance while in flight, but their notorious inaccuracy meant that they were prone to land most anywhere, inflicting both fear and unexpected civilian pain. It was their image streaking across the night sky that caused Francis Scott Key to write about "the rocket's red glare" during the War of 1812. A curious observer at Veracruz thought the rockets looked like meteors. Talcott's rocket company fired forty Congreves at Veracruz on Wednesday, and the next day, they loosed ten of the more modern, improved Hale rockets. Named for another British officer, William Hale, these new models no longer had the guide stick, and their spinning motion gave them better accuracy. Both types had a range of two thousand to three thousand yards.[30]

The escalated artillery duel also created an intense panorama for the soldiers to behold, especially after dark. "Every second a shell or a round shot is in the air either from our cannon or theirs," wrote William Walker to his wife. Lieutenant Theodore Laidley described to his father what he saw: "The air was rent with the whistling of balls, the roaring of our own mortars, and the bustle and confusion incident to such an exciting time." Another soldier named Bradford reported that at times he saw as many as five American shells in the air at one time, rendering few areas of the city safe. "At night the spectacle was grand," remembered Kirby Smith, "the air being filled with shells crossing each other in every direction their tracks marked by the burning fuses. The havoc was terrible, the crash of buildings, the shrieks and moans of the poor creatures within the walls could be plainly heard at night within our lines." Smith believed that the Veracruz example would make the conquest of other Mexican cities easier as the army marched inland, but regarding this tremendous display of firepower, he wrote that the shelling of Veracruz was "a horrid business" with its "shower of iron falling upon the . . . city." It was "justifiable by the usages of war," he assured his correspondent, but "I desire never to witness another bombardment."[31]

A young lieutenant from Virginia named Thomas J. Jackson, who had graduated from West Point the previous year, experienced his first action at Veracruz. Not for fourteen more years would Jackson acquire the nickname "Stonewall" for his stubborn stand on the First Bull Run battlefield, but even at this early stage of his career, he left such an impression that fellow officer and former West Point instructor Captain Francis Taylor believed that "Jackson will make his mark in this war." Before landing on Collado Beach, Jackson, in a frank conversation with his future brother-in-law, D. H. Hill, wondered what it was really like to be in combat and how it felt to handle troops in the heat of battle. "I really envy you men who have been in action," he admitted to Hill. Then with a smile, he said, "I want to be in one battle." Assigned to Company "K" of the First Artillery, he helped man one of the batteries during the bombardment and got his wish. On one occasion, as he informed his sister, "a cannon ball came in about five steps of me." Those around him took note of his calm demeanor during the noise and confusion of combat, and his superiors were impressed with the ability he displayed in fighting his guns. One soldier commented that Jackson was "as calm in the midst of a hurricane of bullets as though he were on dress parade at West Point."[32]

One indication that the increased rate of fire was having an impact in the city came in the form of a note dated March 24 and delivered to General Scott, requesting a cease-fire to allow foreign consuls, along with Mexican women and children, to leave the city. Scott responded in the negative, saying that the American guns would stop firing only when the city's garrison surrendered, and he reminded them that they had rejected an opportunity to leave the city before the bombardment began. By one account, the American officer who allowed the letter bearer in the camp without Scott's approval was arrested.[33]

Critics have contended that Scott should have yielded to the request and allowed one day for the evacuation of foreign consuls, women, and children and that his justification for not doing so, the approach of yellow fever season, was disingenuous because he did not start his march away from the coast until three weeks after the city's surrender. Such criticism falls short on several counts. Although modern-day historians know that the city garrison capitulated three days later, they apparently assume that Scott also knew the date that the surrender would occur, knew that the siege would not extend into April, and knew that he would have a short respite before the onset of yellow fever. But he knew none of these things. Besides, he wanted to march inland immediately, but could not do so for lack of transportation. Those who wish to censor Scott also fail to mention that he had previously offered safe passage out of the city for all foreign diplomats, allowing them several days to evacuate. Also citizens had had almost two weeks to leave, and some had. Furthermore, a consideration for the safety of the civilians works both ways. The Mexican commander, while clearly feeling an obligation to defend the city's inhabitants, nevertheless chose to use the city itself as a fort rather than fight outside its confines.

Scott has also been charged with contradicting himself in his *Memoirs* in an effort to justify the continuation of the bombardment. On one page, he wrote: "Detachments of the enemy too were accumulating behind us, and rumors spread, by them, that a formidable army would soon approach to raise the siege." Thus the need for haste in capturing the city. Yet half a dozen pages earlier, he wrote that Santa Anna "had returned to his capital, and was busy in collecting additional troops" with intentions to stop the invasion at an inland mountain pass.[34] These two statements, however, are not contradictory. "Detachments" of enemy troops were indeed all about the countryside "accumulating," and Scott nowhere implied that the "formidable army" that he feared might attack him from behind would be led by Santa Anna. He certainly knew that Santa Anna soon would march east from Mexico City with a sizable force, and that he might try to block a mountain pass, as he did at Cerro Gordo. Or if the siege continued indefinitely, the Mexican leader could have chosen to attack Scott at Veracruz—not Santa Anna's most likely option, but one for which the city's inhabitants certainly held out hope. In truth, Scott did not know what course his opponent would take, but any competent general must consider and prepare for all contingencies.

By March 25, some of Scott's officers were becoming disenchanted with the "slow, scientific process." By that time, the Americans had been ashore for over two weeks, and the city had been heavily bombarded for three days, with no results. Meade had grown tired of the idleness and wished that he had been present at Buena Vista the previous month. "My great regret now is that I was separated from General Taylor." He was now convinced that Veracruz could "only be carried at the point of the bayonet." Worth had also grown impatient. He had gained notoriety as a result of aggressive action during the assault on Monterey the previous fall, and he had been an advocate of attack since the landing on March 9. Despite his longtime friendship with Scott, he "condemned the operations at Vera Cruz as tedious." Other officers, however, worried lest there be such ambition for glory among some of the generals "that they will be willing to make any sacrifice of human life to gratify their ambition." Scott knew that many of his troops favored a quick, decisive victory through a head-on assault. He also knew that the general public back home would not appreciate the significance, would not understand the finesse of capturing the city without "a long butcher's bill" as evidence of hard fighting. But he also knew that a bloody assault, although capturing the city, could effectively end the operation. With only 10,000 men, he could not risk a costly battle, especially at the beginning of a long, audacious campaign into the heart of enemy country.[35]

An attack was the last thing Scott wanted to consider, but that was exactly what circumstances forced him to contemplate by March 25. If he remained immobile on the coast, he would risk the effects of disease, which could kill more of his men than a frontal assault. An additional battery opened on that day as the rate of fire continued to increase, but because of the recent norther and the inability to bring supplies ashore, ammunition was running low. He had already ordered some of his guns to reduce their rate of fire to no greater than one round every five minutes. Commodore Perry also reported that within a few days, the Naval Battery would be out of ammunition with no possibility of resupply. With such news in hand, Scott decided that a direct attack might be necessary after all, but he would give the artillery one more day to see if a surrender might yet result. Accordingly, he sent orders to Batteries Four and Five to concentrate their fire in the same area the next morning. He told them to first knock out as many Mexican batteries as possible, then to train their guns on the same spot on the wall in an attempt to create a breach that infantry could charge through. If the city did not surrender on March 26, then Scott would prepare to storm the wall with his army from the land side and with Perry's marines from the sea side.[36]

Meanwhile, another report came into headquarters that a body of mounted enemy troops had arrived outside the American lines and that they might attempt to break through and get into the city. Rumors abounded that Mexican troops were gathering to relieve Veracruz and that Santa Anna was on his way with several thousand soldiers. When a small number of Mexican troops attacked a beef party from the First Tennessee, Scott sent a hundred dragoons to investigate on the afternoon of March 25. They discovered about 150 Mexican troops entrenched at a stone bridge nine miles behind the center of the American lines, which some sources refer to as the Medelline Bridge. General Patterson immediately dispatched eight companies of Tennesseans, two artillery pieces, and additional dragoons as reinforcements, and after a fast march, they found themselves at a lagoon in the midst of a thick chaparral. Their officers aligned them for combat, and they immediately opened fire on what appeared to be a hastily fortified Mexican position. The artillery opened with grape, and after about a dozen rounds, the enemy line began to crumble. The Americans surged forward, led by such officers as Captain Benjamin Franklin Cheatham, company commander of the Nashville Blues, First Tennessee, who had led the way in a charge at Monterey the previous year and would lead many Confederate charges in places like Shiloh, Stones River, and Franklin. Major William Hardee of the dragoons also distinguished himself. When the Mexicans broke and ran, a four-mile pursuit ensued, during which the dragoons overtook and killed several of the enemy. General Patterson, who had come up with the reinforcements and was overwhelmed with excitement, stood in his stirrups and shouted, "Hurrah for Tennessee!" The Tennesseans responded with loud cheers of their own. After the brief clash, and with the sun rapidly descending, the Americans strapped their two dead comrades over horses, put their nine wounded on litters, and started back to camp. Along the way, they looted and burned deserted ranch houses.[37]

By the end of Monday, March 25, as Patterson's men returned to their camps, the situation inside the city was becoming critical. The heavy U.S. ordnance had pounded the city for four days, with devastating effect. According to Colonel Hitchcock, the shelling "was very destructive—perfectly terific—nothing can exceed its horrors." Houses and shops had been demolished. Buildings burned from the exploding shells. At times the ground shook so much that church bells rang. One shell went through the roof of a church and killed a woman and her son while they prayed. On the previous day, a shell had hit a powder magazine, igniting three powder kegs and killing the men who were at work inside. According to another account, a shell had hit a hospital and killed nineteen people. A story was later told of the wives of two Mexican officers who left their homes and took refuge in a seventeenth-century church. The church was heavily damaged and both women killed, but their houses were untouched. The fifteen-year-old daughter of the British consul was also killed, and the proprietor of a "French store" lost a limb when a shell came through the roof of the establishment. Debris made some streets impassable while panicked and confused citizens roamed about.[38]

After such destruction, and with growing hunger and chaos among the people, Morales began to seriously consider surrender. It seemed clear to everyone that no help was coming, and both soldiers and civilians began to talk of raising the white flag. Even the foreign consuls, thwarted in their attempt to leave the city on March 24, began to press for surrender, as did a group of Mexican officers who met during the night. Accordingly, the next day, as Americans were preparing to open with additional batteries, Morales, not wanting to be the one to surrender and receive Santa Anna's wrath, turned command over to Brigadier General José Landero. The new commander sent a message under a flag of truce to Scott requesting that he appoint commissioners to discuss surrender terms. Scott suspended fire on the city at 8:00 A.M. and appointed Worth, Totten, and Pillow as peace commissioners. He also honored the navy's role by allowing one of its captains, John H. Aulick, to participate as a negotiator.[39]

The U.S. commissioners met with three Mexican colonels, José Guiterrez Villanueva, Pedro Miguel Herrera, and Manuel Robles, to work out the terms of the surrender. Negotiations began in the midst of a roaring norther that had blown in the previous night. Meeting later in the day in a lime kiln near the beach, the opposing sides presented very different sets of demands. The Americans demanded the surrender of the city, the castle garrison, and all war matériel. However, their counterparts responded with a demand that the garrison be allowed to march out of the city with their weapons and repair to the interior of the country, and that their national flag not be taken down until they were gone. Furthermore, national guard troops who had participated in the defense of the city should be allowed to remain at home unmolested. Such terms were reminiscent of Taylor's lenient and imprudent agreement at Monterey the previous year and were wholly rejected. Worth, who had been spoiling for a fight from the beginning, advised that the talks cease and the infantry assault that Scott had contemplated be executed immediately. Scott, however, understood that victory was in reach without further bloodshed, and that Landero was likely searching for a way to save face. On March 27, Scott proposed and Landero accepted the following terms. The entire garrison must surrender but would be allowed to march out of the city with full military honors before being paroled. Officers could keep their guns, horses, and other personal effects. The property and safety of the civilians left behind would be respected. Both parties signed the terms on March 28, and the Mexican army evacuated the city and the castle the next day.[40]

Two aspects of the surrender terms warrant further notice. First, the capitulation of the castle in addition to the city was significant. Scott had concerns about the prospects of occupying Veracruz with hostile forces still in San Juan de Ulúa, but that potential problem was eliminated. Also, the agreement to parole the Mexican troops was an issue because under the laws of war, the term means that paroled Mexican soldiers pledge not to fight against the Americans again unless formally exchanged. This was a dubious understanding; many of the American soldiers did not like the provision, and it soon became obvious that countless Mexican soldiers did not consider it binding.

The bombardment lasted from 4:00 P.M. on Monday, March 22, until 8:00 A.M. Friday, a total of eighty-eight hours. In all, the American guns, both

land and sea, fired about 6,700 rounds of shot and shell at the city, for a total of 463,600 pounds of ordnance. The 10-inch mortars that fired ninety
pound shells were responsible for three thousand rounds, while the heavy
Naval Battery accounted for 1,800 of the total. American casualty reports
vary. Scott placed the number of killed and wounded at sixty-four, while the
number reported in other sources ranges from sixty-eight to eighty-two. The
most likely estimate would place the number at sixty-eight: thirteen killed
and fifty-five wounded. Casualties inside the city are more difficult to ascertain. Mexican sources put their numbers at about a thousand, with the total
somewhat equally divided between soldiers and civilians, depending on the
source consulted. However, it was in their best interest to inflate the number
so as to better justify the decision to surrender. A neutral British observer
estimated the number killed at a hundred civilians and eighty soldiers. However, a more recent Mexican source offered the following breakdown: 350
soldiers killed, 400 civilians killed, 250 people injured. Property damage in
Veracruz amounted to between $5 million and $6 million, with the heaviest
toll falling on the southwest quadrant of the city. "Your battery has smashed
that side of the town," wrote Captain Lee to his brother Smith Lee.[41]

Light American casualties did not mean an absence of gruesome scenes.
Near the end of the bombardment, a lieutenant named Thomas Williams
wrote to his father that "a man must be an eyewitness to realize what are
called the horrors of war." The young subaltern recounted how a wounded
man was in the process of having his leg amputated when he received a second wound, presumably from a shell fragment, that killed him. "To see these
bodies," he lamented, "as they are picked up by surviving comrades drop
their shattered heads upon the sand,—brains falling out, & their gore pouring out in a thick stream." Capturing the city may have been the result of a
slow, scientific process, but it was also, as Kirby Smith described it, "a horrid
business."[42]

The official surrender and evacuation of Veracruz occurred on the morning of March 29. American troops occupied an open plain in front of the
city. They formed two lines a mile long and two hundred feet apart on either
side of the Alvarado Road, Worth's men on one side and Patterson's on the
other. A navy contingent, including some marines, took part in the ceremony,
and one soldier noted that they were the neatest and cleanest dressed of the
bunch. At the head of this gauntlet through which the Mexicans were to
march was Talcott's rocket company, with its howitzers loaded and matches
lit as a form of insurance against mischief. Harney's dragoons were positioned off to the side, and the rest of the army occupied nearby sand hills. A
gun from the castle fired a signal shot for the procession to begin, and the
city gates opened. Out came the enemy army, some dressed in bright green,

Bombardment of Veracruz. Courtesy of Special Collections Division, University of Texas at Arlington Libraries.

some in bright blue, and others in white, all trimmed in red. The officers "were fine-looking men, of light complexion, and exceedingly polite in their manners; saluting our generals with their drawn swords, as they passed."[43]

Once outside the city, the procession stopped for about an hour, and the Mexican soldiers, by previous arrangement, stacked their muskets, filed to the right, and submitted their regimental rolls to be checked by American officers. While looking to be sure that the number of troops leaving the city matched the tallies on the regimental rolls, Lieutenant Roswell Ripley detected a variety of expressions on the faces of the Mexican soldiers: "Some indifferent or apparently so, others trying to look dignified & unconcerned, but with the traces of mortification too distinctly visible to be hidden, others giving way to their grief. One Commandante de Battalon could not restrain his tears." But Ripley's view was up close; from a distance "it was the most glorious & splendid sight I ever beheld," thought another American. George Kendall thought that their evacuation reminded him of the "'Departure of the Israelites' . . . the long procession of soldiers, national militia, & people of all classes & sexes as they poured out of the walls" of the city.[44]

The camp followers who came out after the soldiers attracted much attention and comment. One volunteer simply noted the "women and children following with great loads on their backs." Another witness marveled at the "throng of camp women, carrying every conceivable implement of ornament

& use, . . . to say nothing of the innumerable parrots, poodle dogs, & absurdities of a kindred nature. It is a singular fact that the poorer the people in every country, the greater number of dogs they must have about them." After wives and families came the lancers, dismounted, who laid down their lances and *escopetas* before following the crowd. The long procession, accompanied by Mexican bands, took two hours. The numbers associated with the Mexican surrender were approximately five thousand soldiers, five generals, eighteen colonels, and over 350 cannon.[45]

The Veracruz siege made a lasting impression on young American officers. Lieutenant George McClellan, who described the bombardment as "superb," would later choose to begin his 1862 Peninsula Campaign in Virginia in the same fashion. As a Union general, he decided not to assault General John Magruder's fortified position at Yorktown, opting instead to take time to place his batteries before bombarding the town. The Veracruz experience gave Captain Robert E. Lee opportunity to hone his considerable engineering skills while he helped place the American batteries. Lieutenant Ulysses S. Grant, who was more of the Zachary Taylor mold, nevertheless was just beginning to see that wars are more often won as a result of campaigns rather than battles. Veracruz was just the first step of a process that would not end until the enemy capital was captured and its government agreed to terms. No advance, fight, and retreat here. This would be a sustained, ongoing operation with the army either maintaining its ground or advancing until the enemy capitulated. It was Grant who became the master strategist and victor of the Civil War, and he succeeded because of a bulldog tenacity that was developed from an understanding of sustained campaigning. His willingness to think beyond a single battle is best epitomized by his famous statement in May 1864 that he would "fight it out on this line if it takes all summer." In 1864, Grant knew from experience—it had taken him months to capture Richmond and Petersburg, just as it would take Scott months to capture Mexico City—that success would not come with a single engagement.

CHAPTER THREE

The Army Advances

Olive Branch and Sword

*The whole of the southwest side of the city was most exposed to
the storm of destructive missiles, and was a scene of desolation
calculated to make the most strenuous advocates of physical force
pause and reflect.*
—George Ballentine, Englishman in U.S. First Artillery

As the Mexican army marched into the distance, American troops filed into
Veracruz, field guns and naval vessels fired a national salute, and the stars
and stripes were raised over the city. General Scott rode into Veracruz to the
customary cannon salute that greeted the commanding general and set up his
headquarters in the governor's palace. Scott's methods had resulted in a stun-
ning victory, but as news traveled north, many people were dumbfounded by
the low casualty figures. A few days earlier, as the Mexican commissioners
were negotiating the surrender of the city, back in the United States, the
Niles' National Register had expressed with certainty that news from Scott's
army would arrive soon. It cautioned the public that whether the news would
be of victory or defeat, it would certainly be a tale of blood and death. It was
not. Because of its scant death toll, Veracruz was overshadowed by the bloody
and dramatic battle at Buena Vista, where Taylor had lost 665 men just the
previous month. The slow, scientific process did not satisfy the martial appetite of people back home—not like the account of two armies entangled in
a deadly struggle. Society favors a direct approach and straight-on solutions,
and it often frowns on indirect methods. Military professionals are often the
same, but great leaders know how to resist the temptation to rush into battle.
Others did not appreciate Scott's accomplishment. The British criticized the
siege and its accompanying bombardment as cruel and unnecessary, as if a
frontal assault would have been a more humane approach. Mexicans naturally censured the invaders as cowards. They called the bombardment a bar-
baric act because the "first victims were women and children."[1]

But Scott's men appreciated the results. A Tennessee volunteer named
Samuel Lauderdale wrote to his brother that "a more splendid nor bloodless victory ever adorned the historic page," while Edmund Kirby Smith

called it "a glorious consummation to reduce works of such strength with so little loss." Barna Upton of the Third Infantry wrote to his brother that had Veracruz "been taken by storm (which was generally expected) it must have cost thousands of life." William S. Johnson, of South Carolina's Palmetto Regiment, wrote in his diary about the light American casualties and he described the victory as "Dog cheap *to the living*." Other soldiers tried to describe the nature of the fighting at Veracruz, characterizing it as the "science of dodgeing" and "an affair of trenches and artillery." Thomas Jackson wrote that the capture of Veracruz and the army's performance around the city "excell any military operations known in the history of our country." The young artillery officer came to regard Scott as "the most talented and scientific" general in the army, but Jackson was quick to add that he was also the "most vain and conceited." The only aspect of the operation in which he disapproved was Scott's decision to parole the Mexican troops rather than take them unconditionally as prisoners. William B. Campbell of Tennessee proclaimed Scott "an intelligent and accomplished man," but unlike Taylor, who made everyone feel like an equal, Scott was always intent that people feel his superiority.[2] Many of the soldiers who had transferred from Taylor's army with disappointment and regret began to show respect and admiration for Old Fuss and Feathers, who, despite his arrogant and peculiar ways, had shown unexpected care for the lives of his men.

Scott's accomplishment was indeed impressive, and his friends hoped that he would receive the credit he deserved. However, others wanted to share in the accolades. Low casualties among the artillery crews were due to the skill of the engineers who constructed the battery emplacements, and Totten wanted the work of his engineers acknowledged. Hitchcock agreed that the engineers deserved much of the credit, and in a letter home, he stated, "Our approach and our entire proceedings have been conducted under the direction of scientific Engineers & everything has proceeded according to the known rules of the art of war. Hence the loss has been very slight." Commodore Perry wanted his share of the glory too. It did not sit well with some in the army when Perry informed Scott that he wanted to join in the signing of the surrender document—a request that Scott approved.[3]

And then there was Gideon Pillow, who, after the fall of Veracruz, began to speculate about his future and fortune with the army. He knew that Congress would soon authorize ten new volunteer regiments, if it had not already done so, and he hoped that the need for new officers would provide him with an opportunity for promotion. Knowing the Democrats needed a major general in the army "to counter-act that . . . which is exclusively whig," and believing that other top candidates lacked his qualifications, he saw himself as the best person to hold such a title in a successful and growing army. In addition, he had a powerful friend in the White House who could facilitate his rise. Pillow likely felt a growing sense of self-importance because of the deference that Scott showed him. The commanding general was "putting forward Pillow on all occasions," wrote Colonel William Campbell, who referred to Scott, Worth, and Pillow as "a sort of triumvirate" because they were seen together so often. In giving Pillow a prominent role, "Scott is paying Polk for letting him come here," Campbell concluded.[4]

Upon entering Veracruz, some soldiers, like Thomas Jackson and his former West Point instructor, Daniel Frost, were surprised to find so little damage, and D. H. Hill saw sparse firsthand evidence of destruction caused by the bombardment. Conversely, other soldiers commented on the widespread damage. Arthur Manigault, a South Carolinian and future Confederate general, wrote a letter to his brother describing the "great havoc amongst the houses, scarce one that does not show some bullet hole or other damage." Another soldier estimated that the bombardment had affected a fourth of the city. Barna Upton, an enlisted man from Massachusetts, "was surprised at the almost entire destruction of a considerable part of the town." He went on to surmise that the devastation "reminded me of the description I have read of cities destroyed by earthquakes."[5]

The curious Americans also observed that the city had been well fortified. When he first entered the city, Hill was impressed with the twelve-foot wall around it, the loopholes for muskets, and the periodic forts that ringed it with their scores of cannon. In some of these forts, the destructive effect of the bombardment remained evident—holes in the fortifications that had been filled with sandbags, damaged artillery pieces, and bloodstained walls. Then there was the mighty fortress of San Juan de Ulúa, with all of its guns. When Americans entered the castle, they found over 7,500 artillery shells and 900 barrels of powder. They had never seen such a fortress, with its "thick walls, solid roofs, and its excellent adaptation for defence, and its durability, . . . [all of which] excite wonder and astonishment in the mind of the beholder," wrote Lee to his fifteen-year-old son. Lieutenant Edmund Kirby Smith boasted with an air of superiority that if such a strong bastion had been in American hands, no army in the world could have taken it. Another soldier, in a statement that demonstrated a similar vein of thought, asserted with confidence that "now, with an American garrison in it, it would bid successful defiance to the navies of the world."[6]

Once in possession of Veracruz, Scott's primary objectives were to secure civil control, round up supplies and draft animals, and move inland as soon as possible. He appointed Worth military governor of the city, regulated food prices, issued 10,000 rations to the poor, and paid idle citizens to clean debris out of the streets. In addition to the rubble from the bombardment, the

Americans were astonished to find piles of garbage in the streets, along with a stench that hung over the city. "Vera Cruz," thought Lieutenant Roswell Ripley, "deserves from its filth to have all the diseases which ever issued from Pandoras box." Lieutenant Isaac Stevens also commented on the "miserable, dirty" condition of the city, and also described as "troublesome" the number of fleas and mosquitoes. The houses in Veracruz were made of brick or stone with tile roofs, but many of them appeared "much worn by time." Aside from its imposing strength, the next most commonly mentioned characteristic of the castle of San Juan de Ulúa was its filth, and work crews cleaned the city as well as the castle. Just as American soldiers had shared their rations with the departing Mexican soldiers, they also loaned money to and shared their food with needy residents, who "clamor[ed] about [the] commissaries' depots for bread."[7]

Scott and Worth worked quickly to put the city in order so that preparations could be made to move inland. The docks were reopened for trade, and, in accordance with a system of duties established by the Polk administration to help pay for the war, duties collected at Veracruz went to pay for the occupation. Also, straightway Scott issued General Order No. 20 proclaiming the city under martial law. This order had been first articulated at Tampico, one of the army's collection points, but since landing below Veracruz, many of the soldiers had seemingly ignored its provisions. The immediate imperatives of the siege had apparently resulted in lax discipline, because numerous soldiers engaged in lawlessness in the latter stages of the bombardment. Groups of volunteers and sailors had robbed and looted in the suburbs outside the city wall the day before the cease-fire, and even some regulars, having gotten drunk, became unmanageable. Some had to be "tied and gagged," and Lieutenant Hill went so far as to "give one of them a sound drubbing with my own hands" in order to gain control. With Scott's martial law proclamation, he served notice that past indiscretions would no longer be tolerated. Thus, murder, rape, assaults, and robbery were forbidden, as was desecration of religious, personal, and public property and interruption of religious ceremonies. Scott's purpose for using martial law to maintain discipline was for "the welfare of the military service, for the interest of humanity, and for the honor of the United States." Both Mexicans and Americans were subject to the general's directive, and violators were subject to strict punishment. Although American offenders would be tried by court-martial, Scott allowed the Mexicans to choose their own magistrates to mete out punishment to their countrymen.[8]

Within three days after the reissue of the martial law order, two military commissions had been established and were preparing to hear cases against both regulars and volunteers. Some soldiers, however, worried lest the influence of politics result in inequities, especially in the volunteer units. Soldiers in those units came from the same communities back home, and selection as an officer often resulted from past political connections or future political aspirations. Under such circumstances, how could officers assigned to adjudicate cases render impartial judgment against potential future voters? There is no direct evidence of such corruption plaguing the courts, but military commissions from different states often handed down widely divergent punishment for the same offense. Assault, theft, and public drunkenness seemed to be the most common crimes. One soldier had gotten drunk and assaulted a Mexican woman, for which he received twelve lashes, then was ordered to perform hard labor in ball and chain for the war's duration. Two soldiers were sent to the dungeon of the castle for stealing. Three volunteers were tried for stealing jewelry, furniture, and other items worth $300 from the home of Rosalie Lopez. All three were convicted and sentenced to confinement, a fine, and the return of the stolen property. Lopez was so astonished when American officials returned her belongings that she wrote a letter of gratitude to Scott.[9]

Isaac Kirk, "a free man of color," who worked as a teamster for the army, was arrested for theft and rape. Lieutenant George Turnbull Davis, a staff officer on Brigadier General James Shields's staff and acting judge advocate of the Volunteer Military Commission, knew that Kirk was of "a degraded and friendless race" and as a consequence would receive no special sympathy. So he was vigilant in his oversight of this trial to be sure that Kirk received a capable defense and that the evidence was compelling. Evidently it was, for the court convicted Kirk and sentenced him to hang. In writing the court's findings and the punishment to which Kirk was sentenced, Davis concluded with, "And may God have mercy upon your soul." According to Davis, when Scott's military secretary, Lieutenant George Washington Lay, read that part of the court proceedings to the commanding general, Scott liked it so much that he ordered that those words be included in the records of all future capital cases that ended with a guilty verdict.[10]

Public intoxication became a problem. Sutlers and army followers opened liquor shops in the city, and within days, the Americans had to designate a guardhouse for the detainment of soldiers found drunk in the streets. The building used was more like a large stable approximately a hundred feet by forty feet, and all of the doors and windows were locked except one, which was blocked by guards. According to John Smith, who visited the guardhouse a few days after the surrender, about 150 men were confined: some had passed out on the floor, while others leaned against the wall in a drunken stupor. Occasionally one would make a dash for the door to try to get into the street, but would be blocked by the sentinels and often "knocked down by a blow" from a musket butt—the nose apparently being the favorite target for the guards.[11]

Rigid discipline did not eliminate crimes by American soldiers, and dealing with lawless behavior was an ongoing concern. Some of the men seemed indifferent to the strict regulations; others simply failed to understand why they could not act as they pleased in a foreign country against a race of people that they did not respect. Why, some wondered, could they not take whatever they wanted—food, drink, souvenirs of war—and just live off the land? Breaches of discipline thus continued. A company of Pennsylvania volunteers stationed outside the city walls adopted the practice of luring into their camp Mexicans who they knew to be carrying liquor, whereupon they "confiscated" the strong drink. In this fashion, the Pennsylvanians succeeded in accumulating quite a bit of the beverage.[12]

In the days after the announcement of martial law, the commanding general continued to receive reports that American soldiers were stealing cattle, produce, and other provisions. Scott lamented the shameful acts committed by "worthless soldiers," and on April 1, he issued a general appeal to his men. The actions of a few had dishonored the entire army, he wrote, and "every good soldier" should help maintain order, discipline, and honor by turning in those who violate orders. He implored his men not to allow a small minority to bring dishonor to the whole army, and he reminded them that the army had made provisions to purchase its food, and individuals must pay for items in a fair and honest fashion, "as at home." Even though such behavior was not eliminated, Scott's diligence, along with that of other officers, did limit such acts—enough to enable Isaac Stevens of the engineers to inform his wife a week later that "scarcely an outrage has been committed in the city." He may have exaggerated, but the surprising degree to which the American soldiers were kept in check demonstrated to the Mexican people that their rights would not be lost during the occupation. "Every exertion is made to protect the whole city in its rights," continued the officer. And according to Robert Anderson, "Genl. Scott will be as liberal towards the Vera Cruzians as his duty to his own Govt. will permit."[13]

In this manner, Scott hoped to prevent a hostile uprising by the civilian population—a guerrilla war that could potentially peck away at his small army, thus rendering it unable to march on the capital. And while guerrilla attacks were a constant menace, attacking supply trains and reinforcements, they were never widespread to the point of threatening the survival of the army. Partisan bands that roamed the countryside were a constant concern and annoyance, and Scott had to make adjustments to meet the threat they posed. However, he never did have to significantly alter his plan in a way that deterred him from his march to the capital. And because guerrilla bands preyed on Mexican civilians as well as American soldiers, they never won the universal support of their own people. Internal dissension among the various classes of Mexican people also prevented them from unifying against, or even identifying, a common enemy. Scott's pacification plan was, for its time, a sophisticated model for waging war in a foreign country and occupying enemy territory without alienating the civilian population. As America's first foreign war, the government had no experience in such matters, but Scott's system of martial law, despite its imperfections, established a noteworthy pattern for waging war in another country.

As proof that his pacification plan worked, Mexican citizens who had either fled the city or hidden in their homes began to return and enter the streets to mingle with the foreigners. Learning that the army would pay for, rather than take, their goods, they reopened their shops two days after the surrender, and merchants and street vendors began to make a profit off the Americans. The soldiers could purchase all manner of produce in the streets' open markets. Eggs sold for fifty cents a dozen and chickens for $1.50. Some merchants advertised turkey eggs for sale, but once the soldiers discovered that they were really buzzard eggs, they stayed away from anyone with such advertisements. Some of the troops especially liked Mexican honey, until they learned that it was generally transported to market in cowhide sacks sewn together with the hair turned inward. American atrocities against Mexicans were the exceptions, while civility and commerce were the rule.[14]

Respect for religious services and property was another aspect of Scott's pacification program. The anti-Catholic, anti-immigrant sentiment of the nativist movement back home influenced the attitudes of many soldiers, who were predominately Protestant. They often viewed the Mexican peasantry as ignorant and superstitious because of their devotion to the church, and they considered the church, with its wealth and influence, a corrupt institution that rivaled the Mexican government in oppression. But Scott understood that winning the hearts and minds of the civilian population had to be done within the context of their own culture, and many Mexicans were devout Catholics. So, American prejudices notwithstanding, soldiers were required to show proper reverence and respect for Mexico's religious heritage. After Veracruz surrendered, news circulated that the churches would not be conducting their normal services for fear that the American "heretics" would desecrate their services. As a way of placating the clergy and the church faithful, Scott saw to it that churches were open the following Sunday, and he made a public display of attending mass at a church outside the city walls. His staff, other officers, and quite a crowd of soldiers also attended.[15]

It was concerning one of these services in Veracruz that Joseph E. Johnston later related the following ribald anecdote regarding Robert E. Lee. The antecedent to the story actually occurred three years earlier, when Lee and Johnston were stationed at Fort Hamilton in New York during the Oxford Movement, also called Tractarianism, in England. Among its advocates in England was a man named Edward Pusey. This controversial religious movement sought to introduce high church practices into the Anglican church, and some American Episcopalians were concerned lest its influence spill over into the United States, thus moving their religion in the direction of Catholicism. Lee was a vestryman in the local parish, but he usually refrained from discussing Tractarianism when it was the topic of conversation. During one particularly heated debate among several officers at Fort Hamilton, they made an effort to draw Captain Lee into the discussion, to which he simply advised that they not get involved in the questionable movement. Then in a playful and vulgar use of a double entendre, he warned them to *"Beware of Pussyism! Pussyism is always bad, and may lead to unchristian feeling; therefore beware of Pussyism!"*

Three years later in Veracruz, General Scott, along with a host of other officers and men, attended a religious service, and Johnston found himself seated next to Lee in the crowded assembly. At one point, a church official brought to Scott, and to the officers seated around him, candles, and they were instructed to rise and walk around the building in a procession that to many of the Protestant Americans looked very high church. Johnston and Lee were walking shoulder to shoulder, candles in hand, just behind Scott, when Johnston touched Lee on the elbow. Lee looked dignified and graceful as he pretended to know what the ceremony was about, and he gave his friend a quiet but "rebuking look." Johnston touched him again, and this time Lee leaned over and whispered, "What is it?" To which Johnston responded, "I really hope there is no *Pussyism* in all this." Lee tried to keep a straight face, but "the corners of his eyes and mouth were twitching in the struggle to preserve his gravity."[16]

In the days after the surrender, lack of transport remained Scott's most pressing problem. The army had 185 wagons and 1,100 mules, but he informed Marcy that he needed an additional 60 wagons and enough mules to pull them in order to begin his march inland. The army's persistent and unfulfilled transportation needs seemingly induced the secretary to wash his hands of the problem. "What embarrassments may attend your forward movements, arriving from the difficulties of obtaining supplies and the means of transportation, cannot be foreseen or anticipated here," came Marcy's response.[17]

To fill his needs, he sent Brigadier General John A. Quitman's brigade, a contingent of dragoons, and the navy to Alvarado fifty miles to the south. Located near the mouth of the Río Papaloapán, it was an ideal site for an

American naval base, but Conner had tried and failed to capture it the previous fall. Scott and Perry wanted to try again, and they hoped that in the process, the army would be able to procure an abundance of cattle and horses from the farms in the area. Accordingly, Perry ordered Lieutenant Charles G. Hunter, commander of the iron-screw steamer *U.S.S. Scourge,* to blockade the mouth of the river until the army-navy expedition arrived. However, the overly aggressive Hunter arrived on March 30 and bombarded the city. The Mexican troops spiked the guns and fled, the town surrendered, and Hunter garrisoned Alvarado with half a dozen sailors. When Perry arrived with twelve vessels and Quitman with his infantry on April 2, Hunter had already sailed further upriver to capture other towns, and in so doing, had alerted the surrounding countryside. The inhabitants drove their cattle and horses away and burned supplies to prevent them from falling into American hands, and the net result was that Quitman came away from the lush ranching area with few animals.[18]

The Alvarado expedition proved frustrating for all involved. The infantry had marched under extreme conditions of heat and lack of food and water, at one point quenching their thirst out of a muddy pond from which their horses refused to drink. Upon arriving, they were angry at having endured such hardships for no apparent reason. As one soldier put it, with a bit of exaggeration, the town had surrendered to "a midshipman & four men." Many in the brigade suffered from dehydration, dysentery, and other illnesses and had to be carried back to Veracruz on board naval vessels. After two days of rest in Alvarado, Quitman ordered the brigade back to Veracruz, and once again the oppressive heat took its toll. Quitman pushed them to get back in three days, even though several died along the way. "We were marched back in a deuce of a hurry," remarked an annoyed William Johnson. Scott and Perry were also angry about Hunter's independent action, Scott because the army so desperately needed the animals and Perry because he wanted to be the one to capture Alvarado. Perry had Hunter court-martialed, and the court found him guilty. Although U.S. newspapers portrayed Hunter as a hero, he was no longer allowed to serve in Perry's squadron. Later his aggressive nature landed him in trouble again while commanding a ship as part of the Union naval blockade in the Civil War. He pursued a British blockade runner in Cuban waters, was again court-martialed, and was dismissed from the service.[19]

Meanwhile, Colonel William S. Harney and his dragoons combed the area around Antigua for animals and supplies. He brought back some of both and a few enemy prisoners as well, but still the army needed more. Scott's lack of transportation on both water and land had already cost him six weeks in January and February, and he knew that he could not linger on the coast much longer. The periodic northers that had wreaked havoc on the army and beached dozens of vessels had at least kept the mosquitoes away. Soon the northers would end, and the mosquitoes would arrive, bearing their debilitating and often deadly diseases. The soldiers were aware of the approaching yellow fever season and worried about its potentially "dreadful ravages." Early symptoms of the *vomito,* as Americans called it, included jaundice, fever, headache, and vomiting. In severe cases, blood vessels ruptured, which caused black-and-blue spots to appear on the skin. The hemorrhaging blood began to fill the lungs, and eventually the victim began to vomit dark, coagulated blood. In the nineteenth century, people commonly believed that yellow fever resulted when the wind stopped blowing and the spring rains created stagnant pools in the lowlands, especially in marshes or close to the coast. These factors, they believed, created an unhealthy environment that could be avoided by moving inland to higher elevations, and they were correct to a point. They just did not know that the mosquitoes that bred in such places were the actual carriers of the disease. So as the first week of April drew to a close, Scott knew the clock was ticking and that he had to get his army inland.[20]

News of political chaos in Mexico City reached the coast in early April. The fall of Veracruz, coupled with the recent Polkos Rebellion, caused a "great sensation" in the capital. Two of President Polk's agents, Moses Beach and Jane Storms, had gone to Mexico City two months earlier and had helped finance the rebellion. In addition, Beach had succeeded in winning limited support, or at least sympathy, from clergy for Scott's invading army. When Santa Anna arrived in the capital after his defeat at Buena Vista, Beach helped Storms slip out of the city so she could travel to Veracruz and report to Scott. Storms's knowledge of the Mexican people allowed her to offer perceptive insights. She believed that "Gen. Scott can have the people with him—or at least passive—while he exterminates their old oppressors." Instinctively understanding Scott's carrot-and-stick approach, she continued, "he can march to Mexico [City] without the loss of a single man in battle, if he will pursue the wise, explanatory, protecting system . . . but if, like brave Old Taylor, he will use no argument but the sword, it will cost many lives." Although her sentiments conformed precisely with Scott's objectives, the haughty general did not appreciate having his views validated by "a plenipotentiary in petticoats." Hoping to take advantage of the political turmoil and thinking that the Mexican government might be ready to negotiate, Scott sent word to the capital that the United States was prepared to receive peace overtures. Meanwhile, he said that "the army would continue to advance—presenting at once the olive branch & the sword."[21]

As his army began its march on April 8, Scott sat down and penned a proclamation to "the good people of Mexico." It was itself an enunciation of the carrot-and-stick approach that he intended to pursue as the army advanced. He opened by warning that he commanded "a powerful army" and that another army in northern Mexico was poised to march south. (Taylor's army in northern Mexico actually was not poised for such a march, but saying so added weight to Scott's pronouncement.) Then he extended the olive branch: "*Mexicans!* Americans are not your enemies; but the enemies, for a time, of the men who, a year ago, misgoverned you, and brought about this unnatural war." It was a psychological approach, an attempt to position his army on the side of the Mexican people. "We are the friends of the peaceful inhabitants of the country we occupy, and the friends of your Holy Religion, its Hierarchy and its Priesthood." In addition, he assured them that there were "devout Catholics" in the United States and that the church was "respected by our government, laws and people." (He failed to mention that one of his own daughters had converted to Catholicism and in so doing had caused Mrs. Scott considerable grief.) He went on to guarantee the safety of "unoffending inhabitants" by explaining that the "few bad men in this army" were being severely punished. "Is that not proof of good faith?" he asked. He further promised cash payments for residents who wanted to sell animals and food to the army. The proclamation contained one more threat with the sword for civilians who attempted to bring injury to "any . . . person or property belonging to this army." Such offending parties "shall be punished with rigor," he warned.[22]

As Twiggs's division of regulars led the army inland on April 8, the ground seemed to move slowly under them. With each difficult step, their feet sank ankle deep into the hot sand as they trudged under a burning sun. For several miles north and then turning west, American soldiers labored on the road that led away from Veracruz, away from the coast, and away from yellow fever country. One soldier thought it was "the hottest day I ever did see. Our men were loaded down notwithstanding the hot weather." Massachusetts native Barna Upton described the heat as "extreme . . . as hot as any weather we have in the summer in the north." Romeyn B. Ayres, a future Union general from New York, remembered, "I was nearly used up with fatigue." Sometimes the sand was so deep that wagon wheels sank to the hub, and teamsters used the whip and "all the oaths of the catalogue" to keep mules moving forward. Despite the difficulty of the march, the men left Veracruz in high spirits.[23]

As they moved further inland, the soft sand turned into a wide highway built of heavy stone and covered with cement. It was the National Road, long noted for its sturdy construction, and although parts of it had fallen into disrepair, it made the difficult march a bit easier. The flat, sandy, coastal region looked much like a desert, but after several miles, the soldiers began to pass palm trees, then thick tropical vegetation as the National Road made a

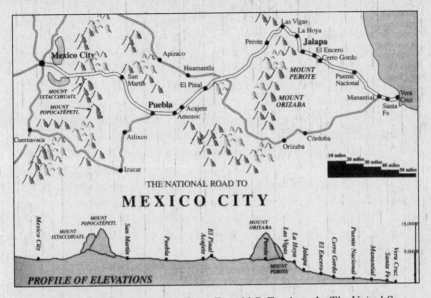

U.S. Army's route to Mexico City. From Donald S. Frazier, ed., *The United States and Mexico at War* (New York: Macmillan, 1998). Reprinted by permission of The Gale Group.

gradual ascent up the Sierra Madres and wound its way inland through and eventually out of the *tierra caliente,* or hot country. The steady uphill trek exhausted the men. A volunteer private from Pennsylvania noted that despite the sand, heat, and incline, his regiment covered over twenty miles the first day, but in the process left men "scattered for miles back." After the long day's march, men wearily entered the designated campsite, clothes drenched with perspiration, and as soon as the sun set, the temperature dropped so that the cold night winds made their uniforms feel like ice blankets. Building fires was a top priority, and despite protests from local inhabitants, fence rails or boards taken from nearby farms and villages served as fuel.[24]

At the outset of the march, friction arose within the army high command. When striking out from Veracruz, Scott gave Twiggs the place of honor by allowing his division to lead. It was an obvious choice since Twiggs's division was located on the northern end of the siege line and thus was closest to the point where the National Road turned inland. Because Worth's division had been allowed to land on the beach first, and given his position on the extreme south, Scott, in a spirit of fairness, thought Twiggs should have his turn at the head of the army. The day after Twiggs's division marched, Patterson's volunteer division followed (except for Quitman's brigade, which was still too sickly and broken down from the Alvarado expedition). Meanwhile, Scott ordered Worth's division to remain in Veracruz until additional wagons arrived. The marching orders infuriated Worth and renewed the dispute over seniority that had occurred with Twiggs the previous year. Now Worth believed that he was being superseded by his old antagonist, and he "became almost outrageous, burning up as he was with hatred & jealousy of Twiggs."[25]

Worth's dissatisfaction drew comments from various soldiers. According to Lieutenant George Davis, a staff officer in Brigadier General James Shields's brigade, everyone assumed from the outset of the campaign that Worth's division was to have the post of honor in all of the army's actions. That his men landed first on Collado Beach seemed to confirm the supposition, thereby fostering a "spirit of jealousy and unrest" in the volunteer division. John Gardner, an officer in Twiggs's division, thought he perceived blatant favoritism in the placement of the batteries for the Veracruz siege. Most of them had been located in front of Worth's division, making his section of the investment line the focal point. The "design from the first was to pile all the honor on Worths division, and accordingly little or no notice was taken of the services of any part of Twiggs'." After getting all the credit at Veracruz, Worth "could not even play 'second fiddle' in this concert," complained Gardner.[26]

After starting along the National Road, however, they had little time for such squabbling and were happy to be on the move. The soldiers knew that the road inland carried them to a healthier climate. Their destination was Jalapa, some sixty-five miles from the coast, which, at an altitude of 4,700 feet, was safely above the yellow fever region. The course of the road took them roughly along the same path that Hernando Cortes had followed three centuries earlier when he conquered the Aztec empire. However, as they left the coast behind them, many Americans believed the rumors that Scott would meet with Mexican officials at Jalapa to negotiate a peace, which, if true, would make their conquest of the country much faster and less costly than their Spanish predecessor.[27]

Early in the march, Colonel Henry L. Kinney, beef contractor with the army's quartermaster department, entered into an interesting arrangement to supply the army with cattle. The colorful Kinney was a well-known Texan who had served in the republic's congress before it was annexed to the United States. A native of Pennsylvania and a former land agent in Illinois, Kinney had established a trading outpost in 1838 that later became Corpus Christi, Texas. Known for a multitude of business enterprises, one of which was smuggling, Kinney served in Zachary Taylor's army as a quartermaster officer before joining Scott's command. Before leaving Veracruz, Kinney had scouted the army's inland route as far as Mango de Clavo, one of Santa Anna's estates, which boasted thousands of cattle. There Kinney contracted to purchase some of the livestock, and Santa Anna, careful to conceal his involvement in the affair, had his agent, Manuel Garcia, arrange the terms of the sale. Then Garcia informed Kinney that another individual named Nicholas Dorich, whose nationality is unknown, would collect payment and finalize the transaction. When Twiggs's lead division passed through the village where Dorich was staying, which was near Mango de Clavo, the army paid him $500 in silver and gold for an unspecified number of cattle. However, rowdy volunteers of Patterson's division delayed the delivery of the animals when they came through. According to Dorich, they broke down his door, struck him, and demanded whiskey. When one of their officers came in and tried to control them, they attacked him also. Dorich ran to some nearby woods but the soldiers found him and stripped him of his clothes. Dragoons had to be called up to restore order, collect the cattle, and deliver them to quartermaster officials. In reporting this incident, Kinney claimed that "bandits" had prevented the transfer of the cattle into American hands. Records are unclear as to whether this was a one-time deal with Santa Anna or an ongoing enterprise, but it is evident that the Mexican leader made money from the war.[28]

CHAPTER FOUR

Cerro Gordo

A Brilliant Affair

*One of the surest ways of forming good combinations in war would
be to order movements only after obtaining perfect information of
the enemy's proceedings. . . . As it is unquestionably of the highest
importance to gain this information, so it is . . . one of the chief
causes of the great difference between the theory and the practice
of war. From this cause arise the mistakes of the generals who are
simply learned men without a natural talent for war.*
—Henri Jomini, *The Art of War*

Despite the hopes that enemy resistance would evaporate, Antonio López de
Santa Anna planned to stop the Americans before they reached Jalapa. Santa
Anna was a longtime military and political leader in Mexico, admired and
respected by some but distrusted and despised by others. First elected president in 1833, he dominated twenty years of Mexican history and has been
referred to as both an eagle and an enigma. He became a national hero in 1838
when he lost a leg while defending Mexico from an invading French army,
and he fancied himself the Napoleon of the West. However, the most recent
study of Santa Anna calls him a "political opportunist" and "a curse upon
Mexico." Returning to the capital after his disappointing defeat at Buena
Vista, the Mexican leader had reorganized the government and negotiated
a loan from the church for two million pesos to help finance the war. Santa
Anna, calling the capitulation of Veracruz a "shameful surrender," decided
that his talents were required to stop the American invasion. On April 5, he
arrived at his hacienda, El Encero, near Jalapa, and immediately went to work
organizing a defensive position east of Jalapa. Although some in Scott's army
believed that the war was practically over, others instinctively knew that a
battle awaited them.[1]

On April 11, the Americans reached the National Bridge, which crossed
the Antigua River thirty miles from Veracruz and about halfway to Jalapa.
The bridge, an impressive stone structure, had five arches supporting its span
of four hundred yards. Its road surface was over fifty feet wide, and it gently
curved in a half-moon shape. The river was a hundred yards wide with steep

Antonio López de Santa Anna. Courtesy of Special Collections Division, University of Texas at Arlington Libraries.

hills all around. The well-watered area produced a lush, dark green foliage that covered the hills and cliff faces as far as the eye could see, and flowers in a variety of brilliant colors dotted the landscape. The scenery was breathtaking; a "wild and romantic place," as one soldier described it. Lieutenant A. P. Hill described the bridge in a letter to his parents as "the most beautiful specimen of Bridge architecture I ever saw." Another soldier named Fitzgerald wrote that the "National Bridge . . . is the grandest structure of the kind I ever saw."[2]

The cliffs overlooking the bridge bore evidence of a recently aborted attempt to defend the area. Indeed, before leaving the capital, Santa Anna had sent orders to his generals to defend the road that led inland. To General Valentín Canalizo, commander in chief of the eastern division, Santa Anna sent instructions to oppose the American advance at various points. He also issued a broadside to the Mexican people challenging them to "Awake!" and defend their country. One of the points that he implored Canalizo to fortify was the National Bridge, but construction of defensive works had only begun as the news of Veracruz's surrender filtered down to Canalizo's soldiers. This demoralizing news prompted most of the workers to flee in panic. Rather than a desperate fight, the only thing the Americans encountered at this place was a splendid vista of colors and architecture.[3]

The beautiful and majestic encounter with the National Bridge was followed later in the day by a far more serious encounter. Fifteen miles up the road, in the vicinity of a village called Plan del Río, Colonel William S. Harney's cavalry screen ran into a body of Mexican lancers, who fired a few ineffective shots before retiring. Harney sent word back to Twiggs of the contact with hostile troops, and the general accurately ascertained that this was likely the advance guard of a Mexican army rumored to be in the area. Regardless, Twiggs was determined to act. He ordered a courier to ride back toward the coast, find General Scott, and inform him of the discovery. Then Twiggs rushed his division up to Plan del Río late in the day to encamp for the night, intending to conduct a strong reconnaissance the next morning. At least that is what Twiggs later called it—a "reconnaissance"—as have historians. However, a dispatch rider overheard the general say at his headquarters, "I shall fight them. . . . tomorrow I shall march out, whip them, and return to my camp."[4]

At Plan del Río, the National Road ran north, crossing a rushing stream called Río del Plan. After winding through the rugged terrain, it turned west about a mile above the village, angled back toward the river, then turned and ran roughly parallel to it. After making its westward turn, the road ran through a deep gorge that ended three miles away at the town of Cerro Gordo. Hills and ridges dotted the landscape and lined both sides of the road before it reached the town and open country. Like a funnel, the road carried everything on it into the narrow Cerro Gordo pass—a deadly trap for an unsuspecting army. Any number of positions on this stretch of road would make ideal locations for the Mexican army to make a stand. This was on the edge of the *vomito* region, so if the Americans could be beaten back and forced to remain relatively close to the coast, they might yet feel the ravages of the deadly disease. Santa Anna's hacienda with its thousands of acres was a few miles west of Cerro Gordo, giving him a personal interest in resisting further American advances in this area.

Aware of Harney's clash with enemy cavalry, the men in Twiggs's division knew that it must be an advance patrol and that a Mexican army of unknown strength could not be far away. That evening before going to bed, Joseph R. Smith recorded in his diary his expectation that he was "on the eve of a severe battle." That his thoughts dwelt on both his immediate and his eternal future is evident in the way he closed his entry on April 11: "O, my God, in Thee do I put my trust. Let me not be confounded, still watch over me and shield me. Protect me in the hour of conflict and the day of battle. Preserve my life." The last sentence of his prayer indicated his willingness to accept his fate: "Yet, oh God, not my will but Thine, be done."[5] As it turned out, Smith's foreboding about the morrow was premature by five days.

On the morning of April 12, Twiggs impetuously sent forward a reconnaissance force supported by the advance of his entire division. Without knowing the size or location of the enemy in his front, and without waiting for the rest of the army to come up or for instructions from the commanding general, he formed his division and started up the road toward the gorge. In his battle report written a week later, Twiggs explained his intentions "if practicable, to make an effective attack on all his works." As historian K. Jack Bauer aptly described him, "'Old Davy' Twiggs . . . was not one of the army's intellectuals." Alfred Hoyt Bill, another chronicler of the conflict, wrote that in pressing the issue without adequate preparation, Twiggs was "disdainful as ever of all finesse." In his classic study of the war, Justin H. Smith asserted that Twiggs's "brains were, in fact, merely what happened to be left over from the making of his spinal cord." A volunteer officer, Colonel William Campbell, wrote in a letter the next day that he had no confidence in General Twiggs, and neither did "the intelligent officers of the army."[6]

Leading the reconnaissance and at the vanguard of the entire forward movement were Captain Joseph E. Johnston of the Voltigeurs and Lieutenant Zealous B. Tower of the engineers sent out by Twiggs to gather and relay information about enemy positions. From local inhabitants, Johnston learned of the strong enemy position in and around Cerro Gordo, and upon communicating such to Twiggs, he was instructed to push forward and get a closer look. Johnston's scouting party, however, got too close, and when Mexican pickets spotted it, they opened fire. Johnston fell to the ground, severely wounded, and three Mexican soldiers were killed in the skirmish that followed. Four Americans rushed to the captain's aid, laid him on a blanket, and, each grabbing a corner, carried the suffering Johnston to the rear. Doctors removed two musket balls, one from his arm and the other from just above the hip, and ordered a couple of weeks of bed rest. It would not be the last time Johnston would be wounded in the line of duty.[7] Had the Mexicans waited until the Americans were well into the gorge, they might have destroyed Twiggs's division with a devastating fire from three sides. Among the seven companies designated to attack the Mexican works was that of Joseph Smith, whose dramatic prayer the night before might indeed have been his last. As it was, Santa Anna's gunners fired prematurely, thus surrendering the element of surprise and allowing Twiggs to avoid a potential disaster.

With the reconnaissance party driven back, and with his appreciation of the strength of the Mexican position enhanced, Twiggs ordered his division back. He sent out more scouts in the afternoon of April 12 to get a better picture of what he was up against and to provide time for Major General Patterson's volunteer division to arrive at Plan del Río. Patterson's subordinate officers worked tirelessly to bring up the division. Israel Uncapher recorded in his diary on the evening of April 12: "Started early & travelled fast. The road was . . . very dusty . . . very hot." The arrival of the volunteers would have ordinarily put the whole force at hand under Patterson's charge, because he was the superior officer, but he had reported sick, leaving Twiggs in command. Accordingly, "Old Davy" Twiggs made plans to attack at 4:00 A.M. next morning. But Patterson's men were tired and "much broken down" from the march, so his brigade commanders, Gideon Pillow and James Shields, requested that Twiggs give the volunteers time to rest. Therefore, Twiggs postponed the attack twenty-four hours, or until the morning of April 14.[8]

With the Americans idle on April 13, Twiggs fortunately used the day to gather additional intelligence. Lieutenant Pierre G. T. Beauregard (attached to Patterson's division) and other engineer officers led several companies around to the north through rough terrain to try to ascertain the strength of the Mexican left flank. The topography on the north side of the road consisted of endless hills and ridges as far as the eye could see. For a while the engineers followed what appeared to be a mule trail, and as they went, they dropped off troops along the way to guard the route. The trail eventually disappeared, which slowed their progress, but the reconnaissance party pressed on, probing for a passage to the enemy flank and rear. At length Beauregard reached the base of a hill called La Atalaya, and, leaving the remainder of the party there, he and a few sharpshooters crept to the top to take a look around.

For over an hour, Beauregard scanned the surrounding countryside, but what most attracted his attention was an adjacent hill to the southwest called El Telégrafo or Cerro Gordo (Fat Hill), which commanded a long stretch of the road leading into the town of Cerro Gordo. The bases of the two hills very nearly met, while their peaks, standing roughly equal height at about six hundred feet, were perhaps four hundred yards apart. From this distance, Beauregard could see that several dozen infantry and four cannon occupied the top of El Telégrafo. He also perceived that he was on the extreme left flank of the Mexican army—that, in fact, El Telégrafo anchored this end of the enemy line, and with but a few infantry and a scant four guns, was very lightly defended. He was about a mile behind the forwardmost Mexican position on the south side of the road, and capturing these hills would put the whole enemy line in jeopardy.[9]

While Beauregard and the others scouted the countryside, Scott, escorted by cavalry under Captain Philip Kearny, hurried to catch up to the head of

La Atalaya as seen from El Telégrafo (top). From El Telégrafo looking southeast at the three ridges running parallel to the National Road (bottom). Courtesy of the author.

his army. Having received word from Twiggs on April 12 of the enemy encounter, the commanding general had left Veracruz and traveled all day on April 13. Always scrupulously jealous of his title and authority, Scott was not inclined to look favorably on a subordinate officer who exceeded instructions or initiated a battle without his approval. Besides, Scott was dubious of Twiggs's ability and may have put him in the lead position because he did not expect a battle before the army reached Jalapa. Indeed, Scott thought Twiggs ill-suited "to command an army—either in the presence, or in the absence of an enemy." But a fight is what Twiggs wanted, and on April 13, he seemed determined to bring one on. Meanwhile, Worth, stuck on the coast without adequate transportation and ordered to bring up the rear, cautioned that the enemy should not be attacked until the entire American army arrived. Worth did not want to be absent when a general engagement took place.[10]

Two days of reconnaissance, however, began to reveal the strength of the enemy position, bringing the location of Mexican forces into clearer focus. Santa Anna and his chief engineer, Lieutenant Colonel Manuel M. Robles, had been busy for days studying the topography and issuing orders for the construction of defensive works. Robles had an eye for detail, and he had earlier reported that, while the Cerro Gordo Pass was an ideal place to harass the Americans, it was not the best place to make a determined stand. The position could be flanked easily, Robles thought, and, in his opinion, Corral Falso a little farther west was more defensible. The engineer reported his assessment to General Valentín Canalizo, but Santa Anna, intending to bring about a decisive battle at Cerro Gordo, unwisely dismissed Robles's concerns. Not only was Santa Anna's position faulty, but also his finances were lacking. From Cerro Gordo, he wrote back to officials in Mexico City stating that unless the government could send money at the "velocity of lightning," there was little hope of stopping the American advance, and, he continued, if the government did not meet the army's financial and supply needs, he would "in no way consider myself responsible for any bad result."[11] Even before the battle commenced, the crafty generalissimo was shifting the blame elsewhere should things go badly.

Despite certain weaknesses, the Mexican position was not unimpressive. Santa Anna had roughly 12,000 men with which to defend the Cerro Gordo Pass, an ample number. Despite having only limited time to prepare defenses, Robles had wasted no time. What he had accomplished in just a few days was laudable. To defend the positions that his engineer had prepared, Santa Anna deployed his army as follows. On the western end of the gorge, just before the road reached the town and near the base of El Telégrafo, he posted half a dozen pieces of artillery and 1,400 supporting infantry, all protected by breastworks. This force anchored the center of the Mexican line and was favorably positioned to seal the western end of the pass while raining a sheet of grape and musketry onto the road. The south side of the road, or the Mexican right flank, was protected by the Río del Plan and by three ridges that ran parallel to each other between the road and the river. At the eastern tip of each ridge, the Mexicans erected breastworks to protect artillery—nineteen guns in all, supported by nearly 2,000 infantry. It was here that Santa Anna fixed much of his attention in preparing for the Americans' arrival. This southernmost position was forward of the other defensive works, and it commanded a stretch of the road in the eastern half of the gorge. In this area, they had cut down trees east of the ridges and along the road to give their gunners an open field of fire.[12]

The weakest point of the line was the left flank or northern end. However, the terrain was so rugged north of the road with hills, ridges, and gullies, not to mention thornbushes and underbrush, that Santa Anna considered it impassable for even a rabbit, let alone wagons and cannon. Such a natural geographic barrier did not warrant much attention, thought the Mexican commander. So he posted four 4-pound cannon and about a hundred infantry on El Telégrafo, not to protect his left flank from attack, but because it overlooked the road, and from there, one could see the entire area. This was the scant collection that Beauregard had observed from atop La Atalaya. On the slightly rounded summit of El Telégrafo, there was perhaps no more than an acre of defensible terrain before the ground began its steady downward slope. Here the Mexicans dug breastworks that enclosed the remains of an ancient stone-and-concrete tower. In centuries past, the old tower had been part of a series of signal stations used to relay messages from the coast to Mexico City—thus the hill's name.[13] Here also they had cleared brush to provide a field of fire. The location was an excellent observation post, but, as Beauregard discovered, it was too lightly manned to withstand a determined attack.[14]

This the young engineer reported to General Twiggs on the afternoon of April 13: the Mexican left was inadequately defended and could be taken with a flank attack. Armed with a fairly accurate description of the enemy line, Twiggs, despite being outnumbered about two to one, decided to attack the Mexicans in front and flank simultaneously, and accordingly, that evening he sent his orders to officers in the two divisions present. Next morning, Patterson's division would attack in front while Twiggs's division, led by Beauregard, would swing around to the north and hit the Mexicans in flank. The plan worried the young lieutenant, who saw this as a violation of one of the basic maxims of warfare: never divide your force in the face of a superior foe. Furthermore, with the Americans attacking on the outside of an imaginary arch, the enemy would enjoy the advantage of interior lines. Beauregard was skeptical of the plan and of the commander, as was the rest of the army.

That evening, as word of the pending attack passed through the ranks, an air of gloom descended over the troops. They were reluctant to go into battle under Twiggs and also leery of initiating a major battle without the rest of the army or the commanding general on hand. Patterson, still incapacitated by illness, summoned Beauregard to his tent and asked his opinion of the battle plan. The lieutenant frankly expressed his belief that the army should not be divided as Twiggs intended, that the bulk of the army should be directed to attack the weak Mexican position at El Telégrafo. At Patterson's urging, Beauregard went back to Twiggs that night and expressed his reservations, but Twiggs simply responded by saying that his orders had been sent, and it was too late to make changes. Then, as if he had second thoughts, he asked Beauregard, "Don't you think we will succeed any how?" "Certainly Sir," the dutiful young lieutenant replied.[15]

Patterson did not share his engineer's optimism. Determined to stop Old Davy's premature undertaking, he rose from his bed, removed himself from the sick roll, assumed command of the forces, and at 11:00 P.M. suspended Twiggs's attack order. Pulling the rug out from under Twiggs in such fashion did little to enhance the relationship between the two generals. Patterson was not a professional soldier, and if he was known for anything, it was a penchant for being slow, which he would demonstrate fourteen years later at First Bull Run. However, he was a veteran of the War of 1812 and he possessed enough experience to understand the wisdom of waiting for the commanding general to arrive on the scene.

The next day, around noon, Scott did arrive. He took in all the information that had been gathered from Beauregard's reconnaissance north of the road and Lieutenant Zealous Tower's reconnaissance of the three ridges south of the road, and he opted not to adopt Twiggs's plan for an immediate attack in front and flank. Such an approach, noted one soldier, "would sacrifice to much of the Army." But he did see the value of Beauregard's information regarding the weak Mexican flank and considered an attack north of the road a viable option. Before formulating his plan of attack, however, Scott wanted more definitive information from officers he knew and trusted. So on April 15 and 16, he directed his engineers to continue reconnoitering the Mexican positions.[16]

All of the scouting before and after Scott's arrival provided the troops with four days of leisure time which they filled with foraging and exploring. Apple, peach, orange, banana, and lime trees grew around Plan del Río, and countless soldiers took the liberty to relieve some of the trees of their delectable fruit. Limes, they discovered, "make a very refreshing drink." Some of the soldiers took the time to wash off the dust from days of marching by bathing in the Río del Plan and other clear springs in the vicinity. On April 14, about a dozen hungry Pennsylvania volunteers, being "pretty near starved," decided that the minor infraction of plucking an occasional piece of fruit was not enough to satisfy their desires. So they slipped out of camp in search of beef. They found two cows in a corn field, and despite the owner's presence, they shot both of them and skinned them. After quartering them, the men carried them back to camp "slyly," making sure to stay off the road so as not to be spotted by a superior officer.[17]

Much of the activity around Plan del Río was legitimate contractors' work. On one occasion, four wagons went out looking for forage and found six hundred bushels that farmers had just loaded on mules to carry to the Mexican army. From April 14 to 16, beef contractors busied themselves in the surrounding countryside searching for cattle to buy from the locals in a never-ending quest to provide the army with an ambulatory supply of food. On April 16, a group of Tennessee volunteers (Company "K" Mounted Infantry, or, as they were also known, the Knoxville Dragoons) escorted one of the beef parties on its search. Their activity took them from ranch to ranch until, at one point, they spotted a band of Mexican soldiers who fired at them and quickly bolted off the road and into the thick chaparral. The volunteers dismounted and pursued, leaving behind John Roberson and one other to guard the horses. Soon Roberson heard a rustling, then saw movement in the brush just off the road, but he held his fire for fear that it might be a comrade. His caution cost him his life, for it was a lone Mexican soldier who raised his gun and fired before disappearing in the thick undergrowth. The musket ball struck Roberson in the upper thigh, shattering the bone, and his companions had to carry him back to camp in one of the wagons. Roberson lingered in great pain for two days before dying.[18]

Other fatalities occurred while the army was camped at Plan del Río. On the same day that Roberson was mortally wounded, Chauncey Sargent, purporting to be an eyewitness, wrote in his journal about another fatal result from one of the food searches. Not knowing what had happened, he simply recounted that "a Tennessean who was shot in seven places, . . . died a few minutes after he was brought to camp, he was out with a beef party, two of them getting separated from the rest were attacked by Lancers one was killed instantly." Another incident of a different nature had equally tragic results. After loading his musket, a soldier enlisted the aid of a comrade to remove the charge from the barrel. While using the ramrod to try to dig the ball and powder out, the gun went off, shooting one of the men in the chest and killing him instantly, while the ramrod flew out and lodged in the neck of a nearby soldier.[19]

While engineers assessed the enemy position, the Mexicans worked to strengthen their defenses. Santa Anna on occasion mounted his horse and, with his staff, rode from location to location inspecting his lines. Given his disregard of his engineer's advice, perhaps he felt a false sense of confidence. Some of the officers in his army were not so confident, and a few privately voiced their concern about "important defects in the general plan of defence." Santa Anna had relatively comfortable quarters in Cerro Gordo, and he dined in the evenings with his aides and officers. Meanwhile, his soldiers became increasingly fidgety with each passing day, anxious to fight the Americans. And so was Santa Anna. Hoping to strike a blow against the invaders and growing impatient, he sent out units of his cavalry to ride through the narrow defile along the river in an effort to get as close as possible to the American camp at Plan del Río. However, the terrain was so rugged that after losing several men and horses over cliffs, they turned back.[20]

Meanwhile, Scott's engineers continued their observations of Mexican positions. On April 15, young Lieutenant George H. Derby, only one year out of the military academy, conducted a thorough reconnaissance of the three ridges south of the road. Working his way through cacti and chaparral for over four miles, he came to a spot behind the Mexican right flank where he counted the guns, estimated the strength of the troops, and drew a sketch of the area. The following day, Lieutenant Isaac Stevens did additional scouting in the area beyond the Mexican right. He earlier had seen several hundred lancers along the south bank of the Rio del Plan and assumed that their location indicated the presence of a nearby ford. Stevens secured permission to take fifty dragoons and push up the south side of the river to investigate. His reconnaissance lasted for several hours, but the unexpected return of an old groin injury forced him to return to camp that afternoon before he had completed his search.[21]

Also on April 15, Beauregard led Captain Robert E. Lee and three companies around to the north to take another look at the area that Beauregard had covered two days earlier. Again dropping off portions of their party as they went, Lee and a sergeant finally reached La Atalaya, from whence he was able to see the entire area. Lee spent the day lurking about on the Mexican left flank, pushing on beyond La Atalaya to see if he could find a path to the National Road behind Santa Anna's army. At one point he was near a stream when he heard approaching footsteps and Spanish voices. He ducked behind a fallen tree, pressing himself as close to the ground and as far under the log as possible. There he lay for hours while enemy soldiers milled around, filled their canteens in the stream, and even occasionally sat on the log just above his motionless body. The seemingly endless procession of Mexican soldiers lasted much of the afternoon, and not until after dark was the shaken captain able to slip away and return to camp.[22]

After surveying the Cerro Gordo Pass and the terrain around it, Lee described it as "impassable" and "unscalable." What he did believe was possible, however, was what Beauregard had already suggested: an attack in the vicinity of El Telégrafo coupled with an effort to get to the rear of the Mexican army. Accordingly, Scott ordered the narrow path that Lee charted to be improved and widened to make it passable for infantry and artillery. Thus the ownership of Beauregard's information and idea for a flank attack was transferred to Lee, who would later receive the lion's share of the credit. Scott spent April 16, a Friday, poring over the various reconnaissance reports that had come in and found them altogether thorough and valuable. With all possible information in front of him and with "the eye of a skillful general," he formulated his plan of attack. He assigned General Gideon Pillow's four regiments of volunteers, the First and Second Tennessee and the First and Second Pennsylvania, to attack the Mexican positions on the three ridges south of the road, and he directed Twiggs to take the bulk of his division through the rough terrain north of the road and attack the enemy left flank on El Telégrafo. Scott's plan would placate Twiggs, who originally sought to attack, and it would give Pillow an active role while keeping him away from what Scott expected to be the vital portion of the battlefield north of the road. Thus Pillow could be made to feel as if he played a crucial role while in actuality Scott was putting him in a location where he could do no harm.[23]

Scott's battle plan was much like Beauregard's proposal to Twiggs earlier in the week, though the lieutenant never received the credit he was due. Unlike Old Davy, who wanted to aggressively attack in front and flank at the same time, Scott's tactics were a bit more refined and Napoleonic. Whenever he could do otherwise, Napoleon never made a frontal assault. His most common approach was to hold an enemy in check with a diversionary force in front, while maneuvering around to attack in flank and rear. Scott, a thorough student of the Corsican, followed the pattern precisely. With a thorough knowledge of the countryside, Scott decided not to do what Santa Anna wanted him to do, which was to advance directly and force his way through the gorge. Because of the strength of the Mexican position, he would, as at Veracruz, take the course of least resistance. Having the volunteers advance at the opposite end of the battle line would merely create a diversion and hold in place the Mexican units south of the road. The problem of dividing his army in the face of a superior foe Scott intended to overcome by using surprise—a surprise that would so threaten the enemy army as to prevent it from utilizing its advantage of interior lines. Looking back at the battle a month later, Lieutenant E. Kirby Smith thought that it indeed exhibited a Napoleonic flair, and in retrospect, he described the battle as "a brilliant affair."[24]

On that Friday evening, Scott met with Twiggs personally, instructing him to take his division the next morning and, with Lee as a guide, move it along the path north of the road until he was on the Mexican flank. Scott directed him to avoid a clash with enemy troops and to reach a position from which he could move on the road behind the enemy army. Upon achieving that objective, he was to stand ready and await instructions while the remainder of the army got into position. Later in the evening, after Scott's conference with Twiggs, General Worth arrived at Plan del Río. Fearing that he would miss an opportunity to participate in the coming battle and upset that he had been left behind, he departed Veracruz on April 13 with 1,600 men and arrived late Friday evening. His presence gave the army a sizable reserve, and Scott assigned his division to follow up Twiggs's attack so as to be in position to pursue in the event of a Mexican retreat.[25]

Saturday morning, April 17, Twiggs got his division up at 4:30, and by 7:00 they were on the march. The division consisted of Brigadier General Persifor F. Smith's brigade and Colonel Bennet C. Riley's brigade. Although not a West Point graduate, Smith was regular army. The Princeton-educated New Orleans lawyer had been a leader in the Louisiana militia and was a veteran of the Seminole War in Florida. Now almost fifty, Smith was brave, competent, and respected. Here at Cerro Gordo, however, illness prevented him from directing his troops. In his stead, Colonel Harney acted as temporary brigade commander. The sixty-year-old Riley had been an officer in the army since 1813 and was a veteran of the War of 1812 and the Seminole War. An outstanding soldier, he would later serve as provisional governor of California.[26]

Twiggs's division marched up the National Road from Plan del Río until, coming to the appropriate point east of the gorge, Lee directed the column to turn right into the rough terrain to the north. It was here at the spot where the troops veered off the main road that Lieutenant Thomas Claiborne of the rifle regiment got his first look at Lee. General Scott was there too, and he and Lee were sitting on their mounts conversing. Lee "looked in the fullest vigor of manhood, a most striking figure dressed in a shell jacket with gold lace, mounted on a fine horse, which he sat with superb grace. . . . He impressed me then in a manner I could not forget."[27]

During the previous day, engineers had worked to clear brush and improve the path so that not only troops but cannon could be moved to the flank. The rolling hills and ridges made the progress slow. Some of the "chasms . . . were so steep that men could barely climb them," recalled Lieutenant Ulysses S. Grant. The topography, along with vegetation, low-growing mesquite trees, and chaparral, shielded much of the path from view, except for a stretch of about thirty feet with no cover. When they reached that point, Lee wanted to take a few minutes to pile up brush along this section, so as to further conceal the Americans' movement, but Old Davy did not want to halt his men and did not see the importance of the suggestion. But Lee's advice was prudent. As a precaution, a body of Mexican troops had occupied La Atalaya, and, as Lee feared, they spotted the Americans in the distance as they filed past this opening in the terrain. Now amply warned, the Mexicans prepared the hill as a defensive position while Twiggs brought his division around.[28]

By late morning, Twiggs had his men in position seven hundred yards from the Mexican flank. Continuing along his present course, he would have to turn left to regain the National Road, which as yet lay too far away to see. Rather than trust his guide who had reconnoitered the entire area, Twiggs wanted to get his bearings and locate the enemy flank, so he decided to send a company to occupy a nearby hill and take a look around. He called for Lieutenant John Gardner, a company commander in the Seventh Infantry Regiment, and in his usual gruff voice, he ordered him to "go up there and see if they are occupied." Now able to see this movement, the Mexicans responded by pushing some of their own units forward, and a general engagement began. Twiggs's instructions had been to work his way toward the National Road for a surprise attack, but now after carelessly giving away his flank march, he brought about a brisk fight that fully alerted Santa Anna that an American column was moving in strength to the north. Gardner's company became pinned down when the enemy "opened a strong fire upon us," but Harney rushed forward in relief with the Mounted Rifles and the First Artillery (both units fighting as infantry without horses or cannon). Together the Americans pushed the Mexican force back to its fortified position on La Atalaya, then, stopping to catch their breaths, waited for orders.[29]

They did not wait long, for orders soon came from Harney to advance and seize the hill in their front. They sprang forward and rushed toward La Atalaya, "hollering and yelling" as they went. Under heavy fire, the Americans charged up the northeast slope of the hill, some stopping occasionally to get off a shot. At one point, in the midst of all of the noise and confusion, Lieutenant Claiborne looked to one side and saw a soldier "loading [his musket] mechanically" and firing without aiming. Looking ahead again, he saw a sergeant coming back down the hill, clutching his wounded left arm. The men should fall back, he yelled to Claiborne over the noise of battle. No sooner had he spoken than a "debonnaire" and "handsome" young lieutenant named Earl Van Dorn came up, tied a white handkerchief tightly around the sergeant's bleeding arm, and continued up the hill. With shouts of encouragement from their officers, the men pushed their way to the top and swept into the makeshift Mexican works, breaking their line and forcing enemy soldiers to run from the summit down the back side of the hill. Near the front of the charging Americans was the young engineer officer, Lieutenant George Derby, who was known in the army as a practical joker, a young man who loved to have fun at someone else's expense—but this was no laughing matter. As he rushed across the top of the hill, he shot and wounded a Mexican officer, told him to lay still and no one would hurt him, then continued in pursuit.[30]

Having gained the crest, a captain asked Twiggs how much farther they should charge, to which the crusty old general retorted, "Charge 'em to hell!" So the lead units of the American attacking force ran down the back side of the hill, chasing the Mexicans, who were scampering into their next fortified position on the brow of El Telégrafo. This aggressive pursuit proved to be a mistake. The Mexican soldiers could not resist such tempting targets on the exposed southwest slope of La Atalaya, and they opened a blaze of fire that pinned down many of the Americans. All along the hillside, men scurried for whatever cover they could find as casualties began to mount. Claiborne dove into a goat trail, hoping its shallow depression would shield him from enemy fire. A few feet away, he saw a man crouched behind a bush and yelled to him to get out of there. The soldier pointed to a nearby corpse and yelled back, "He tried to get away."[31] Neither of them went anywhere for a while.

Major Edwin V. Sumner, realizing that some of his comrades were trapped, brought forward reinforcements from the Rifle Regiment to cover a withdrawal. Sumner, a veteran with twenty-eight years' experience, was from Massachusetts, and he later gained notoriety as a corps commander in the Union army. "He was of the old school, rugged and stern, honest and brave," wrote Thomas Claiborne. "He detested frivolity, was austerely sober, and always reminded me of Cromwell's best puritan soldiers." His bravery on this day, however, resulted in a serious wound to the head. A musket ball hit the star on his cap, slowing its momentum before hitting his forehead. He recovered from the wound, and as a result of it acquired the nickname "Old Bull." The story became embellished over time to the point that later accounts asserted that Old Bull was so bull-headed that the bullet bounced off of his skull.[32]

Despite the danger, most of the Americans made it back up to the crest of La Atalaya, and the subsequent lull allowed time for Harney, the commanding officer on the scene, to care for the wounded. Derby went back to check on the wounded Mexican officer, whom he had instructed to lay still, only to discover that he had been killed by another American soldier. Lieutenant Dabney Maury, a Virginian and West Point graduate, received a serious wound in the left arm during the assault, requiring a friend to help him to the rear. A surgeon examined the wound and concluded that it required amputation. "You've a very bad arm," said the doctor. "I shall have to cut it off." Upon hearing the grim diagnosis, Maury gestured to a more seriously wounded soldier lying nearby and suggested that the doctor take care of him first, and, with that distraction, made his getaway. On a borrowed horse, he rode back to Plan del Río, where he presented himself to another doctor, John Cuyler. "We can save that arm," Cuyler told him. Maury replied, "Do it at all risks. I will die before I will lose it, and I assume all responsibility." Maury indeed recovered, his arm intact, and later rose to the rank of major general in the Confederate army, commanding troops in the trans-Mississippi and western theaters of the Civil War. The doctor who saved his arm went on to serve in the medical department of the Union army, retiring as a brigadier general in 1882.[33]

The sharp fighting resulted in about ninety American casualties, but it was over by noon. In the afternoon from within the Mexican lines atop El Telégrafo came the shrill blast of trumpets that announced their intentions to resume the fight. Simultaneous with the sound of the horns, there emerged from the brow of the hill a line of Mexican soldiers arrayed for battle, advancing down the hill and toward Harney's men on La Atalaya. George Wilkins Kendall from the New Orleans *Picayune* newspaper had attached himself to the army and was on hand at Cerro Gordo. Along with a few other Americans, he had crept down, under cover of trees and bushes, into the valley between the two hills and recorded the scene that unfolded. "[S]oon we could see a long line of infantry marching down the steep hillside & making directly for the height now occupied by Col H. & his small but gallant band." Kendall thought that the furious noise might, all by itself, be "sufficient to drive every Yankee completely from the heroic & sacred soil of Mexico." And as the enemy soldiers pressed on, "louder came the blasts from the trumpets." In the valley between the two hills, the Mexicans stopped to dress their lines and, by all appearances, prepare for a charge up La Atalaya.

Atop La Atalaya, Harney had the Seventh Infantry, the Rifle Regiment, and the First Artillery—not overwhelming numbers. To make his situation more precarious, he had detailed some of his men as litter bearers to carry the wounded to the rear. So just as the Mexican lines stopped to form for the final assault, "Col H. improved the occasion to play off a regular trick upon them." With his position partially hidden by the curvature of the terrain, Harney stood up in view of the enemy below and "commenced a harangue which would have served for an army of 20,000 men. . . . 'Don't shoot yet!'" Harney bellowed, "'wait till they come closer, & then give them h–ll! Don't draw a trigger, I tell you—double charge those cannons, there, with grape & cannister, & wait till I give the word. I don't want one of them ever to get back alive!'" According to Kendall, Harney's shouting could have been heard from a mile away, and after some of the English-speaking Mexicans translated the speech to some of their officers, they turned their men around and marched back up El Telégrafo.[34]

During the afternoon General James Shields's brigade (Patterson's division) arrived to reinforce Twiggs's division. Shields, a thirty-seven-year-old Irishman, had served in the Illinois state legislature and as a justice on that state's supreme court. He performed admirably at Cerro Gordo but was a failure as a Union commander fifteen years later. He had appeared at Scott's headquarters three days earlier to protest rumors that his brigade would be held in reserve in the upcoming battle. It was not the first time Shields had complained to the commanding general about a subordinate role in the army's movements. Scott yielded, and now Shields arrived on the American right to reinforce the flanking column. It was a role that almost cost him his life.[35] In the vicinity of La Atalaya, Twiggs now had almost 5,000 men with which to renew the fight on the morrow.

That evening, General Scott sent written orders to the various parts of his dispersed army with instructions for the next day. Twiggs commanded the bulk of the army. Scott gave him two objectives: seize the road in the enemy's rear so as to cut off their retreat to Jalapa and capture and hold El Telégrafo so as prevent Mexican guns on that hill from enfilading the flanking column. To the rear or the American left, Pillow was to get his brigade of volunteers in position opposite the three artillery laden ridges south of the road by early morning. Upon hearing the noise of battle in Twiggs's sector, Pillow was to attack the ridges and "pierce" the enemy's line of artillery. Worth, who had left Veracruz late and had arrived the previous evening with 1,600 men, was to follow Twiggs's division and join in the pursuit. Scott's written orders turned out to be a phenomenally accurate prediction of the next morning's events. "The enemy's whole line of intrencments & batteries will be . . . turned, early in the day tomorrow—probably before 10 o'clock A.M." He ordered his cavalry to be in the National Road out of range of Mexican guns and ready to pursue by 9:00. Then he went on to assert that the retreating enemy force would be pursued for several miles "until stopped by darkness or fortified positions."[36] What Scott wrote twelve hours in advance proved to be a nearly exact blueprint of the way the battle would unfold.

The Seventh Infantry and the Rifles slept as best they could on La Atalaya that night while Lee and Captain Gustavus W. Smith directed a work party in the construction of a battery emplacement. It would be a laborious task, but during the night, the Americans intended to pull two howitzers and a 24-pounder up to the top of La Atalaya to add to their firepower for the next day's fight. Lee, after indicating where he wanted the battery located, instructed Smith to oversee the work of preparing gun mounts. The ground was rocky and digging was difficult as a work party attempted to throw up an embankment and build platforms. Smith and other engineers had marched twenty-four hours since the previous night to get to Plan del Río on April 17, arriving at 11:00 P.M., hours after the fighting had ended. It must have been sometime after midnight before he found Lee on the right flank and started to work. At 3:00 A.M., he was too exhausted to continue, so he summoned another officer who was sleeping at the bottom of the hill to come take over.

Upon being relieved, Smith began his weary trek down the hill, and while walking along, he dozed off. While upright but still slumbering, he stumbled on the uneven ground, fell forward, and landed on top of a dead Mexican soldier; the corpse's face, "eyes wide open, within a few inches of mine." Before he could come to his senses and get to his feet, he heard a stampede of men rush by, followed by a familiar voice shouting in the darkness. It was Lieutenant Peter V. Hagner yelling at the men to stop. Smith hopped up and helped bring the men under control before inquiring what had happened. They had been detailed earlier in the night to pull one of the cannon up La Atalaya and had left their muskets at the bottom of the hill. Using drag ropes, they inched the piece slowly up the slope until they reached a point where their path was blocked by trees. While the trees were cleared, the men rested. They all, having fallen asleep, became startled when someone shouted that the Mexicans were upon them, and they leapt to their feet and took off down the hill to retrieve their weapons. The officers calmed the rumor-induced panic, restored order, and eventually the way was cleared for the work to continue.[37]

Twiggs's clumsiness had eliminated the possibility of catching the Mexicans completely off guard. Santa Anna spent the night strengthening his left flank to guard against another American push in that area. He sent more troops, the Second Light Infantry and the Fourth Regular Infantry under General Ciriaco Vásquez, to protect El Telégrafo, and he instructed Captain Robles to construct fortifications for an additional battery of three guns. He also personally oversaw the work on an additional battery near the road just west of the hill to protect the main camp. These steps, however, were just a precaution, for he continued to focus his attention myopically on the defense of the three ridges south of the road, expecting the main American advance to come there. In fact, the Mexicans believed that on the morning of April 17, they had stopped an all-out American attack, thus proving that their flank was impregnable. However, the next day's events would prove that the Mexican fortifications along their main line on El Telégrafo were incomplete and inadequate to halt an attack in force.[38]

Although the battle was not yet over, Joseph Smith, who had penned the prayer for protection on April 11, got out his diary and, sitting atop La Atalaya, expressed his gratitude that he had survived the day. "Many times during this day has my life been in peril from the enemy's shots, but God still spared me in answer to my prayers. Praised be his name."[39]

CHAPTER FIVE

Cerro Gordo

Tomorrow Will Settle the Affair

*The attack was made as ordered, and perhaps there was not a
battle of the Mexican war, or of any other, where orders issued
before an engagement were nearer being a correct report of what
afterwards took place.*
—Ulysses S. Grant, Fourth Infantry Regiment

Some soldiers spent the night of April 17–18 trying to rest, but anxious about
what the morrow might hold. William Campbell wrote to his wife during the
evening that "tomorrow will settle the affair between Genl. Scott & Genl
Santa Anna." Captain Ephraim Kirby Smith, the forty-year-old brother of
Confederate General Edmund Kirby Smith and the son of an infantryman
who had fought with distinction at Lundy's Lane in 1814, was with the Fifth
Infantry in Worth's division at Plan del Río. After hearing the distant cannon fire of battle on April 17, he and his comrades discussed the prospects of
battle for the next day. "We all think it will be the last fight of the war."[1]

Before dawn on Sunday, April 18, General Pillow prepared his brigade to
march from Plan del Río five miles southeast of Harney's and Twiggs's position at La Atalaya. By 6:00 A.M., the brigade of volunteers (First and Second
Tennessee and First and Second Pennsylvania) was on the road heading for
the Cerro Gordo Pass. They marched for three miles before reaching the
designated spot where they were supposed to leave the road to the left and
start their trek through the hills and underbrush to an attack position in front
of the three defended ridges. Scott had intended this attack on the Mexican
right to occupy that portion of the enemy army and distract attention away
from Twiggs's action on their left flank. But some in the army thought this
"a most foolish and unnecessary move" and that it had been pressed on Scott
by Pillow, who wanted an opportunity for glory.[2]

On April 13, 15, and 16, Lieutenant Zealous Tower and Lieutenant George
McClellan, accompanied at least part of the time by Pillow, had conducted
extensive reconnaissance in the area to determine enemy strength and to
chart the best route for an approach on the position. Now, as the infantry
filed off the road to get into position, Pillow rode up to McClellan and told

him that he wanted to change the approach route that McClellan and Tower had chosen. After learning of Pillow's impulsive desire, Tower protested, but he did not insist that they stick with the original plan. The new route took the troops down a narrow trail, which had to be traversed single file. Consequently, they became strung out for a long distance, which slowed their progress. They could already hear the sound of battle in the vicinity of El Telégrafo, which signaled their tardiness in getting into position.[3]

As the sun came up, at the other end of the battlefield, Captain Gustavus Smith was back up on La Atalaya standing next to the battery that he had helped prepare. Lee, who was everywhere on the American right flank and seemed never to sleep, appeared and instructed Smith to send him several men who could cut a road around the base of the hill to facilitate the movement of more artillery, then to report to Colonel Harney, who was preparing to attack. Lee then headed back down the north face of the hill to begin leading other units in a wide-arching circle around the hill and toward the road in the rear of Santa Anna's army. The Second Infantry and the Fourth Artillery of Colonel Riley's brigade, followed by three volunteer regiments, the Third and Fourth Illinois and the New York Regiment, under General Shields, followed Lee's lead and began their movement at the same time an artillery duel atop the two hills began.[4]

Soon after daylight, the American battery on La Atalaya opened fire on the enemy position on the adjacent hill. Mexican trumpeters blew their horns, and soon their artillery opened in response. At 7:00 A.M., Harney took off his coat and rolled up his sleeves, signaling that he was ready to get down to business. Then, with sword in hand, he shouted in his thunderous voice, "Come on, boys," and led the brigade forward. Down the hill and into the valley they went, then up the steep northeastern side of El Telégrafo. Keeping their footing was difficult because in places the hillsides were "almost perpendicular," and some of the men used the butts of their muskets for support. The Mexican guns were firing grape and canister, and the fire was so heavy that they "thined our ranks with vengence," reported Benjamin Wingate. The enemy fire was so thick that "it appeared to me like I could have reached out my hands in any direction and found shots thrown at us from the Mexican batterys." Another described the hillside as a "sheet of belching flame & smoke."[5]

Even so, the men pressed steadily onward, yelling as they went. Future Confederate general Richard Ewell was with the dragoons, who were being held in reserve in the rear, but his brother Tom, a lieutenant with the Rifle Regiment, walked "deliberately down the slope . . . in full view of the Mexicans" without flinching or ducking a single time. Just before reaching the top of El Telégrafo, the officers halted the men and instructed them to lie down so that they were shielded by the curvature of the ground. While in this position, barely fifty yards from the Mexican works, they caught their breath and prepared for the order to charge.[6]

At this point, Captain Smith asked for and received permission to creep up the hill to get a closer look at the enemy, and he came back and reported to Colonel Harney that "we could dash over their works without a halt." While Smith was making his report, a steady fire of musketry opened on Harney's left flank from the direction of the road to the south. They were men of the Mexican Sixth Infantry, reinforcements that had been dispatched from the Mexican center, and they occupied "a nest of surface quarry holes which gave them protection." Harney told two companies of riflemen to turn left to meet this threat, and he instructed them to advance when he gave the order to charge.[7]

Meanwhile, Lee had been guiding Riley's and Shields's men in a westerly direction across the northern base of El Telégrafo in an attempt to envelop the Mexican left and seize the road in the rear. From atop the hill, General Vásquez had spotted this movement in the distance and had sent his Fourth Infantry and a piece of artillery to a spur that jutted out along the northwest side of the hill. From there, the Mexicans had commenced an annoying fire on the flanking column. General Twiggs, who was in command of those troops, first sent two companies then the entire Second Infantry and Fourth Artillery under Riley to engage these enemy troops.[8] Riley wheeled his units left and attacked, while Shields maintained his original course and continued to push on toward the road with his three regiments. Riley's men were now advancing on El Telégrafo's northwest slope, and Harney's brigade was poised for a charge along a line that ran from the north to the east side of the hill. This placed Vásquez in a dangerous vice with Riley threatening to cut off his line of retreat to the town.

On the northern and eastern slopes, men of Harney's brigade sprang up and rushed forward at his command. In seconds, they were jumping over the Mexicans' improvised stone and dirt defenses. What followed was "a short, but bloody, hand to hand struggle, in which bayonets, swords, pistols, and butts of muskets were freely used." Tom Ewell of the Rifles was among the first to reach the enemy line. With a leap, he was inside the works and instantly saw "about 200 men lying down ready to fire, . . . I passed my sword through the first man. The next was aiming at me." Just as Ewell struck the musket with his sword to deflect the Mexican's aim, it discharged, and the round entered his abdomen just left of his navel. He was gut shot—a wound generally considered to be fatal. Earl Van Dorn, a veteran of the Battle of Monterey the previous year, went over the works with the Seventh Infantry and killed two of the defenders during the melee.[9]

The Mexicans abandoned their first defensive line and fell back to a second position. The opposing lines exchanged several rounds in a close range duel of musketry until the Americans once again sprang forward, bringing about another deadly hand-to-hand struggle. It was "a kind of fighting which I hope never to see again," remembered Barna Upton, who thought "it seemed like murder to see men running bayonets into one anothers breasts." Lieutenant Barnard Bee, who fifteen years later would use the term "Stonewall" to describe Thomas Jackson at First Bull Run, ran into the works and found a Mexican soldier coming at him with bayonet lowered. With his sword, Bee parried the enemy's thrust but suffered a cut on his hand in the process. The lieutenant then ran his opponent through with his sword, and his own blood, along with that of the Mexican, mingled together staining the entire blade to the hilt.[10]

The Mexicans fought bravely, but they could not withstand the converging assaults of Harney's and Riley's troops. By the time Harney's men crossed bayonets with the enemy on the crest, Riley had cleared his opponents from the spur. The struggle atop the hill lasted several minutes, but soon Mexican troops began to melt away and retreat down the back side of the hill. Some tried to mix in with the wounded who were retiring down the southwest slope, causing Santa Anna to send staff officers to stop their retreat and order them back to their posts. Some of them did return to the chaotic fighting, but the trickle of retreating soldiers quickly turned into a flood, and the Mexican line gave way to the growing number of American soldiers who breached the works. As one Mexican source reported, as soon as American attackers fell, they "were instantly replaced by others, who seemed to reproduce them." General Vásquez was among the growing number of Mexican casualties, mortally wounded by a shot in the face.[11]

Among the storming party was Captain John B. Magruder, whose First Artillery fought as infantrymen. Magruder was a West Point graduate from Virginia and had a reputation for being hot tempered. When the enemy line broke, he and a few others gravitated to the abandoned enemy cannon, and they turned the guns on the retreating foe—a deed for which Magruder won a brevet to major. Panic was beginning to grip the Mexican army; they began to run "like a flock of frightened sheep." Young Lieutenant Thomas Jackson observed Magruder and was impressed by his fearless and decisive action. A few weeks later, when the opportunity arose, Jackson got himself transferred to Magruder's command.[12]

As the enemy line broke, Riley turned his men toward the village and ordered them to charge directly into the main Mexican camp. They did so, firing at will at the fleeing enemy troops. Almost simultaneously, Shields's men, having completed their wide arch under Lee's direction, burst out of the chaparral and literally into the enemy camp adjacent to the road and the town. Their progress had been slow through the thorny and almost impenetrable thickets, and in some places, they had to move in single file through the rough terrain. As they emerged into the clearing, some Mexican soldiers panicked, while others began to fire their muskets and turn cannon in their direction. Shields quickly formed five companies of the Fourth Illinois and ordered them to attack. As they did, six enemy guns opened fire with grapeshot, seriously wounding Shields in the process. As the Americans rushed into the camp, they overran ranches and buildings that were being used by the Mexican army, and within minutes, they had accomplished Scott's objective by taking up a position to block the Mexican retreat. In the confusion, Lee came across a young Mexican boy, a bugler or perhaps a drummer, who had been wounded in the arm. He was pinned underneath a wounded Mexican soldier, and nearby, a little girl sobbed helplessly over the plight of her young friend. Lee looked at the barefoot girl with waist-length hair, her "large black eyes . . . streaming with tears" and took pity on her and the boy. He gave instructions to a subordinate to lift the man off of the youngster and see that they both received medical treatment.[13]

Chaos reigned in the Mexican army. Santa Anna, who had started the battle near the middle of his lines on the National Road, funneled reinforcements over to his left as the threat mounted on El Telégrafo, and eventually went over to that part of the battlefield to personally take charge. Now with that end of his line disintegrating, he, like many of his men, began to look for the fastest way off of the battlefield and out of harm's way.[14]

On the Mexican right, south of the road, it was the Americans who had been having a tough go of it since early morning. When the sun rose in the eastern sky, the battle already underway, Pillow and his brigade were hustling to catch up with the day's events. At 8:30, they still were not in position to attack the batteries firmly ensconced at the end of the three ridges. Progress over the rough terrain had been slowed by the need to cut away the dense chaparral that dotted the area. The narrow, unfamiliar path resulted in the four regiments being strung out for an extended distance. According to the original plan, Pillow's brigade was to attack the enemy battery closest to the river, or on the extreme Mexican right. Such an approach would protect the Americans' left flank, and it would negate the northernmost battery closest to the road.

To further support the attack, the Americans had placed, with great difficulty, a howitzer, commanded by Lieutenant Roswell Ripley, on a ridge south of the river. Under Ripley's supervision, three companies of New York volunteers had spent the better part of twelve hours pulling the heavy gun for two and a half miles over hills and through gullies to get it in place in

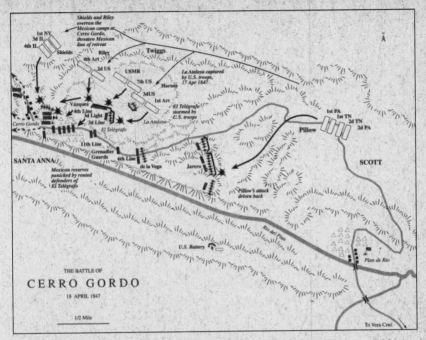

THE BATTLE OF

CERRO GORDO

18 APRIL 1847

1/2 Mile

Battle of Cerro Gordo. From Donald S. Frazier, ed., *The United States and Mexico at War* (New York: Macmillan, 1998). Reprinted by permission of The Gale Group.

time to support Pillow's attack. But Pillow nullified his advantage by deciding to attack two of the enemy batteries: the one closest to the river and the one next to it on the middle ridge. Thus, artillery (nineteen guns in all) and musketry (almost 2,000 infantrymen) from all three ridges would now be in play. Ripley later commented that if Pillow had stayed with the original attack plan, he would have "availed himself of the support" offered by the howitzer's covering fire, thus improving his chances of success.[15]

Pillow had designated the First Pennsylvania and the Second Tennessee as the assaulting units supported by the First Tennessee and the Second Pennsylvania, respectively. Now, at close to 9 o'clock, Colonel William T. Haskell worked, with some difficulty, to get his Second Tennessee aligned to attack the middle ridge with its eight guns and a thousand defenders. Meanwhile, Colonel Francis M. Wynkoop was having even less luck getting his badly scattered First Pennsylvania deployed for an attack on the five cannon and five hundred infantry posted on the southern ridge. Worse, Pillow's two other regiments were not in position to offer support.[16] The situation on the American left was a mess.

The Americans were concealed by the terrain and the underbrush but were close enough to hear Mexican officers barking orders in the distance. Haskell had only two of his companies in position when Pillow shouted, "Why the Hell don't Colonel Wynkoop file to the right?" Whereupon a bugle from the Mexican lines sounded an alarm, and enemy artillery opened with grape and canister. Pillow immediately ordered Haskell to attack, but the colonel did not know whether to advance in such a disorganized state or to disobey orders and remain under cover. Haskell was a twenty-eight-year-old lawyer and a veteran of the Seminole War. His brother, Charles, was among those massacred by Mexican troops at Goliad in 1836, and his desire for revenge got the better of him. He gave the order to charge, and the companies that were not yet in line simply left the trail, pushed their way through the chaparral, and, in pell-mell fashion, joined the unorganized assault.[17]

They were three hundred yards from their objective; much of it covered with thick underbrush "so dense and full of thorns that we were obliged to cut our way through it with *bill hooks*." At a distance of about two hundred yards, the Mexicans had cut away most of the chaparral and had stacked the bushes along their front to form a "thorny brush entanglement . . . about waist high." It was a crude abatis, which the Americans found difficult to wade through. Then, at about a hundred yards, the attackers burst into open terrain, where they were easily picked off by the well-protected Mexican troops. The entire area became deadly ground for the volunteers—a "bloody spectacle," as one Tennessean described it.[18]

The Second Tennessee rushed forward into a hail of enemy fire that stopped its initial charge. Haskell had his hat shot away by canister, leaving his long hair flowing free. Wynkoop's First Pennsylvania, which had been assigned to go into battle on Haskell's left, was nowhere in sight. They were to the rear, still trying to get organized but taking enemy fire nonetheless. The Second Pennsylvania, assigned to support Haskell's regiment, was still not up. Pillow dispatched staff officers to both Pennsylvania regiments in an effort to get the former to initiate its designated assault and to get the latter to hurry along so as to assist in the attack. It is likely that the lieutenant bearing orders for Wynkoop never made his way through the thick brush and enemy fire to deliver Pillow's orders. Thus, the Second Tennessee went into the battle unsupported and as a result suffered heavy casualties. Some of the men tried to find cover behind bushes, while others ran to the rear. Several dozen "retreating" Tennesseans ran through the lines of the recently arrived Second Pennsylvania, causing that support unit to withdraw. An angry Haskell went to find Pillow.[19]

General Pillow was in the rear squatting behind a bush talking to Lieutenant McClellan. When the lieutenant suggested that they needed regulars to break the enemy line and capture the ridges, Pillow consented to allow him to ride back, find General Scott, and request that he send some regulars to reinforce the volunteers. While they conversed, a canister shot ripped into Pillow's right arm above the elbow, breaking the bone and tearing the muscle. As Pillow made his way further to the rear, he came upon Colonel William B. Campbell, who commanded the First Tennessee. Campbell's orders had been to support Wynkoop's regiment in his attack on the southern ridge, but the First Tennessee was far to the rear during the march and consequently was just arriving in the vicinity. The wounded Pillow turned over command of his entire brigade to Campbell and ordered him to press his men forward quickly to join Wynkoop.[20]

Campbell, a Whig politician and no friend of Pillow's, "was in a most furious humor" over the way the battle had been managed—or rather mis-managed—thus far. He pushed his men forward, but even while trying to get them into position, they fell under heavy fire from Mexican artillery. His men had fought under Taylor at Monterey the previous year, but some of his veterans later said that they had never experienced such heavy fire. Just try-ing to get into position on the far left, they had to pass under the fire of the enemy guns. Samuel Lauderdale, from Sumner County, Tennessee, was a member of the regiment. His father, Major William Lauderdale, had built a block house fort on the southeast coast of Florida during the Seminole War, and the city that eventually grew up around it bears his name. The younger Lauderdale stopped to wipe the sweat from his face not far from where Pillow had been wounded only minutes earlier when canister struck him in the forehead, just above the right eye. He died within two hours, and friends later carried his body back to camp and buried him near the Río del Plan.[21]

When Haskell found Pillow in the rear, the scene was not pleasant. Over the noise of battle, the two Tennesseans exchanged angry words. Haskell was mad because his men had rushed into the fight without support and as a result were being badly mauled, and Pillow was obviously frustrated because thus far he had been unable to accomplish his assigned task with any degree of coordination. Pillow accused the colonel of neglecting his duty by leaving his men and ordered him to return to his regiment immediately and resume the attack. Then he berated the Second Pennsylvania troops and went off to find Campbell, who was trying desperately to press the attack. Campbell had ordered the Pennsylvanians to advance, but because he did not specify First or Second Pennsylvania, neither obeyed. Mad and with a "perfectly rampant" disposition, Campbell "damned the Pennsylvanians for a set of cowards." When Pillow found Campbell, the former resumed command of the brigade, and was trying to help bring order to his chaotic situation when word arrived from General Scott that the Mexicans on other parts of the battlefield were retreating.[22]

Earlier McClellan had ridden off to find Scott and ask for reinforcements. He found the general with elements of Worth's division, following Twiggs's path around the north flank. By this time, Harney had captured El Telégrafo and Shields had blocked the road, leaving Worth's men nothing to do but join the pursuit. When McClellan rode up and asked for regulars to assist in Pillow's attack, Scott refused, saying that he could not spare them. The bulk of the Mexican army was retreating toward Jalapa, but Scott wanted to be ready in case Santa Anna turned to fight. Besides, the enemy in Pillow's front was now cut off, and Scott knew that their surrender would be imminent. Upon receiving the news from Pillow's front, the commanding general was "not much surprised and not much 'put out' that Pillow was thrashed," and according to McClellan, he seemingly "attached no importance to [Pillow's] future movements." He simply instructed McClellan to tell Pillow that he could attack or not attack again—whatever he wished to do. McClellan's description suggests that Scott's battle plans had been designed to pacify the president's friend and keep him occupied on the American left. No doubt he hoped that something positive might result from Pillow's attack, but he knew all along that the real battle was on the American right. This idea was borne out in a letter written several days later by future Union general John Sedgwick, who asserted that Pillow's attack on the American left "was thought unimportant, as the fall of the hill would give us command of all their works."[23]

When McClellan returned to the left flank, the first officer he encountered was Colonel Wynkoop, who reported having seen a white flag raised over the Mexican works. Obviously by this time, around 10:00 A.M. or shortly after, the Mexicans were aware that the rest of their army was in flight toward Jalapa, and as Scott predicted, they understood the hopelessness of their situation. But Wynkoop did not know what the flag meant, and when told that it was a sign of surrender, he declared that he was going to attack anyway, orders or not. As historian Justin H. Smith asserted, "Wynkoop felt . . . eager [to attack] when it was too late."[24]

The battle on the American left had lasted about forty-five minutes, and it had been ugly. Most observers blamed Pillow, as have subsequent historians. A sergeant in the Second Pennsylvania thought that Pillow would "always be censured" for his faulty approach to the enemy position. Campbell wrote to his wife that Pillow "as I expected . . . managed the whole affair most badly." A few days later, in a letter to another relative, he emphatically asserted that Pillow "is no part of a Genl. or military man and as light as a feather and is always making himself ridiculous by his foolishness." Lieutenant Roswell Ripley leveled harsh criticism at Pillow, saying that because he was a volunteer he did not know what he was doing. Consequently, "he was most confoundedly well thrashed."[25] Historians like Justin H. Smith and K. Jack Bauer have also criticized Pillow's handling of the attack. He indeed made critical mistakes, including the way he arranged the regiments in their march to the jump-off point, his spontaneous decision to change the approach route, and his sheer inability to create order out of chaos. These are all mistakes of an inexperienced and naive commander who was too anxious to win glory. And frankly, some of his subordinates did not like him or did not trust him—or both. What Pillow most lacked was modesty and military skill, but as Nathaniel Cheairs Hughes and Roy P. Stonesifer assert in their biography of the Tennessean, he was no coward.

In Pillow's front, the furious noise of battle gradually gave way to an occasional musket shot. Some Mexican soldiers fled in an effort to escape the American trap and get to Jalapa, while others simply gave up and handed over their weapons. The units defending the three ridges surrendered virtually intact, having suffered, according to one source, only one casualty. In a letter home, Hiram Yeager instructed his brother to tell one of his friends that after the battle, "I kicked a Mexicans behind after he gave me his musket." As they collected their prisoners, the Tennesseans and Pennsylvanians also began the arduous task of carrying the wounded from the field. One Tennessean, wounded in the hip, made his way to the rear complaining of his great agony, and upon reaching a doctor, he moaned, "Oh! I am killed. . . . I believe I shall die." After examining him, the doctor assured him he would be fine and would only suffer temporary discomfort in sitting.[26]

On the American right, troops were also beginning to care for the wounded, Mexican and American alike, while many of Twiggs's men pursued the retreating enemy soldiers up the National Road toward Jalapa. Atop El Telégrafo, Mexican corpses lay along their breastworks, some of them stacked two and three deep.[27] A future Union general and veteran of the 1862 Peninsula Campaign, Lieutenant Napoleon Dana, charged El Telégrafo with the Seventh Infantry. He was seriously wounded in the side and left for dead by his comrades, only to be discovered a day and a half later by a burial party. Also lying among the bodies, conscious but suffering, was Tom Ewell, who had been shot in the abdomen inside the Mexican works. His friend, Thomas Claiborne, found him "prone on his hands, head and knees," and tried to offer comfort as other comrades gathered round. Upon examination, they found that the musket ball had not quite passed all the way through his body. It was just beneath the skin, next to the spine. Knowing that he was dying,

Brigadier General Gideon J. Pillow. The Nathaniel and Bucky Hughes Collection, courtesy of Lupton Library, University of Tennessee at Chattanooga.

Ewell requested opium to relieve him of his excruciating pain. Among the Mexican dead on top of the hill was General Vasquez and also a colonel, "his face handsome and composed," whose chest had been blown away.[28]

Scott was with elements of Worth's division and was following Twiggs's path in pursuit. Along the way, they passed through the hilly terrain and around the north side of La Atalaya, getting their first glimpse of the grisly aftermath. The aristocratic Scott always showed his soft side when caring for his men, even if he was sometimes clumsy in his well-intended efforts. Wishing to see the top of El Telégrafo up close, he made his way to the crest, where he came upon staff officer and prankster Lieutenant George Derby. The lieutenant, whose name was pronounced "Durby," was lying on the ground suffering from his wound when Scott spotted him and said, "My God, *Darby*, you're wounded!" Derby responded, "Yes, General *Scatt*." To which the general retorted in a testy manner, "[M]y name is *Scott*, not *Scatt!*" "And my name is *Derby*, not *Darby!*" said the lieutenant.[29]

At some point, Scott came upon a group of soldiers huddled around the wounded Tom Ewell. He pushed his way through, knelt by Ewell's side, and, grasping his hand, said, "Mr. Ewell you are an honor to your name, an honor to the service to which you belong." Then, proclaiming the lieutenant a hero, he concluded, "you must not die." A short time later, Ewell's brother, Richard, ascended the hill to see him. Dick, as he was called, had advanced with the dragoons, and while riding along the base of the hill, an acquaintance had told him of Tom's condition. The brothers exchanged words in the brief moments before Dick rejoined the pursuit. Tom told him that he knew he was going to die, and he asked Dick to write a letter to the family. Before the two parted, Tom told him that his commanding officer had his watch and purse. Dick then rode off, but he returned in the evening and spent the remaining hours of Tom's life by his side.[30]

Despite the unpleasant sights, Scott was exuberant about the day's events. He had already told McClellan that he had watched the attack on El Telégrafo and that it was "the most beautiful sight that he had ever witnessed." When he happened upon Harney, Scott reportedly exclaimed, "I cannot now adequately express my admiration of your gallant achievement, but at the proper time I shall take great pleasure in thanking you in proper terms." He was especially proud of the reconnaissance work done by the West Point officers and remarked to Lieutenant Isaac Stevens, "You engineers are too daring. You require to be held back."[31]

General Shields's condition was grave and his pain intense. As he led the charge on the Mexican camp, only thirty yards from the enemy battery, he had been hit in the right side of the chest by grapeshot that broke his ribs before exiting his back. He vomited the coffee that he had drunk that morning, and Captain George Davis thought that it was tinged with blood. Davis quickly detailed eight men to take him to the surgeon's station two miles away, and he accompanied them to the rear. Four men would carry him at a time, one under each arm and one under each bent knee. When they tired, they would switch and the other four would take their turn. The bouncing movement caused excruciating agony, evidently because of broken ribs "raking into his flesh." In his suffering, Shields begged them to put him down and let him die in peace, and once, when they stopped to comply with the general's wishes, Davis drew his sword and threatened anyone who tried to lay him down. When they reached the field hospital, a doctor named McMillan stuffed lint into the entrance and exit wounds, then instructed that Shields be placed in a comfortable place to die.[32] Working in the rear of the American army was Belgian-born Dr. Pedro Vanderlinden, who was actually a surgeon in the Mexican army. He attended to the Mexican wounded who had fallen into American hands, and at some point during the afternoon, he examined Shields and left with him a bottle of wine. In defiance of all expectations, the general did not die that evening—indeed, he survived the wound after an extended convalescence. Vanderlinden continued to look in on him in the days after the battle, and he later surmised that Shields had survived only because the grape ball had entered at such close range and with such force that it went through his body at maximum velocity, thus doing less damage than it might have otherwise.[33]

While Shields's men were carrying him to the rear, both mounted troops and infantry chased the Mexicans up the road for several hours. At dusk and eight miles west of Cerro Gordo, the Americans reached Santa Anna's "magnificent Hacienda," Encero. With darkness setting in and the chase hindered by a drizzling rain and tired horses, the pursuit halted. Just as Scott had predicted the previous evening while writing his orders, the enemy's batteries would be "carried or abandoned," and the ensuing American pursuit "may be continued many miles, until stopped by darkness or fortified positions, toward Jalapa."[34]

Casualty figures for the battle of Cerro Gordo were lopsided. Out of approximately 8,500 engaged, the Americans lost 63 killed and 368 wounded. The cost for the Mexican army was most assuredly high, although exact numbers are more difficult to ascertain, and the number captured—approximately three thousand, including five generals and two hundred other officers—was significant. Justin Smith's dated but still useful study of the war put the Mexican killed and wounded at approximately a thousand. The morning after the battle, Scott wrote his initial report of the engagement before setting out for Jalapa, and he estimated the Mexican killed and wounded at 350. Scott's preliminary report, written less than twenty-four hours after the battle, may have been grossly inaccurate, but the commanding general's numbers probably included only the enemy casualties around the immediate vicinity of the Cerro Gordo battlefield. In the days ahead, additional reports from the American units that pursued the enemy west to Jalapa would no doubt increase Scott's initial estimate. If this accounts for the disparity in the numbers, then the Mexican retreat was bloody indeed.[35]

Trained American officers were certainly aware of the vulnerability of an army during a retreat, and they took full advantage. Henri Jomini wrote in his classic work, *The Art of War,* that a "retreat, even when executed in the most skillful manner and by an army in good condition, always gives an advantage to the pursuing army; and this is particularly the case after a defeat." Jomini also wrote that "preservation of order is the only means of saving a body of troops harassed by the enemy during a retrograde movement." The Mexican army lost all semblance of order after the battle, and its officers ceased any attempt to maintain organization. Napoleon's maxim that retreats always cost an army more than the bloodiest of engagements certainly held true at Cerro Gordo. An American correspondent reported that there were dead horses and Mexican soldiers from El Telégrafo to Encero, and at places where the pursuing Americans overtook the retreating Mexicans, their bodies lay in heaps. Benjamin Wingate of the Mounted Rifles asserted a few days later that the reason his regiment went to Mexico was "to kill some of them Mexicans which we have shorly don."[36]

The Battle of Cerro Gordo was a disaster for the Mexicans, and the soldiers of both armies knew it. They "never expected to be defeated at this place," wrote Wingate. "Santa Anna told the citizens of Jalapa when he was on his way to Cerra Gordo that he defied all europe to take it away from him." Cerro Gordo was "a perfect place for a blunderer to sacrifice an army. But Scott was no blunderer." Rather than walk into an enemy trap, he sprang one of his own. Later Santa Anna reportedly told an American officer that Cerro Gordo was the greatest American victory of the war. Contemporary accounts notwithstanding, Santa Anna overestimated the strength of his position at Cerro Gordo, and he should have listened to his engineers. Although he commanded the high ground overlooking the road, his various strong points were not interconnected and were thus incapable of providing mutual support. Therefore, when one position fell, the rest were put in peril. Finally the failure to stop the Americans at the Cerro Gordo Pass cost the Mexicans their most important ally; yellow fever and other diseases that were just beginning to arrive in the coastal lowlands.[37]

The victory at Cerro Gordo awed young officers in the army and probably influenced the way they viewed military operations. Lee called it a "great victory." He was impressed with the Mexican defenses, but he was even more impressed with the manner by which they were defeated. "[T]heir whole line was turned by the left. It was a beautiful operation & came in well after our turning San Juan de Ulua by first taking Vera Cruz." In the first two encounters of the campaign, Lee learned the value of flanking enemy positions. Captain Robert Anderson, future commander at Fort Sumter and a general in the Union army, was learning another lesson from Scott's leadership. Having previously served under Zachary Taylor, he made a perceptive comparison of the two commanders. Taylor took few prisoners, Anderson observed, but Scott had captured over 7,000 at Veracruz and Cerro Gordo, and even more astonishing to the young captain was the low casualty rate in Scott's army. Taylor's bravery was unquestioned, but in battle, all must remain under his immediate supervision, whereas Scott's generalship was more sophisticated. He went to great lengths to reconnoiter in an effort to find any advantage that could be gained through science and skill, and the result was that his casualties were fewer. In sum, Anderson concluded, "matters are managed here differently."[38]

Two final observations of the battle deserve notice—one from a general's perspective, the other from that of an infantryman. From a general's viewpoint, this was a textbook Napoleonic battle with its holding action in front and its sweeping flank attack. Lieutenant Kirby Smith thought that it had been "marked by high strategic merit, not unlike the operations of Bonaparte, first consul, among the mountains of Italy." It had been made possible only by the skill of Scott's staff and engineers, then the plan carefully laid out by Scott himself, and finally executed with skill and bravery by the commanders in the field. Scott was able to concentrate the bulk of his army against the weak point of the enemy, and ultimately he forced the Mexican army to fight from extreme disadvantage. Military historian Bevin Alexander, in his analysis of the leadership characteristics that make for great generals, asserted that "an enemy [that] is forced to change front, . . . tends to be dislocated and unable to . . . fight effectively." This is exactly what Scott intended—and what he accomplished at Cerro Gordo. However, battle plans drawn up on paper mean very little to the infantryman when bullets are whizzing by, sabers are clashing, and opposing soldiers are locked in deadly combat. His perspective of battle is different. Once the troops were deployed and the shooting started, Cerro Gordo became essentially a soldier's fight. Infantryman Hiram Yeager described Veracruz as the "science of dodgeing," but concerning Cerro Gordo, he concluded that "dodgeing was out of the question[;] every man for himself." An enlisted man reflected a few weeks later that the "fight at Cerro Gordo was, while it lasted the fiercest one I was ever in."[39]

The battle was over by noon on April 18, and Mexican troops fled west through Jalapa to Perote. The road was heavily strewn with animal carcasses and with dead and wounded Mexican soldiers who had tried to fend off an enthusiastic American pursuit. Along the way, retreating soldiers had shed weapons, ammunition, rations, and all sorts of supplies. In a terrible state of disorganization, the fragmented elements of the Mexican army acted in their own self-interest, eluding their pursuers and taking what they wanted from local inhabitants as they saw fit. Santa Anna, too, had fled. He narrowly escaped Shields's flanking column, unhitching a horse from his carriage team to make his getaway. He, along with a few staff officers, spent the remainder of the day traveling west on a course parallel to but a safe distance from the main road. His abandoned carriage fell into American hands along with its contents: one of his artificial legs, food, fine wine, "highly flavored cigars," personal papers, and several thousand dollars in cash. According to George Kendall of the *Picayune*, two American captains were among the ones who captured the prize, and they climbed in and found the booty. They ate the food, drank the wine, and each smoked one of the cigars.[40]

As darkness fell over the battlefield, gathering and caring for the wounded continued. Dabney Maury, who had been wounded in the arm the previous day and had narrowly escaped amputation, found himself on April 18 in

Plan del Río in a reed hut that was serving as a makeshift medical ward for wounded officers. Among the injured was Captain Joe Johnston, who had been wounded several days earlier. His friend Captain Lee paid him a visit and expressed for the second, but not the last, time in the campaign his pity for his friend. The first was two months earlier during the voyage, when Johnston had become terribly seasick. "[M]y poor Joe," Lee lamented, "I can do nothing with him." After visiting Johnston in the field hospital, Lee reported in a letter home that "my poor Joe Johnston," who had been seriously wounded by two balls, had now had both of them removed and was "comfortable." Captain Stevens Mason of the Mounted Rifles, like Maury a Virginian, also shared the hut, having lost a leg to a cannonball. Mason and Maury often joked and laughed about getting back home to Virginia. Another officer, George Derby, also ended up convalescing there. A recent West Point graduate and classmate of Maury's, he had acquired the nickname "Squibob." The fun-loving Derby talked incessantly, but beneath the surface, he was an officer and engineer of considerable talent who had finished seventh in his class. Maury apparently did not mind Derby's constant chatter, but Johnston became quite annoyed. One day a herd of goats passed by the hut and Derby instructed a servant to go out and apprehend one of them, to which a testy Johnston responded, "If you dare to do that, I'll have you court-martialed and cashiered or shot!"[41]

Each of these officers experienced different results from their Cerro Gordo wounds. Within a few days Johnston departed on a litter. He was carried all the way to Jalapa, where he continued to recuperate before returning to active duty. He, of course, went on to be one of the highest-ranking officers in the Confederate army, but he lost his command to Lee in 1862 after suffering another wound. Maury also recovered, and in June, when he was well enough to travel, he was sent back to the United States, arm in sling, to recruit for the army. At Louisville, Kentucky, a man asked Maury if it was true that he had been wounded at Cerro Gordo, to which Maury responded in the affirmative. "Well, come, please, and take a drink with me," the man said, and upon entering the bar at the Galt House, instructed the bartender to give Maury "the best you have in the house, no matter what it costs." Like Johnston, he later became a Confederate general, seeing service at Pea Ridge, Vicksburg, and Mobile, and after the Civil War, he founded the Southern Historical Society and served as a diplomat. Derby went on to see extensive duty in the West, where he became a noted explorer and surveyor for the army. He was in California during the gold rush and later helped open the Arizona Territory with his exploration of the Colorado River. His wit was on full display once when dining in a San Francisco hotel. He watched with curiosity as the proprietor cut a slab of beef into ever smaller pieces, and at length he inquired as to why the man was serving such small portions. The owner responded that he did not have much and he wanted to make it go as far as possible. Derby then retorted that in that case, he would take a large piece because he was on his way to San Diego and thus could make it go as far as anyone. Mason, who talked so much about getting back home, died of his wounds three weeks later.[42]

There were many other victims of the battle, particularly Mexicans, whose names are forgotten to history. Private Richard Coulter from Pennsylvania recorded in his journal that the western slope of El Telégrafo down which the Mexicans fled was strewn with bodies. It was "an ugly sight; men shot in every position." Mexican women, wives and girlfriends who accompanied the army, soon started to arrive to care for the wounded and captured, particularly atop the hill where many of the Mexican wounded had gathered. Enemy bodies continued to lie throughout the battlefield, and within a couple of days, "the smell was very bad."[43]

After pursuing the enemy as far as Jalapa, Dick Ewell returned to the battlefield in the evening to be with his brother. The pain from Tom's abdomen wound was unrelenting, and Tom expressed the desire to die rather than continue to endure. He knew his wound was fatal and was resigned to his fate. To Dick he said that "he hoped his great sufferings might be an expiation for his sins." Tom lived until about 1:00 A.M. on April 19—about sixteen hours. Shortly before his death, his legs became numb, and when he passed away, he did so with such "calmness" that Dick, who was by his side, could not even tell when he had taken his last breath. Dick procured a coffin, and brother and friends buried him near the spot where he fell. At least Tom and those around him knew he was dying; one Pennsylvania volunteer had a very different experience. He was wounded on April 18 and under a doctor's care for a week and a half after the battle. On April 29, the doctor declared him fit for duty and ordered him back to his post, but on April 30, he died.[44]

How to handle the 3,000 or more enemy captured posed an immediate logistical problem for Scott and his army. The day after the battle, the commissary department issued pork and bread to the prisoners as well as to the women who were attending them. Despite caring for their immediate physical needs, many of the American soldiers nevertheless viewed their captives with disdain. Coulter referred to one huddled group of them as "a promiscuous crowd." Thomas Barclay called them "a miserable looking set," and his attitude toward officers was no better: "The officers appear to be as great scamps as the men." Ultimately, Scott chose to parole the prisoners as he had done at Veracruz. It was well known within the U.S. Army, however, that many of the Veracruz prisoners had violated their parole and that most likely so too would those captured at Cerro Gordo. However, as Barclay speculated, "Gen. Scott considers it easier to take them prisoners again than to lead and guard them." Some of the Mexicans, including two generals, chose to remain prisoners rather than accept their parole, and Scott ordered that they march under their own recognizance to Veracruz and report to the military governor Colonel Henry Wilson. Once in the port city, Wilson locked them in the castle.[45]

Captured personnel were only part of the problem; confiscated hardware created additional difficulties. The Americans captured at least 4,000 muskets and some forty cannon. The muskets were dealt with by bending the barrels and breaking the stocks, some of which the soldiers used to fuel campfires. Scott took one Mexican battery for the army's use but had no means of transporting the rest. We are "embarrassed with the pieces of artillery—all bronze—which we have captured," he wrote to Secretary Marcy. He had most of the cannon spiked and left behind, but when he learned that one of the captured pieces was named "El Terror del Norte Americano," he ordered it, along with five others, shipped back to the States as trophies.[46]

Later some soldiers paused to reflect on what they had witnessed at the Battle of Cerro Gordo. In mid-May, Barna Upton wrote such a reflective letter to his brother: "Four weeks ago today (Sunday!) While you were engaged in the worship of God at church—I was in a foreign land witnessing and participating in a scene of wholesale carnage and bloodshed." What irony he must have felt to consider that instead of "listening to prayer and songs of praise to our Creator I heard only the thunder of hostile cannon the rattleing of musketry, the clashing of shell, the groans of the wounded men, and the shouts of victory as the victors rushed onward trampling on . . . fallen foes." In a poignant passage that illustrates the loss of innocence that soldiers experience, Upton admitted that he was not "by nature" intended to be a soldier, but after Cerro Gordo, he was "astonished at the calmness and almost indifference which I now experience, in walking over a battlefield . . . [and] seeing hundreds of our fellow beings cut down instantly in the bloom of manhood, and laying in heaps on every side." Then in a passage that reflects his idealism and religious commitment, he went on to write, "how strange and inconsistent is the idea of thousands of intelligent men, meeting together to mangle and kill each other."[47]

CHAPTER SIX

Jalapa

Garden of Mexico

*Scott must now be near Jallapa. . . . He would give any thing to
get ahead of Old Zack, but his ridiculous fears of "a fire in the
rear" lost him a position which he will never be able to regain.*
—William L. Marcy, Secretary of War

"The war is nearly up," exulted W. L. Bliss, predicting that he would be in
the Halls of the Montezumas in two weeks. Cerro Gordo was "the greatest
victory ever won by the Americans in Mexico," bragged Jacob Hoffer to his
parents. Even Scott, basking in the recent victory, wrote to Taylor proclaiming that "Mexico has no longer an army." Optimism abounded as Scott put
Worth's division back in the lead for the remaining fifteen miles to Jalapa. On
April 19, Worth's men took up the march in a steady rain. For the next few
days, the rest of the army collected itself and filed away from Cerro Gordo,
leaving behind a small garrison at Plan del Río to care for the wounded. Their
march afforded them grisly sights of the recent carnage, and along the way,
they saw ample evidence of the shattered enemy army. "Dead Mexicans lay
along the road, & dead horses & mules literally putrified the air," while disabled guns and smashed carriages served as a grim clue of the areas of most
desperate fighting. Limbs were scattered about while decaying bodies "torn
and mangled by cannon balls, [lay] . . . half devoured by the beasts and birds
of prey." Vultures circled overhead and perched on trees and bushes throughout the area. By one soldier's count, two hundred Mexican corpses remained
atop El Telégrafo four days after the battle. "The smell . . . is sickening,"
wrote a volunteer.[1]

The defeat came as such a blow to the Mexicans because it was so unexpected, and as its news spread, so too did panic and confusion. Lieutenant
Isaac Stevens said that the "decisive blow" at Cerro Gordo came on the "Mexicans like a thunderbolt." It was made all the more difficult to accept given
Santa Anna's prebattle boasting. Many Mexicans wondered in disbelief how
the outnumbered Americans could hand their army such a thorough drubbing. Some suspected Santa Anna of treachery and thought that perhaps the

Major General
William J. Worth.
Courtesy of the
Library of Congress.

outcome of both of the battles at Buena Vista and Cerro Gordo had been pre-arranged. "Bribery & corruption" must be the motive. After entering Jalapa, George Kendall reported that "the Mexicans here, one & all, denounce Santa Anna for a coward, a traitor, & everything else that is bad." Some citizens, when asked about their chieftain, "will draw their hands across their throats showing what they would do with him." Sergeant Thomas Barclay summed up the Americans' attitude when he penned in his journal that the Mexicans "are now dispersed and dishonoured. A plentiful and healthy country is now in our possession and the road is open to the City of Mexico."[2]

And that open road to the capital is just what the government feared. When the discouraging news of the battle arrived, the Mexican Congress sprang into action, passing legislation that forbade the executive branch (Santa Anna) from opening negotiations with the United States government, especially if they involved the cession of Mexican land. Distrustful of Santa Anna, the legislative body took more vigorous steps to prosecute the war and at the same time tried to enlist the British government to act as an arbitra-tor. Meanwhile, Santa Anna engaged in the kind of political maneuvering to which he was so adept. Knowing that he faced growing opposition in the Congress, he submitted his resignation, but worded it in such a way as to suggest that if accepted, it would be because Congress was opposed to the staunch resistance that he advocated. On learning that the government would likely accept his resignation, he withdrew it, publicly exclaiming that it was news of his pending abdication that had emboldened the Americans to advance further.[3] While it strove mightily to resist, the Mexican government possessed neither the trust nor the sympathy of many of its citizens. The impact that Cerro Gordo had on Mexico was political and psychological as well as military.

In Scott's army, Lieutenant E. Kirby Smith thought that the battle would teach the "bigoted fanatics" among the Mexican leadership of the "futility of waging war against us & cease prating about national honor." But he and others mistook the defeatism of the citizenry as an indication that the government was in complete disarray. Kendall admitted that he had no solid news from the capital, but "an intelligent Spaniard" told him that the "most unparalleled distress prevails" there. This, some Americans thought, presented an opportunity to rush to the capital and seize control. Worth thought that the army could be there by the end of May. Raphael Semmes thought that Scott should hasten to Mexico City while the enemy army was reeling and unable to offer resistance, and that a failure to do so could only be a result of the general's lethargy.[4]

However, while Scott had remedied many of his transportation needs, insurmountable logistical problems would have accompanied such a rapid march. Even if the reports of government disorganization were true, that was, for Scott, sufficient reason not to advance. His goal from the beginning was to win a peace, and that could only be accomplished through authoritative negotiations with a stable and intact Mexican government. Also, Scott intended to fight only as long as it took to win a peace settlement, and with his sword and olive branch approach, he deemed it imperative to give the Mexicans time after each battle to meet his olive branch with one of their own. Throughout the campaign, Scott never hurried, but always allowed Mexican authorities to regain their balance in the hopes that they would extend a peace offering. Indeed, during his brief stay in Jalapa, Scott half expected to receive a proposal from Mexico City. Just the previous month, Roswell Ripley, an artillery officer who would later become a Scott critic, wrote in a letter home a passage that demonstrated an instinctive understanding of what the commanding general was doing. While encamped in the siege line south of Veracruz, he wrote to his mother of his desire for a rapid conclusion of the war, which might be possible with the quick capture of Veracruz and a rapid march inland, if we "are careful to give the Mexicans an opportunity to keep up a Government with whom we can treat."[5]

In its efforts to resist the Americans, the government in Mexico City began to actively promote exactly what Scott hoped to avoid. Less than two weeks after Cerro Gordo, the interim president, Pedro María Anaya, signed an order to create a light corps or a cadre of irregulars to engage in unconventional warfare against the invaders.[6] With its army in disarray, the government hoped to foment a guerrilla war that could hinder, if not entirely halt, the American advance, and it pinned its hopes on citizens of influence and wealth to raise and lead these quasi–national guard units. As envisioned by the government, a wealthy man would recruit a unit of about two hundred partisans and outfit them with the necessary equipment and supplies at an estimated cost of 24,500 pesos. Of the seventy individuals who applied and received authorization by the government to raise such units, nearly half (thirty) were located in the three states where Scott's army operated: Veracruz, Puebla, and Mexico. However, such a cadre system made personal wealth a prerequisite for citizens who wanted to resist the Americans. Thus, rather than serve as a unifying plea, Anaya's decree only exacerbated social divisions that already existed along class lines, thereby preventing a guerrilla strategy from reaching its full potential.[7] It would take several weeks for this new development to affect the movement of troops and supplies, but Scott met the growing threat with calmness and skill as he marched deeper into the interior of the country.

The trip to Jalapa was a short one. Along the way, they saw several places that had been prepared as defensive positions—all abandoned. Some of the paroled Mexican prisoners had already plundered their way through the town. When Scott's army arrived, the volunteer units were marched through and beyond Jalapa to keep them out of the city and thus out of trouble. Sentinels stood guard to ensure that the angry volunteers did not enter. For the most part, however, American spirits lifted as they arrived in this "paradise." With an altitude of 4,700 feet, crisp mountain air, and a refreshing climate, it was "one of the finest places in Mexico." The 12,000 inhabitants cultivated the rich soil of the region, producing pears, oranges, bananas, cherries, and peaches, along with corn, oats, coffee, and rye. "Everything is plenty here," wrote Hiram Yeager. Jalapa looked different from the previous towns that Americans had seen, especially Veracruz. Here the buildings were neat, sturdy, and clean, and all had red tile roofs. The area was covered with lush foliage and exotic, brilliantly colored flowers. It is called "the Garden of the country," wrote W. L. Bliss, and is "one of the most delightful spots that I have ever seen in all my life." "Jalapa is one of the prettiest places I ever

[saw]," agreed Captain Robert E. Lee. Their observations of the pleasant city quickly confirmed for them the reason why Mexicans refer to Jalapa as the "Heaven of Mexico" and "Vera Cruz, the hell."[8]

The Americans commented freely on their new hosts, and in so doing displayed their sense of cultural and racial superiority. They generally believed that Jalapans were more industrious, advanced, and civilized than Mexicans they had seen elsewhere, and they were particularly impressed with members of the opposite sex. "The women are very handsome," thought Private Israel Uncapher. Another, Ralph Kirkham, wrote to his wife that the only pretty girl he had seen in Mexico was in Jalapa, and he fearlessly added, "she was pretty! Such beautiful large, dark eyes and such a graceful figure." Later in the same letter—and perhaps remembering to whom he was writing—he added, "The Mexican women are very graceful, more so than ours; but as for being handsome, or even pretty, it is all a mistake. Nine-tenths of the people resemble the Cherokee Indians." George McClellan disagreed, penning in his diary, "The white faces of the ladies struck us as being exceedingly beautiful—they formed so pleasing a contrast to the black and brown complexions of the Indians and negroes who had for so long been the only human beings to greet our sight." The consensus was that Jalapa was home to some of the "most beautiful Ladies" who "dress so very gay and neat that a fellow almost falls in love with them."[9]

Scott was optimistic when he arrived in Jalapa just before noon on April 20. After sending Worth's division ahead to Perote, he made his headquarters in the governor's palace, and the bulk of the army nestled into the garden surroundings, where it would remain for about a month. From there, the commanding general sent an upbeat dispatch to Colonel Henry Wilson, military governor of Veracruz. "Our dangers & difficulties are all in the rear between this place & V Cruz," and he now believed that he could take all of Mexico without losing a hundred men. He instructed Wilson to forward medicine, blankets, flour, bacon, ammunition, and other supplies as soon as possible. The commanding officer of each department—commissary, medical, ordnance, and quartermasters—wrote to their corresponding chief in Veracruz with specific lists of needs for the army, and Scott ordered Wilson to give "rigid attention to those requisitions." Jalapa was still on the edge of the yellow fever region. Scott did not intend to stay there long, and he wanted to be prepared to press on after accumulating necessary stores and seeing to the wounded. Also, for the safety of the troops, the general instructed that if a yellow fever epidemic existed in Veracruz when new troops arrived from the States, the soldiers were not to be allowed off their vessels until adequate transportation was available for their journey inland. Then they were to be brought ashore and quickly gotten out of the city.[10]

Back on the coast, the Veracruz garrison was stretched thin, but it worked long hours guarding the city and forwarding supplies to the army. The number of men assigned to guard the city gates and batteries was reduced from eighty-one to fifty-eight in an effort to provide more rest for the men. A week after Scott's request, the Ordnance Department in Veracruz reported having 900 muskets on hand, and out of 4,000 captured Mexican muskets, Captain Joseph Daniels estimated that perhaps 1,500 could be made serviceable for the army if proper ammunition could be located. To supplement the food supply and to remedy such problems as spoiled bacon, 311 barrels of which had to be discarded from the Veracruz supplies, Wilson actively sought to contract with local inhabitants for the purchase of additional beef.[11]

After securing the army in its new camp, Scott sent wagons and litters along with a heavy guard back to Plan del Río to bring up the wounded. The return trip took two days, and it was unpleasant for both the wounded and the litter bearers. The National Highway, although mostly paved, was by no means smooth, and while it made for easy marching, its uneven surface was magnified by the wooden wheels of a wagon. Private Thomas Tennery from Illinois had been shot through both legs during Shields's flank attack, and he rode up to Jalapa in a wagon with three others, an experience that he described as being "jostled almost to death." Being carried on a stretcher by weary, stumbling comrades was not much better. "Poor fellows! They suffered very much," remembered Joseph R. Smith. Dabney Maury, who had thwarted a doctor's attempt to amputate his arm, returned with the wounded and was well enough to walk, but Joe Johnston remained in bed and required daily care. Maury visited him daily, but Preston Johnston, a nephew, was his most assiduous caregiver. Before leaving Jalapa, General Scott visited the hospital and made a point to talk to each man, inquiring about his health, his unit, and the like. About Johnston, Scott reportedly said, he "is a great soldier, but he has an unfortunate knack of getting himself shot in nearly every engagement."[12]

Many of the soldiers had a low opinion of the army's medical staff. The doctors who accompanied the volunteer units did not have to meet the same stringent requirements as the regular medical doctors, and the resulting difference in care was predictable. Also, unit commanders often assigned the worst soldiers and the misfits to work as orderlies. Furthermore, the hospitals were usually dank, unsanitary places where one was more likely to catch a disease rather than be cured of one. A common problem in Mexico was the infestation of maggots in wounds, especially the stumps of amputated limbs. Under such conditions, staff members, working long hours under adverse conditions, tended to be rude, callous, and disrespectful to the soldiers. On visiting one hospital, a soldier became depressed to see the once energetic youth of the patients waste away, "exposed to the carelessness of nurses and attendants and daily insulted by ruffians." While in Jalapa, news arrived in one of the Pennsylvania regiments that seemed to confirm their contemptuous feelings. Two of their sick friends had been left behind in Veracruz and had died. The doctor had refused to discharge one of them when he became ill because he said the man was not serious enough to justify it. Later, when his condition worsened, the same doctor judged him too serious to discharge because he would not survive the trip home.[13]

Disease rapidly became a concern in the army by late April and early May. Even though yellow fever was no longer a primary concern, doctors still had to contend with malaria, dysentery, and measles. Dysentery and diarrhea sapped the body of necessary fluids, and all too often, thirsty soldiers then drank from dirty, bacteria-infested ponds. The volunteer units compounded the problems through their own ignorance of basic sanitation. They rarely saw to proper drainage and they often lacked adequate protection from the elements, with the result being that their camps usually became "miasmic sink-holes of filth and squalor." Dysentery was often fatal, but it frequently took a long time to claim its victim—months or in some cases years. There were still veterans, who, having contracted the disease in Mexico, were dying in 1849. For all soldiers who served in Mexico, there was an 11 percent mortality rate from disease.[14]

While in Jalapa, Scott showed courtesy and respect for local sensibilities at every opportunity. When a Mexican colonel who had been wounded at Cerro Gordo died, he provided an elaborate funeral for his fallen foe. Scott, Twiggs, and other U.S. officers attended the somber affair, at which five priests presided and an American band played. "It was a splendid pageant," thought Uncapher, and the effort to honor one of their countrymen was "much to the satisfaction of the people," recalled Richard Coulter. But Americans mocked their opponents, as was the case when a troop of dragoons happened on one of Santa Anna's nearby estates. There they found an outbuilding that housed the general's fighting cocks, and they picked two out of the group. One, a "fierce looking rooster . . . not so large as some but with game sticking out all over him," they named General Taylor. The other, a "heavy but clumsy bird, with but little fight in him," they designated Santa Anna. When they turned the birds loose on each other, General Taylor struck several quick blows, and Santa Anna disengaged "as fast as his two legs would carry him." General Taylor was "crowing right lustily" as, no doubt, were the dragoons.[15]

As proof that Scott's pacification plan worked, the inhabitants freely mingled with the foreigners, showing an indifference and lack of hostility that surprised the Americans. Markets were open as usual, especially on Sunday, when the streets filled with vendors selling red peppers, cabbage, fruits, eggs, chickens, tomatoes, rice, and other delectable supplements to the soldiers' rations. The prices were high, but the variety was a welcome change to standard army fare. Meanwhile, the commissary department bought large quantities of supplies from the surrounding rancheros.[16] The attitude was business as usual, at least for a segment of the community, and both the Americans and the Jalapan merchants benefited. This would be a typical scene for occupied Mexican cities. However, it would be simplistic to assert that the favorable environment was entirely due to Scott's pacification policy, for he benefited greatly from a latent class conflict that predated the war.

It also would be too simplistic to say that all Mexicans succumbed to this army of invaders. The way that locals responded to the foreigners often depended on their status in society. A sailor named William Harrison was posted at Veracruz for much of 1847, and he made numerous excursions into the city, talking to as many of the residents as possible in an attempt to improve his Spanish. In so doing, he learned much and detected a pattern of Mexican attitudes that seems to hold true when compared with other accounts. He found that most of the upper class, those privileged Mexicans who were comfortable with things as they had been previously, fled Veracruz, and those who remained "do not, if possible, show themselves in the streets." When they did come out, they gave every passing American "such a scowl & look of hatred as to leave no doubt in the mind of the latter as to what would be his fate, if the other had his wish." The lower class—beggars, *leperos*, and the like—were perfectly indifferent to the American presence. Likely their lot in life made them so disposed. The "merchants, tradesmen, mechanics," however, "seem in their glory. Such a harvest they never had. Heretofore, their customers have been an impoverished set, but now . . . the city is filled with American troops, most of whom have money to spend." This industrious middle class, which benefited financially from the American presence, constituted the majority of the polite, welcoming natives. This class distinction was borne out by Lieutenant Daniel Harvey Hill's observations. While serving in northern Mexico the previous year, rancheros had told him of their "bitterness" toward the rich, the military, and the clergy, causing Hill to conclude that "we are fighting the Army and the Aristocracy *not* the *people* of Mexico."[17]

Despite the heavy hand of punishment that threatened those who broke Scott's martial law order, violations did occur. On one occasion, the troops assembled in Jalapa to witness the whipping of four soldiers, three volunteers and one regular, for robbery. A punishment of thirty-nine lashes had been ordered by the strict Colonel Thomas Childs, whom Scott had appointed military governor of the town. Many of the volunteers who gathered had "a general feeling of disgust . . . that such a punishment could be inflicted under the laws of our country." Seeing "free born Americans tied up and whipped like dogs . . . in a foreign land" was sobering to behold, and the penalty tended to result in sympathy for the criminals. Although many American soldiers regarded Scott's law and order policies as unfair, they were not entirely one-sided. While in Jalapa, he issued General Order No. 127, which made all local alcaldes responsible for tracking down and punishing bandits and guerrillas in their areas. Failure to do so would result in a $300 fine.[18]

Most soldiers tried to show respect for their hosts, especially when it came to their religious practices. Many Americans, particularly immigrants from Ireland, were Catholic and attended mass with the Jalapans, but for the majority who had Protestant backgrounds, Catholicism was a different and sometimes strange religion. Captain Joseph Smith penned this succinct opinion of Catholicism in a letter home: "And then their *religion!* Such su-perstitious mummery and idolatry!" Some soldiers commented on the "rak-ish look" of the priests who "live on the fat of the land" and who ignored the church's mandate of sexual abstinence. They are supposedly celibate, wrote John Dodd, "but unless common report belie them, they make up for it." Robert Anderson concluded that the priests were corrupt and afflicted some of the best families in the country, making "love at the same time to mother and daughters." The church seemed to maintain its wealth by drawing from the poverty-stricken masses. Anderson wrote to his sister that the power of the church is what had kept the country together, "and the church is even more corrupt than the state." A general feeling among the soldiers was that the Mexican government and the Catholic church constituted a twin tyranny, both serving to keep the people impoverished and ignorant. Robert E. Lee thought that the country would be better if "free opinions of government & religion" were introduced and "the power & iniquity of the church" were broken.[19]

Among Zachary Taylor's troops in northern Mexico, news of the Battle of Cerro Gordo began to arrive in the early days of May. Initial rumors brought the depressing but inaccurate news of a Mexican victory and of the capture of Generals Patterson, Smith, and Twiggs. Some accounts even claimed that both Santa Anna and Scott had been killed. But as additional reports came in, a very different picture emerged, as they learned that Scott had turned the Mexican army in a brilliant flanking movement. With some exaggeration, William Fraser wrote in his diary that Scott had crossed a river and "placed his whole army in rear of the Mexicans." One of Taylor's colonels, Henry S. Lane, thought that the victory at Cerro Gordo "will place Scott on high ground as a general." In Washington, Secretary Marcy thought that even though Scott wanted to outshine Taylor, his "ridiculous" letter writing cost him too much.[20]

Scott's and Taylor's was not the only rivalry in the army. In the weeks after the battle, several officers expressed discontent over the official reports of the engagement and the lack of credit they had received. Lieutenant Pierre G. T. Beauregard had already felt slighted when Colonel Joseph Totten's report of the Veracruz siege failed to single him out for recognition as the engineer who selected the spot for the placement of three of the batteries. Now friction erupted over the Cerro Gordo reports. Worth, whose division was reduced to acting as the reserve, thought that Scott's summary of the battle was too glowing and that both Pillow and Twiggs deserved censorship. In a letter to a family member, he called the commanding general's report "a lie from beginning to end." Colonel Bennet Riley also felt slighted because his division commander, General Twiggs, failed to properly acknowledge the role of Riley's brigade in storming El Telégrafo. His dissatisfaction was such that he requested a court of inquiry to vindicate his men—a request that Scott denied.[21]

Finally there was Lieutenant Roswell Ripley, who, with herculean effort, succeeded in positioning a howitzer south of Río del Plan to protect Pillow's flank, only to have his gun's utility nullified by Pillow's last-minute change of plans. Just getting his gun into position had been a great feat, but Scott's official report did not recognize his contributions, and he wrote to army headquarters to inform the general of the discrepancy. Scott informed the lieutenant that his contributions would be brought out more fully in a subsequent report, but no such follow-up account appeared. After the war, Ripley, still wanting credit for what he mistakenly believed to be a significant contribution to the battle, wrote directly to the War Department. Pillow, by that time a staunch ally of Ripley's, likewise wrote an accompanying letter to Marcy to set the record straight. With so many officers, from the commanding general down, seeking credit and fame (and perhaps a political future), rivalries and disputes became the rule rather than the exception as the campaign wore on, creating a friction that ultimately fractured the chain of command. As historian Otis Singletary put it, the United States fought two wars in Mexico, "one against the Mexicans and the other within the American military establishment." Captain Robert Anderson of the Third Artillery clearly voiced his opinion about soldiers who tried to ensure that they received a place of prominence in after action reports. After Veracruz surrendered, Major George H. Talcott approached Colonel William Bankhead, commander of Scott's artillery, "importuning" the colonel to highlight his actions in the trenches during the siege. Anderson wrote, "I would cut my tongue out before I would allow it to commit so great an act of indelicacy."[22]

After a couple of weeks at Jalapa, paradise began to give way to grumbling as discontent filtered down into the ranks. While some soldiers wrote home about the variety of food they were able to purchase on the street, some of the volunteers could not enjoy that luxury. With their camp two miles away from town and money in short supply (they sometimes went months without pay), it was often impossible for them to supplement their rations. They tried to be inventive with their allotment of flour but found that all one could cook with it were "Slap Jacks," which contained enough grease to "give an ostrich dyspepsia." Daily rains also made for damp quarters, wet blankets, and generally uncomfortable and unhealthy living conditions. Neither the Second Pennsylvanians nor the South Carolinians had tents, so they slept out in the elements. Disease, coupled with wounds, combined to make for a steady death rate of half a dozen or more each day at Jalapa. Men of the Pennsylvania regiments had had enough. When some companies went to their colonel's headquarters tent and demanded either money or more rations, the officer promised to look into the situation. Not satisfied with his answer, they charged a Mexican fruit stand, but were stopped short by armed guards.[23]

When several of the volunteer regiments were released to go home in the first week of May, it eliminated some of the breeding ground for such discontent, but it intensified a dilemma for Scott. Since arriving at Jalapa, the approaching expiration of the enlistments for the twelve-month volunteers had been a growing concern. The War Department had been promising to send enough new volunteer regiments to raise his army's strength to 20,000, and those guarantees would continue into the summer, but as yet, none had arrived. General Patterson had advised Scott to push deep into the interior of the country so that when their time expired, the volunteers would opt to reenlist rather than hazard the long journey back to the coast. Scott chose otherwise. He released the regiments early so that they could return to Veracruz and get out of the country before the height of the yellow fever season. He also sent them home early because he knew that as the expiration date of their enlistment approached, they would likely become increasingly difficult to control. Also, because Scott did not anticipate another battle in the immediate future, it did not make sense to keep the volunteers around just to consume supplies. So on May 6, seven regiments from Tennessee, Georgia, Alabama, and Illinois began the trek home. Only four volunteer regiments remained in the army, two from Pennsylvania, one from New York, and the Palmetto Regiment from South Carolina, and their enlistments were for the war's duration. Scott's numbers had dwindled to just over 7,100 men.[24]

As the volunteers were packing their gear and heading for the coast, the U.S. cutter *Ewing* was dropping its anchor at Veracruz with a passenger on board whose presence in Mexico seemed to confirm Scott's suspicion about the administration. It was Polk's special agent from the State Department, Nicholas P. Trist, whose assignment was to conduct peace negotiations with the Mexican government when the opportunity arose. When news had arrived in Washington on April 10 of the fall of Veracruz, the president immediately engaged Secretary of State James Buchanan to select a suitable representative to go to Mexico and take charge of the government's diplomatic efforts to secure a treaty. Buchanan suggested Trist because of his knowledge and diplomatic skill. In addition to being married to Thomas Jefferson's granddaughter, he had served as consul to Havana, Cuba, was fluent in Spanish, and familiar with Hispanic culture. As the chief clerk of the State Department, Buchanan had entrusted him with responsibilities akin to that of an undersecretary. In fact, his unfortunate title was not very descriptive of the level of duties that he fulfilled for Buchanan. Trist was a moderate expansionist, but like Scott, he was arrogant and stubborn. Polk thought the candidate's qualifications suited the mission, so he made the appointment, and Buchanan drafted a peace proposal to the Mexican government, sealed it, and gave it to the envoy. Before Trist left Washington on April 17, Polk gave him the astonishing advice that he need not bother Scott with the particulars of his assignment. Instead, the president recommended that if he required consultation, he should feel free to approach Polk's friend Gideon Pillow.[25]

The sealed proposal that Buchanan gave Trist embodied the administration's demands for a Rio Grande boundary, and a large cession of land that included California and the New Mexico territory (this territory would eventually become the states of New Mexico, Arizona, Nevada, Utah, and part of Colorado and Wyoming). The United States government in turn would pay a price that Trist had the latitude to negotiate. Polk hoped to pay no more than $25 million, but he instructed Trist that if he could also obtain lower California and right of passage across the Isthmus of Tehuantepec, he could go as high as $30 million. Trist's instructions called for him to present the proposal to the Mexican government at the earliest possible date.[26]

When Trist arrived in Veracruz, problems arose immediately. Once there, he learned of the American victory at Cerro Gordo, and he considered it urgent to get the administration's peace proposal to Mexican representatives. So while waiting on the coast for an armed escort to carry him safely to Scott's army at Jalapa, he decided to send the proposal ahead with a troop of dragoons, along with a letter from Marcy to Scott. Unfortunately, the secretary's letter was written in such a way as to send the general into a tirade. In it, Marcy had written that Trist was "clothed with . . . diplomatic powers as will authorize him to enter into arrangements with the government of Mexico for the suspension of hostilities." It went on to say that if "the contingency has occurred" wherein Trist instructs Scott to suspend military operations, Scott should consider it as if it were "a direction from the President."[27] The wording left Scott with the impression that he, the commanding general of the army, would be in a subservient role, taking orders from a civilian State Department employee regarding military operations. Moreover, it was evident that the administration wanted to circumvent Scott in the negotiation process, an impression that seemed obvious by the fact that he had not been made privy to the contents of the sealed proposal. And a last insult was Trist's accompanying note instructing Scott to forward Buchanan's proposal to the Mexican government.

Scott could not control his anger. It was an insult to be answerable to a low-level official sent by an administration that did not understand that he alone could determine, for reasons of safety and security, the appropriateness of halting his army's operations. Nor did the administration appreciate the current state of the Mexican government, or the essential role that Scott would have to play if Trist were to make contact. These shortcomings constituted a "stupendous blind spot in Polk's thinking," as Trist biographer Wallace Ohrt put it. Convinced that this represented a "fire from the rear," Scott sat down and wrote a defiant response to Trist. In it he sarcastically commented on the diplomat's assignment as being "considered too important to be entrusted to my agency!" Knowing that his letter would be forwarded to Washington, he probably wrote that statement more for Polk than for Trist. In a derisive tone, Scott went on to assert, "I see that the Secretary of War proposes to degrade me, by requiring that I, the commander of this army, shall defer to you, the chief clerk of the Department of State, the question of continuing or discontinuing hostilities." Scott made it clear that regardless of the diplomatic powers with which Trist was clothed, unless he held "military rank over me, . . . I shall demand" that if peace negotiations require a cease-fire, "you refer that question to me." He also pointed out that the present state of the Mexican government, as well as a recent law making it illegal for a Mexican official to enter into peace negotiations with the Americans, made it quite impossible for him to forward Buchanan's proposal.[28]

Ironically, just the previous month, Scott had made it clear to the administration that he was willing to have someone with the army who could negotiate a treaty. In an April 5 letter to Marcy, he indicated that he had laid the groundwork for a treaty by passing along to influential Mexicans the administration's desire for a "just and honorable" peace based on certain territorial considerations. He went on to invite the presence of "American commissioners at the head-quarters of this army," which he thought would be necessary at least by the time he reached Puebla.[29] But he envisioned peace commissioners who would follow his lead and act when he told them to act. Marcy's letter now made it sound as if Scott was being subordinated to a civilian, with his role only ancillary to that of Trist. This Scott could not tolerate. After clearly defining his turf and his unwillingness to yield, he sent his intemperate letter to Trist.

But Trist could be just as arrogant and defensive as Scott, and their opening exchange did little to dispel the negative impression of Scott that the diplomat had carried with him to Mexico. The two men were acquaintances from a couple of previous meetings, but they did not really know each other. Trist, having left Veracruz with a heavily guarded wagon train, received Scott's letter while on the road. In a lecturing manner, the diplomat demonstrated his own resolve in an eighteen-page rejoinder. After chiding Scott for not providing him with a timely escort to conduct him to Jalapa, he tried, in a condescending tone, to explain that Buchanan's letter was sealed to give it the weight of an official document and not to hide its contents. He further informed the general that he was in Mexico at the behest of the president, the constitutional commander-in-chief of the armed forces. He pointed out that the administration's course of action was "what any man of plain, unsophisticated common-sense would take for granted" to be the proper conduct, but Scott, with his "over-cultivated imagination," seemed to think that it was his prerogative to determine whether the federal government would be permitted to engage in its diplomatic functions. Then, in a transparent gesture of pretended modesty, Trist described his role as that of a mere military aide, and he closed by suggesting that perhaps Scott would have been a better choice to conduct the negotiations. Be that as it may, the president had appointed him. Trist need not have spent so much time on his lengthy missive, for Scott did not bother to open it for almost two weeks.[30]

When Trist arrived at Jalapa on May 14, Scott took no notice or interest in him other than arranging for him to share lodging with the amiable Brigadier General Persifor Smith. Nor did Trist pay a courtesy call on Scott. The two men simply forwarded copies of their acrid correspondence to their respective superiors in Washington and fumed at each other in silence for the next week. In his anger, however, Scott rescinded his previous approval to assist Lieutenant Raphael Semmes of the navy in making contact with the Mexican government. Semmes had been sent from Veracruz by Commodore Perry on a mission to seek the release of a midshipman whom the Mexicans had captured, and Scott had indicated a willingness to help Semmes open a channel of communication. Now the general was beginning to feel the sting of insult by serving as a mere intermediary for both Trist and Semmes—men of inferior status and rank. In addition, his badly needed resources and mounted troops were being siphoned off to escort these individuals from the coast to Jalapa. Consequently, he informed Semmes that he would not facilitate his efforts, a reversal that turned Semmes into a lifelong Scott critic.[31]

The anger that Scott directed at Trist may have been a way of venting for a variety of frustrations, for when the diplomat arrived, the general was heavily engaged in logistical matters related to the next leg of the army's march. The return home of several regiments had dangerously diminished his strength, and he was anxious that the promised reinforcements arrive. He needed them not only to increase the size of his modest force, but also to keep the road open from Veracruz as he moved inland. His desire was that as new regiments arrived, large detachments would move from the coast inland in successive marches frequently enough to keep the road clear of guerrillas, and their arrival would augment his numbers sufficiently to allow him to leave strong garrisons at Jalapa and Perote as the army pushed deeper into the interior. By early May, however, he had learned that the War Department had directed 3,000 of the new troops to Taylor's army rather than to his—a revelation that was as surprising as it was disappointing. An additional disappointment came when Major General John A. Quitman's brigade arrived in Jalapa without bringing extra rations. Scott's explicit order before leaving Veracruz was that no body of soldiers was to move inland without bringing additional food so that the army's supplies would be increased rather than diminished as its numbers grew.[32]

Before leaving Jalapa, Scott issued another proclamation designed to drive a wedge between the Mexican people and their government. His first public statement, issued after the fall of Veracruz, had a more conciliatory, olive branch and sword tenor, but this one was a harsh indictment of Mexican political and military leadership, indicating an awareness of class and social schisms in the country. In it Scott declared that the Mexican government had "criminally concealed" the truth about the cause and course of the war. He leveled harsh criticism at Santa Anna, who had deceived both the Mexican people and the United States government, and also at incompetent Mexican generals who had been "paid without service rendered." He went on to assert that the stories circulating about American atrocities against citizens were false. "We have not profaned your temples, nor abused your women, nor seized your property. . . . The army of the United States respects, and will ever respect, private property of every class, and the property of the Mexican church." He concluded by warning the people not to resort to guerrilla war, for such would not harm the American army but would "produce only evils to this country."[33]

The last part of his proclamation addressed what was potentially the greatest source of danger to his army: widespread guerrilla activity. Such an uprising had the potential of not only cutting off his supplies from the coast, but completely debilitating his little army. Of this, Scott was well aware. With inducements and encouragement from the Mexican government, guerrilla

American troops fend off an attack on a supply train. Courtesy of Special Collections Division, University of Texas at Arlington Libraries.

bands of various sizes commenced raids on Scott's supply line soon after Cerro Gordo. It was not a surprising development considering that Mexico's conventional army had been shattered and, at least for the time being, rendered useless. Two weeks after arriving in Jalapa, Scott had sent infantry to the National Bridge halfway back to Veracruz to protect westward-bound supplies that were rumored to be vulnerable to attack in that area. A few days later, he ordered part of the First Dragoons, his own escort, back to protect a supply train coming up from the coast. Guerrillas attacked another train, killing three teamsters, before it arrived in Jalapa on May 20.[34]

Stragglers were particularly vulnerable to roaming guerrilla bands. Reports came in almost daily of the discovery of the corpses of soldiers who had strayed too far from the army either in camp or on the road. A private who lagged behind his unit on its march from Cerro Gordo to Jalapa was attacked and almost beaten to death before dragoons happened along and saved him. A wagon in one of the supply trains broke down just after leaving Veracruz and the driver, thinking his proximity to the army made him immune to attack, stayed with his wagon on the side of the road as the rest of the train continued inland. Next day, American soldiers found his body with three bullet holes in it. Even in Jalapa, where the Mexicans had offered no organized resistance, random acts of violence served as reminders to Americans that they were not universally welcome. During the army's six-week presence there, frequent confrontations occurred between U.S. soldiers and Mexicans. On at least one occasion, a guard on picket duty was found stabbed to death. Such attacks often resulted from angry Mexicans who, although hostile to the foreign invaders, were nevertheless unconnected to guerrilla partisans.[35]

But a guerrilla war is exactly what many American soldiers expected after Cerro Gordo. "The Mexicans have resolved on a guerrilla mode of warfare," wrote Ralph Kirkham. It is "a cowardly mode of warfare . . . not countenanced by any civilized nation," wrote Moses Barnard, and resort to such strategy will never work, thought Isaac Stevens. In a letter to his sister, Lieutenant Roswell Ripley warned what he anticipated would happen if Mexicans embarked on guerrilla warfare. "We have not yet commenced anything like the operations which a guerrilla war would compel us to carry on & which would of course have all this country a desert never to be repeopled until by the Anglo Saxon Races." But Ripley was wrong. His proposed solution was exactly how the French had responded to the Spanish uprising in 1808, with such disastrous results. Scott's approach, conversely, was designed to avoid such a degeneration, and Lieutenant Isaac Stevens displayed an instinctive grasp of the commanding general's objectives. A guerrilla strategy will not work because "General Scott will enforce the strictest discipline, and the people of the country will remain undisturbed in their houses," Stevens wrote to his wife. "A fair price will be paid for everything that is consumed. The war will be made to bear with a heavy hand upon all connected with the government."[36]

CHAPTER SEVEN

Puebla

Waiting All Summer

Waiting for reenforcements, the halt, at Puebla, was protracted and irksome. . . . We were also kept on the alert by an army sometimes of superior numbers, hovering about us, and often assuming a menacing attitude. . . . On these occasions it was painful to restrain the ardor of the troops. But I steadily held to the policy not to wear out patience and sole leather by running to the right or left in the pursuit of small game. I played for the big stakes. Keeping the army massed and the mind fixed upon the capital.

—Winfield Scott, Commanding General

Marching deep into the enemy's country is sometimes treacherous and always audacious. Keeping the American army dispersed while on the move was a logistical necessity because feeding the men and animals was no simple affair. When Worth's lead division had pushed forward thirty-five miles to Perote the previous month, Scott had instructed him "to gather from the country" most of his supplies and all of his forage. And, of course, all forms of subsistence gathered in the country had to be purchased from citizens in accord with Scott's pacification policy, or else "they will be withheld, concealed, or destroyed by the owners." Not only must provisions be purchased, but they also had to be distributed and consumed with economy. Now as Worth prepared for the next leg of the journey, an eighty-mile march to Puebla, Scott reminded him of his "lively desire of conciliating the unoffending inhabitants of the country, by protecting their persons and property."[1]

The administration in Washington did not adequately appreciate—nor have subsequent historical accounts—the intricate orchestration involved in the army's westward push to Mexico City. Before Scott could roll up the army's tail, he had to push the head forward so that the larger area occupied would be able to sustain his men. Thus, as the Jalapa troops began marching out in stages beginning with Quitman's command on May 7, Worth's lead division prepared to vacate Perote and proceed to Puebla. For a time, his army would be spread over some sixty miles from Jalapa to Puebla—a significant risk in a foreign country. None "but our gallant officers and troops would have dared such a movement," thought Joseph Smith.[2] However, Scott knew his enemy, knew that Santa Anna's army was unable to offer stiff resistance so soon after Cerro Gordo, and on a more practical level, knew that such was necessary in order to live off the land. Scott had an adequate understanding of the limitations of his opponent, but he also possessed the audacity that was born out of self-confidence—a trait that Captain Robert E. Lee may well have picked up from his commanding general in Mexico. In addition, Scott knew from Jane Storm's messages and other intelligence sources that he was not likely to face opposition in the cities. Moses Beach had succeeded in gaining cooperation from the priests in Mexico City, along with assurances that they would cultivate an attitude of nonresistance among the clergy in Puebla, Jalapa, and other towns.

Two weeks after Quitman marched out of Jalapa, Scott departed with the remainder of the army, the bulk of which was composed of Twiggs's division of 2,600 men. A small garrison under Colonel Thomas Childs and consisting of Second Pennsylvania volunteers and some detachments of regulars remained in Jalapa, much to their displeasure. A few days after Scott's departure, Lieutenant Thomas Jackson, on May 25, wrote to his sister of his "mortification of being left to garrison the town of Jalapa," but he surmised that it was God's way of "diminishing my excessive ambition."[3] Their stay there was of short duration, but for the time being, their presence was necessary to help keep the army's lifeline to Veracruz open.

The road to Perote passed through some of the "most picturesque and romantic country" the men had seen as they gradually ascended higher into the Sierra Madres. Majestic peaks, cold mountain streams, and lush vegetation lined the route. Along the thirty-five-mile trek, the army marched through the Black Pass near the village of La Hoya, where, for over a mile, the road was tightly pressed between two mountains. The Americans knew this area as a location where guerrillas and bandits liked to attack, but Twiggs's men only found several cannon spiked and abandoned at the site, and they passed on through the town. A few miles farther, they reached the village of Las Vigas, another place worthy of suspicion. Because of the steady climb into the mountains, many of Twiggs's men fell behind, and the road became littered with discarded equipment. Although a few American soldiers were ambushed and killed along the way, the Mexicans offered no major resistance to Twiggs's advance.[4]

Once through the mountain passes the ground became level at an altitude of almost 8,000 feet, and for the last few miles before reaching Perote, the men passed through handsomely cultivated fields of barley, corn, and wheat.

The town itself was unimpressive, even a "dismal place," wrote one soldier, "cold [and] disagreeable," wrote another. The water seemed to be "impregnated with some mineral that renders it unpalatable." "The town is small and like all Mexico going to rack," thought one man. Americans, having grown accustomed to purchasing fruits and vegetables in the streets of other towns, described the markets of Perote as "very poor," and this despite the abundant produce grown all around—perhaps an indication that here the Mexicans did not welcome the occupying troops. Gambling seemed to be a favorite occupation of the locals.[5]

The most impressive feature about Perote was its famous castle. Built by the Spaniards in the 1770s as a fortress to defend a major trade route, it had served primarily as a prison. In fact, Santa Anna had had Juan Morales and José Landero locked away in the castle for surrendering Veracruz, but they were released just before the Americans arrived. Made of dark lava rocks with sixty-foot-tall walls and a twenty-foot-deep moat around it, the castle looked ominous and sinister. The bastions of the fort could accommodate a hundred cannon. When American troops of General William Worth's division had arrived there earlier, they found it, like all other Mexican fortifications after the Cerro Gordo debacle, deserted, with significant ordnance left behind. A lone Mexican colonel remained to surrender the town to the Americans. The abandoned matériel included more than sixty guns, including mortars and howitzers, 25,000 rounds of artillery ammunition, and hundreds of muskets. Had the enemy decided to stay and fight, thought Lieutenant John Wilkins of the Third Infantry, it would have taken a month to capture the fortress. The Americans converted it into a hospital.[6]

The first brigade of Worth's division had first marched into Perote on April 22, and under orders from Scott, he began to evacuate the town and advance on Puebla on May 10. Quitman's brigade followed a few days behind Worth, with Twiggs bringing up the rear. Although Scott had left Jalapa at the same time as Twiggs's division, he and his escort rode ahead of the main body, arrived in Perote early, and left for Puebla on May 25, the day that Old Davy's men arrived. When Scott departed Perote, Worth had been in Puebla for ten days. Just before Worth started for Puebla earlier in the month, he had used some of his infantry and dragoons to round up and punish local officials west of Perote who were trying to prevent citizens from selling provisions to the army. Artillery officer Robert Anderson approved the action. "Our paying the Mexicans liberally for what they bring will induce them to come, our punishing those who prevent them, will show them that we know and feel our strength, and that it will be exerted when necessity demands it."[7] That Anderson could make such a comment about knowing and feeling the strength of a small army in the middle of a hostile country is due entirely to the success of Scott's plan to neutralize the population so that the outcome of the war would be decided by purely conventional means.

The eighty-mile march to Puebla took Worth's men six days. They passed through several towns and villages along the way, none very impressive. Private William Johnson thought that in many locations, the large, ornate cathedrals cost more than the rest of the villages' combined value. He also concluded that the inhabitants along the road to Puebla were generally "a miserable looking set." Worth pushed his men hard. One soldier, remembering General Scott's much publicized embarrassment of the previous year, wrote in his journal that one morning the men awoke and ate a "hasty plate of soup" before setting out. After a few grueling days of long marches, most of them were worn out, and many were sick with diarrhea and other afflictions. The main body had even left a few stragglers on the side of the road to die.[8]

Meanwhile, Santa Anna waited in Puebla determined to make another stand. After Cerro Gordo, he had fled south to Orizaba, where he began to patch together another army, and at about the time Worth was leaving Perote, Santa Anna arrived in Puebla with about 4,000 cavalry and infantry. He seized horses in the area, exacted money from the citizens, and chastised the city authorities for not providing more stalwart support to help prosecute the war. Many of the residents were circulating Scott's May 11 proclamation, which had either created or reinforced a discernible apathy among the residents. Some Pueblans, to escape Santa Anna's heavy-handed authority, fled the city. The Mexican general knew that Worth's lead brigade was but the head of a thinly spread American army that stretched back to Jalapa and beyond, and he had received reports that Quitman's brigade, along with a heavy supply train, was twenty-five miles behind Worth, or a march of about a day and a half. When both brigades arrived in Puebla, Worth's unified division would consist of 4,200 men, so Santa Anna decided to swing around the vanguard with his cavalry and strike at Quitman's isolated and more lucrative column.[9]

Worth did not advance blindly. By various accounts, he was nervous and edgy during the time that his detached division was at the army's forefront, but to his credit, he took wise precaution as he approached Puebla from the east. He knew that Santa Anna was there, and he suspected that his or Quitman's column might be subject to an attack. So he slowed his pace to allow the second brigade and wagon train to close the gap, and on May 13, he stopped at Amozoc, about ten miles from Puebla, to bring his division together. That night, a couple of hours after midnight, the long roll beat, signaling the soldiers to stand under arms, and the men assumed that a battle was imminent. They watched and waited until daylight, but nothing happened.

However, later that morning, the warning sounded again, and this time Mexican lancers approached from the north. Worth sent portions of the Second Artillery and Sixth Infantry to confront them, but they avoided contact and moved off to the American right. They were trying to get around Worth's men and get into position to advance on Quitman, but the Mexicans did not know that the gap between the two factions was, by this time, only about two or three miles. For their part, the Americans did not know that the enemy had another target in mind farther east, so as the lancers kept their distance and continued moving away from Amozoc, the Americans continued to follow in an effort to bring on a battle. Eventually, men of the Second Artillery got close enough to unlimber a battery and open fire, which caused the enemy to scatter. By this time, the Mexicans knew that the two portions of the U.S. Army were not as far apart as they previously thought and that surprise was out of the question. So they returned to Puebla and joined Santa Anna in a retreat to Mexico City. Thus ended the skirmish of Amozoc.[10]

Worth met with some of Puebla's officials to make arrangements for the American occupation, and at 10 A.M. on May 15, his column entered the city. Men of the Fifth Infantry occupied two abandoned forts, Loreto and Guadalupe, that were situated on hills just north and east of town. Curiosity induced many of the town's 80,000 residents to line the streets and pack balconies, windows, and rooftops to get a look at the North Americans as they marched in—these fearful, powerful warriors who had seized Veracruz and shattered the Mexican army at Cerro Gordo. The appearance of the weary, hungry, very average-looking men in their tattered and dusty uniforms must have fallen well short of their expectations. Some of the inhabitants looked on with angry faces as the troops filed through the streets and eventually packed into the plaza in the center of town. Once there, some of the soldiers simply laid down and went to sleep, while others stacked arms and began to roam about or purchase food in the street markets.[11]

Most of the inhabitants seemed resigned to the occupation. Few, if any, exhibited fear, and, although it would have been easy for such a large population to rise up and destroy the small occupying force, this did not occur. Hiram Yeager wondered how their small army could garrison such a densely populated city in the heart of enemy territory without fear of molestation. He speculated in a letter home that "if the Mexicans had the least drop of Native pride," thousands of them would unite and crush the vulnerable Americans. Then he answered his own question by asserting that they do not oppose us because they "have found out that we are not the Sort of People that was represented to them." They know that we are "not waring against their Religion nor do we want to interfere with their daily pursuits that all we wish is peace."

If this be an accurate assessment, then Scott's pacification plan worked beautifully.[12]

Over the next few days, the troops settled into their new surroundings, and their letters and diaries indicate that most of them liked what they saw. To the Americans, Puebla looked more modern than Perote, Jalapa, and Veracruz. Its buildings were sturdy, the streets were paved and clean, and the houses appeared to be well kept, and some soldiers noted the unusual fact that they detected no foul odors as they explored the city. It was nicknamed the City of Angels because, according to lore, an angel had indicated to the founders where to build. There were gardens throughout the city, and colorful flowers adorned most of the houses. After some time in Puebla, Ralph Kirkham discovered that many of the residents were fond of birds and kept them in cages in their houses. He also concluded that "there is not a house or a room occupied by Mexicans in the city of Puebla which has not from one to twenty paintings and engravings," all "on religious subjects." James Fitzgerald wrote that "upon the whole I am delighted with Puebla, and it is the only place in Mexico that I would live in if I could."[13]

Puebla is located on an extensive plain, and in the cultivated fields surrounding the city, fruit of every variety grew: oranges, pineapples, bananas, peaches, apples, figs, and more. As in other towns, the residents quickly learned that they could make money off the Americans, and so in the abundant markets, they sold eggs for twenty-five cents a dozen, tomatoes for $6 a bushel, and chickens for thirty-seven cents each. By the pound, they sold butter, coffee, rice, and salted beef for a dollar, twenty cents, eight cents, and thirteen cents, respectively. Some of the men took advantage of the favorable cantinas and eating establishments in the city, and on Sundays, many were drawn to the plaza, where they could buy everything from fruit and mint juleps to "the finest Ice Cream in the world."[14]

While the soldiers praised the scenery and surroundings, they made few favorable comments about the people. There was a considerable number of "idelers and . . . rabble" who roamed the streets or loitered around the plazas and cathedrals. They were "filthy in the extreme," and their dark complexion made it easy for everyone of European descent to consider them an "inferior race." The troops were quick to conclude that the lower class dominated the population, and among that element, the women did most of the work. The Pueblans are "poor, miserable beings who are as ignorant and superstitious as it is possible to be," wrote Lieutenant Ralph Kirkham. Another soldier, William Johnson, quickly surmised that they were "a miserable cut throat looking set—generaly." After a few weeks in Puebla, Kirby Smith described the whole country in a letter home by writing that "everything is stamped by ignorance, vice, and misery." A week later, he wrote with humor that "lying is so universal here that I am almost afraid I shall fall into the habit myself." Robert E. Lee offered this opinion long before arriving in Puebla: "The Mexicans are an amiable but weak people. Primitive in their habits and tastes."[15]

Several days into the occupation, curiosity turned to caution. There were nightly murders of Mexicans and Americans alike and constant rumors of planned attacks on the troops by the citizens. Worth wisely issued orders for his men to always be armed when they left their quarters, and he directed patrols to police the streets at night. He placed sentinels on top of buildings throughout the city and kept a third of his force on post at all times. However, just as he had during the march to the city, he seemed anxious and jittery—insecure is probably a better description—calling the men to arms on the slightest rumor. "Worth had the troops under arms the greater portion of the time constantly expecting an attack," complained Lieutenant Theodore Laidley. "He is famous for getting up *stampedes* and [he exhibits] a want of confidence that a General should not." His "constant fear . . . harasses . . . his troops." The frequency of his false alarms led some of his men to refer to "Worth's scarecrows." Lieutenant Ulysses S. Grant believed it a part of the general's personality to be "nervous, impatient and restless on the march, or when important or responsible duty confronted him."[16] Perhaps it was from that example, or from a comparison of the way Worth and Scott behaved under stress, that Grant learned to be calm and resolute in the face of danger.

On Friday, May 28, Scott galloped into Puebla escorted by two troops of Colonel William S. Harney's cavalry. The Mounted Rifles rode into town first, followed by Captain Philip Kearny's First Dragoons, all mounted on gray steeds. It was a splendid entry. As was customary, pomp and ceremony accompanied everything Scott did, but he could get away with it because he had both style and substance. The commanding general's presence reduced the tension in the army, because, as historian Justin H. Smith put it, "a wiser mind and steadier hand now took charge." Gone were the false alarms and phantom enemies that had plagued the men, for Scott's experience told him not to believe every report about enemy movements. His presence in the city had a calming effect on the entire army.

The circumstances surrounding the commanding general's arrival in the city is a case in point. Worth had received "positive information" that an enemy army of 20,000 was approaching to attack Puebla before nightfall. Furthermore, reports indicated that a general uprising in the city would accompany the attack. So Worth sent riders dashing off to the east to report to Scott who was known to be on his way. The couriers reached Scott three miles away and reported the alarming news. The general listened, then told the messenger to take the report to Colonel Harney, after which he calmly resumed his discussion with members of his staff. According to one of the troopers with Scott's column, they continued to the city cautiously, only to find "the army and insurrection altogether creations of Worth's imagination." The story of Scott's calm reaction made the rounds in the army, and although it was an insignificant anecdote, it precisely demonstrated the contrast with Worth's behavior. It was while in Puebla that an army doctor supposedly overheard General Twiggs say that Scott was the greatest living general and that Taylor's name "ought not to be mentioned in the same day with him." Scott's steady leadership, thorough planning, and masterful strategy had long since won over the skeptics who had transferred from Taylor's army. Two weeks after his arrival in Puebla, artillery officer Robert Anderson concluded that with every battle and important movement, Scott "gains warm friends."[17]

On his first full day in Puebla, Scott revisited the Nicholas Trist problem. As Scott was leaving Jalapa, he had received another letter from Trist dated May 20, which requested that Scott return the sealed letter from Secretary Buchanan. The diplomat also indulged in renewed criticism of Scott for not forwarding the dispatch to Mexican officials as requested. Just as he had done with Trist's earlier missive of May 9, Scott set it aside without opening it. On May 22, Scott had an aide open both letters and read to him what totaled thirty pages of sarcastic insults and chastisements. As Scott was at that time on the road to Perote then Puebla, he waited several days to respond. Once established in his headquarters in the city, the general took pen in hand and wrote a venomous rejoinder. Even though a week had passed, Scott's anger had cooled very little. He referred to Trist's letters as a "farrago of insolence, conceit, and arrogance," indicating that his first inclination had been to return them, but instead he decided to "preserve the letters as a choice specimen of diplomatic literature and manners." He said that he was actually thankful that he had not been "degraded" by being appointed to serve with Trist on a peace commission, and he asked the diplomat to be brief in future correspondence, for Scott was very busy with army matters. In addition, he warned that if Trist ever sent him such condescending or "discourteous" letters again, "I shall throw back the communication with the contempt & scorn which you merit at my hands."[18]

Trist had accompanied the army to Puebla, had in fact been with the army for six weeks but still had not met with the commanding general. Nor had he had any contact with the Mexican government or succeeded in delivering Buchanan's secret dispatch. So on June 6, Trist wrote to his old acquaintance Charles Bankhead, the British minister to Mexico, requesting that the Englishman open a channel of communication with the government in Mexico

City by forwarding Buchanan's dispatch. Bankhead agreed and sent the secretary of the British Legation, Edward Thornton, to Puebla to retrieve the documents. Thornton arrived on June 10, and he and Trist discussed the best possible means of bringing about peace negotiations. When Trist mentioned that he had the authority to draw $3 million from the Treasury Department to facilitate negotiations, Thornton apparently suggested that spreading the money around to the right people would help move the process along. Thornton returned to the capital, the British passed along Buchanan's sealed documents to the new Mexican foreign minister, Domingo Ibarra, and there the situation stood for two weeks.[19]

In Washington, Secretary Marcy and Polk had read copies of Scott's and Trist's earlier exchanges, and the Secretary of War scrambled to do damage control. He penned a thirteen-page letter to the general assuring him that Trist did not have the authority to supersede his direction of the military aspects of the war and that hostilities could only be ceased at Scott's discretion. The "strange mistake into which . . . [Scott had] fallen," Marcy wrote, resulted from poor sentence structure and word usage in the secretary's April 14 letter. Regarding Scott's complaint about being excluded from the contents of Buchanan's secret communication with the Mexican government, Marcy explained that Trist had a copy of the document, which Scott could have read if he and Trist had met. It was all a misunderstanding, according to Marcy, and he thought that Scott would regret his harsh letter to Trist when he became better informed.[20]

Scott was unaware of Trist's under-the-table machinations with the British, but for the present, it did not matter because the general was up to his neck in military matters and a variety of personality issues that created friction within the army. The first problem arose during Scott's first few days in Puebla, and this one involved General Quitman, who had recently learned of his promotion to major general. Soon after Scott's arrival, Quitman wrote him two letters in which he expressed his desire to command a full division of regulars rather than his current below-strength division of volunteers. He knew that commanding regulars carried more prestige, and he wanted the full allotment of regiments as stipulated by regulations, thereby solidifying his position in the army hierarchy as the second ranking general of the army. In a letter to his wife, Quitman even pondered his ascent to army commander if anything happened to Scott. This was just the kind of personal glory seeking that Scott did not have time to deal with. On May 31, the commanding general sent Quitman a mild rebuke, explaining that he was too busy with "the high duties of the campaign" for such issues. All of the army's divisions had been depleted by leaving detachments in Veracruz, Jalapa, and Perote, Scott explained, and he could not justify breaking up another division just to bring Quitman's to full strength. Then Scott made a suggestion calculated to derail his subordinate's ambition. He offered to transfer Quitman to the Rio Grande, where there were an adequate number of regiments to give him command of a full division. Quitman was not likely to accept a transfer out of the theater of operations. Scott then concluded his letter by soothing Quitman's ego. You are "a good soldier . . . & a good man" he wrote, and he asked him to "bend to circumstances." "Your post is still one of honour, & you can fill it with distinction. Remain then & give me your cordial aid & support." Quitman ceased his remonstrations for the time being.[21]

Another personnel issue came in the form of a crack that developed in his relationship with Worth that, over the next four months, widened into an impassable chasm separating the two old friends. The problems originated from the lenient terms that Worth granted to local officials when he occupied Puebla. He agreed to allow Mexican citizens accused of crimes against Americans to be tried in Mexican courts. This contradicted the terms of Scott's martial law order, which not only held American soldiers accountable for crimes against Mexicans, but also made Mexicans accountable in a military court for offenses against U.S. soldiers. And since the army's arrival, a local court had acquitted a Pueblan who had been accused of murdering an American. A member of Scott's staff, Lieutenant Colonel Ethan A. Hitchcock, thought Worth's concession ridiculous, and Scott let his subordinate know of his anger. He wrote to Worth asking if it was true and if so, he demanded to know how Worth could make such an imprimatur. Scott wanted to see a copy of the terms. He even considered marching the army out of Puebla, then returning without granting any terms, but he knew such action would be a farce, so he bound himself to abide by the original agreement.[22]

Soon after this initial disagreement, Worth made another misstep. When he heard rumors of a plan to put poison in the Americans' food supply, he wrote a warning and circulated it among his division. Scott learned about it and was furious on two counts. First, Worth had not bothered to inform the commanding general or to warn anyone other than his own troops. Second, in his circular, he used language calculated to insult the Mexican people when he referred to them as "cowards" who would "poison those from whom they habitually fly in battle." Then he likened such a contemptible act as something "familiar in Spanish history." Such an affront ran contrary to Scott's pacification efforts, and he wrote Worth a stern rebuke, followed by an order that he withdraw the poison circular. Scott's harsh criticism injured Worth's pride, so the division commander requested a court of inquiry to determine if his actions had been appropriate and to consider whether he had been wronged by the commanding general. The court, made up of Generals Quitman, Twiggs, and Persifor Smith, met on June 25, and it ruled that

Worth had acted inappropriately in both the occupation agreement and the poison circular and that he deserved the reprimand.[23]

This was but the beginning of the fissures in a fault line that would eventually erupt into an earthquake. Worth's biographer, Edward S. Wallace, blamed Scott and "his porcupine act" for the break. Naval officer Raphael Semmes also thought that Scott was at fault because he failed to show Worth the respect he deserved. Scott's aide, Colonel Hitchcock, placed significance in a minor episode that occurred just days before the poison food rumor surfaced. Worth had invited Scott and other officers to dine at his headquarters, a common practice among the army's brass. During the meal, Scott began to tell a story, which turned into a rather lengthy tale—also a common practice with the commanding general. All who knew Scott knew that he was usually the topic of his stories and that he expected the full attention of everyone present. During his monologue, Worth began to whisper with one of the other guests, thus displeasing the commanding general immensely. Scott stopped talking, and when encouraged to proceed, he snorted, "I'll not say another word—my host is engaged in a private tete a tete & I'll not interupt him." Tension filled the air for the remainder of the evening. This may not have been the only time that Scott received such a snub from his subordinate. According to Hitchcock, Worth evidently had a habit of acting disinterested during Scott's frequent dinner narratives.[24]

It was a trivial incident, but it underscores Scott's legendary arrogance, his rigidity regarding military etiquette, and his constant effort to subordinate everyone around him to the role of disciple. He had indeed earned his nickname "Old Fuss and Feathers." However, from Scott's perspective, the break with Worth came after several instances of insubordination. Worth had opposed the slow siege craft that Scott used to reduce Veracruz; he had protested when Twiggs and his division got to lead the way inland in early April; he had described Scott's report of the Battle of Cerro Gordo in the most insulting terms, calling it "a lie from beginning to end"; and most recently, he had revised Scott's plan for the civil government of an occupied city. So, as Scott saw it, his friend of over thirty years, his former aid from the War of 1812, was actually the one who had habitually failed to show proper respect to his superior officer. According to Hitchcock, Scott had expressed the opinion that Worth was spoiled and jealous of power, and that even though Scott regretted the deterioration in their relationship, the commanding general had simply run out of patience. Hitchcock went even further, speculating that Worth fancied himself a presidential candidate in 1848. Evidently, Worth, who had been a Whig since that party's inception in the mid-1830s, had been trying to put the word out that he was a Democrat because he knew how desperate that party was for a military hero to nominate for president. A week after Worth's court adjourned, he sent Scott a "half apologetic" letter that seemingly helped the antagonists to put their differences behind them. However, their problems would resurface later.[25]

In addition to dealing with Worth in those early days in Puebla, Scott had to make the usual assessments required of a commanding general: learn the disposition of all of his troops, see to the army's logistical needs, determine the most likely approaches by a hostile force, prepare for the defense of the city should an attack occur, conduct reconnaissance, and prepare for the army's next move. The army, however, would stay put until its numbers were augmented by new volunteer units currently being raised in the States. The War Department continued to assure him that he would receive ample reinforcements before his final push to Mexico City. Indeed, on April 30 and May 20, Secretary of War Marcy wrote letters to Scott in which he reiterated his earlier commitment to increase the army to 20,000 by the end of June. Marcy also explained the diversion of the 3,000 new troops to Taylor's army earlier in the year. It had resulted from rumors of a Mexican attack on Taylor's forces at Saltillo and the fear in Washington that he might be forced to retreat to Monterey or, worse, be cut off from the Rio Grande. Of course, none of that came to pass, and the panic in Washington along with the resulting reassignment of troops came before the administration heard of Taylor's victory at Buena Vista. Apparently, Scott had nervous and fidgety superiors in Washington as well as subordinates in his own army, and despite the administration's assurances, he never had an army that came near to 20,000 men until the fighting was over. Out of frustration, Scott wrote to Marcy in early June regarding the "cruel disappointments and mortifications" that he had felt as a result of the "want of support and sympathy on the part of the War Department."[26]

Among the more significant aspects of army business in which Scott involved himself was the employment of Manuel Dominguez and a group of Mexican bandits. Supposedly Dominguez, an honest businessman, took up a life of crime after he was "robbed and ruined" by an officer in the Mexican army, and he subsequently went on to become the well-known leader of a band of highwaymen. When some Pueblans identified Dominguez as a common criminal, U.S. officials arrested him, then recruited him to go on the American payroll. He became the leader of a group of outlaws, twelve of whom he got released from jail in order to join him. At first Dominguez had a few dozen men, but eventually his numbers grew to over a hundred, and by one account, his band ultimately reached about two hundred. Many of them were simply bandits who had worked the roads between Mexico City and Veracruz for years. One of the group was a native Virginian named Spooner who reportedly had been a highwayman in Mexico before the war started.

Dominguez's group, which was most commonly referred to as the Mexican spy company, worked with the American army as scouts, couriers, spies, and guides. They also conducted a security function by keeping an eye on the towns surrounding Puebla in search of suspicious activity and enemy troop movements. In addition to conducting routine checks on the roads running west toward Mexico City, they also made sweeps to the east to keep the roads clear of guerrillas. Dominguez and his cohorts provided valuable intelligence during the remainder of the campaign, and they ensured that Scott's dispatches arrived at their destinations. According to Lieutenant Henry Moses Judah of the Fourth Infantry, Dominguez could control 10,000 bandits between Mexico City and the coast. They looked rough, like the robbers and thieves that they were, but they wore green coatees with red collars and cuffs, and red bands around their wide-brimmed black felt hats to identify them as friendly. Whenever they needed something—a horse or piece of equipment—they simply went to the nearest Mexican resident and politely took what they wanted "apologizing in a regular robber style." Some Americans thought they were an untrustworthy set of rogues. Ralph Kirkham referred to them as "Mexican Rascals" and D. H. Hill described them as "a wild, savage looking set of fellows," but Edmund Bradford believed that they were "perfectly faithful" to the Americans. At $20 a month, they made almost three times the pay of an American private.[27]

The army remained in Puebla for about ten weeks while they awaited reinforcements, and the men found many ways to occupy their time. An American acting troupe performed nightly at a theater, gambling establishments featuring a variety of games flourished, and restaurants and bars, many of them run by Americans, sprang up around the soldiers' quarters. Many of the men saw their first bullfight while in Puebla. Ralph Kirkham described the 5,000-seat arena he visited and the way the crowd's excitement fluctuated depending on the pain inflicted on the bull and the level of danger for the bullfighter. He concluded that a bullfight "is certainly the most cruel amusement that I ever witnessed." Other soldiers visited the nearby ruins of Cholula, the ancient Aztec city with its huge temple mound.[28]

Of course, liquor was abundant and easy to find, and the most common drink that many of the Americans commented on in letters and journals was pulque. It was the drink of choice for lower-class Mexicans because it was cheap and readily available. Pulque, made from the maguey plant, which grows all over Mexico, was especially abundant around Puebla. The plant is a stout evergreen that reaches a height of about six feet, and its center stem is large and funnel shaped. Its long leaves drape over on all sides, and their ends have a sharp point that can penetrate flesh. By one soldier's description, it resembled the "head of a Pine Apple," only much larger. Many of the residents used the plant as a fence row. When a maguey plant is about seven or eight years old, the stem is tapped to draw off the juice for fermentation, and one plant can produce several gallons a week. Once tapped, the plant will live several more years yielding its liquid, but if left untapped, the century plant, as some called it, will live up to a hundred years. The finished product of the fermentation process is the bitter drink pulque, which has an unpleasant smell, a "fiery, smoky taste," and a flavor, as some remarked at the time, "more like green tobacco than anything else." It is a white color and "about the strength of New England cider." The Mexicans drank it in large quantities. They sold it on the streets from hogskin containers, and a quart was sufficient to "intoxicate twenty men," according to George Furber, a Tennessee volunteer.[29]

The extended leisure in Puebla was punctuated by regular drill, but over the weeks, the men had ample time to send letters and receive information about loved ones. Joseph Smith worried about his brother Henry, who had become sick with yellow fever while the army was still in Veracruz. Henry was a member of Scott's staff, but his illness caused him to be left behind when the army marched inland. While at Puebla, Joseph received the depressing news that his brother had died, causing him to write a prayer in his diary asking God for "support and comfort." At the opposite emotional extreme, William Walker wrote his wife a love letter from Puebla. "Molly," he wrote, "I love you more (if possible) this moment than I did when at the alter in the sight of God and man." Later he mentioned his throbbing heart and referred to Molly as the "gentlest, kindest of her sex." Then he speculated on the chances of his letter falling into the hands of bandits who roamed the roads from Puebla to Veracruz. What if this letter ends up in Mexico City and is published in the papers? If that were to happen, he assured Molly, "I will pin the Editor of the paper by the ears to his front door." Then he drifted away from his wife and began to write directly to his imagined bandits. "Highwayman I give you notice that if you do get this letter and make it public that *the day of retribution* will come." Next he issued a warning to an editor who might consider publishing the letter: "look out . . . for I shall be in the city of Mexico soon."[30]

The preeminence of the Church in Puebla, more omnipresent than in other cities, tended to reinforce negative opinions already garnered before the army got there. Especially impressive to the Americans was the ornate seventeenth-century cathedral, Cathedral de las Angelos, with its marble floor, silver candelabras, and gold gilding. Will Lytle went inside and was "overwhelmed by the gorgeous magnificence of everything around me." Its splendor seemed to confirm the impression that the church fleeced the impoverished masses. Thomas Barclay, a Pennsylvania volunteer, thought that

"The holy fathers . . . are content with vast possessions . . . treasures amassed by a system of robberies for centuries and with palaces both as residences and places of worship. . . . Clothed in silk they fare sumptuously every day . . . and woe to the Mexican who incurs their displeasure." He went on to assert that those "who rule Mexico endeavor to keep down every feeling of progress or improvement. Two great parties here divide all power and wealth—the Church and the Army. . . . [T]hey wink at the tyranny and excesses of each other."[31]

Such circumstances, however, proved to be good for the American army. The agreement of church officials to accept the American occupation was crucial, and if the church members "blindly" followed their lead, it was a significant advantage for the army. The American high command had indeed redoubled its efforts to appease the clergy in Puebla, even though soldiers often resented such efforts. On Sunday, May 23, General Worth and his entire staff attended worship at the great cathedral, and as one observer reported, they all knelt on the marble floor like everyone else. The church hierarchy could not but notice the stark contrast between the Americans' magnanimous treatment and that of their own government, which had begun to tax the church heavily to pay for the war. By showing deference to church officials, Scott also hoped to lend moral support to a rumored political revolt by the Clerical Party in Mexico City. Meanwhile, Santa Anna attempted to counteract Scott's skillful pacification. After hearing of American efforts to placate the priests, the Mexican leader issued through a Mexico City newspaper a warning regarding the crafty Yankees, who paid much attention to the pretty women of Jalapa, but on arriving in the pious environs of Puebla suddenly became devout.[32]

Army discipline remained a top priority both for the safety of the troops and the pacification of the people. In accord with Scott's orders, no one could leave their quarters without a pass and a weapon. No one could venture out into the city in groups of fewer than six, one of whom had to be a noncommissioned officer, and it was a punishable offense for a soldier to be caught in the streets of Puebla alone and unarmed. One-fourth of each regiment had to remain under arms and on guard at all times. After the poison scare, special precautions had to be taken in the preparation of food, and the men were forbidden to eat anything except what their company cook prepared. In trying to enforce this regulation on the volunteers, who wished to maintain their customary habit of cooking and eating in small groups, the men refused to obey. Their messmates formed an important group for social interaction, and they did not like being told when and where to eat. After reading the order, one soldier called his commanding officer "an ignorant jackass." Despite the regulations, soldiers often wandered off on their own to do as they pleased, and despite the precautions, Americans were frequent victims of attack and murder.[33]

American behavior ran the gamut as typical vices afflicted the army in Puebla, but generally they conducted themselves quite well. After about a month in the city, Lieutenant Kirkham wrote to his wife, "I cannot describe the amount of wickedness in the way of profanity, sabbath-breaking, intemperance, and gambling which is daily practiced. . . . Temptation in every form is being presented to the army." The treatment of Mexican citizens was surprisingly good. Atrocities committed by Americans were the exception, not the rule, and when they did occur, they were often in retaliation for some Mexican deed. The arrival of Scott's army generally brought a degree of order and security to townspeople rather than chaos and plunder. In fact, American troops did less looting than the Mexican soldiers had done when they passed through. Women freely mingled with the Americans in the streets, which indicated that they felt safe; however, many of them rejected romantic advances for fear of retribution after the occupiers departed. In sum, the pacification efforts made many of the Pueblans feel "more secure in their persons and property than they have ever been under their own authorities."[34]

In addition to the effect of the pacification efforts in preventing a general uprising, another factor was the perception that Mexican citizens had of the guerrilla fighters. Many people saw them as nothing but "notorious Bandits" who are encouraged and "supported by the government." D. H. Hill asserted that "the peaceable citizens of Mexico have long been satisfied that these robbers injure far more their own people than they do the North Americans and are strenuously opposed to the whole Guerrilleros System." Another soldier claimed that Mexicans were frequently the victims of the numerous robberies and murders perpetrated by the guerrilla bands that roamed the roads. These sentiments were also indicative of the social and political conflict going on inside Mexico. Since the beginning of the war, there had been internal revolts, especially of the lower classes, against the ruling elites in Mexico, and Puebla had been a site of such upheavals.[35] Consequently, some of the locals were unwilling to embrace the government's efforts in 1847 to organize guerrilla units as a way of resisting the Americans. They might not like the foreigners in their midst, but Scott's pacification efforts helped them to see the Americans as the lesser of two evils.

Punishment for disobedient soldiers was, by today's standards, harsh in the extreme. One private thought that soldiers were "treated more like a vicious dog, than a civilized, intelligent, human being." Among the traditional forms of punishment was a method referred to as "riding the horse," wherein the soldier was made to straddle the narrow wooden beam of a sawhorse contraption for hours. It stood high enough that his legs could not touch the ground, and weights were tied to the ankles while hands were tied behind the back. It was a painful ride, and on occasion, men were known to fall over and break their necks. Beatings with a whip, carrying a cannonball or rock for an extended period of time, branding on the face or forehead, forfeiture of pay, confinement, and hard labor with ball and chain were other forms of punishment used, depending on the seriousness of the offense. Another common and painful method was to be "bucked and gagged." Here the soldier was seated with knees drawn up to the chest, ankles tied, arms wrapped around the legs, and wrists tied in front. A pole or stick was passed under the knees. Then a large object like a tent peg was forced into the mouth and used as a gag. All of the joints, including the jawbone, sent searing pain through the body by being fixed in such a position for several hours at a time. Eventually the body would grow numb, and when the soldier was released, the movement of returning the arms, legs, and mouth to their normal positions would again cause excruciating pain.[36]

Officers could mete out most of these and other forms of punishment for the slightest offenses, and often did so with unreasonable capriciousness. General Twiggs once grabbed a man by the hair, pulling out a handful for the offense of buying a drink of whiskey. While in Puebla, Captain John H. Winder struck some soldiers with his sword because they refused to kneel as ordered when a Catholic procession passed. After two months in Puebla, a dozen volunteers refused to join the rest of General Quitman's division for drill one day and also refused to clean their camp. Before the day was out, they were "bucked and set in a row in the guard house." And while American soldiers were punished severely and sometimes arbitrarily, Pueblan offenders occasionally received unusual leniency as a way of placating the residents. "There are great complaints and very just ones among the men," thought a Pennsylvania volunteer, because "Gen. Scott is watching with a paternal eye the interests of the Mexicans." A soldier commented that more Americans had been executed in Mexico than would have been put to death in the entire United States in a ten-year span.[37]

Such harsh punishment and discontent among the troops occasionally led to desertions—over two hundred while the army was in Jalapa. Before the Americans arrived in Puebla, a covert Mexican plan got underway to try to debilitate Scott's army through desertions once it arrived in the city. Santa Anna and the Minister of Foreign Relations Manuel Baranda placed agents in Puebla with money and instructions to entice as many U.S. troops away from the army as possible. According to one account, "Baranda's Puebla agents, sometimes friendly foreign nationals, sometimes lovely young women, did their part to spark desertions from May to August 1847, and so did the buck and gag and the rawhide lash." William Austine of General Worth's division wrote about "Recruiting depots" in the city where "rewards of every kind are promised" to American soldiers for changing their allegiance to the other side. Army officials in June arrested a German merchant in the city for trying to entice soldiers of German descent to desert. Martin Tritschler, tall and blond, was a naturalized Mexican citizen, an officer in the city's National Guard, and a wounded veteran of the Battle of Cerro Gordo. He began handing out leaflets written in German as soon as the U.S. Army arrived. A court sentenced him to a firing squad, but for days after his conviction, local residents and the bishop of Puebla visited Scott to plead for his pardon. Many testified to Tritschler's insanity, and on those grounds, Scott indeed pardoned and released him. After his release, however, some Americans thought he made an extraordinary recovery—as Austine reported, "We thought his madness had a method at least." The overall results of the plan disappointed Mexican officials, but it did have some impact. Foreigners who had immigrated to the United States and had ended up joining the army tended to be singled out for harsh, sometimes tyrannical, treatment by their superiors and, not surprisingly, these persecuted individuals seemed more inclined to desert while the army was in Mexico. As Austine reported, the soldiers who deserted while in Puebla were "principally foreigners." This, as shall be seen, would have dire consequences before the campaign ended.[38]

Punishment, low and erratic pay, disease, long marches, constant danger, foul weather, cramped quarters, and the countless other hardships that make up a soldier's life caused some of the volunteers to rethink their decisions to enlist. They discovered that real army life was much different from the naive images of glory that induced many of them to join, and that gathering laurels in Mexico was not all it was cracked up to be. A South Carolina volunteer remembered "a Scene in a certain Court House when there was a perfect tempest raised against Mexico" by emotional speakers who harangued the crowd with challenges for brave young men to come forward. "But lo! of all the valient men who stired up the more quiet country-loving audience by loud declamation and invective—of those men of wind I have not seen one of them in Mexico. Nor do I know of one of their descendants—one honorable exception—representing them here." Another man, later and from another area, similarly observed that "'sodgering in Mexico' is not quite so agreeable as Texas orators, who remain at home, would have the young, chivalrous & patriotic believe."[39]

CHAPTER EIGHT

Puebla

Between the Devil and the Deep Sea

An army ought only to have one line of operations. This should
be preserved with care, and never abandoned but in the last
extremity. Every army that acts from a distant base and is not
careful to keep this line perfectly open, marches upon a precipice.
—Napoleon Bonaparte

One of the frictions of war that can alter or destroy a general's plan is the debilitating effect of disease, which began to take its toll during the army's ten weeks in Puebla. On elevated and dry terrain, yellow fever was not the culprit; rather, it was dysentery. Caused from unclean water and unsanitary cooking and living conditions, or from eating fruit and vegetables contaminated by human feces, its chief symptoms were nausea, intestinal pain, fever, headache, and diarrhea. In severe cases, the diarrhea became chronic, dehydration occurred, and the body gradually withered away until the patient died. Kirby Smith described one of his friends who was suffering from the disease: he "looks like death and is wasted to a very skeleton."[1]

That malady, along with others, began to have an impact by June and July, with over two thousand soldiers on the sick rolls in Puebla, Perote, Jalapa, and Veracruz. The South Carolinians were hit especially hard. "Our men are dying off very fast," wrote one of them. Fourteen South Carolinians died of disease in the first half of June, and during July fifty-four died, eight in one day. According to George McClellan, the volunteers, who were notoriously negligent regarding personal hygiene and camp sanitation, died at a higher rate than the more disciplined regulars. "They literally die like dogs," he wrote. Burial processions occurred daily. The deceased were usually buried in a $5 wooden coffin made of thin planks and painted black. Often at night Mexicans would return to the cemetery and dig up the bodies so that they could take the blanket that the corpse was wrapped in as well as the coffin. The bare body then dumped back into the grave was filled over with dirt. According to one report, stolen coffins were sometimes resold two and three times.[2]

The prospects of continuing the campaign were quickly becoming a numbers game. Disease, casualties, and the expiration of enlistments began to take a toll, putting Scott in an increasingly perilous situation. He was stuck in Puebla and could do nothing until more troops arrived. The War Department had been pushing for and the Congress had been working on legislation to raise new regiments since late 1846. In February 1847, the Ten Regiment Bill passed, and with it the opportunity for the administration to appoint new officers. It was in conjunction with these new troops and officer appointments that Polk had embarked on his failed effort to make Senator Thomas Hart Benton a lieutenant general. After delays and diversions of troops, new units, mostly company strength, began arriving in Veracruz in May and June, and as sizable numbers of men collected, they marched in stages into the interior of the country to reinforce the army at Puebla.

By the summer, however, bandits and irregulars swarmed the roads between Veracruz and Perote, making the passage particularly treacherous for the mostly inexperienced new soldiers. The guerrillas "take every advantage to anoy our sick . . . and also to plunder our trains that might be without sufficient guard," wrote Hiram Yeager. The Americans viewed them as "cowardly [because] they never show themselves in the open." In fact, many of the Americans viewed these quasi-military bands as a collection of brigands whose primary object was not military resistance but opportunistic thievery. As William Austine of Worth's division wrote, "The whole country is infested with robbers, and hardly a vehicle escapes their hands." It was in this atmosphere that Colonel James S. McIntosh marched out of Veracruz on June 4 with nearly 700 men, a long supply train of 130 wagons and 500 pack mules, and over a quarter of a million dollars in specie. Aware of the convoy's value, guerrillas struck soon after it departed the coast, with three separate attacks coming on the sixth. McIntosh lost over twenty of his wagons, and his column suffered twenty-five casualties. Because he was unable to keep the ranks closed on his long and vulnerable column, he halted at Paso de Ovejas and called for help from Veracruz. So for several days the Americans sat in camp awaiting assistance. On numerous occasions, they spotted Mexican irregulars on the surrounding hilltops, who at least once rode toward the camp and fired a few shots before scampering away. McIntosh's caution appeared to his men as confusion. "He does not appear to know what to do," wrote surgeon Madison Mills.[3]

On the coast, George Cadwalader, a Philadelphia native and brigadier general of volunteers, was awaiting the arrival of the rest of his men. When he learned of the beleaguered condition of McIntosh's troops, he immediately gathered the five hundred men on hand and rushed to give aid, arriving on the eleventh. That evening, the combined force reached the National Bridge around dusk and discovered that Mexicans had piled rocks in the road to block access to the bridge. With darkness approaching, and knowing that guerrillas were in the area, the prudent course of action would have been to establish a secure campsite for the night. However, Cadwalader ordered the rocks cleared and the bridge crossed. It was near dark when the head of the column began to march onto the bridge, and as it reached the far side, some four hundred yards distant, guerrillas opened fire from the cliffs above on both the right and left. Some of the inexperienced drivers jumped off of their horses and let the wagon teams go, which caused havoc and disorder. Horses were killed and wagons turned over, clogging the road with wreckage. The bridge became a bottleneck of confusion as the raw recruits began to fire on each other. Thrown from his mount, Mills became "lodged between the wheel and body" of a wagon and was spared being crushed to death only because the wagon was stalled in the congestion.[4]

The ordeal on the bridge lasted longer than just a few minutes. Cadwalader ordered the debris removed from the road and the enemy cleared from the high ground to the right, but inexplicably, he left the Mexicans firmly ensconced in their fortified position to the left of the road. He then continued to push his men across. Ten Americans were killed and about thirty wounded in the fight. Afterward, Dr. Mills began to treat the wounded, and after removing American musket balls from several of them, he quickly surmised that friendly fire had claimed some of the victims. Cadwalader evidently thought that attempting to cross the bridge at night while under fire was brave and daring, but his subordinates disagreed. "His conduct . . . deserved to be punished," wrote Mills in his diary. "He is not sustained by a single officer, except by Capt. [Joseph] Hooker, his Asst. Adj. Genl. who was probably his advisor in the matter." The doctor harshly condemned Cadwalader as "pompous, overbearing[,]. . . . Ignorant and conceited. He is an ass." In short, Mills believed that "the Gen. ought to be dammed for this affair," which the embittered Mills believed resulted from "too much brandy."[5]

Two days later, the column was again ambushed before reaching the relative safety of Jalapa on June 15. A week earlier, the Jalapa garrison had received orders from General Scott to evacuate the town and proceed to Puebla. This resulted from Scott's manpower dilemma and his decision to consolidate all available troops for the push to Mexico City. When he realized that the promised 20,000-man army would not materialize, he took the fearless step of drawing in most of his garrisons, thus cutting himself off from the coast. It was indeed a bold decision made by an audacious and confident commander, but one that raised eyebrows back home. When President Polk heard about it, he declared, "I cannot approve" of such a "hazardous" decision, and later he suggested that Scott had "acted very unwisely." Major Patrick Galt of the Second Artillery thought the perilous move put Scott in "a most delicate position," and considering the way the president felt about the general, the "poor fellow [is] between the devil and the deep sea."[6]

Cutting his line of communication, however, probably was not as risky as some people have portrayed it. Most observers understood that Scott's decision constituted a violation of one of Jomini's maxims regarding the necessity of maintaining at all times a secure line of communications back to the army's base. When the Duke of Wellington, victor at Waterloo, heard the news, he supposedly proclaimed, "Scott is lost. He has been carried away by successes. He can't take the city, and he can't fall back upon his base."[7] However, keeping garrisons in Perote and Jalapa—towns that already had demonstrated an unwillingness to rebel against the American occupation—had not rendered the road to Veracruz safe from guerrillas. Even with those posts occupied, American troops had been forced to travel in strength to discourage or defeat guerrilla attacks. What would he lose by abandoning the towns? Besides, he knew that they could be reoccupied at a time of his choosing. In the face of the enemy's guerrilla efforts, Scott did just the opposite of what might be expected. Rather than strengthen outposts and guard his supply lines, he simply eliminated them as potential targets for partisan bands, and in so doing, added strength to his limited numbers. Taking into account that his pacification program had allowed him to consistently purchase supplies in country, he chose to simply continue that practice. Adequate ammunition might become a concern, but food would not. Ultimately, in a game of numbers, Scott realized that he stood to gain more by consolidating his forces than by keeping them dispersed.

So when Cadwalader continued his march on June 18, he took the Jalapa garrison with him, bringing his total to about two thousand men. The next leg of the journey was perhaps the most treacherous because it took the troops through La Hoya, with its notorious Black Pass. The town had a reputation for cooperating with guerrilla bands. One volunteer described it as "a most villainous hole" and "a perfect settlement of ladrones" (thieves). Located about a dozen miles west of Jalapa and close to Las Vigas, where Father Caledonio Domeco Jarauta commanded seven hundred irregular Mexican guerrillas, the Americans knew to expect trouble there, and Jarauta was waiting for the five-mile-long column when it approached. However, Colonel Francis M. Wyncoop, the garrison commander at Perote, which was twenty miles farther west, heard rumors of an ambush and responded by marching to the Black Pass with four companies of infantry and Captain Samuel Walker's company of Mounted Rifles to disrupt Jarauta's plan. On the evening of June 19, Wyncoop attacked the guerrilla position in the pass from the west. After an inconclusive skirmish against overwhelming numbers, Wyncoop inexplicably ordered his men back to Perote with Cadwalader's column on the other side of the pass, just a few miles away.

Walker, however, refused to obey the order. As a Texas Ranger, Walker was a fearless leader, and as a member of the 1842 Mier Expedition (an invasion of Texans into northern Mexico) who had spent time in a Mexican prison, he had a thirst for revenge. Next morning, about fifty of Walker's Mounted Rifles attacked Jarauta's irregulars again, and for close to an hour, the opposing forces were locked in a sharp battle. Then a forewarned Cadwalader entered the pass and attacked from the east, causing Jarauta's guerrillas to break and run. Walker had a horse shot from under him and he lost one man while the guerrillas suffered significantly higher losses. The American losses were minimal in terms of personnel, but they lost several more supply wagons and many of their pack mules. The confrontation at La Hoya was, at times, hand to hand, and the young Lieutenant Thomas Jackson, traveling with Cadwalader's column, came away with a Mexican sword as a prize for his role in the fighting.[8]

After routing the guerrillas, Walker and his men went on a rampage. In the words of one volunteer, Walker's "inveterate hatred against the Mexicans" caused him to wage war "according to his own peculiar feelings." Wheeling their mounts around, they galloped into nearby Las Vigas and burned every building in the town as punishment for providing safe haven for guerrillas. The log houses of Las Vigas gave the town a notably different look from the typical adobe huts; they were also easier to burn. Cadwalader's men followed close behind and found many of the houses still in flames as they marched through. Sergeant Thomas Barclay, a Pennsylvania volunteer, feared the repercussions of such destruction. If the Mexican "people are once aroused either by an attack upon their religion or property, a resistance will be made similar to the Spanish campaigns of 1813 & '14."[9] And if such were to happen, no number of American troops could prevail. Of course, Barclay's perceptive analysis painted precisely the picture that Scott had hoped to avoid, but he was willing to overlook such wanton destruction when it was directed against those who harbored and facilitated unconventional war. It was a lesson in the hard hand of war.

On the same day that Cadwalader marched out of Jalapa, Gideon Pillow left Veracruz to join him with two thousand men. Pillow had returned to his Columbia, Tennessee, home after his Cerro Gordo wound. While there, he fended off charges of incompetence made by subordinate officers in the disbanded Second Tennessee Regiment before President Polk promoted him to major general. Now a division commander, Pillow had been in Veracruz preparing troops for the inland march before departing from the coast on June 18. When he arrived at Jalapa ten days later, he was surprised to find the town abandoned by the army, and he sent a letter to Polk censoring Scott's decision to vacate the post and asking the president to hurry more men to Mexico so that the army's communication line could be restored. From Jalapa Pillow also sent orders ahead to Cadwalader, instructing him to wait at Perote until his arrival so they could finish the march to Puebla united and with overwhelming strength.[10]

Pillow arrived in Perote a few days behind Cadwalader, and within two days, he had incorporated the latter's troops along with the local garrison and set out for Puebla. The march was "long and tedious," and guerrillas continued to swarm around the long column. Attacks occurred almost daily, one coming at 2:00 A.M. on July 6 while the column was still thirty miles from their destination. It was an insignificant skirmish instigated by fifty irregular Mexican cavalry, but on receiving news of the attack, Scott dispatched Colonel Harney with cavalry and infantry to escort the column the rest of the way in. On the afternoon of July 8, Pillow's dirty and weary troops reached Puebla with a strength of over four thousand and with over four hundred wagons laden with badly needed supplies.[11]

Pillow's arrival with provisions, money, and especially reinforcements came as a relief to Scott and the rest of the army. However, by the time he got to Puebla, Nicholas Trist had opened a diplomatic channel that he hoped would render further military operations unnecessary, for his efforts to use the British as intermediaries had borne fruit. Two weeks after Edward Thornton's initial visit to Puebla, wherein he had agreed to deliver correspondence from Trist to Mexican authorities, he returned with a reply. In his visit to Trist, he took with him two other Englishmen, one named Turnbull, a merchant living in Puebla, and Ewen Macintosh of the Manning and Macintosh banking firm and also the British consul general in Mexico. Macintosh's firm had investments in the country and had helped refinance Mexico's debt in 1845, giving him a vested interest in the return of peace. The three delivered Foreign Minister Domingo Ibarra's response, which indicated a willingness on the part of Santa Anna to propose negotiations based on Polk's territorial demands. They also told Trist that the Mexican congress had been called together to consider the proposal. The prospects looked promising, but, of course, the financial incentives—bribery—that Thornton and Trist had discussed earlier was an understood prerequisite for a peace treaty.[12]

This development created an opportunity for Scott and Trist to break the ice of their frigid relationship, and as author Wallace Ohrt put it, the two "gentlemen began to feel foolish and then to behave like grown men." In the last week of June, Trist notified Scott of this potential avenue of communication with the Mexicans, and the general responded courteously. Soon after, Trist fell ill and was confined to bed for two weeks with his host, General Persifor Smith, acting as nursemaid. It was on July 6, during his convalescence, that Scott penned the following note to Smith: "Looking over my stores, I find a box of Guava marmalade which, perhaps, the physician may not consider improper to make part of the diet of your sick companion." This simple gesture transformed their mutual contempt into a warm working relationship, and the thaw occurred just as Pillow arrived.[13]

From Scott's perspective, the potential for peace talks could not have come at a better time. Knowing that his numbers and resources were limited, he welcomed a possible end to the fighting, and he knew that the resumption of active military operations would hamper the political process in Mexico City. Indeed, Santa Anna intimated that an American advance on the capital would diminish the influence of peace advocates in the Mexican congress. Scott liked the possibility of ending the war without further bloodshed, but he also understood the controversy associated with paying a bribe to achieve peace. Just five months earlier on the floor of the House, Congressman Henry J. Seaman of New York had expressed a view that many held regarding the question of bribery. During a debate on an appropriations bill, Seaman wondered if some of the money requested by the administration was to be used "to bribe the Mexican General, and make him a traitor to his country." If it were true, the congressman thought it to be "as wicked as it is ridiculous." Further, he suggested that such would dishonor the country, and Scott certainly understood the disdain with which members of the administration would view a bribery attempt.[14] However, he obviously concluded that if there was any dishonor associated with bribery, surely it would attach to those soliciting and accepting it.

During the second week of July, the major players in the so-called bribery scheme danced around the issue in an effort to discover who favored it and who opposed it. Polk had instructed Trist to freely consult with his friend and informant Pillow, which he did. The diplomat explained the situation to the new major general and asked his opinion, and, according to Scott's aide, Ethan A. Hitchcock, Pillow "sanctioned" the action. Trist then consulted the commanding general, who actually had the funds on hand to initiate the process. At some point, the two decided to make an initial payment of $10,000 from Scott's contingency funds to get negotiations underway with the promise of $1 million for the conclusion of a treaty. However, Scott was not willing to go forward without consulting his top-ranking officers. He probably already knew what he wanted to do, but he needed to feel out Pillow, who was known to be Polk's surrogate in Mexico.[15]

On July 17, Scott called together Generals Cadwalader, Pillow, Quitman, Shields, and Twiggs "to post them up," as Scott called it, regarding army matters. First he told them that General Franklin Pierce would soon arrive with additional reinforcements, and he asked their opinion as to whether they should wait or go ahead and push on to Mexico City. The council advised waiting. Then Scott got to the business at hand. He explained the bribery offer and the money Trist needed to go forward with the plan. He further said that he did not like the notion of tempting the "fidelity or patriotism" of the Mexicans, but that he saw nothing wrong with taking advantage of the situation if Mexican officials were willing to be bribed. Then he asked his subordinates for their opinions. Pillow was the first to speak "fully and eloquently" in favor of the plan, and he even bragged about his role in helping Trist decide to pursue this course. Quitman, who regularly played chess with Scott and had grown close to the commanding general since the army arrived in Puebla, was careful not to offend. He had reservations about using such a shady measure to try to purchase a peace, and he feared the public outcry that would result from its disclosure. Shields, a former Illinois supreme court justice, also offered mild opposition to the plan, and Cadwalader, when asked to weigh in, refused comment and simply shook his head. Davy Twiggs, who easily could have assumed Zachary Taylor's nickname "Old Rough and Ready" and who possessed a healthy dislike for Mexicans, thought the plan was more political than military, but he endorsed it nevertheless.[16]

The plan ultimately accomplished nothing and probably caused more controversy than it deserved. Scott proceeded with the initial payment of $10,000, which many assumed went into Santa Anna's pocket. Historian Justin Smith, however, asserted that the recipient was Miguel Arroyo, who later served on the Mexican peace commission. After sending the money, Scott received word from Santa Anna that he had been unable to get the legislature to agree to open negotiations, but the exceedingly manipulative generalissimo suggested that perhaps another opportunity would arise as the Americans approached the outskirts of Mexico City. Thus ended an unsuccessful attempt to use money as a lubricant to engineer a peace treaty. The one positive thing to come out of the effort was that it brought Scott and Trist together into a close working relationship.[17]

William Worth's absence from the generals' council indicated how far he had fallen out of favor. He criticized Scott for the long delay at Puebla while the Mexicans strengthened the capital's defenses. "We gain victories and halt until all the moral advantages are lost," he complained. Others protested as well, arguing that the bribery intrigue was nothing but a ploy by Santa Anna to delay the American advance while he prepared to defend the city. It did not, however, delay Scott's army a single day. It was not that Scott decided to wait in Puebla to see if the bribery plan would work; it was rather that, because the army was stuck in Puebla awaiting reinforcements, he decided to pursue this avenue.[18] And it was consistent with his desire to win a peace through negotiations.

As July turned to August, the army continued to wait for General Pierce, who marched out of Veracruz on July 15 with 2,500 men. While the New Hampshire native and future president was en route, another one of New Hampshire's sons made an unexpected visit in Puebla, and his role in the final weeks of the campaign, although significant, has been all but forgotten. In early August, this unexpected rider came into Puebla from Mexico City bearing dispatches from the British minister, Charles Bankhead. The nature of the documents is unknown—they may have related to the bribery project—but the importance of the event was the messenger, not the message. It was Noah E. Smith who arrived at Scott's headquarters in the middle of the night, and after some cajoling, he convinced the guards to awaken the general. The two men had a long conversation in which Smith shared with Scott all that he knew about the capital, and Scott discovered that he possessed such a wealth of information about Mexico, the terrain, influential citizens, and such that he bade Smith to remain with the army.[19]

A native of New Hampshire, where his father had served in the state legislature, Smith had moved to Mexico in the early 1830s to work for a stagecoach company that ran a line from Mexico City to Veracruz. Later he started his own business in the capital, buying and selling Mexican horses and importing larger, more expensive horses from the United States. His business became lucrative, and through it, he gained access to many of the capital's financial and political elites. By the time the war started, he was wealthy and well known, but because he was an American, local officials viewed him with increasing suspicion. In the summer of 1847, with the U.S. Army eighty miles away in Puebla, the authorities ordered all Americans out of the capital. Fearing for his life, Smith adopted a disguise, paid a last visit to his friend Minister Bankhead, hired a guerrilla band as an escort, and, leaving his family behind, slipped out of the capital. Several days later, he arrived at Scott's headquarters, where the commanding general quickly recognized his value to the army, not the least of which was his knowledge of the roads, garnered from his stagecoach experience. He agreed to guide the army back to Mexico City and thus became a de facto member of Scott's staff.[20]

As they waited to start the last leg of the journey, the troops wondered whether there would be another fight. Opinions varied, just as they had after the fall of Veracruz and the victory at Cerro Gordo. Some "predict that not a shot will be fired," while others believed that heavy fighting lay ahead. "If we do fight," wrote Lieutenant Ralph Kirkham, "many an honest and brave heart that now beats will beat no more." Despite a shortage of artillery ammunition, the men were generally sanguine about their ability to triumph. In Washington, President Polk was also optimistic. He had some weeks earlier expressed the opinion that the brave American soldiers would win battles even "if there was not an officer among them." But the men did not always share the same optimistic feelings for Polk as he felt for them. Hiram Yeager asserted that "there is a general Condemnation of Polk . . . in the army." He was particularly frustrated because "our government is not furnishing men to carry on this war. . . . We want men and money if we have not those two principle thing[s] we might just as well be called home. There is a great fault somewhere and where it is, is more than the poor soldier can tell."[21]

One more attitude that constituted a prevalent theme in soldiers' writings deserves notice. It was a notion that began to take root in the second year of the conflict, not just in the army but back in the States as well, and that was the growing conviction that most, if not all, of Mexico should fall under U.S. control. Few people doubted that the war was about land and that some territorial concessions would be required of Mexico in order to consummate a peace, and by 1847, the American appetite for land was growing. Back in the spring, Secretary Marcy had written to General Scott instructing him to look for "the most effective way in your power" to encourage the severing of political ties between the government in Mexico City and any region wherein the people seem to favor the idea. Later in the year, William P. Chambliss, while on duty with a Tennessee regiment, noted a particularly beautiful spot near the National Bridge that he thought would make an ideal manufacturing location because of the power that could be generated by the rapidly flowing river. And he speculated that the area would be host to just such an enterprise "at no distant day, should this country become a part of the U.S."[22]

Other soldiers began to harbor similar assumptions as the war progressed, believing that the United States should absorb its southern neighbor because of its inferior institutions and backward culture. "They are a poor excuse for a nation, and dont deserve the beautiful country with which heaven has blessed them," wrote John Dodd to his wife. In the latter stages of the campaign, Roswell Ripley wrote to his mother regarding the dishonesty and corruption that prevailed in Mexico. Then he opined that if a treaty is made and broken by the enemy, "we shall be ultimately obliged to take possession of the country, as an outlet to the superfluous energy of our own, and a corrective to the exuberant rascality of this." In a later letter, Ripley expressed the opinion that conditions in Mexico would improve only with a prolonged American presence in the country. William Austine echoed the same sentiments when he decried the state of disrepair into which many of the roads and buildings had fallen. The "Mexicans never repair . . . any of these great works except when absolutely compelled to do so," he complained. "If the country is not soon taken possession of by some enlightened nation it will eventually return to its primitive state." Even Robert E. Lee weighed in on the idea of taking over the country: "They will oblige us in spite of ourselves to overrun the country & drive them into the sea. I believe it would be our best plan to commence at once."[23]

All of that speculation, however, had to give way to the business at hand, which was marching on to the Mexican capital and ending the war. The want of money and men was somewhat remedied when General Pierce arrived with both on August 6. Sporadic guerrilla attacks had also plagued this column as it marched from Veracruz, including a major skirmish with over a thousand irregulars at the National Bridge. Just before reaching Cerro Gordo, they discovered that guerrillas had destroyed the bridge across the Río del Plan, and after spending a day and a half making repairs, they continued on to Jalapa and beyond. West of Perote, guerrilla activity had been temporarily quelled by the time Pierce's troops marched through, thanks to a surprise raid the previous week by American dragoons from Puebla under Captain Charles F. Ruff. In that skirmish near Ojo de Agua, some forty guerrillas were killed. Manuel Dominguez's Mexican spy company also did its part to suppress the presence of irregulars on the roads and in the mountain passes.[24]

The difficulties that Pillow, Cadwalader, McIntosh, Pierce, and others faced illustrate that the guerrilla threat had grown in magnitude. By summer, it had become a constant nuisance and worry for Scott, to the extent that the safe movement of troops and supplies between the coast and the army became an important consideration for the commanding general. Scott realized that to ensure security his troops could no longer travel in groups of a few dozen or even a few hundred; rather, they needed to march in strong columns numbering a thousand or more. It was obviously with this concern at the forefront of his mind that he drew in his vulnerable garrisons at Jalapa and Perote. Ultimately, though, the guerrilla war that emerged was never more than a significant irritant, a thorn in the flesh. It did not cause Scott to alter his plans or slow down his operations, and it never rose to an unmanageable proportion. In short, it never threatened the outcome of the conflict. Certainly columns of troops and supplies had difficulty traveling the roads, but none ever failed to reach its destination.

The nature of these partisan attacks and the Americans' attitude toward them are best illustrated by quotes from two officers, Major William B. Taliaferro and Captain Benjamin S. Roberts. While traveling inland from Veracruz with a body of reinforcements in September, Taliaferro recorded the following comments about an encounter with irregulars. After a skirmish near the National Bridge, he recounted how they drove the guerrillas away with artillery: "Our shells burst all over them, and we could see them leave the fort . . .

without a shot being fired" by the enemy. The major then commented on the sporadic gunfire that went on all night: "Indeed it is so common to hear the reports of escopettes that I hardly care to get up at night to go out and see where they are fired from, and sleep soundly although I may be called to a fierce conflict before morning." The former quote illustrates the common knowledge that the guerrillas would not stand and fight in a set battle, while the latter demonstrates such a lack of fear that Taliaferro did not even bother to get out of bed to investigate the sounds of gunfire. Such indifference was reiterated by Roberts, a member of the Mounted Rifles, who wrote several weeks after the army left Puebla that his regiment had "marched for hours without paying attention to their firing upon our train and rear. They have kept in the hills beyond our musket and rifle range and their escopeta balls if they hit a man would seldom break the skin." Such was Roberts's disdain for the military prowess of the guerrillas that he concluded that "One hundred riflemen would consider it an amusement to fight a thousand guerillas daily."[25]

One more development that occurred before the army left Puebla warrants notice, for it provides clues about Scott's motivations once he reached the vicinity of Mexico City. This involves a revealing exchange of notes between the commanding general and his British contacts inside the capital. Clearly Scott and Trist had cultivated relationships with Minister Bankhead, Secretary Thornton, and undoubtedly others, and these well-placed individuals had acted as unofficial intermediaries between the American army and Mexican officials, both political and military, for much of the campaign, as evidenced by the aborted bribery scheme. Before leaving Puebla, Scott received a letter from one of these sources indicating that if the Americans marched only part way to the capital—say, to San Martin, which was a third of the distance—then halted, the Mexican government might extend a request for peace talks. If Scott, however, decided to march all the way to the capital, the letter went on to make the incredible request that he identify the point of the city that he intended to attack. The nature of the letter made it suspect as to which side the correspondent was attempting to aid, but Scott did not fall into the trap. He responded by writing a note that Lieutenant Colonel Hitchcock called "the most remarkable ever penned by any commander in any campaign on record." Hitchcock read the note (in fact, he saw it more than once), and several months later, he recounted its contents. Scott audaciously informed his contact that he intended to advance to the capital and would "either defeat the enemy in view of the city, if they would give him battle, or he would take a strong position from the enemy, and then, if he could restrain the enthusiasm of his troops, he would halt outside of the city and take measures to give those in the city an opportunity to save the capital by making a peace."[26]

On its surface, it was a bold assertion from a confident army commander, but on deeper reflection, it also served as a signal of Scott's moderate approach. It clearly indicated that capturing Mexico City was not his primary objective and that he would use only as much military leverage as necessary to win a peace. Thus, when he reached the outskirts of the capital, he would look for that signal victory "in view of the city," then give his opponent time to seek peace. It was Scott's consistent strategy throughout the campaign: sword, then olive branch; fight, then wait.

Pierce's column brought the army's fighting strength to 10,700 with an additional 2,500 hospitalized with illness and wounds. Preparations for departure were already underway when Pierce arrived, and on Saturday, August 7, the army began marching out of Puebla by division. The four division commanders were David Twiggs, who led the army out of the city and away from their ten-week hiatus; William Worth, who just days earlier had written a "half apology" to Scott for the problems he had caused; John Quitman, who continued to command volunteer troops; and Gideon Pillow, whose deficient military mind caused him to rely heavily on his new adjutant general, Captain Joseph Hooker. Pillow once said to Hooker, "When you see occasion for issuing an order, give it without reference to me. You understand these matters." It was just as well, for many of the soldiers, especially subordinate officers, resented orders from Pillow. For him to give orders, thought Captain George Davis, was like "the tail attempting to wag the dog."[27]

With bands playing and regimental flags flying, the army departed the city with a flash of pageantry that suited the commanding general nicely. As Twiggs's lead division began its exodus from the city, he yelled with his thunderous voice for his boys to "give them a Cerro Gordo shout!" Quitman, Worth, and Pillow followed, on successive days through August 10, and covered only a half day's march initially so that each division would remain within supporting distance of the ones in its front and rear. The order of march each day consisted first of mounted troops, then light infantry and artillery, followed by the main infantry regiments. Behind them came the supply train, and finally a strong rear guard to protect the wagons from attack.[28]

As they marched out, some of the soldiers were struck by the level of disinterest exhibited by the Pueblans, who appeared to pay little attention to their departure. William Austine expressed disappointment when a "market woman," who had sold pigs to the troops, and whom Austine had visited on numerous occasions, acted entirely indifferent as he left town. "I must confess my mortification when on mounting my . . . horse, neither the mother, daughter or even the babies . . . deigned a look, not even a parting glance, at one who for three months had daily . . . taken the liveliest interest in their secular affairs, what base ingratitude."[29]

Scott's tentative plans for his final advance on the capital dictated the order by which each division left Puebla, and he had formulated his plans on the basis of long-range reconnaissance by Captain Lee and Major William Turnbull, Scott's chief topographical engineer. During the army's long summer encampment, Lee and Turnbull had scouted the roads between Puebla and Mexico City, talked to residents along the way, and made crude pencil maps of the possible approaches to the capital. They each made their own maps on the basis of separate reconnaissance missions and without consulting each other. Also after each mission, Scott called them to his headquarters, where he questioned them separately to see if he got the same answers from each. Their maps slowly developed over time "from information procured in every possible way you can imagine." When they were confident in their finished products, they compared their maps and corrected any discrepancies. Scott assigned great responsibility to his engineers, especially to Lee, in whom he placed considerable trust. As a result of their findings and recommendations, Scott decided to advance on the city from the south, and to placate his old friend, he would give Worth's division the honor of leading the way. No one but Scott knew about the plan that was percolating in his head while in Puebla, but to pursue what he envisioned, Worth's command needed to be the third to depart. The reason for his placement there would become apparent after the army arrived in the Valley of Mexico.[30]

Having pulled in his garrisons, except for a small one to remain in Puebla to care for the convalescent soldiers, and cut off his communications with the coast, Scott displayed bold leadership. Like the Spaniard Hernando Cortez who burned his ships on the coast before striking out to conquer the Aztec empire, Scott's decision signaled that there was no turning back. The advance, not the rear, was where the Americans must focus their attention. According to intelligence from the capital, Santa Anna had spent the previous ten weeks strengthening the city's defenses and building an army that exceeded 20,000 men. He enjoyed several advantages in addition to his significant numerical superiority. Now that he would be fighting in and around the capital, his previously long line of communication was nil. Most importantly, he would be fighting with interior lines. Operating with interior lines, he would be able to shift troops and communicate with his officers much more quickly and easily than could the Americans. Conversely, Scott's army, by severing its ties to the coast, had no choice but to fight while isolated and deep within hostile territory. Clearly, there was no room for error. "But we are ready for anything," recorded Lieutenant Kirkham, and come what may, "General Scott will do the thing up in the most scientific order."[31]

CHAPTER NINE

Into the Valley of Mexico

No Room for Error

Santa Anna had now had nearly four months (since the battle of Cerro Gordo) to collect and reorganize the entire means of the Republic for a last vigorous attempt to crush the invasion. A single error on our part—a single victory on his, might have effected that great end.
—Winfield Scott, Commanding General

After leaving Puebla, the climate changed rapidly. With the volcanic peak of Popocatépetl visible in the distance, the army gradually approached the last mountain range, which made up the eastern rim of the Valley of Mexico. On the third day, the road began to ascend, and the men marched for hours uphill through a uneven terrain covered with pine woods. The mounted troops must have been fuming over the elevated march into the mountains because some of their horses had been taken from them before leaving Puebla for use in wagon teams. The temperature became "quite cold" and the air damp as the men continued their trudge up the mountains. As they ascended, the altitude made breathing difficult and eardrums bore witness to the effects of the pressure, but up they marched until they had to look down at the clouds. Still on the eastern side of the range, the army came to Rio Frio, which has an altitude of more than 10,000 feet. It was a small stream that flowed from the mountain tops, and true to its name, it was "nearly as cold as ice." Now the volcano, Mount Popo, as the locals called it, was on the left, still twenty miles away but jutting up seven thousand feet higher than their current altitude.[1]

The army continued unopposed through the mountain passes. Here and there, abandoned log breastworks served as clues that they would not have another fight until they reached the capital. At the Cordilleras Pass, just beyond the summit where the troops stopped to rest, Noah Smith told Scott that he had something to show him and asked if the commander would ride with him a short distance. The two men left the road and in a few minutes came to a spot that Smith knew about where the Mexican capital was visible, and from that location, Scott got his first glimpse of his objective, far in the distance in the valley below. In his *Memoirs,* he described the spellbinding vista as a "sublime trance." The "surrounding lakes, sparkling under a bright sun seemed, in the distance, pendant diamonds." Below stretched the valley floor, and several thousand feet above him towered mountain peaks. Taking it all in "filled the mind with religious awe," Scott wrote years later. Before leaving the spot, he called for his staff officers so he could show them the sight and the place where the army's journey would end.[2]

At this point, the road began a rapid ten-mile descent into the valley below, and after going a short distance down the west face, the troops made a turn in the road. Suddenly they marched into an opening where "the luxurious valley of Mexico burst upon us." Several thousand feet below, they saw the entire breadth of the valley, thirty miles wide and forty-five miles long, all the way to the dark mountains that surrounded it on all sides. Lakes and small villages dotted the panorama, but there, twenty-five miles distant, was the object of their quest: Mexico City, with its domes and towers clearly visible. Numerous descriptions in letters and diaries indicated that the sight was as unforgettable for the soldiers as it had been for the commanding general. "The Valley of Mexico shut out from the surrounding world by a range of lofty mountains which completely encircles it, was spread out far below us," wrote Lieutenant Simon Bolivar Buckner to a relative. "From the height at which we viewed it, we gazed upon the many beauties which it unfolded;— upon the highly cultivated fields, upon the villages, and cities, and spires, . . . upon the distant mountains which bounded the horizon, and which were mirrored in the smooth surface of the lakes which reposed tranquilly beneath." The Englishman George Ballentine remembered "the uniform appearance of a green-swept plain dotted with white churches, spires, and *haciendas,* and containing several large sheets of water." The clear air allowed them to discern an incredible amount of detail for a great distance. "It is certainly the most magnificent view in Mexico," Ballentine concluded, "perhaps the finest in the world." During the long trek through the mountains, the tired marchers had trudged on in "sullen silence," but on catching their first glimpse of the Mexican capital, their mood changed as they began "briskly chatting and laughing most merrily."[3]

Understanding the historic nature of their enterprise, some of the soldiers could not resist making comparisons between their campaign and Cortez's sixteenth-century march into this same valley to conquer the Aztecs. Moses Barnard pondered the fact that he was beholding the same sights that the Spaniard had seen as he crossed the mountains. "We were treading the same ground, gazing on the same scenes, experiencing the same delight that Cortez & his gallant little band of Cavaliers experienced three centuries before us. Our expedition was as full of hazard & romance & I have the vanity to think our hearts were as stout." Cortez, with a tiny army, had defeated a magnificent empire, and here in 1521 he had captured the great Aztec capital Tenochtitlan, the ruins of which lay beneath Mexico City. Now the Americans imagined that if they could pull off the same feat, their fame would equal that of Cortez.[4]

Their steady march took them to the valley floor later that day, but as they descended to the fields, villages, and lakes, the view that appeared enchanting from a distance slowly disappeared. Ballentine revised his description, remembering that "as we come closer its beauty vanishes. The lakes turn to marshes, the fields are not cultivated, the villages are mud, and the residents are wretched-looking Indian *peons* in rags and squalid misery." This account is borne out by Captain William Lytle, who asserted that "the most magnificent sight in the world is to behold from a distance, a Mexican city. The immense number of domes and turrets rearing their lofty heads far above everything around them, makes the view most striking and picturesque." However, on entering the cities, "how great the disappointment" to find yourself surrounded by unhappiness and misery.[5]

As they arrived in the valley, Scott sent out a detachment to purchase food, and because Noah Smith knew the surrounding area, he consented to Scott's request to lead the expedition. Smith asserted that he could get all that the army needed. However, when he learned that he was to go out with Manuel Dominguez's band of spies and cutthroats, he demurred. Not only did Smith fear for his own safety, but he also was certain that the "Forty Thieves," as he called the spy company, would cause problems with the farmers and ranchers along the way. When he asked Scott for regular troops to accompany him, the general responded, "you shall have what you want," and he sent Edwin Sumner's dragoons along. At the hacienda of San Borke, the first place they came to, the residents told Smith that they were not afraid because they knew that the Americans protected individual rights and private property. The overseer, however, said that the owner was away and that he could not sell to the Americans for fear of retribution from the authorities. So Smith and the overseer had a private conversation wherein the two agreed that the army would take what it wanted by "force," and later the proprietor could present a receipt at headquarters and receive compensation. The overseer then called together all the laborers and told them they would all be shot if they did not cooperate, thereby tricking them into loading supplies onto the pack mules that the Americans had brought. They left with barley, grain, and a hundred head of cattle.[6]

Meanwhile, the army arrived in echelon, and Scott sent out his engineers to gather information about the roads and terrain around Mexico City. Three large lakes covered much of the eastern side of the city—Texcoco, Chalco, and Xochimilco. The National Road, the main approach from the east, ran between Texcoco and Chalco, but the ground from the lakes to the city, a nine-mile stretch, was a marsh. Because this wet land extended from the east around to the southern side of the city, most of the roads were elevated causeways. An army approaching on the National Road would have to march along a raised roadbed, thus rendering itself vulnerable prey for an opposing force. In addition, Santa Anna had been busy fortifying a hill at the southern end of Lake Texcoco called El Peñon, where he intended to turn the Americans back. The alternatives to this route would take the army around the lakes to attack from either the north or south. To go north around the larger Lake Texcoco would greatly increase the distance for the army, and because a Mexican force was positioned at Texcoco blocking the road and because other fortified positions studded this route, Scott never seriously considered it. The other direction, south around the bottom of Lakes Chalco and Xochimilco, then turning right to approach the city from the south, provided a third option—the one he had already decided on before leaving Puebla.

By Thursday, August 12, five days after leaving Puebla, Twiggs's division had marched straight across the intersection with the Texcoco Road and encamped in Ayotla on the north shore of Lake Chalco, where Scott established his headquarters. Quitman's men set up camp just behind Twiggs, and Harney's dragoons brushed back enemy pickets and took a position a mile and a half west of Ayotla. This gave the appearance that Scott intended to continue his advance along the National Road and approach the capital from the east, and that was just the impression that Scott wanted to give. However, he had already decided to take the southern approach, or the Chalco route. To that end, he ordered Worth, whose division was third in line of march, to turn left at the lake and set up camp at the town of Chalco with Pillow following him and posting his men nearby. Thus the two divisions at Ayotla would mask the real movement to the south, and Scott positioned his old friend to take the leading role. Worth was unaware of Scott's intentions when he halted his division at Chalco.[7]

After receiving reports that the Chalco route might be impassable, Scott kept the army stationary in these locations for three days while his engineers gathered additional intelligence. As Robert Anderson put it, "Genl. Scott has his battle-fields well reconnoitred, and avails himself of all the advantages which science or skill may suggest." The Chalco road south of the lakes had fallen into disuse since the early 1800s and was little more than a rough wagon trail, and Noah Smith had warned Scott that it traversed ravines and was not practical for an army.[8] Santa Anna did not suspect that it could be used by the Americans, but for good measure, he had instructed that rocks be rolled onto it from the adjacent ridges and trees felled across it to impede an advance. This prompted the reports that Scott had received advising against

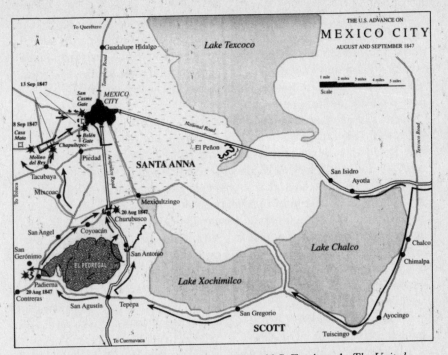

U.S. Army's advance on Mexico City. From Donald S. Frazier, ed., *The United States and Mexico at War* (New York: Macmillan, 1998). Reprinted by permission of The Gale Group.

this route, so he waited and rethought his options. After reconnoitering around Lake Chalco, Lee and Lieutenant Beauregard reported on the twelfth that the southern route would indeed pose difficulties but was passable. Before entirely ruling out an eastern approach, Scott sent his engineers out to gather every piece of information they could about the Mexican position at El Peñon.

Lee, along with Captain James L. Mason and Lieutenant Isaac I. Stevens, reported on its formidable defenses. Part of the lake wrapped around the front of El Peñon, giving the appearance that it rose up out of the water—indeed, Lee indicated that it "stands in the waters of Lake Tezcuco." It was perhaps four hundred feet high and a thousand yards long, and its location adjacent to the road allowed it to completely dominate an approach from that direction. The hill had three levels or plateaus, each with breastworks, and Santa Anna had interspersed thirty pieces of artillery among the fortifications. On the causeway and four hundred yards in front of El Peñon was another battery. In addition to posting seven thousand defenders on the hill, Santa Anna had made his headquarters there, as he deemed this to be Scott's most likely approach. Clearly, Santa Anna intended to make his stand here, and he had rallied his army and focused his people's attention to defending the capital at this spot. And it was a good one. The water and marsh that surrounded it made a flank attack impossible. To approach from the east, the Americans would have to attack El Peñon straight on and take it at the point of the bayonet—a bloody proposition.[9]

Scott had an important decision to make. Captain Joseph R. Smith of Twiggs's division recorded in his diary, "I know not what our great general will decide upon. He is most prudent and will not sacrifice a life if he can avoid it." But an attack on El Peñon would come with a heavy sacrifice—perhaps 1,500 men. Scott knew that he could not take such a risk with his limited numbers and the uncertainty of reinforcements. He also knew that even if he could capture El Peñon, he would have to fight another, perhaps more desperate, battle to seize the city, and he simply could not afford the kind of fight that an approach from the east would necessitate. Discretion had to dictate whatever strategy he devised, for his paramount concern had to be preserving his army. Santa Anna hoped that Scott would batter his army against his defensive works, but although Scott indeed was willing to use his army as a battering ram, he realized that he could take that chance only as a means of gaining entry into the city itself.[10]

If El Peñon could not be attacked in flank, could the entire position be turned by swinging around it? To answer that question, he sent Lieutenants Beauregard and George McClellan, along with Mason and Stevens, out to conduct reconnaissance in front of Mexicalzingo on August 13. If he could seize that town, he could bypass El Peñon entirely. Scott even accompanied this group part of the way, stopping at Chalco to consult with Worth. He told his division commander that he had reconnaissance parties out, and although he had not yet decided on a course of action, he would do so by August 15. He then instructed Worth to send out some of his own officers to examine the Chalco route. He remained at Worth's headquarters an hour, and before leaving, he assured his division commander that he would be prudent and cautious in planning his advance on the city. "[I]f a place could be taken, it should be done with the minimum loss of life." Scott told Worth that Scott would hold "himself responsible" for unnecessary casualties.[11]

Meanwhile, Beauregard and party found that Mexicalzingo was also well fortified and strongly defended by infantry and artillery, although it was not as strong a position as El Peñon. And like El Peñon, the surrounding water and wetland made the only practical approach along a raised causeway. Furthermore, the road leading to Mexicalzingo could be fired on by the guns atop El Peñon. However, they believed that the town's location would make it more difficult for Santa Anna to reinforce. The Mexicalzingo option would also be difficult, but what appeared to trouble Scott most was that, like at El Peñon, if the position could be taken, the remaining distance to the city would be along an exposed causeway; thus the army's location, after a potentially tough fight, would still be unfavorable. That fact notwithstanding, Scott was leaning toward the Mexicalzingo approach by the fourteenth.[12]

That afternoon, Colonel James Duncan, an artillery officer whom Worth had sent to scout the Chalco route, returned and reported that there were no enemy troops along the road and that with some work, the road was serviceable. Worth wrote a note recommending that approach, and he immediately sent it with Duncan to report to the commanding general at Ayotla. Duncan's party went about as far as had Lee and Beauregard two days earlier, and they essentially confirmed what they had previously reported to Scott—that the road could be used, but with some difficulty. Scott had harbored misgivings about attacking Mexicalzingo all along and considered it the lesser of two evils. Duncan's report prompted him to reconsider, and after doing so, he returned to his original plan. So on August 15, he ordered the army to march to San Agustin via the Chalco route, thus bypassing both El Peñon and Mexicalzingo. Unaware of Scott's original plan, Worth and Duncan incorrectly assumed that Duncan's findings had opened an entirely new possibility for the army. They concluded that the march to San Agustin resulted solely from their recommendations, and they felt slighted later when the commanding general's official reports did not acknowledge their contribution. As it became clear that taking the southern approach was one of the decisive moves of the campaign, they adamantly sought to claim the credit. Duncan was quiet, obedient, and reliable, and many regarded him as one of the best artillerists in the army, but his reconnaissance, while important, did not add materially to what Scott already knew.[13]

Scott's decision meant that he would be leaving fortified positions in his rear, which was a violation of the accepted mode of conducting a campaign. However, because Scott had cut off his own line of communication, he in effect had no rear to worry about. An earlier decision to maintain an open line back to the coast would have rendered this course of action inadvisable, if not impossible. He once again did the unexpected by shifting the battle front to an area that his opponent had not anticipated and had even believed to be impractical. In so doing, he turned two enemy positions by marching around them, "thus leaving the enemy to ruminate on the beauty of their works & the immense labour & expense it had cost them, without the pleasure of firing a gun."[14]

On August 15, Worth's division, followed by Pillow's, led the way around the southern edge of Lakes Chalco and Xochimilco with the engineer company and a five-hundred-man work detail to clear the way. At the same time,

Twiggs's and Quitman's divisions advanced from Ayotla toward El Peñon to mask the army's true movement and hold Mexican troops east of the city. Next day, Twiggs and Quitman turned and followed the lead divisions along the Chalco route—a reversal that confused some of the volunteers. Such a sweeping flank march with his entire army would have violated one of Henri Jomini's rules, except that the lakes offered an insurmountable barrier completely covering the American flank as it moved to the city's south side. On the sixteenth and seventeenth, the army closed ranks in order to better protect the wagon train, but frequent delays in Pillow's division proved annoying to the units behind it and made it impossible for it to remain close to those in its front. Despite Scott's effort to tighten up his units, his army of almost 11,000 and its supply train of a thousand wagons stretched for twelve miles.[15]

The ruse did not last long. When a frustrated Santa Anna learned that the Americans were en route to San Agustin, he immediately began to shift units to the southwest. By the time Scott's army began to arrive at the intersection where the Acapulco Road runs north to the capital, hundreds of Mexican laborers were busy with picks and shovels building fortifications west of Xochimilco. Anchored by the town of San Antonio, the enemy hastily built an impressive line of breastworks and gun emplacements that stretched across a two-mile-wide neck of flat land between the lake and a lava field. Called the Pedregal, this lava bed consisted of black, jagged rocks and crevices that extended for about three miles across. By Lieutenant William S. Walker's account, it looked like "an ocean petrified in a storm."[16] This geographic anomaly could be traversed only with great difficulty on foot, and not at all on horseback or with artillery. It protected one of the Mexican flanks at San Antonio, while the lake shielded the other.

On Wednesday the eighteenth, Scott ordered Worth to turn his division at San Agustin and push north toward San Antonio to ascertain the enemy's location and strength. With Edwin Sumner's Second Dragoons leading the way, they pressed forward two miles along the Acapulco Road. "Grand" and "impressive" was the way one soldier described their march along the "beautiful avenue." When ordered to halt, they knew they were close to San Antonio but could not yet see the town. Worth ordered his infantry to rest while the dragoons advanced to reconnoiter the Mexican line. Captain Seth B. Thornton was a member of Sumner's unit, and he had been a participant in the war literally from the day it began. On April 25 of the previous year, he had led an American patrol into an ambush along the Rio Grande—the act that had precipitated the war. He was captured that day but later exchanged. On this day, Thornton rode forward with the dragoons to examine the enemy lines at San Antonio. He had ventured forward somewhat carelessly and was sitting with one leg over the pommel of his saddle when two heavy guns shattered the silence. An 18-pound shot struck him in the body, killing him instantly. The ball "tore him to pieces," and as Lieutenant Ralph Kirkham put it, he "probably did not know what killed him." According to Robert Anderson, the shot took "off his arm, and a good deal of his breast & side." Comrades carried his "mutilated body" to the rear and buried him on the side of the road.[17]

Worth's lead brigade immediately formed into battle line as a precaution despite being behind a cornfield and still unable to see anything. The other brigade remained on the road. When a group of skirmishers crept forward and peered out the other side of a cornfield, they were surprised at what they saw. Across a thousand yards of marsh, they saw a line of fieldworks running from building to building with sandbag parapets stacked on each roof. Thousands of soldiers and civilians were piling dirt here and carrying sandbags there to create a long line of connected forts that completely dominated the approach to the town. A large number of lancers sat on their mounts in the road watching the Americans. Now taking a more cautious approach, Worth sent engineers Mason, Stevens, Tower, and Smith forward to survey the enemy line. Mason crept forward to a nearby church, climbed up into the steeple, and looked in vain for a way to get around to the Mexican rear. All of the engineers came back and reported that the unusually strong position could not be flanked.[18]

While the engineers continued their dangerous work, Worth pulled the rest of his division back 1,500 yards and awaited orders. His men located a nearby hacienda that was both magnificent and deserted—just the right combination for curious and hungry soldiers. The hacienda was within sight and range of the Mexicans, who soon opened a sporadic fire on the Americans. The soldiers explored the estate but were careful to dodge or take cover in an effort to avoid the enemy shot and shells. "Keep one eye on the muzzles of the 'big guns,'" the officers warned as the men roamed about. They quickly discovered that the establishment was a dairy farm owned by a wealthy Spaniard who had fled so quickly that "all the valuables were left behind." William Austine recounted in a letter to his cousin how "we milked the cows and of course drank the milk for our services, and seriously thought of eating the animals themselves before quitting the premises." The artillery fire continued throughout the day, and whenever one of the men, peering around the corner of a building at the enemy line, saw a puff of smoke belch from a cannon's mouth, he would shout "jump" and everyone would take cover. Worth's men held this position through the night.[19]

Meanwhile, the impetuous and foul-mouthed Davy Twiggs was struggling to bring up the rear with his division on the south side of the lakes. He heard when the firing erupted in Worth's front and became impatient lest his chief rival get ahead of him in battlefield exploits. So he diligently pressed his men forward, hoping to get into position to join the fight, but his column was hopelessly snarled on the narrow road. Upon investigation, he discovered that the bottleneck was the result of a single broken-down wagon. Twiggs exploded with fury, and he shouted expletives until his face turned red. "Here I am . . . lying in the road, firing ahead and me unable to go on," and all because of an "old waggon not worth two dollars." He condemned the wagon to everlasting damnation, then yelled at the driver, "Why the hell don't you throw it into the ditch?"[20]

While these events unfolded on the eighteenth, Lee and Beauregard had been busy west of San Agustin. Along with Captain Philip Kearny's First Dragoons and an infantry escort, they spent the day scouting along an old mule path that ran along the southern edge of the Pedregal. They pushed along until they came to the southwest edge of the lava field, and there they ascended a hill called Zacatepec, the highest point in the area. The excellent location gave them a clear view of the San Angel Road that they had heard locals talk about during the previous days. It came up from the south and ran through the villages of Contreras, Padierna, and San Angel, all the while skirting the western edge of the Pedregal before bending around its northern edge and running into the Acapulco Road. The two engineers immediately discerned Mexican soldiers moving along the road—not many, but enough to confirm an enemy presence west of the Pedregal. Looking straight ahead, or due west, they saw more Mexicans preparing a defensive position on the high ground behind the village of Padierna. Almost as quickly as the engineers appeared on the hill, a body of Mexican lancers opened fire on the dragoons that accompanied them. Despite the enemy's greater number, Lieutenant Richard Ewell spurred his mount and led his platoon in an attack across the rugged terrain. After failing to swing around behind the lancers, the dragoons dismounted and fought as infantry until the enemy retreated. Then, having gathered all the information they needed, the Americans retired back to San Agustin.[21]

The Mexican troops that Lee and Beauregard had seen belonged to General Gabriel Valencia, commander of the army of the north. Santa Anna had ordered him to take positions so as to block the American advance from San Agustin, which he had done. By the seventeenth, Valencia had wisely placed troops in San Angel to block a move on the western side of the Pedregal, but by the eighteenth, he was unwisely moving his men further south and away from the bulk of the Mexican army to a location near Padierna. Having chosen favorable high ground behind the town, he intended to dig in and create an impregnable defensive line. This was the activity that Lee and Beauregard

Fighting around the Pedregal. From Donald S. Frazier, ed., *The United States and Mexico at War* (New York: Macmillan, 1998). Reprinted by permission of The Gale Group.

had witnessed from Zacatepec, although they mistook Padierna for Contreras. It was a mistake that others repeated, and one that would permanently and inaccurately label the action at Padierna as the Battle of Contreras. By moving that far south, Valencia was somewhat isolated and would need cooperation from Santa Anna to successfully hold the San Angel Road. Such was impossible, for Santa Anna and Valencia disliked and distrusted each other. When Santa Anna realized the peril that Valencia had placed himself in, he ordered him, on the night of the eighteenth, to withdraw to San Angel. Valencia refused.[22]

That night, Scott summoned his officers and engineers to discuss the army's next move. He listened to the reports of his engineers, one by one. Mason argued for an assault on San Antonio, which he believed would be successful if infantry could pick their way through the eastern edge of the Pedregal and attack the enemy in flank. Lee believed that the path he had traveled that day could be widened, cleared, and made accessible to infantry and artillery. He argued for an advance to the San Angel Road, which was not as heavily defended, and an advance up the western side of the Pedregal. Scott relied heavily on his staff officers and engineers, and he considered their advice carefully, but he had learned to place particular weight on Lee's assessment because of the captain's skillful insights. According to Lieutenant Raphael Semmes of the navy, who was serving on Worth's staff, Lee possessed "a mind which has no superior" among the engineers, and he "advised [Scott] with a judgment, tact, and discretion worthy of all praise. His talent for topography was peculiar, and he seemed to receive impressions intuitively, which it cost other men much labor to acquire." But Scott did not dismiss Mason's recommendation. In fact, he ordered work parties from Pillow's division to cut a road along the southern edge of the lava field, but he issued no definitive orders about the direction the army would take. His desire was to turn the enemy at San Antonio, but he would wait to see how the situation developed.[23]

Next day, several hundred men of Pillow's division began work widening the mule path to Padierna into a road, while the remainder of the division, along with that of Twiggs, advanced to cover the work party. Meanwhile, Worth held his ground so as to threaten San Antonio, and Quitman unhappily sat idle at San Agustin, protecting the wagon train and supplies. Although the ground south of the Pedregal was rough and had occasional rock outcroppings, the work of improvising a road went well all morning. They had covered over a mile when Pillow received instructions from Scott. The commanding general had made his headquarters in a hotel in San Agustin, which was the tallest building in the town. From the roof, he had watched Pillow's progress, and he also could see what the undulation of the ground hid from Pillow's view. About a mile in front of the work detail, Scott observed enemy troops in the vicinity of Padierna, where Lee and Beauregard had seen the activity the day before. He warned Pillow that the Mexicans appeared to be gathered in strength in his front and directed him to avoid a general engagement so that the work on the road could be completed.[24]

When the road work reached the vicinity of the hill called Zacatepec, Pillow ascended it and looked west, getting his first look at what lay beyond the Pedregal. For six hundred yards, the ground, broken by jagged rocks, crevices, and defiles, sloped steadily down to a ravine through which a swift stream passed, and running roughly adjacent to it was the San Angel Road. Hidden among the rock fissures were two hundred Mexicans, waiting to pick off American soldiers as they advanced. Upon reaching the ravine and the road, the lava rocks ended, but the terrain remained rugged. At the road stood the hamlet of Padierna, which the Americans repeatedly referred to as Contreras, and there Pillow could see enemy soldiers milling about. Beyond Padierna the ground sloped up gently, and several hundreds yards from the road—perhaps a mile from where Pillow stood—was the high ground that Valencia had so painstakingly fortified. There he had positioned twenty-two guns, including 16-pound and 24-pound artillery along with howitzers. Protecting the guns were seven thousand well-entrenched infantry along with many lancers. He considered his position unassailable, and it should have been. The rough, broken ground, with its deep ravines, made it impossible for cavalry and artillery to negotiate and exceedingly difficult for infantry to maneuver.[25]

Pillow's immediate concern was the Mexican skirmishers scattered among the rocks on the slope leading down to the San Angel Road. Fearing for the safety of his approaching work parties, he decided to try to push them back toward Padierna. So at about 1 o'clock in the afternoon, Pillow ordered Major William W. Loring's Mounted Rifles forward to clear the enemy troops from his front. Two companies (dismounted) went into the rocks and crevices, exchanging musket fire with the Mexican skirmishers as Valencia opened fire with his artillery. Loring ordered three more of his companies forward, and after an extended skirmish, they succeeded in scattering the enemy and taking possession of not only the slope but of Padierna as well.[26] To counter the Mexican artillery fire, Pillow began to feed more men into the fight, and he ordered Twiggs to hurry his division up the newly cut road, thus bringing on the general engagement that Scott had hoped to avoid. Pillow ordered artillery into the ravine to fire on Valencia's position, and he needed Twiggs's men to cover the guns and hold on to the town.

Twiggs arrived at the front a half hour after Loring's Rifles descended on Padierna, and he immediately sent Brigadier General Persifor Smith's brigade down the slope to cover the guns that Pillow had ordered forward. At the same time, his other brigade under Colonel Bennet Riley turned northwest and began to cross the southwest edge of the Pedregal in an attempt to take up a blocking position between Valencia's troops and San Angel. The artillery that Pillow brought up was Captain John Magruder's battery from Twiggs's division and from his own division, Lieutenant Franklin Callender's mountain howitzers and a rocket company under Lieutenant Jesse Reno. Valencia laughed in disbelief when he received a report of American artillery pieces moving across the lava field. "The birds couldn't cross that Pedregal," he scoffed, but his demeanor changed when shells began to fall on his position.[27]

The Voltigeurs had also come forward and were atop Zacatepec with General Pillow in the early afternoon. From this vantage point, Lieutenant William S. Walker, nephew of the Secretary of the Treasury, Robert J. Walker, could see for miles around. Looking north, he peered across the tall, jagged, black rock of the Pedregal and remarked to a fellow officer that it looked "like hell burnt out." Beyond that and about seven miles away, he caught a glimpse of Mexico City "crowned with her antique towers." Off to the west, fifteen hundred yards away, he could see the enemy works commanding the road down below. He watched as Twiggs's division marched forward, "a forest of bayonets," Smith's men scurrying down the slope toward Padierna to provide cover for Magruder's guns, and Riley's troops angling off to the north and scattering as they worked their way over the deep crevices and through the rocks that jutted out of the ground, some as tall as a man. For a few brief moments, the Voltigeurs watched as the panorama of battle unfolded beneath them. Then their brigade commander, Brigadier General George Cadwalader, rode up with orders. Looking north along the road, Pillow had seen Mexican reinforcements coming down from San Angel, and he wanted Cadwalader to take his brigade through the Pedregal and join Riley's troops beyond the road near San Geronimo. Cadwalader, turning to his men, shouted, "Voltigeurs, I am going to lay out something for you to do! Will you do it?" Straightway he ordered them to follow Riley's brigade through the Pedregal and join that unit along the San Angel Road.[28]

It was after 2:30 P.M. when Cadwalader began his flanking move with the Voltigeurs and more than an hour after Riley's brigade started across the Pedregal. Most accounts portray Riley's flank march that afternoon as Gideon Pillow's initiative because he was the one who issued the order. However, Lieutenant Isaac Stevens of the engineers claimed that he himself pressed on Twiggs the need to flank the Mexicans to the north or on Valencia's left. "Attack his left, you cut him off from his reserves," Stevens said to Twiggs. The general concurred with the engineer's assessment. Stevens then went to Riley and personally delivered Twiggs's orders for him to cut the road north of Padierna. Pillow later heaped praise on himself for the tactical genius he supposedly displayed on this day, while the veteran Twiggs remained angry for being subordinated to an inexperienced politico. As a major general, Pillow was the senior officer and technically in charge of the operations, and he certainly was aware of all the troops' movements. However, if Isaac Stevens's account is accurate, after the battle commenced, Pillow was more an observer than an innovator.[29]

Magruder and his comrades accomplished the impossible by getting their guns down the rugged slope and into position along the San Angel Road while under fire from the enemy guns. Major James Smith, the supervising engineer, had suggested putting the artillery in the ravine as the best possible location to shield them from enemy fire. However, it was Captain Lee, who had been directing the road work all morning and had actually gone forward with the first two companies of Rifles, who charted a path for the artillery and found the most favorable location for the guns. When Magruder arrived with his four-gun battery, he sent two of the guns to the left under Lieutenant Preston Johnston and the other two up the road to the right under Lieutenant Thomas Jackson. Between those two positions, he placed Callender's little howitzers. The American artillery was decidedly outmatched by the heavier and more numerous Mexican guns, and they quickly began to take a beating. Jackson realized that his guns were having little effect on the enemy, but although his men were falling all around, he never considered withdrawing.[30]

The infantry fared no better. "The enemy cannon caused much destruction in our ranks," wrote Guy Carleton, "and grape shot flew about us at a terrible rate." Lieutenant George McClellan had two horses shot from under him on this portion of the battlefield that afternoon. Some men became pinned down among the lava rocks, while others made it to the ravine and crossed the road and the stream, only to get stuck on the far bank, unable to go farther. Their instincts told them to push forward and attack the enemy position on the hill, but the advance became completely stalled.[31]

Lee was still with the artillery an hour later when young Preston, the nephew of Colonel Joseph E. Johnston, fell mortally wounded. A solid shot had taken off his leg, and he died a few hours later. Magruder ordered Jackson to move left, locate Johnston's two guns, and take command. However, the deadly duel did not last much longer. The mountain howitzers were soon knocked out, and Smith's infantry could not get across the ravine to directly threaten the enemy position. Smith, seeing that a direct approach would not work, began to move the majority of his brigade off to the right as Magruder tried to provide covering fire with his guns. Soon Magruder pulled his own men back to safety. An officer in the Rifle Regiment asserted that the casualties around Padierna and the consequent American withdrawal resulted from "the shameful mismanagement of the fool Pillow." Lieutenant D. H. Hill, whose negative opinion of Pillow predated the battle, thought that "of all the absurd things that the ass Pillow has ever done this was the most silly. Human stupidity can go no farther than this, the ordering of six and twelve pounders to batter a Fort garnished with long sixteens, twenty-fours and heavy mortars!!"[32]

When Scott saw that a full-scale battle was developing in Pillow's front, he made ready to go there himself. The ever-ready Quitman also wanted to follow the sound of the guns, so he went to Scott and said that his passive assignment guarding the supply train had "cast a gloom" over his men. He protested that the volunteers had not been given an opportunity to distinguish themselves since the campaign began. But his protests were a bit too harsh, and when an agitated Scott "showed considerable excitement," Quitman apologized and excused himself. Before leaving San Agustin, however, Scott changed his mind and ordered Brigadier General James Shields's brigade of

Quitman's division to reinforce Pillow. It was some time after 2 o'clock when Scott headed west to find Pillow.[33]

Meanwhile, Riley's and Cadwalader's brigades struggled to work their way through the hazardous Pedregal. In and out of ravines they went, jumping from rock to rock, scrambling to keep their feet under them, all producing "considerable fatigue." As they reached the western side of this maze of rocks, they filtered out and crossed the San Angel Road near San Geronimo. The units had become badly scattered and separated while picking their way through the rocks, and the first group to emerge numbered perhaps four hundred. They were on Valencia's flank and in position to cut him off from the capital and the rest of Santa Anna's army. However, when they looked north, they discovered that their situation was more perilous than Valencia's, for eight hundred yards away, they saw an endless column of Mexicans, infantry and lancers, advancing toward them. The force, seven thousand strong and commanded by Santa Anna himself, was on its way from San Angel to reinforce Valencia at Padierna. The Americans, although greatly outnumbered, were resigned to their fate and determined to fight. They quickly and quietly wheeled about and formed for battle while the Mexicans prepared to attack. As their bugles blew, the Mexican soldiers shouted and cheered, but across the way, the Americans, with only a few hundred men, held their position in cold, determined silence.[34]

Santa Anna's menacing force grew as his lines formed. About half a mile separated the two sides, but the imposing Mexican lines stretched across a seven-hundred-yard front. The lancers were in formation across a ridge, and in front of them, in their multicolored uniforms, were several thousand infantry. Two coincidences probably prevented a Mexican attack and saved the small band of Americans from being cut to pieces. One was the fact that as they hastily formed into battle lines, their left happened to extend into an orchard, which partially obscured the weakness of their numbers. The other occurred only moments later when additional U.S. troops arrived—those of Persifor Smith's brigade.

After being stymied earlier in the afternoon while supporting Magruder's guns in front of Padierna, Smith had taken it upon himself to move most of his brigade north in an attempt to outflank Valencia. Guided by Captain Lee, Smith's men began to work their way through the edge of the Pedregal in search of a safe place to pop out of the rocks and cross the road. When they did so near San Geronimo, they could see the Mexican force gathering to the north, so Smith got them across the road and stream and hustled them to the outskirts of the village just in time to help ward off Santa Anna's attack. The isolated little band was relieved to see not only the additional troops but also Smith, the Princeton-educated lawyer turned soldier. Popular and respected,

Smith had won a brevet to brigadier general at the Battle of Monterey the previous year and would be breveted major general for his conduct on this day. Beauregard believed that Smith possessed skill and judgment that was second only to Scott's, and some of Riley's men reportedly cried when they learned that Smith had joined them. Confidence rose as the remnants of Riley's and Cadwalader's brigades continued to arrive, along with the Fifteenth Infantry Regiment from Brigadier General Franklin Pierce's brigade ordered over to San Geronimo in midafternoon. As the senior officer on the field, Smith now commanded the bulk of three brigades totaling 3,300 men.[35]

For the time being, the Americans lost sight of their original goal of attacking Valencia's left flank. Necessity forced them to focus their attention on the larger body of Mexicans to their north. Although the Mexicans had opted not to attack, they remained in position half a mile away with their bands playing and soldiers yelling. At one point, Santa Anna came out on horseback and pranced back and forth in front of his lines with his staff in tow. "We calculated upon a fight to a certainty, but were disappointed," remembered Walker. After Smith sized up the situation, he made preparations to take the offensive. Riley's brigade would swing around and attack Santa Anna on the left, while Cadwalader hit him on the right. However, by the time all was ready, it was late in the afternoon, and with darkness approaching, Smith ordered his men simply to maintain their defensive posture. At dusk, Santa Anna left his lancers and artillery in place but withdrew the rest of his force to the comforts of San Angel.[36]

It was about 4:00 in the afternoon when an angry Scott arrived on the western edge of the Pedregal and joined Pillow atop Zacatepec. In violation of Scott's orders, Pillow had brought on a battle, and as historian James W. Pohl described it, he had gotten "himself in a box." A frontal assault on Valencia's fortified and concentrated position violated the precepts of warfare, of which Pillow was ignorant. However, because Pillow was who he was, Scott did not reprimand him. Beauregard thought that Pillow had mismanaged the affair all afternoon, that the situation was "confusion worse confounded," and that by the time Scott arrived, the army was facing a "crisis." Scott, however, did not seem overly alarmed, and for several minutes, he calmly surveyed his surroundings with a discerning eye. According to Beauregard, "he beheld in dismay his forces in the d—dest *scattertion* that perhaps he or any other general ever saw before."[37] He could see the remnants of American units sprinkled across his front among the rocks all the way down to the ravine and Valencia's imposing position beyond Padierna. Scanning right, he saw the wooded area that hid San Geronimo, where three of his brigades sat isolated. He knew that the enemy was in force around San Angel and that the road through that town and on to Coyoacán was the key to turning the enemy out of San

Antonio. He also knew that a large portion of his army was in something of a vice at San Geronimo, sitting between two enemy forces, each of which was stronger than the Americans between them. The potential for disaster was great.

Great generals can bend events to their will and turn adverse circumstances into a positive outcome. Combat is always tense for a commander, but Scott showed no fear as he soberly examined the disposition of the troops and decided what needed to be done. Indeed, he saw the situation as a possible opportunity, so he ordered Brigadier General James Shields's brigade from Quitman's division to cross the Pedregal and join the other three brigades. He hoped that the additional numbers would provide the San Geronimo force with adequate strength to ensure its security while preventing reinforcements from reaching Valencia. Scott knew how to create situations on the battlefield that were most likely to lead to success, and he also knew his opponent and what he could get away with—a skill at which Lee would excel in the Civil War. Before returning to his headquarters at San Agustin, the commanding general promised to send Worth's and the remainder of Quitman's divisions in the morning to help force the issue with Valencia, and finally he suggested to Pillow that he and Twiggs might want to proceed over to San Geronimo and join their troops.[38]

After dark, Generals Smith and Cadwalader met with Captain Lee in San Geronimo to plan their next move. A steady rain had begun to fall, making it a miserable and unusually dark night. Smith knew that he could not just sit until dawn and react to whatever his opponent did; rather, he needed to take the initiative. Engineers had been reconnoitering the area around the village, and they reported that a ravine to the south appeared to lead to the rear of Valencia's position. Armed with this valuable information, Smith knew what to do. In the middle of the night, he would march his troops around Valencia's force and attack it in the rear at dawn, hoping to defeat Valencia quickly, before the San Angel force to the north could respond. It was a move forced out of desperation. A demonstration by the troops that remained in front of Padierna would be most beneficial to Smith's plans if only he could get word to Scott. So Lee volunteered to work his way back through the Pedregal and report Smith's plan to the commanding general, and at 8:00 P.M., he set out with a few other men. In the Pedregal, he ran into men of Shields's brigade, who were on their way to reinforce Smith. They had left San Agustin at 3:00 that afternoon and were, as Private William Johnson put it, working their way "through the confines of Purgitory . . . [in an] incesant Rain." Lee assigned one of his comrades to direct Shields back to San Geronimo before continuing his trek through the sharp rocks. In the blackness of the night, he was guided by an occasional glimpse of Zacatepec afforded by unpredictable flashes of lightning. That Lee was able to navigate the broken terrain in pitch darkness, feeling his way among the rocks, was remarkable.[39]

Meanwhile, Santa Anna had missed his best opportunity to inflict a damaging blow on Scott's army. Combined with Valencia's force, he had over 13,000 men west of the Pedregal with which he could have crushed the 3,300 or so Americans at San Geronimo. But Santa Anna let the opportunity slip away, he declined to attack on his own, and he gave up on trying to link his column with Valencia's. After falling back to San Angel with the bulk of his troops, Santa Anna ordered Valencia to march north with his Padierna force and join him. But Valencia was full of himself on the night of the nineteenth, thinking that he had won a spectacular victory that afternoon. He refused to obey. Valencia tried in vain to get Santa Anna to do something about the Americans lodged at San Geronimo, but the Mexican commander opted to remain inactive, leaving his subordinate to fend for himself. Two enormous egos that refused to cooperate with each other would spell disaster for the Mexicans at daybreak.[40]

Scott's headquarters at San Agustin was a buzz of activity late into the night. His concern for the 40 percent of his army at San Geronimo induced him to send several staff officers through the Pedregal in an effort to ascertain their situation. None of them could find their way through, but late in the evening, Lee arrived and outlined Smith's plan to attack Valencia from the rear. Scott liked what he heard, gave his approval, and promised to provide the necessary diversion in front of Padierna at dawn. Sometime after Lee arrived, Twiggs and Pillow also showed up, having failed in an attempt to comply with Scott's desire for them to join their troops at San Geronimo. At dusk, Pillow had approached Isaac Stevens of the engineers and asked, "in much perplexity," to be guided across the lava field to San Geronimo. Stevens, however, was unable to comply, so Pillow and Twiggs struck out on their own. The darkness made it impossible for them to know where they were going, and the rain made for slippery footing on the jagged rocks. Twiggs fell in one of the crevices, injuring his foot, and to add insult to injury, they got lost. At length they decided to retrace their steps back to Zacatepec, and from there, they made their way to San Agustin.[41]

It was after midnight when Scott sent orders for Worth to be ready to move his men before daylight in clockwise motion around the Pedregal toward Padierna. If Smith's night march and dawn attack worked, he wanted Worth's division in striking distance to exploit circumstances. Scott then ordered the indefatigable Lee to go to the far end of the Pedregal and prepare Pierce's brigade and the remains of various units for the dawn diversionary attack in Valencia's front, and he directed Twiggs to accompany him. It was 1:00 A.M. when Lee, assisting the crippled Twiggs, left San Agustin.

Scott instructed Pillow to remain at headquarters for the night. From Pillow's perspective, it was probably a well-deserved opportunity for rest, but from Scott's view, it was likely just a diplomatic way of keeping Pillow out of the way when the real action started. Scott tried to handle Polk's friend with great care and tried to make him feel important without giving him too much responsibility. Everyone knew that Pillow was the president's informant, so there was a price to pay by having him with the army and staying on favorable terms. Thus far, Scott had managed the situation admirably. He had given Pillow an important but secondary role at Cerro Gordo, away from the decisive action. He had included Pillow in important conferences like the discussion regarding the bribery scheme. Clearly if Scott and Trist had pursued that course of action, the commanding general needed the cover that Pillow's acquiescence would provide. And just that morning, Scott had given the Tennessean an important role in preparing a road for the army's advance, but with instructions to avoid a general engagement. Now that a battle was in the offing, Scott successfully but gingerly removed Pillow from a crucial decision-making role.

It was a miserable night, difficult for sleeping. In Worth's division in front of San Antonio, word arrived of an American defeat that afternoon at Padierna. The same false reports had made it into the Mexican ranks along the San Antonio line, prompting cheers and celebration that kept John Sedgwick of the Second Artillery, and doubtless many other Americans, awake all night. Across the Pedregal, Twiggs, limping and exhausted, sat down near Zacatepec to rest, leaving a sleepless Lee to organize Pierce's brigade, a portion of the Mounted Rifles, and the remains of Magruder's battery for their dawn attack in Valencia's front. There men huddled together in the open with the cold rain beating down on them. Lieutenant Thomas Jackson was among them. He had received his baptism by fire that day and impressed both Magruder and Twiggs with his coolness in the heat of battle. Although it would be fourteen years before he would acquire the nickname "Stonewall," that was an apt description of his conduct in front of Padierna on August 19. He spent that night drenched to the bone, worrying that "the fire would not be hot enough for me to distinguish myself." At San Geronimo, some of the men found shelter in the village, but others remained outdoors. John Wilkins of the Third Infantry found it impossible to sleep in the downpour. He and Israel Bush Richardson shared a blanket that night. First they put it under them so that they would not have to lie on the wet ground, but it quickly became soaked. Then they put it on top of them, seeking protection and warmth, but it provided neither. The night was full of misery for American soldiers all around the Pedregal, but back in San Agustin, Gideon Pillow slid into a soft, dry bed and went to sleep.[42]

CHAPTER TEN

The Battle of the Pedregal

Padierna and Churubusco

*The road and its vicinity on both sides, for most of the three miles,
were covered with dead and dying, bodies without heads, arms and
legs, and disfigured in every horrible way! Oh, it was awful and
never can I forget this day!*
—Ralph Kirkham, Sixth Infantry Regiment

The rain continued to beat down on the weary soldiers at San Geronimo, but
some had dozed off when their officers came around to awaken them at 2:00
A.M. They had hunkered down a few hours earlier cold, wet, and hungry, and
without any knowledge of General Smith's plan for a dawn attack. Warren
Lothrop of the Company of Engineers was roused by his lieutenant, who
told him that the enemy guns had "to be taken before Sunrise." As Lothrop
cleared his head, he "thought of home & then thought of what I was A going
to do & . . . I thought of my musket & put on A new cap." Captain Moses Barnard of the Voltigeurs was awakened when his sergeant shook him and told
him to get up: "the troops are moving off by the left flank." Quickly and quietly, men in wet uniforms arose, got their soaked gear together, and prepared
to march as word of Smith's intentions filtered through the ranks.[1]

When Smith had decided the previous evening to attack Valencia's force
to the south, he worried most about Santa Anna to the north. He anticipated
that Santa Anna would return to San Geronimo and attack at dawn—maybe
earlier. So Smith had taken precautions. He posted pickets so close to the
enemy lines that they could hear voices from their camp all night. He also
sent the First Artillery to occupy a hacienda that was favorably positioned to
defend the road, and during the night, the unit captured over a dozen enemy
soldiers who tried to pass. General James Shields's arrival during the evening
had eased his mind, for now Shields's New York and South Carolina volunteer regiments would remain at San Geronimo and cover the back of Smith's
flanking column. Shields's men would also be in position, should Smith's
attack succeed in routing Valencia's troops, to block their retreat north to
San Angel.[2] Perhaps the greatest contribution that Shields made that evening, however, was his agreement to allow Smith, his junior in rank, to retain

command and see his plan through to completion. The Mexican army failed because its senior officers did not coordinate and cooperate, but the American army succeeded because its senior officers did.

The march to their point of attack began around 3:00 A.M., but it was a difficult undertaking. Bennett Riley's brigade (Second Infantry, Seventh Infantry, Fourth Artillery) led the way because his men—about a thousand—constituted the main assault group. George Cadwalader's brigade (Eleventh Infantry, Fourteenth Infantry, Voltigeurs) followed Riley's, but because his regiments consisted largely of raw recruits, his men were slow to move. Finally Smith's brigade, temporarily commanded by Major Justin Dimick, brought up the rear. The extreme darkness made it difficult to keep the units together. It was "darker than any night I had every seen," remembered Barnard. "The night was black as a wolf's mouth," thought William Walker, and "You could not recognize a man a yard off." Lieutenant D. H. Hill recalled that it was "scarcely possible to see the hand before the face." Footing was treacherous as well. The muddy ground was slippery, and in some places, water was ankle deep. "Silently we moved off plunging into mud & water at every step," remembered Barnard. Another described the clay under foot in the trough of the ravine that was as slippery as "soft soap." Major John Gardner of Riley's brigade summarized the difficulties of the march in his battle report: "the darkness of the night, the flooding rain, the clayey and precipitous nature of the ground, and the intricacies of the way baffled the best intentions." Despite the obstacles, the ridges and ravines concealed their march.[3]

To try to keep the ranks closed, Smith ordered the men to stay "within touch of each other," and that worked pretty well except when someone allowed too much distance to come between himself and the person in front. When that happened in the Fourth Artillery Regiment, an entire company got separated from the rest of the brigade. Cadwalader's slow start created a space between his brigade and Riley's, which resulted in some of his men losing their way. An engineer had to be detached to find them and put them back on track. The entire column was guided by the engineers, who had already been over the ground, with Lieutenant Zealous Tower taking the lead. The troops were halted on a few occasions, either to close gaps in the line or to allow the guides to get their bearings, and during those delays, some soldiers took the opportunity to remove damp charges from their muskets and replace them with fresh loads. Quietly and slowly, they continued their march around the Mexican left at a distance of eight hundred yards until they were directly behind them.[4]

The eastern sky was beginning to turn gray, and a light fog had replaced the rain as Smith's men neared their designated position for attack. But despite their stealth, their movements had not gone undetected. Mexican cavalry commander General Anastasio Torréjon had discovered and reported movement on the flank several hours earlier. Valencia had responded by detaching a strong force of infantry to face the rear "several hundred yards" from his main works, but surprisingly, he failed to assign pickets to the ravines and ridges that led to the back of his camp. He may have suspected that something was afoot, but by failing to take proper precautions, he ensured that the American attack would remain a surprise.[5]

It was daylight when Riley's men formed into two ranks in their concealed position, and after checking their muskets and taking off their knapsacks to lighten their load, they turned left to face east. The Voltigeurs and other units from Cadwalader's brigade got into position to follow Riley's first wave and support his right flank. Because Dimick's brigade (Smith's) brought up the rear, it was further north, but in an ideal position to come in on Riley's left. While the troops were aligning themselves, Smith had gone to the top of a nearby ridge, where he could see the enemy in his front. From there, he saw the detachment facing in his direction about halfway between his line and Valencia's main force, so he directed the Rifles along a concealed route to a flanking position near the Mexican detachment. Meanwhile, a mile to the east, beyond the Mexican position, the men of Pierce's brigade had been active for over an hour. They had scurried down the long, rocky slope of the Pedregal and were already drawing Valencia's attention toward Padierna.

All was ready at 6:00 A.M., and Smith ordered Riley's men up out of the ravine, where they remained momentarily, still shielded by a rise in the terrain. Then they proceeded forward until they were "in full view of the enemy." The Mexican advanced detachment fired a volley at them, only to be surprised when men of Major William W. Loring's Rifle Regiment rose from behind a ridge on their flank and fired at them from fifty yards. Riley's men also fired a volley at them, and they immediately broke to the rear to rejoin the main force. By now Riley's and Loring's men were in a full charge but still two or three hundred yards from their objective. "We rushed on to them yelling like so many Devils," Lothrop recalled. Two hundred yards behind them were the men of Cadwalader's brigade, who made up the second attack wave.[6]

Within Valencia's camp, there was sudden activity as his soldiers scampered about in surprise. The entire camp appeared to be in a "hubbub." "They seem not to have believed in the possibility or rather probability of an attack in the rear." They hastily improvised a defensive line that faced west and succeeded in turning two of their guns and opening fire with grape and canister. As Riley's spearhead smashed into their ranks, the Seventh Infantry and Rifle Regiment charged right into the Mexican guns. Enemies fired at each other from point-blank range, but hand-to-hand fighting quickly became the prevalent mode of combat. As the Voltigeurs approached the Mexican position a minute later, the enemy line still maintained enough integrity to fire a volley into the oncoming second wave. Nevertheless, the hilltop was already covered with Americans and Mexicans locked in close, desperate struggles: clubbing with musket butts, thrusting with bayonets, and slashing with sabers. Unit cohesion within Valencia's command quickly melted away as infantry and lancers became intermingled in the confusion. Within minutes, confusion turned to panic and panic to flight.[7]

Mexican troops ran in every direction, some of them "firing a farewell shot at the detested yankees" as they left the field. Pierce's troops around Padierna could see what was happening atop the ridge, knew what the pell-mell disorder within the Mexican camp meant, and charged up the hill from the east. Riley's Fourth Artillery, commanded by Major John L. Gardner, led a dash for the artillery pieces. While fighting hand to hand amid the guns, a Mexican soldier knocked Gardner's sword away with a musket, but just as he lurched forward with his bayonet, he was shot down by another American. The gunners spiked their pieces and joined their comrades in flight. The natural direction for the Mexican troops to flee was north toward the rest of their army and the safety of the capital, and many ran in that direction. However, General Smith had held the tail of his flanking column in reserve slightly north and still concealed in the ravine. These troops emerged and began to fire into the Mexican flank as they ran, and still further north, Shields's brigade, which had remained at San Geronimo to keep an eye on Santa Anna, was ideally situated to cut off their retreat. Shields had placed the volunteers of the Palmetto Regiment and the New York Regiment along the side of the road leading to San Angel, and they "opened a most destructive fire upon the mingled masses of Infantry and Cavalry."[8]

The typical American soldier took pride in bloodshed, whether it be the blood of friend or foe, as is borne out by the following comments. Several days after the successful charge, D. H. Hill wrote that he would "always feel proud to have commanded the company which suffered most severely." Warren Lothrop wrote to his family about his part in the battle, telling them that he fired his musket eleven times during the melee. "I know what affect A part of my shots had but I do not feel like boasting of it." Another soldier wrote home to tell his mother about the assault and the pursuit that followed. We "murdered the wretched enemy for 3 miles in retreat," he wrote. Then he gave a synopsis of his role in all of the battles. "I think I have killed personally about 10 but am unable to say of which rank as I fired at a column and had not time to show a preference. I think though I have blood enough on my hands to satisfy the largest patriotism."[9]

The field remained a dangerous place, with shots being fired all around, when Gardner leaned against one of the captured guns to catch his breath. Here and there, pockets of Mexicans still resisted; others were either surrendering or trying to evade capture. Amid the confusion, George McClellan, a West Point classmate, came up and, with a smile on his face, slapped Gardner on the back. Then he introduced his friend and fellow engineer Beauregard. The twenty-three-year-old Gardner would later serve as a general in the Civil War, like McClellan and Beauregard, but unlike the other two, a severe leg wound at First Bull Run would limit his role and relegate him to obscurity. The two guns they were standing next to, they later discovered, were the two that had been captured from the Fourth Artillery six months earlier at the Battle of Buena Vista when that unit was in Zachary Taylor's army.[10]

The battle quickly subsided, and most of the gunfire gradually shifted north as U.S. troops pursued Valencia and his disorganized mob toward San Angel. Nearby, General Persifor Smith looked at his watch then commented to his staff: "It has taken just seventeen minutes." The field was strewn with muskets, cartridge boxes, caps, and other accoutrements along with the dead and dying, and a trail of such accessories, although scattered in every direction, generally led north. While other units joined the pursuit, Riley's brigade rounded up prisoners. Fabian Brydolf, an Iowan and a sergeant serving in the Fifteenth Infantry, had lost his boots in the march around Valencia's flank. Writing about his experiences years later, he recalled that "my Shoes wher some waat large and stuck in the mud." He charged the enemy line barefooted, and after the battle, he found a dead Mexican officer, pulled off his boots, and tried them on. He discovered to his delight that "they fittet me to perfection. Such is War."[11]

Lee had followed Pierce's men from Padierna up the hill to the Mexican camp and arrived there just after the battle ended. He saw his friend Joe Johnston, who had stormed the position from the other direction with the Voltigeurs. Lee had been present the previous day near Padierna when Johnston's nephew, Preston, received his mortal wound while servicing Magruder's battery. Johnston was exuberant over the quick and decisive victory when Lee approached his old friend with a solemn look on his face. He extended his hand and told Johnston that his nephew had died during the night. Johnston slumped into the abandoned trenches, and his body "shivered with agony" as he wept. Preston was the son Joe Johnston never had, and Preston had faithfully nursed his uncle back to health after his Cerro Gordo wound. His nephew's death was a devastating blow. Five days later, Johnston wrote to his brother about the "full bitterness of grief" that he felt. "I loved him more than my own heart," Johnston wrote. Such is war.[12]

American losses were severe from Johnston's grieving perspective, but actually they were relatively few in number. Most accounts repeat Scott's statement in his battle report, which places American losses at sixty, but Riley, whose brigade led the charge and suffered most of the casualties, gave his losses as eighty-three killed and wounded. Mexican losses, however, were staggering—in fact, Valencia's force essentially ceased to exist. Seven hundred killed, over eight hundred captured, including four generals and eighty-eight officers, seven hundred pack mules, and twenty-two cannon, along with small arms and ammunition, all constituted the Mexican losses in personnel and matériel.[13]

The brief engagement at Padierna, typically called the Battle of Contreras, was only the beginning of a long day of fighting. By 7:00 A.M., scattered American units from Pillow's and Twiggs's division were pursuing the remnants of Valencia's shocked command toward San Angel. The Mexicans stopped and made a brief stand near San Geronimo before resuming their retreat through cornfields and ravines. Santa Anna, who had been reinforced during the night, made plans to push south again that morning in an effort to reestablish communications with Valencia. However, no sooner had he begun to venture forth from San Angel than he began to run into panicked Mexican soldiers streaming north. Now Santa Anna exploded with rage. He was angry at Valencia for not obeying his order to withdraw the previous day, and he ordered Valencia shot by the first person who found him. He took out his frustration on the retreating soldiers by striking them with his riding crop as they fled past him. At the moment, all he could do was assign Brigadier General Joaquín Rangel's brigade as a rear guard to delay the American pursuit while he tried to organize a new defensive line farther north.[14]

The Americans pursued the retreating Mexicans to San Angel, and Pillow and Twiggs soon joined their commands there. Pillow had arisen early and was crossing the southern edge of the Pedregal when the rout began. He joined Smith and Twiggs on the road north of Padierna, and the three generals fell in behind their men. When they arrived at San Angel, Pillow sent word to Scott that he would continue to press the enemy north. In the early morning, the commanding general was also on the move. Leaving San Agustin, he rode to Padierna, saw the littered landscape of battle and the groups of prisoners held under guard, then issued orders to take advantage of the circumstances that were unfolding. The previous night, Scott had instructed Quitman and Worth to march their men west at dawn so that he could throw the entire weight of his army at Valencia, but seeing the situation, he immediately sent orders to the two division commanders to turn their units around and head for San Antonio. In this three-day-old chess match, Scott had been probing and searching for the best way to get his army around natural and man-made obstacles of rock and enemy troops. Now an unexpected opportunity presented itself to turn the San Antonio defenders out of their position by having Worth and Quitman attack them in front while Pillow and Twiggs marched across the north of the Pedregal to trap them in a vice. Scott wanted to settle this day's affair by utilizing movement and position, an aspect of combat in which this author of a tactical manual excelled.

Before he followed the path of his men up the San Angel Road, he came across Lieutenant Beauregard. The commanding general knew that the young lieutenant was but one of a host of engineers who had once again played a crucial role in gathering intelligence, mapping roads, and locating enemy weaknesses. With pride and gratitude, he looked at the twenty-nine-year-old and said, "Young man, if I were not on horseback, I would embrace you." Then, turning to his staff, he exclaimed, "Gentlemen, if West Point had only produced the Corps of Engineers, the Country ought to be proud of that institution." The commanding general also came across members of the Fourth Artillery, complimenting the men in "the most extravagant manner." Then, having learned about the two brass guns that the regiment had repossessed, he asserted that the pieces should henceforth bear the inscription: "Lost by the 4th Artillery at Buena Vista without dishonor and recovered by the same with glory at Mexico."[15]

As Scott and his staff rode north along the road, he passed soldiers who stopped and cheered when they saw the commanding general. The men were exuberant about the ease with which they routed the enemy that morning. Reflecting a few days later, Lieutenant Roswell Ripley of Pillow's staff called it the "most glorious" victory the army had won to date. It seemed amazing that just the previous night, half of Scott's army was in peril of being crushed by two larger enemy forces, but in William Walker's words, "we extricated ourselves from a dangerous position before a superior foe by a brilliant victory."[16] Much of the credit belonged to brigade commanders who, through bold leadership, sought ways to translate a bad situation into success.

Winfield Scott also deserved acknowledgment for avoiding Santa Anna's traps and consistently placing his army in a position to exploit enemy mistakes. With each battle, respect for the commander rose. Lieutenant Isaac Stevens observed that during the entire affair around the Pedregal, Scott was "perfectly composed and assured." Even before leaving Puebla, Lieutenant John Sedgwick had informed his sister that he viewed Scott "as one of the great men of the day, and it would be the greatest misfortune to this army if anything should befall him." Four days after the battle, John Wilkins of the Third Infantry wrote that Scott's "generalship, dignity, coolness & forsight have placed him ahead of any general living." Twenty-three-year-old Thomas Jackson acknowledged that in casual conversation, Scott came across as arrogant and opinionated, but in discussions on military topics, "you may expect to call forth the mighty powers of his mighty mind, and upon information so obtained I would rather rely than on all the other officers in our armies in Mexico." A bond had developed between the general and his army as the men came to realize that beneath his stern and arrogant exterior, Old Fuss and Feathers was wise, fair, and gracious. "He is proud of his officers & men & they have every confidence & faith in him," Wilkins observed. And so as Scott rode north toward San Angel, receiving periodic praise from his men, he stopped on one occasion, took off his hat, and said, "thanks be to God for the Victory & glory to this Gallant little Army." When the soldiers cheered again, he said, "it's not for you to cheer me but me to cheer you." The affection was mutual.[17]

The Mexicans were as demoralized as the Americans were elated. Letters to their families written on August 20 and 21 expressed extreme disappointment on the part of Santa Anna's soldiers. One writer exclaimed, "Judas! All is lost—eternal shame for us. . . . The scene of Cerro Gordo has been repeated exactly." Another summed up what happened at Padierna by lamenting, "In war the Yankees know no rest—no fear." Yet another wrote of his bewilderment about how the American army got between Valencia and Santa Anna without any aid given to the former. A member of the Mexican Congress thought he knew how such a thing could happen: "there is great weakness and ignorance and very little honor shown on the part of our generals." And the defeat was rendered all the more bitter when one considers the confidence that many of the defenders felt just twenty-four hours earlier. After the coming battle, the Americans will not "laugh in their beard, as they have on former occasions," wrote one man. At least some Mexicans agreed with the American assessment of the quality of Scott's leadership, for in one letter, a soldier referred to "Scott, a man of superior talents in the art of war."[18]

Some final assessments of the early morning fighting on August 20 deserve notice. Scott made the following laudatory assertion in his battle report: "I doubt whether a more brilliant or decisive victory—taking into view ground, artificial defences, batteries, and the extreme disparity of numbers—without cavalry or artillery on our side—is to be found on record." D. H. Hill penned this conclusion in his diary a week later: "There has been nothing in the whole war so brilliant as the storming of the heights of Contreras." Also, reflecting a growing lack of respect for Mexican soldiers, Captain Moses Barnard offered this critical appraisal of his opponents: "the Mexicans have naturally a great gift in erecting fortifications, but very little bravery in defending them."[19] But the day's fighting was not over, and the Mexican soldiers would give reason for Barnard to amend his critique that afternoon.

At San Angel, Twiggs and Pillow prepared, after a brief halt, to push on to Coyoacán on the north side of the Pedregal. The latter had recently rejoined his men and assumed command of both divisions along with Shields's brigade (Quitman's division). Pillow ordered General Smith to put the Company of Engineers and the Mounted Rifles in the lead, and Smith sent his staff officer Lieutenant Earl Van Dorn to make the proper disposition. Van Dorn caught up with Lieutenant Gustavus W. Smith of the engineers and relayed Pillow's orders to prepare his company to lead the army forward. Smith explained that he had spotted a tall building near San Angel just a few hundred yards away, and he wished to go there and survey the area from the top of it. Smith believed that he "would be able to get a good view of the level country for miles around, and obtain quite definite knowledge of the positions and movements of the main Mexican forces." It was the kind of thing that Scott certainly would have wanted, but the order came from Pillow, so Smith canceled his reconnaissance initiative and reported at the head of the column.[20]

As they approached Coyoacán, Scott, along with Nicholas Trist, caught up and accompanied the troops into the town. While riding with his generals, they spotted Colonel Riley for the first time since his successful dawn attack and in the commanding general's presence Pillow proclaimed, "You have earned the Yellow sash [of a general officer], Sir, and *you shall have it*." Flushed with the day's success and assigning to himself an inflated amount of the responsibility, it appeared, as Trist put it, that Pillow had become the "dispenser in Mexico, of those rewards and honours." The commanding general likely just bit his tongue, because he knew better than to cross the president's factotum.[21]

By the time they reached Coyoacán, Scott and Santa Anna were probably closer to each other than they had been thus far in the campaign, for the Mexican general was in Churubusco organizing a new defensive line. The town was really just a collection of a few houses scattered on the south side of the river, and its name, Churubusco, was derived from an Aztec word meaning "place of the war god"—appropriate enough for the unfolding events of this day. Santa Anna had earlier ordered Major General Nicolás Bravo to give up his fortifications at San Antonio and retreat to Churubusco. Then, to cover Bravo's withdrawal, Santa Anna improvised a new defensive line around the town where most of his retreating troops were headed. This new line ran from the Convent of San Mateo to a bridge over the Churubusco River 450 yards away. The convent, an old Franciscan monastery built in 1678, sat on the road from Coyoacán, and, located just west of the village of Churubusco, it anchored the Mexican right. Its sturdy walls were four feet thick and twelve feet high. Parapets along the roof, a walled enclosure, earthworks facing Coyoacán, and an irrigation ditch made the convent a formidable bastion. There Santa Anna placed seven artillery pieces and 1,800 infantry consisting of national guard units along with the San Patricio Battalion, all under the command of Major General Manuel Rincón. The Mexican left rested on the bank of the river just north of the village at the fortified southern end of the bridge—the *tête de pont*. This hastily but well-constructed earthen fortification mounted artillery and infantry from General Francisco Pérez's brigade. From the bridge, Pérez extended his line east along the river with two regiments, and his men were determined to hold the river crossing until Bravo's San Antonio force crossed over. Additional Mexican infantry lined fieldworks connecting these two strong points, and Santa Anna placed several reserve regiments on the north side of the river.[22]

The San Patricio (St. Patrick) Battalion constituted the heart of the defenders at the convent. It consisted of deserters from the U.S. Army, many of whom were Irish Catholic. The unit had been organized by John Riley, who deserted from Taylor's army on the Rio Grande in April 1846, because as an immigrant and a Catholic, he was persecuted. Riley, like many of his San Patricio comrades, was not a naturalized American citizen, so he felt no special allegiance to the army or the country. Harsh punishment doled out by American officers seemed to fall most heavily on immigrant soldiers, and as a consequence served as a strong motive for desertion. The Mexicans had circulated leaflets on numerous occasions in an effort to induce disaffected soldiers to desert and join their army. During the army's ten weeks in Puebla, several men had slipped away and joined the San Patricios. The unit had manned a battery at Cerro Gordo, and now at the convent, they would fight with seven guns. Of the 204 battalion members who manned those guns with great effect, 142 were Irishmen.[23]

Several roads converged at Coyoacán, and once there, Scott had a decision to make. He could turn north and take the road to Tacubaya, which would put him only three miles from the capital. Other than a single brigade of defenders under General Joaquín Rangel, the way was open. However, that would lead the two divisions under his immediate supervision away from his other two divisions down at San Antonio and would put the Mexican army between him and his supply train in San Agustin. Although Santa Anna's army was retreating, it was also concentrating around Churubusco, which tends to strengthen, not weaken, a fighting force. Rather than put more distance between himself and General Worth, Scott knew that he needed to force a junction—a decision that meant that his immediate objective would be the enemy army, not the enemy capital.

Lieutenant Isaac Stevens of the engineers went into the tower of the church

Bullet-scarred wall of the Convent of San Mateo. Courtesy of the author.

in Coyoacán to survey the area. Cornfields dotted the terrain, concealing a complete view of the surroundings, but Stevens could tell that Churubusco was the focal point of Mexican activity. Looking southeast, he also saw a flow of personnel coming up the road from San Antonio. Churubusco was a magnet, drawing all Mexican forces to it, and Stevens could clearly see that all retreating forces were being funneled to the bridge across the Churubusco River. The lieutenant also detected defensive works in the area, especially around the San Mateo Convent and on the southern end of the bridge. He reported his findings to Scott, who accordingly sent Captain Phil Kearny's First Dragoons to explore the best approach to San Antonio, and he ordered

Pillow to follow with one of his brigades (Cadwalader's). This move was conceived to correspond with Worth's attack from the south. At the same time, Scott dispatched engineers under Lieutenant Gustavus Smith to reconnoiter the area around the convent, and he ordered Twiggs to follow with Persifor Smith's brigade and Captain Francis Taylor's battery to force an opening to the Churubusco bridge.[24]

Gustavus Smith and his engineers advanced several hundred yards from Coyoacán toward the convent with several companies of infantry in support. They got to within five hundred yards, but their view was largely obstructed by cornfields all around. In the distance, Smith could see the roof of the convent, and through occasional breaks in the corn, he detected Mexican infantry to the right and left. Lieutenant McClellan, who had taken another route and had gotten closer, returned to Smith and reported having seen a battery in front of the church and troops "crowded" on the roof. After capturing a lancer and sending him back to General Twiggs for interrogation, Smith and McClellan ascertained that American units were already making contact with the enemy line in front. All they could hear was musketry, but they knew that the stray units that had pushed forward had to be drastically outnumbered, so they ordered Taylor's battery forward in support. Lieutenant Stevens thought that a few rounds of canister fired at the church would disperse the enemy troops and relieve the Americans on the right from the gradually intensifying musket fire. However, rather than follow Lieutenant Smith's recommendation to bring up one gun to operate from the protection of an adobe hut that he had found, Taylor ordered the entire battery forward to within 150 yards and deployed it in an exposed position. The Mexicans unleashed what Taylor described as "a most terrible fire of artillery and musketry." Thus commenced, at about half past twelve, a destructive artillery duel between Taylor's guns and those of the San Patricios that lasted for an hour and a half.

The battle had originated prematurely when Twiggs ordered a close reconnaissance of the enemy line to determine its strength and the best mode of attacking it. His overanxious infantry, flushed with their easy victory that morning and expecting more of the same, pressed forward, and thinking that they were only attacking a church, they rushed in, only to find themselves "directly in front of a bastioned work and immediately under the fire of their guns." The withering fire from Rincón's men forced the Americans to take cover in cornfields, behind maguey plants, and in irrigation ditches. They had hastily dashed forward without adequate knowledge of what lay ahead, but once there, had no choice but to "make the best of it," as Lieutenant John D. Wilkins of the Third Infantry put it. Engineer Smith, reckoning that he would lose half of his men if he tried to cross the road, instructed them to take cover as best they could and not to move without orders. The American advance on the convent remained stalled more than a half hour later when Worth's division approached from the south.[25]

Worth had not been idle on his part of the battlefield. After starting his men for Padierna that morning, he complied with Scott's order to turn around and return to San Antonio so as to be ready to attack from the south when Pillow and Twiggs arrived from the north. Worth arrived back at his starting point in front of San Antonio around 11:00 A.M. as General Bravo was preparing to evacuate the town. The Mexican general left part of his command in the fortifications to keep Worth in check while he led the remainder north to Churubusco. This is the movement that Stevens had seen from the church tower around noon. Concurrent with Bravo's withdrawal, Worth sent Colonel Newman S. Clarke's brigade to the left to pick its way through the eastern edge of the Pedregal in an effort to cut the road leading north. He deployed his other brigade under Colonel John Garland perpendicular to the road and facing the enemy's San Antonio fortifications with orders to attack the works as soon as Clarke's brigade reached the road above the town. It was a classic turning movement—hold the enemy in front and attack in flank.[26]

Worth probably believed that this was finally his chance to achieve the glory that had eluded him thus far in the campaign. The slow, tedious siege at Veracruz had displeased him, and he had arrived at Cerro Gordo too late to participate. Then came the embarrassing run-in with Scott at Puebla. At last, this would be his opportunity, and he did not disappoint. After hearing of the enemy's route at Padierna but before deploying his troops at San Antonio, he had told his junior officers "that as General Twiggs's Division had covered itself with glory, we must do something," thus indicating that the earlier rivalry between those two division commanders remained alive on the Churubusco battlefield. Both Worth and Clarke were veterans of the War of 1812, and the tactics used by Worth at San Antonio were a replica of those he saw executed by a young General Scott at the Battle of Chippewa in July 1814. There Scott, a brigade commander, had sent one of his regiments into the woods to the left with orders to attack the British flank. That attack had worked beautifully. Now Worth, who was one of Scott's staff officers in 1814, hoped to bag the Mexican force in his front with a similar move, and he intended to do so using his old friend, Clarke, with whom he had shared those bloody experiences along the Niagara River thirty-three years earlier.[27]

Clarke's men slowly picked their way through the Pedregal for two miles. The path they followed was described by Lieutenant Ralph Kirkham of the Sixth Infantry as "all rock, covered here and there with prickly pears, . . . deep chasms, and very uneven at all times." The Mexicans spotted them working their way through the lava field and opened fire on them with small arms, but it had little effect. The brigade came out onto level ground about a mile from the road and a mile north of San Antonio, and they rushed forward and attacked the long, thin enemy column packed on the road. The portion of Bravo's command that was above the point of attack hurried on to Churubusco to join the rest of their army, but those below Clarke's attack began to scatter. To the south, Worth attacked the now lightly manned San Antonio fortifications and easily dispersed the remaining defenders before pressing up the road to form a junction with Clarke. This pincer only intensified the panic among the Mexican soldiers, laborers, and civilians who were trapped between Worth's two brigades. Mud from the previous night's rain created a quagmire that caused wagons and caissons to sink so deep that they had to be abandoned on the road, which only added to the confusion within the retreating column.[28]

Slowed only by abandoned wagons that blocked the road for a mile, Worth pursued the retreating throng up the road to Churubusco in what became a running battle. "Shall I shake out the colors and let them see who are after them?" a corporal in the Second Artillery asked company commander John Sedgwick. "Yes," Sedgwick responded. At one point, Lieutenant Raphael Semmes came upon a U.S. soldier standing over the motionless figure of a heavy-set Mexican. Approaching closer, Semmes saw that it was an officer, and he asked the American if the man was dead. "Oh, no sir," came the reply, "he is only a little out of wind, being a fat man; I have just run him down." Then the officer sat up and explained that in their rush to get away, his aide had taken his horse, leaving him to escape on foot.[29] It was during the pursuit, at about 1:00 P.M., that Pillow, at the head of Cadwalader's brigade, joined Worth's division. Having been ordered by Scott to strike at San Antonio from the north, Pillow discovered that Worth had already pushed through the town and that the battle on his front had become fluid. So Pillow turned the brigade north and with some difficulty crossed two deep irrigation ditches to take a position on Worth's left as they deployed for battle south of the Churubusco River.

Twiggs's division had been engaged for over half an hour when Worth arrived at Churubusco. Bringing his winded soldiers up as quickly as possible, Worth placed Garland's brigade to the right of the road and adjacent to some cornfields. Then he positioned Clarke's brigade nearest the road with two regiments (the Fifth and Eighth) facing northwest and obliquely pointing toward the *tête de pont*. Clarke's remaining regiment (Sixth) was deployed directly across the road staring right at the strength of the Mexican bridgehead. Cadwalader's brigade fell in on the left and deployed itself so that its line extended almost to the convent. The Voltigeurs constituted the reserve. Taking into account Twiggs's division, which faced northeast and north, the Americans, about 8,000 strong, were roughly aligned in a crescent shape around 20,000 Mexicans whose defensive position was strong and compact, and who enjoyed interior lines and a secure line of retreat.[30]

Muskets and cannon from the *tête de pont* opened fire on Worth's men as they deployed for battle. Flushed with his easy push north from San Antonio and determined to best Twiggs by capturing the Mexican strong point, Worth became rash and careless, and he repeated the mistake that Twiggs had made earlier. Lieutenant Nathaniel Lyon believed that since Worth had "no share in the glory of Contreras, [he] determined to bring his division into action under whatever disadvantages." Thus, without any pretext of reconnoitering the enemy position, he ordered Clarke's brigade to attack straight up the road. One of the best regiments in the entire army, the Sixth, commanded by Major Benjamin L. Bonneville, led the brigade forward shortly after 1 o'clock. Other officers in the unit included Simon Bolivar Buckner, Lewis A. Armistead, and Winfield Scott Hancock, all future Civil War generals. Buckner would be wounded within minutes of the regiment's advance, and at some point during the battle, Hancock, the namesake of his army commander, received a slight wound. Armistead and Hancock survived the carnage of this day only to go on to face each other as enemies sixteen years later, when men of Hancock's Union Corps would mortally wound Armistead during Pickett's Charge at Gettysburg. At Churubusco, the Sixth rushed forward, exposed on the causeway and in easy range of Mexican infantry and artillery hidden in a cornfield on the American right. A wall of musket balls and grapeshot coming from two directions stopped the advance and forced it back. Garland's brigade also tried but failed to make headway to the right, and Duncan's battery could not come up and support because of the mushy ground. Clarke ordered his men forward again, but again, they were repulsed. On the left, Cadwalader sent his units forward, but cornfields and irrigation ditches resulted in disorganization as the attack lost momentum.[31]

Worth's division became pinned down in the cornfields and among the irrigation ditches along both sides of the Acapulco Road. It was a "'butt head' attack," concluded Lyon, ordered by a "stupid Officer." Their swift pursuit had led them into the teeth of perhaps the toughest fight the Mexicans put up during the entire campaign. Chaplain John McCarty, an Episcopal priest and New York native, earned the praise and respect of the men of the division that day. As was his custom, he went in with the men, and during that long fight in front of the *tête de pont*, he roamed the ground, looking for the best places to get across the numerous ditches that traversed the ground. Along the way, he frequently stopped to console the wounded, all the while urging the men forward and pointing the way. As George Kendall aptly put it, "Such a Chaplain is worth having in a small army like ours."[32]

All along the concave American lines from the convent around to the bank of the Churubusco River on the far right, units were cut to pieces and stymied in the early afternoon. The stern Mexican resolve and determined resistance surprised American soldiers, whose greatest concern a few hours earlier had been whether they would succeed in catching the retreating enemy host. They had uncharacteristically but hastily rushed into a fight without adequate reconnaissance. The advantages that the Americans enjoyed previously and the relative ease that characterized earlier battles had resulted from careful and extensive study of enemy positions and the surrounding terrain. Scott had sent engineers to survey the areas in front of both Twiggs's and Worth's divisions, but an overzealous pursuit and a lack of patience to wait for the engineers' reports meant that men rushed forward without knowing the hazards in their front and flanks.

Scott remained in Coyoacán about a half mile behind Twiggs's division, issuing orders from horseback. He sat on his mount in the shade of a tree as staff officers came and went, updating him on the latest developments at the front. At one point, an observer heard him exclaim, "My God, I have so many irons in the fire some of them will burn." Moments later, Noah Smith, the self-appointed army guide who, having lived in the area for several years and having an intimate knowledge of the surrounding fields, approached Scott with information about how to flank Santa Anna. The bridge north of Coyoacán could be used to get troops across the river, and Smith knew how to navigate the cornfields to bring a force into the enemy flank and rear north of Churubusco. Scott accordingly ordered Pierce's brigade forward under Captain Lee's supervision and Smith's guidance in an attempt to get part of the army north of the river and on the Mexican right flank. It was another iron into the fire, and when he directed Shields's brigade to follow Pierce in support, he had put virtually all of his men into the fight.[33]

Scott watched as Pierce's men filed through Coyoacán and turned onto the road leading north. From his location under the shade tree, Scott spotted Pierce, who had been badly injured the night before in the Pedregal, when his horse fell and rolled his foot on the rocks. His foot was so tender that he held it away from the animal so that it would not rub or bounce against its side. The commanding general approached and said, "Pierce . . . you are not fit to be in your saddle." "Yes I am . . . in a case like this," responded the division commander. "I ought to order you back to St. Augustine. You cannot touch your foot to the stirrup," Scott countered. "For God sake don't give the order," Pierce pleaded before assuring Scott that one foot in the stirrup was enough. Besides, he believed that this "will be the last great fight, and I must lead my brigade."[34]

The entire American army, except those units guarding the supply train at San Agustin, was now in the fight. Scott, having committed his reserves and sent all troops forward, found that he and his staff were practically alone in the rear of the army, a virtual detachment hundreds of yards away from any significant body of troops, and therefore vulnerable to capture or attack by remnant enemy bands. It was a potentially dangerous situation for an army commander, so he moved up to a position just behind Twiggs's men. There was greater danger of a stray musket ball that close to the fighting, but all things considered, his personal safety depended on relocating.[35]

When Pierce's and Shields's men crossed the river and turned right (east), they were about a mile from the Acapulco Road. Working their way through seemingly endless cornfields, Pierce put out skirmishers in front with orders to fall back on the main body when they made contact with the enemy. At one point, they reached a ditch ten feet wide and six feet deep—impossible to cross on horseback. Some of Pierce's men helped him from the saddle, and he hobbled along on foot until pain and fatigue forced him to stop. As they approached the road about three quarters of a mile north of the river, they began to exchange fire with Santa Anna's reserve units. Pierce's and Shields's brigades deployed for battle, with the latter's extreme left resting among the buildings of the hacienda Portales. Shields attempted to extend his line farther north so as to flank the Mexican troops and occupy the road, but the enemy responded by extending their line farther north with infantry and three thousand lancers. The fighting quickly became intense, and many of the Americans took refuge in the hacienda, refusing to go forward. Lee sent word back to Scott to forward reinforcements, but with no available infantry units, Scott redirected the Second Dragoons and Mounted Rifles to assist. Until they arrived, activity on that part of the battlefield remained stalled.[36]

Back on the south side of the river, Twiggs's men remained in a bloody stalemate with the convent garrison. Captain Taylor had been compelled to withdraw his crippled battery after a daring duel. Here and there, small groups of Americans attempted to crawl forward through the cornfield to gain some advantage, but the enemy fire was deadly and constant. Lieutenant Don Carlos Buell fought with the Third Infantry in the cornfields just west of the convent. Buell, a "robust" man with a "vigorous physique," was known as a strict disciplinarian who often tested his soldiers at night while they did guard duty by seeing how close he could get before they demanded the countersign. If he succeeded in getting close without being challenged, he would jerk the musket out of the guard's hands and give him a tongue-lashing for his carelessness. On this day, Buell was unable to get close to the Mexican line because he was seriously wounded in the chest.[37] The fire of the

San Patricios under John Riley's leadership was not only constant but also accurate and effective. Remembering their harsh treatment in the American army, they exacted revenge by taking careful aim at the dark-coated officers in the cornfield.

Both sides attempted to break the stalemate at the convent by outflanking their opponent along the riverbank. Twiggs sent portions of Riley's brigade toward the river in a futile effort to flank the Mexican right, only to find the fighting in that quarter just as hot. Riley's Second Infantry was hit particularly hard, as evidenced by descriptions offered by three of its lieutenants. As Joseph R. Smith and seven of his men tried to inch their way forward, they came under heavy fire but stubbornly refused to withdraw. Only one of them would escape the battle uninjured. Smith was hit twice—in the hip and the left elbow. The ball that entered the elbow shattered the joint, and although he would later succeed in talking the surgeon out of amputation, he was disabled for life. John Wilkins described this part of the battle four days later in a letter to his mother: "such showers of lead & Iron I have never before heard." Another, Nathaniel Lyon, described his advance amid the corn as "necessarily blind and confused." Twice the Mexican defenders attempted their own flanking move. Several hundred emerged from their concealed positions around the convent and, under cover of the cornstalks, tried to make their way around Twiggs's left, but both times they were beaten back.[38]

It was on Worth's front that the stalemate was finally broken. However, it was Scott's decision to stretch his lines north with Pierce's and Shields's flanking move that made Worth's breakthrough possible. The attack north of the river had not gone particularly well and had become bogged down around the hacienda Portales. Indeed, the behavior of many of Shields's men cowering around the ranch buildings was suspect, and one observer described the New York volunteers who lodged themselves "behind a large building and fence, a position many of them did not quit till the enemy were out of Sight."[39] Nevertheless, the presence of American forces north of the river had forced Santa Anna to take men from the bridgehead to help defend his line of retreat. Worth then complicated Santa Anna's situation by getting some of his men across the river to the east of the road. The Mexican defenders had fought courageously for over two hours, but with constant and determined concentric pressure applied by the Americans, their line finally broke in midafternoon.

At about 3 o'clock, after being pinned down in a cornfield to the right of the road for almost two hours, Captain James V. Bomfield of the Eighth Infantry sprang to his feet and started forward. Instantly, Lieutenant James Longstreet jumped up and followed with the regimental colors in his hands. Others followed their example until the entire Fifth and Eighth Regiments of

Clarke's brigade became the spearhead of a general assault on the *tête de pont*. They splashed through the water-filled trench in front, scaled the parapet by climbing on the shoulders of comrades, and, in the words of one staff officer, "put their muskets in the very faces of the Mexicans." After a sharp hand-to-hand fight, they finally seized the stronghold, and Longstreet planted the regiment's flag atop the walls. Ralph Kirkham of the Sixth Infantry informed his wife that "the troops behaved splendidly, and the wonder is how they had courage enough to storm a fort which poured such an excessive fire upon them." As the defenders took flight toward the capital, the Americans turned one of the captured 4-pounders to the southwest and opened an enfilading fire on the convent.[40]

Duncan at last succeeded in moving his battery forward to a position on the road so as to fire at the same obstinate defenders. For another twenty minutes, the San Patricios, knowing what their fate would be as captured deserters, stubbornly continued to fight. Duncan's guns quickly knocked out three of John Riley's pieces; then a round ignited the remaining powder in the convent, killing several of his gunners. Americans, primarily of the Third Infantry, began to pour into the courtyard, clubbing and bayoneting those defenders who were unable to make it inside the church. Now the San Patricios and their Mexican comrades barricaded themselves inside the building, and when American troops battered down the door, they unleashed a deadly volley of musketry. As the defenders worked their way to the second floor, one of the Mexicans raised a white flag, but another one pulled it down. A second and third time, Mexican soldiers tried to surrender, only to have the white flags torn down by other members of the San Patricios Brigade. In the midst of this hand-to-hand carnage, which packed the upstairs corridor, Captain James Smith of the Third Infantry waved his handkerchief and yelled at his men to stop the bloodbath. The fighting ceased, and a wounded and exhausted Riley, along with his companions in arms, slumped to the floor.[41]

North of the river, reinforcements arrived as Pierce and Shields were organizing their brigades for another effort to take the road. They ordered their units forward through the cornfield, and the fight was just becoming hot when Mexican troops began to fall back and join their comrades, who were by that time streaming north along the road. Worth's men were crossing the river at several points, in full pursuit of Santa Anna's retreating army. After an intense and bloody battle that lasted over two hours, the capture of the *tête de pont* had caused the Mexican line to disintegrate, and the northern flight that started just after dawn at Padierna now resumed in earnest toward the capital. After having their flank attack blunted and finally mustering the courage to try again, the men of Pierce's and Shields's brigades now could only watch as the enemy disappeared up the road.

Soon Captain Phil Kearny rushed by with members of his First Dragoons—and what a fine-looking set of horsemen they were, all mounted on gray steeds. Kearny "went dashing by with rein in one hand & drawn sword in the other his head was bent to his saddle low & his eye flashing fire." The glorious scene created a temptation that Major Frederick D. Mills could not resist. A native of Connecticut, Mills was a member of the Fifteenth Infantry in Pierce's brigade. He had just shared with his sergeant a drink from his flask when the dragoons galloped by, and he impetuously decided to join the pursuit. The sergeant, knowing that Mills was not a good horseman and that his horse was "rather vicious," begged him not to go. "You have done your duty, let the Dragoons attend to theirs, stay with the Regiment," the sergeant implored, but Mills said, "No I am bound to go!" Then, after saying something about capturing Santa Anna, he jumped on his horse and joined the chase.[42]

The infantry pursued for two miles before Scott ordered them to stop. Most of the mounted soldiers heeded the bugle call to halt, but Kearny, Lieutenant Richard Ewell, and several others galloped on toward the San Antonio *garita*, a fortified gate at the southern entrance to Mexico City. There the retreating foe had placed a battery, and Kearny, along with his handful of rash dragoons, were determined to charge the enemy guns. As the horsemen approached the gate, even riding past Mexican infantry who were trying to get to the safety of the city, the gunners unleashed a volley that killed their own men as well as some of the Americans. Ewell had a horse shot from under him for the second time that day, and grapeshot mangled Kearny's left arm.[43]

As for Major Mills, his fate was unknown. His strong, powerful, and spirited horse was reportedly one of the finest in the army. He accompanied the dragoons right up to the city gate, and according to witnesses, his horse leaped over the Mexican works. Because none of the other horses could accomplish such a feat, Mills found himself alone, slashing with his saber before he was overcome by both soldiers and civilians. There were rumors that he actually got close to Santa Anna's carriage just inside the city wall. He was wounded and captured, but what happened after that has remained a mystery. His friends held to the hope that he was a prisoner inside the city, but they tried in vain to discover his fate. Stories persisted that he had been either run through with a lance after surrendering or that he was killed and his body mutilated. Mills, a thirty-year-old lawyer, was a graduate of Yale who had joined the army only because friends had talked him into it.[44]

Some of the same soldiers who had marveled as Kearny bolted north toward the city were stunned to see him an hour later returning "with his arm dangling by his side." A surgeon amputated it near the shoulder. The fearless trooper had studied cavalry tactics in France and had fought with the French army in Algiers, earning the nickname "Kearny the Magnificent." He and his companion, Richard Ewell, who rode together up the causeway that day, as if daring the Mexicans to shoot them, would both rise to the rank of general officer but on opposite sides in the Civil War. In the Second Bull Run Campaign in 1862, Ewell would lose a leg fighting for the South, and Kearny would lose his life fighting for the North.[45]

Grisly scenes were everywhere in the battle's aftermath. Areas all around the Pedregal had been killing fields during the battle's various stages: the terrain surrounding Padierna, the road that ran along its western edge to San Angel, the area where Colonel Clarke's brigade smashed into Bravo's retreating column on the northeast side of the Pedregal, and farther north around the convent and the bridgehead. Corpses, both Mexican and American, were strewn for miles, as were the wounded. For Ralph Kirkham, the sight of "bodies without heads, arms and legs, and disfigured in every horrible way . . . was awful" and unforgettable. One American soldier who had his leg "nearly severed took his knife & completed the amputation." Another who had been wounded in the foot and left behind by his friends crawled on hands and knees and hopped on one foot until he rejoined his unit at 10 o'clock that night. One of the Voltigeurs recalled that even before the battle ended, a wounded sergeant was calmly smoking a cigar while being carried off the battlefield in a "hand barrow" with bullets flying about.[46]

At the San Mateo Convent, the dirty, ragged remnants of the San Patricios Battalion stood segregated from the other one thousand prisoners taken in and around the church. Captain Smith had to step in front of his men to prevent them from bayoneting the deserters on the spot. Customarily, an opponent who "fought like devils," as the Irishmen did at Churubusco, would elicit grudging respect from their foe, but these traitors won no such admiration, especially when captured Mexicans confirmed that the artillerists indeed had been taking aim at the American officers. Word quickly spread through the army that the San Patricios prisoners had exacted a heavy toll that afternoon. "These wretches served the guns . . . and with fatal effect, upon . . . their former comrades," reported General Worth.[47]

The price had been high for the Americans—higher than in the two previous engagements combined. Out of 8,500 engaged, 137 were killed and 877 wounded. The casualties resulted from a stubborn Mexican defense in the afternoon, which their strong position made possible. As the day wore on, Santa Anna's lines constricted into a tightly packed defensive position from which they were able to deliver concentrated firepower. It was not the kind of fight Scott would have chosen, but in the day's fluid movements, it was the way the battle evolved. Still, the advantage that Santa Anna's position afforded was insufficient to bring him a much-needed victory, and ultimately his casualties were significantly higher: out of 25,000 engaged, over 4,000 were killed and wounded and 2,700 captured, including eight generals and 200 other officers. The Americans also captured thirty-seven artillery pieces, a large quantity of muskets and ammunition, and hundreds of wagons. After the day's battle, and despite the heavy losses, Scott was in "fine spirits."[48] The day had been long and the fighting bloody, but the result was another one-sided victory.

In the fighting around the Pedregal, Scott conducted affairs in his customary style. He put his army in the most favorable situation possible, and when he was not present, he gave his subordinates the latitude to make decisions based on circumstances. However, the commanding general was never far from the front, issuing orders, seizing opportunities, and capitalizing on enemy mistakes. And his men noted his omnipresence on the battlefield. John Wilkins recounted how surprised the troops were to see how Scott held up under the rigors of the campaign. The general "always reconnoiters with his engineers, examines for himself, is always about on the field of battle & ever ready to take . . . [any] advantages offered." After almost four decades of reflection, Ulysses S. Grant remembered in his *Memoirs* that the "strategy and tactics displayed by General Scott in these various engagements of the 20th of August, 1847, were faultless as I look upon them now after the lapse of so many years." The one thing that Wilkins did not get entirely correct, as far as the fighting around Churubusco is concerned, is the failure to conduct exhaustive reconnaissance.[49]

The fighting courage of the army's rank and file warrants acknowledgment. Ultimately, as at Cerro Gordo, once the armies were positioned and the battle joined, it became a soldier's fight, and victory or defeat hinged on the conduct of lone soldiers or small groups as well as the execution of orders at the company and regimental levels. Many acts of individual bravery are recorded in correspondence and diaries, but no doubt many more are unknown and lost to history. Forlorn Mexican soldiers tried to explain in letters why the Americans, with only a third as many men, succeeded in such a desperate conflict. One wrote that "We trusted for safety to our numbers," but another concluded that "valor is superior to numbers." Captain Lee was impressed with the day's success, and he wrote home to his wife explaining how it was accomplished: "The whole was done with the bayonet. . . . [and] Santa Anna's force melted away." Perhaps it was a lesson too well learned by the Virginian, for he later would rely on the bayonet on numerous Civil War battlefields after the rifled musket had rendered it obsolete as an effective shock weapon.[50]

Soldiers will risk all if they believe their commander to be worth such sacrifice. Faith in the general's competence and trust in his judgment mean everything on the field of battle. In the same letter in which Wilkins described Scott's movements around the battlefield, he went on to write about the pride

Scott felt for his men and how confident they were in his abilities. "General Scott has the entire confidence of the whole army and is more popular by far than 'Old Zack.' Indeed I have never in my life seen such an entire change of opinion as has taken place in the army with respect to him. Everyone expected to see him quite differently from what he is." D. H. Hill, after writing one of his diary tirades about Pillow, ended a paragraph with a note of gratitude for Scott. "Sage general the Army appreciates you if the Country does not."[51]

CHAPTER ELEVEN

Mortification and Mistake

Armistice and Molino del Rey

*Genl. Scott has mortified his troops and no doubt has displeased
the people of the United States, but he has acted as a patriot and
maybe will succeed in gaining for his country the boon of peace.*
—Daniel Harvey Hill, Fourth Artillery

Next morning officers detached burial parties from each regiment to gather
and bury the dead. The soldiers detailed for such an unpleasant task collected
the corpses by unit, removed their equipment, and placed them in large pits
close to where they fell. Sometimes the bodies were stacked in layers, and in
the case of the dead from Worth's division, many of whom fell in and around
cornfields, stalks were used to separate the layers. When that part of the
chore was completed, a chaplain read a funeral oration, soldiers fired a salute,
and the work crews covered the bodies with dirt. Hospital stations remained
overflowing with the wounded. The dying and the dead littered the floors so
thickly that it was difficult to walk, and the doctors and attendants, who had
worked through the night, remained inundated with suffering men pleading
for assistance.[1]

While the doctors and burial parties worked, Scott made his way toward
Tacubaya to oversee the army's movements as it closed in on the capital. A few
hours earlier, his contacts in the city had sent him word that conditions in the
capital were favorable for peace, which he hoped would signal the end of the
bloodshed. With him rode Nicholas Trist. Before reaching their destination,
they met a "fine carriage" coming toward them, and inside rode the Mexican army's chief engineer, General Ignacio Mora y Villamil, who stopped
them on the road. Scott and Trist dismounted as the Mexican climbed out
of his carriage, and the three walked over to the shade of a tree, where Mora
handed two letters to Scott. One was from the minister of foreign relations,
José Ramón Pacheco, proposing peace negotiations, and the other was from
the British minister, Charles Bankhead, expressing his desire that hostilities
cease and requesting that the Americans not sack the city when they entered.
Their exchange brought about two days of discussions wherein Scott con-

sented to "a short armistice" during which neither army could be reinforced nor could they strengthen their respective positions. Scott agreed that the Mexicans could take provisions into the city in return for permission for his quartermaster department to purchase supplies in the capital. In addition, Scott agreed to release his prisoners, which in fact relieved him of the responsibility of having to house, feed, and guard them. Either commander could end the armistice by giving forty-eight hours' notice.[2]

Halting his operations fit precisely with his strategy of moderation. Scott's intention all along had been to achieve a peace treaty at the earliest possible moment, and he devised his carrot-and-stick approach to accomplish that end. Recall the five-page strategy paper "Vera Cruz & Its Castle," which he had submitted to the president the previous October. It stated Scott's intention to "conquer a peace" by either taking "the city of Mexico, or [placing] it in imminent danger of capture." That was ten months earlier, but Scott's strategy had not changed. Unlike the requested cease-fire at Veracruz, which sought to evacuate noncombatants but offered no prospective conclusion to hostilities, this armistice, if conducted in good faith, might bring the war to an end. Scott hoped that it would, but in the end, his desire for peace proved greater than Santa Anna's. Always sensitive to politics and diplomacy, not merely the military conduct of the war, he had hoped for a peace proposal at every step of the campaign. He had half expected to receive one at Jalapa after the Battle of Cerro Gordo, hoped to bring about a negotiated settlement while at Puebla, and thought he might meet a white flag as he marched to the outskirts of Mexico City. In keeping with his bold note written before leaving Puebla, perhaps Churubusco was the victory "in view of the city" that would finally induce his opponent to seek peace. With the armistice, Scott was doing exactly what he predicted while still in Puebla: he promised that after a victory, he would "take measures to give those in the city an opportunity to save the capital by making a peace."[3] Scott had been remarkably consistent in both his goal and the means for accomplishing it since the campaign began. Now he waited.

An additional reason for agreeing to the armistice stemmed from Scott's assumption that the president wanted the same thing. Polk had always sought the earliest possible end to the war, had hoped it would occur the previous year after Zachary Taylor's victories, and had instructed Scott to do all within his power to bring the conflict to a speedy conclusion. There were strong political ramifications at stake, and the length and expense of the war were of central importance to the administration. The general was keenly aware of this. That Polk had placed a State Department official with Scott's army was a constant reminder that the administration wanted to be prepared for peace negotiations at a moment's notice.

Critics contended that Scott should have forced his way into the capital after Churubusco, but the general would not deviate from his strategy of moderation. He also knew that an intact and functioning Mexican government was a necessary prerequisite for a peace treaty. Toppling the government and scattering its officials would be an appropriate course only if the Americans wanted to dictate terms to a defeated and crushed enemy, but that was not the objective. Unaware of the intricacies of Scott's plan, the army's rank and file thought that capturing the capital was the primary objective and could not understand the delay. For Scott, however, the goal was to apply incremental pressure on the government to induce a peace settlement. Scott (and Trist) simply represented the administration's desire for terms in the form of a land indemnity, and the American army needed only to apply sufficient pressure to exact concessions that the administration would deem acceptable. Scott, from the outset, had understood this as his mission and had conducted his campaign in such a way as to prevent the collapse of the enemy government. In notifying Secretary Marcy of the armistice, Scott explained that he had been advised not to create a hopeless mood of desperation within the capital.

Some of Scott's soldiers—but only some—understood the reason for the armistice. His aide, Lieutenant Colonel Ethan Allen Hitchcock, offered proof that he grasped its necessity in a letter to his wife when he explained that to march into the capital would have caused the government to flee, thereby eliminating the chance for negotiations. Lieutenant Daniel Harvey Hill of the Fourth Artillery recorded in his diary similar understanding. General Scott, he wrote, "knew that if he overthrew Santa Anna that 'twould be impossible to find again a responsible Government with which to make a stable peace." Engineer Lieutenant Isaac I. Stevens, however, expressed the clearest grasp of the purpose of the armistice. Was not peace the primary objective of the campaign, he asked, and is not an armistice the first step? Indeed, throughout the entire campaign, was not the desire for peace the "obvious explication of Gen. Scott's whole course?"[4]

However, Hill also accurately observed that by agreeing to the armistice, "Gen. Scott has mortified his troops." Many of his soldiers were mystified as to why a victorious army with its objective in reach would halt operations and agree to talks. Lieutenant Nathaniel Lyon of the Second Infantry was angry and thought "this stupid twaddle about peace" was a waste of time, and Lieutenant George Davis remembered that "a spirit of indignation" emanated from the troops because of this "national disgrace." Most of the general officers also opposed the armistice, and Worth was particularly critical. He and Pillow were on the same side of this issue, and they began to form an alliance of sorts. Both generals thought that Scott at least should have required the occupation of the Chapultepec castle two miles from the edge of the city as a guarantee of good-faith behavior. Quitman wanted to capture the capital before trying to wring concessions out of the Mexicans. Pillow wrote an angry letter of protest to the commanding general; then, in keeping with his role as Polk informant, he wrote to the president criticizing the cease-fire decision.[5]

Many American troops believed that Santa Anna tricked Scott into halting military operations by dangling the prospects of peace in front of him. Scott understood the possibility that the armistice might be a ruse, but he felt compelled to try negotiations.[6] To do otherwise would have been inconsistent with his strategy. Churubusco proved to be inadequate leverage to force a peace settlement, and he probably erred in making a decision that rested on trust in Santa Anna. Ordinarily, Scott was adept at balancing political and diplomatic issues within a military context. Indeed, his strategy necessitated an equilibrium between the application of violence and the extension of peace, but maintaining the proper balance was a potential dilemma. Scott had skillfully maneuvered his way to the outskirts of Mexico City by knowing when to talk and when to fight, but his generosity after Churubusco was, in retrospect, a mistake. He made a political decision in what was essentially a military situation. While granting the armistice was consistent with his strategy, it was based on the false assumption that his latest application of the sword would be a sufficient inducement to bring about peace. His army would pay a price as a result.

While Trist embarked upon negotiations, the army settled into camp south of the city around the hamlets of Tacubaya, Mixcoac, San Angel, and San Agustin. Scott made his headquarters in the archbishop's palace in Tacubaya, which lay just three miles southwest of the capital and about a thousand yards south of Chapultepec. Meanwhile, he ordered the establishment of patrols to prevent outrages against Mexican civilians, and he issued instructions allowing Mexicans to freely pass through and among American troops. Most of the Americans "behaved better than conquering troops ever behaved before." This liberality did not apply to both sides. The movement of American troops was restricted, and they were especially forbidden to enter Mexico City (except for the Quartermaster Department) under the terms of the armistice.[7]

When the armistice went into effect, the Americans only had two days of rations left, and as a consequence, they needed to procure supplies immediately. This crucial and compelling need may also have been a reason why Scott agreed to the cease-fire. Captain William Hardee commanded a wagon train that went into the countryside looking for corn, and he returned a few days later with a thousand bushels. Similar efforts to purchase provisions in the capital did not produce the same yield. The first time Scott tried to send wagons into the capital, the Mexicans stopped them outside the city and turned them back. Next day the train was allowed in, only to be attacked by a mob shouting, "Here come the friends of Santa Anna!" and "Death to Santa Anna! Death to the Yankees!" The angry citizens pelted the wagons with rocks and beat two of the teamsters to death before the drivers could get the wagons out of the city. It took the Mexican military to restore order, and the government later apologized for this breach of the terms of the armistice. In further violation of the armistice, Santa Anna forbade Mexicans from selling to the Americans, which included the mill owners on the outskirts of the city. When American contractors went to purchase flour, the owners refused to grind the wheat and sell it because they said that to cooperate would cost them their lives. So the army took over the mills, posted heavy guards to protect the Mexican workers, and then paid the owners for the flour they produced. A similar result occurred when a Tacubaya rancher refused to sell cattle to the Americans: the army took the cattle anyway, but paid the owner for them. "Our army is not going to starve," snorted Scott.[8]

In the days following the fighting around the Pedregal, erratic and inaccurate news of the battle began to arrive back in Puebla. Information obviously filtered through Mexican sources caused the U.S. garrison under Colonel Thomas Childs to hear and believe the worst. The first news to arrive on August 22 was that Santa Anna had repulsed the American army on the outskirts of the capital and had inflicted heavy casualties. That their army had been "entirely cut to pieces" was a hard pill to swallow, and some simply refused to believe it. Three days later, additional information arrived indicating that the Americans actually had defeated the Mexicans in the fighting on August 19 and 20 and that the opposing generals had agreed to an armistice. This happy news was followed by the disturbing report that Santa Anna had used the armistice as cover to launch a surprise attack. According to this erroneous account, not only had the American army been destroyed but Worth had been killed and Scott captured. Colonel Childs assured his subordinates that the information came from a reliable Frenchman, and he apparently believed it. So did the Pueblans. Major Madison Mills, a doctor assigned to care for the sick and wounded in Puebla, recorded in his diary that the local inhabitants, emboldened by the news, appeared to be preparing to attack the small garrison and convalescents in the town. Furthermore, rumors circulated that Mexican troops were gathering on the outskirts of Puebla. Mills thought, or at least hoped, that the news from Mexico City was inaccurate, but Childs took no chances and ordered that the wounded be relocated to safer places. The truth surfaced, however, in later reports, causing the locals to return to complacency and easing the tension for the isolated Americans in Puebla.[9]

The respite offered by the armistice unfortunately provided time for the officers to engage in varying degrees of self-puffing. Some of it was simply braggadocio, as in the case of Lieutenant Simon B. Buckner, who, in a letter to his future wife, wrote that he had worn a tartan that she had made for him in the fighting at Churubusco. In describing his role in the battle, he quoted the highland chieftain, Lord Lenox: "I did start my hour upon the stage." Other higher-ranking officers, however, engaged in more serious breaches of military etiquette by trying to claim for themselves greater credit than they deserved. Sometimes they exaggerated their role in letters back home, and sometimes they fudged on the facts in official reports. Battle reports from various unit commanders contained a "mass of discrepancies," and when subordinates felt that their contributions had received inadequate description, they protested. The incentives for misrepresenting one's actions varied. For some it was a desire to go back home as military heroes, and for others it was an effort to acquire political gain. Regardless of the motivations, seeds were sown in the last week of August and first week of September that would erupt into a firestorm after the occupation of Mexico City.[10]

The frictions that a successful army must overcome manifest themselves in a variety of forms. While other officers crowed about their martial exploits, John Quitman remained dissatisfied over his lack of prominence in the army. He commanded the volunteer division made up of four regiments that was actually more like an oversized brigade, while his chief rival, William Worth, had a full division of six regiments. Although some of Quitman's men had been involved in the fighting of August 20, the general had been stuck in San Agustin guarding the supply wagons. He suspected that Scott had kept him in the rear to punish him for his earlier complaints. He was skeptical about what might come out of the armistice and confident that if any more fighting occurred, it would be minor, and if another battle came, he thought that he would likely "be kept in the shade." Staff officer George Davis reminded him that it was impossible to please everyone and that some officers were bound to be dissatisfied after a major engagement. Nevertheless, by the beginning of September, Quitman was determined to resign. Davis's persistence, however, convinced him to remain with the army.[11]

The first official negotiating session between Trist and Mexican officials took place on August 27. At Scott's request, Major Abraham Van Buren, son of the former president, accompanied Trist during the peace talks. The American diplomat immediately proposed a settlement based on President Polk's original territorial demands. This included a Rio Grande boundary for southern Texas and a substantial land concession between Texas and the Pacific Ocean. The Mexican commissioners countered with a demand for a

Nueces River boundary farther north, and when they refused to budge after days of wrangling, Trist asked that the armistice be prolonged so as to allow time for him to submit the boundary question to Washington. It was a foolish request, for Polk was not going to alter the Rio Grande demand. To do so would have negated the whole reason for going to war—Polk's contention that the April 1846 attack by Mexicans on the north bank of the Rio Grande was an act of war. His request for a declaration of war was predicated on the assertion that American blood had been shed on "American soil." For Trist to even submit the question to his superiors suggested that perhaps the Mexican demand for a Nueces boundary had some legitimacy—a point that the administration would not acknowledge.[12] It was now evident that the Mexican government was not serious about acceding to U.S. demands, and here Scott should have realized that his generosity was not being reciprocated. He should have immediately canceled the armistice and resumed military operations rather than give Santa Anna through the first week of September to regain his balance and fortify key sites.

While negotiations continued, seventy-two San Patricio captives went on trial. Two courts heard the cases; one in Tacubaya tried forty-three of the deserters and another one in San Angel tried the remaining twenty-nine. Some of the defendants had willfully deserted and offered no excuses, but sixty of the men pled not guilty, often testifying that they had been taken against their will and forced to serve in the Mexican army. Forty percent of the defendants cited liquor as the culprit. Finding themselves intoxicated and isolated in some back-alley cantina in Puebla or some other town, some of them claimed to have been victims of kidnaping and impressment. Regardless of their pleas, the courts found seventy of the defendants guilty of desertion and sentenced them to death. However, Scott sought any reasonable grounds to overturn the verdicts. After examining each case, he ultimately confirmed the execution of fifty of the men, but he reduced the sentences for fifteen and pardoned five. All fifty were hanged in Mixcoac and San Angel during the second week of September.[13]

By September 5, the negotiations were stalled and Scott began to receive reports that the Mexicans were strengthening the city's defenses, in violation of the armistice. Additional reports confirmed to a disbelieving Scott that he had been duped. Indeed, Santa Anna had been calling in reinforcements from outside Mexico City and strengthening his position south and west of the capital. The Mexican leader was in a predicament when the fighting of August 20 ended, for Scott's decision to march around Lake Chalco and approach the capital from the southwest had caught him off guard. The armistice had come just in time to save him militarily and politically. He entered into the cease-fire hoping for a diplomatic solution that would help him shore up his flagging support in the Mexican congress, but the two governments were too far apart for meaningful negotiations. Perhaps Santa Anna knew that; he had been strengthening the Chapultepec castle and other defensive positions in preparations for renewed hostilities.[14]

After a fruitless negotiating session on September 6, Scott finally gave Santa Anna notice that the armistice would end, citing the facts that his army had been prohibited from procuring supplies and the Mexicans had continued with military preparations. Now that diplomacy had failed, the decision to attempt it looked even more foolhardy than it had before. Scott's decision to halt his army's successful march on August 21 was probably the one major flaw of the campaign, and his men knew it. Roswell Ripley thought it was a bad idea all along, and he believed that "the enemy is trifling with us." Talk around the army during the armistice was that "they were humbugging us" while they secretly reorganized their army. "At last," thought Nathaniel Lyon, General Scott had "blundered into the idea that he was being deceived." Captain Moses Barnard said sarcastically, "We can beat the Mexicans in fighting, but they can excel us far in diplomacy." Then, after referring to how Santa Anna had "vanquished" Scott in the armistice affair, he added contemptuously, "Gen'l Scott met him with the honesty & honour of a veteran. . . . Santa Anna in return gave him . . . promises ending in empty air." The consensus among the troops was that now the price that the Americans would have to pay to occupy Mexico City would be infinitely greater than it would have been two weeks earlier.[15] Of course, by their measurement, the campaign would successfully end only when they captured the city, but Scott saw the campaign ending in victory when both sides agreed to a peace treaty. He still was not certain that the capital would have to be occupied.

In casual conversation with some of his subordinates on the evening of September 6, Scott learned that most of them preferred to attack the city from the south, forcing their way through the Niño Perdido and San Antonio gates. This approach would avoid the strong Mexican position around Chapultepec. With that end in mind, Scott ordered reconnaissance of the southern causeways, and he and his staff, along with his engineers, spent September 7 surveying the entire area. After dark, Lieutenant Beauregard, escorted by four companies, attempted to get as close as possible to the southern gates, but an enemy patrol fired on them, forcing them to go back.[16]

Later that evening, new information prompted Scott to change his mind about an attack from the south—at least for the time being. The day's reconnaissance activity along the southern roads had likely attracted the attention of the Mexicans, but the minor clash between Beauregard and the Mexican patrol after nightfall caused the Mexicans immediate concern. The enemy sounded the alarm, and that evening, Santa Anna began to move men from the southwest side of town to the south side. This unwelcome intelligence reached Scott immediately, and that same night, he received more disconcerting news. Fresh reports indicated that the Mexicans were melting church bells into cannon in a foundry near the Chapultepec castle—that the process was ongoing, and bells were currently being removed from cupolas and steeples within the city for recasting into cannon. This cannon factory was supposedly located in a cluster of buildings where a flour mill operated known as King's Mill, or Molino del Rey. Armed with this information, Scott shifted his attention away from attacking the city and began to consider the necessity of capturing the foundry. Knowing the number of cannon that the Americans had captured during the course of the campaign, it seemed logical to him that the Mexicans would be engaged in efforts to replenish their numbers. If they were indeed casting cannon, then capturing the mill was a sound decision.[17]

Gideon Pillow opposed the attack and tried to get Scott to reconsider. He had reliable information indicating that Santa Anna had moved the machinery for casting and boring cannon into the city weeks earlier. Apparently, numerous residents of Tacubaya attested to the fact. However, Scott had decided to attack the mill and he resolved to stay with his decision. Next, Pillow tried to persuade him to simply cut off the water source that supplied power to the machinery, but still the commanding general remained obstinate.[18] It is conceivable that having realized the mistake of granting the armistice and being angry over what he perceived to be Mexican duplicity, Scott simply wanted to strike a blow at the most readily available target. Or perhaps he was simply looking for additional targets outside the city to seize and hold in the hope of gaining sufficient advantage to win a peace without the danger that would accompany an assault on the city itself. It is doubtful that any of Scott's generals could have persuaded him to reconsider, but certainly he would not do so on Pillow's recommendation. Scott tolerated Pillow, even tried to accommodate him, but he did not trust Pillow's military ability, nor did he value his judgment. He simply refused to consider Pillow's advice. On this occasion, he should have.

This group of sturdy, stone structures was situated a thousand yards west of the castle, and the line of buildings ran north to south for three hundred yards. Santa Anna had posted two brigades to defend the complex, which added weight to the reports that something important was going on there. Sandbags and parapeted roofs added defensive strength to the buildings. A drainage ditch ran north across the front of the buildings, then turned due west for five hundred yards until it crossed the southern face of another large stone building called Casa Mata. Behind the ditch was a row of prickly maguey plants, and in front, the Mexicans had thrown dirt to form an earthwork. A third brigade lined the ditch in support of a four-gun battery, and an additional 1,500 Mexican infantry had been posted at Casa Mata. Altogether it was a formidable position, made even more imposing by almost four thousand cavalry lurking a mile farther west, waiting to pounce on the flank of an attacking American force. The number of Mexicans defending this line is unknown. American officers estimated their strength at 12,000 to 14,000, but the actual number was probably closer to 8,000 or 9,000. The area in front of the Mexican line was clear for six hundred yards except for a cornfield located front and center of their position. Looking south, the ground gently sloped up, thus putting the Mexican line at a lower elevation than an attacking enemy force. This would ordinarily put defenders at a disadvantage, but given the Mexican soldiers' tendency to shoot high, the sloping terrain became an advantage.[19]

At 3:00 A.M. on September 8, Worth got his men up, and after standing in the road at Tacubaya for what seemed like hours, they began to move to their designated position in preparation for the attack. Although other units participated in support, Captain Simon H. Drum's two-gun battery borrowed from Twiggs's division, George Cadwalader's brigade from Pillow's division, and 270 mounted troops under Major Edwin V. Sumner, the Battle of Molino del Rey was principally fought by Worth's division. They moved quietly, trying not to attract attention from the strongly held Chapultepec castle, which was slightly farther back and to the right of the Molino del Rey. It was still dark when they arrived on the high ground several hundred yards south of the Mexican position.

In all, Worth had about 3,450 men arranged in three attacking columns. The main attack on the mill complex would be executed by Brevet Major George Wright and five hundred handpicked veterans chosen from all six regiments of Worth's division. Captain Benjamin Huger's two 24-pound siege guns supported Wright's spearhead, which was also supported on both sides by additional infantry. Five hundred yards to the west, Colonel James S. McIntosh, commanding in the place of the ill Newman Clarke, held his brigade ready to attack Casa Mata supported by James Duncan's battery. On the American right flank and four hundred yards directly south of the Molino del Rey buildings, Colonel John Garland posted his brigade next to Drum's pair of six-pounders. Worth placed supporting units farther back and in position to assist while Sumner's dragoons kept an eye on the American left flank.[20]

When they were in position the officers instructed their men to lie down so that the rising sun would not reveal their location. As the gray sky became lighter, the stone buildings of the mill complex gradually appeared out of the darkness seven hundred yards away. As their objective came into view, the Americans saw that they would be attacking down a gentle slope until they

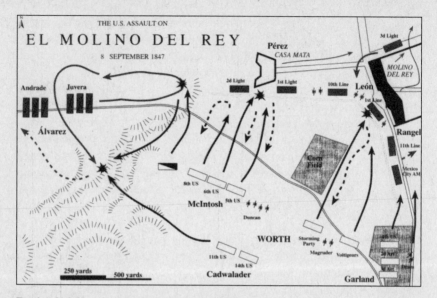

Battle of Molino del Rey. From Donald S. Frazier, ed., *The United States and Mexico at War* (New York: Macmillan, 1998). Reprinted by permission of The Gale Group.

reached the cluster of buildings. Looking beyond and slightly to the right toward the brightening eastern sky, Chapultepec, perched on a tall, steep hill, loomed ominously. There was that eery silence that is unique to dawn, and one wonders what Captain Ephraim Kirby Smith, brother of the more famous Confederate General Edmund Kirby Smith, thought as he prepared to lead the Fifth Infantry against the Mexican right at Casa Mata. Upon learning of the assignment the previous evening, he became depressed and spent the night thinking about his wife and family. In his sleeplessness, he wrote his wife a letter in which he referred to the next day's mission as a "forlorn hope" and asserted his premonition that the morrow would be "a day of slaughter." He closed this, the last letter he ever wrote, by telling his wife, "I am thankful that you do not know the peril we are in. Good night."[21]

The battle commenced just before 6 o'clock, when Huger's big guns shattered the quiet dawn. As the artillery boomed, two engineers, James Mason and John Foster, moved forward three hundred yards to observe the effect of the bombardment. They saw no activity and quickly surmised that the Mexicans had abandoned the position, whereupon they instructed Wright to advance with his five-hundred-man assault column. However, the Mexicans had not vacated the position, and now the main attack was underway prematurely after only a few rounds of artillery support. When they got to within two hundred yards, the enemy opened with grapeshot that tore holes in the American lines. Wright immediately ordered his men to the double quick so as to close on the enemy works rapidly, but within seconds, the entire Mexican line came alive with musketry. Firing from windows, rooftops, and the fortified ditch, they delivered a devastating fire on the advancing Americans. The effectiveness of the enemy fire only intensified the deeper Wright's men advanced into the concave configuration of the defenses, and within minutes, the rapidly rising casualty rate included more than 75 percent of the officers, including Wright. Their momentum carried them far enough to briefly seize the Mexican guns, but a ferocious defense coupled with reinforcements that arrived from Chapultepec forced the attackers to retreat, leaving the ground strewn with bodies.[22]

To the left, the going had been equally difficult for McIntosh's column. Soon after Wright's initial advance, and after an all too brief artillery bombardment, McIntosh's (Clarke's) brigade attacked Casa Mata. The men advanced in battle line, and when they were a hundred yards away, a sheet of musket fire poured into their ranks from the strongly fortified stone structure and the ditch that ran across the front of it. The brigade halted to fire a volley before rushing forward with bayonets fixed. As they charged, their casualties rapidly mounted, and according to George Kendall of the New Orleans *Picayune*, who witnessed the battle, losses were heaviest on this part of the battlefield. Ralph Kirkham described the Mexican fire as "continuous, like the roll of drums." McIntosh fell, mortally wounded. He was first shot in the thigh, then while lying on the ground another musket ball hit him in the leg and traveled up and lodged in his groin. Major Martin Scott, a respected veteran of thirty years, assumed command, but he was instantly killed. Third in line of succession was Major Carlos A. Waite, but he was also wounded. As in Wright's column, officers suffered a heavy toll. Among those killed leading their units were Captain Moses E. Merrill of the Fifth Infantry, Lieutenant Colonel William Graham of the Eleventh Infantry, and Captain Ephraim Kirby Smith, also of the Fifth. Smith, who had spent the night worrying about his fate, was shot in the left eye, the musket ball exiting his left ear. "I tried to do it. I tried to push ahead, but they almost killed me." These were among his last words before slipping into a coma and dying three days later.[23]

The brigade got to within thirty yards of Casa Mata before it recoiled and the men began to fall back. Lieutenant William T. Burwell had been shot in the leg just above the knee during the charge. His friend, Lieutenant Kirkham, was next to him when he went down, but judging that his wound was not serious, Kirkham continued forward. When the attacked stalled and the men pulled back, Burwell, like many other wounded, was left on the field. Then, to the outrage of the Americans, the Mexicans came out from their defenses to kill and rob the wounded. One Mexican split Burwell's skull open with a lance, leaving a gash four inches long. Another stabbed him three times with his bayonet before taking his ring, sword, and other valuables from his pockets. George W. Ayres of the Third Artillery was, according to a fellow artilleryman, "one of the bravest and noblest fellows living." He had been breveted captain for gallantry in the Battle of Monterey the previous year, but had been unfortunate enough to be among those wounded in the initial assault and then left behind. He was killed, his body "horribly mangled," and his equipment taken after the Americans retreated. McIntosh, who lay helpless with two painful wounds, escaped mutilation because two of his men dragged him off the field.[24]

Back on the American right, Garland brought his brigade forward to support Wright's beleaguered attackers, and the Americans pushed forward again, this time driving against the front and the southeast end of the Mexican line. Again they met a withering fire that stymied their advance. On the extreme right, along the Tacubaya Road where Garland's men were fighting, Captain Robert Anderson had advanced on the Mexican flank but found a relatively safe place to hunker down with the rest of his men. However, when he saw Captain Drum and his men pushing their two guns forward by hand in an effort to offer close support, he jumped from his concealed position and put a shoulder to one of the cannon wheels. Just as Drum was preparing his guns for action, Anderson felt "a severe blow" to his right shoulder. It was a musket ball that lodged in his body. Minutes later, a spent round hit him in the left arm wounding him again, but only slightly.

Slowly the Americans fought their way past the fortified ditch and up to the outer wall that surrounded the buildings. The Mexicans continued to pour heavy musket fire from every building; the maze of windows and rooftops remained alive with activity. To gain access to the complex, the Americans needed to force open gates that had been barricaded with dirt, rocks, and timber. Once that was accomplished, they poured into the grounds, and in small groups, they began a process of successive close encounters as they fought an urban-style building-to-building contest. Anderson, after being twice wounded in the attack, continued with his men into the labyrinth of buildings, and as he went through one passageway, he was wounded a third time by a musket ball that grazed his leg. In some of the structures, the Mexicans fought to the end, but others began to fall back or surrender.[25]

Lieutenant Ulysses S. Grant was among the first troops to enter the mill. After doing so late in the battle, he noticed some enemy soldiers on the roof of a nearby building. He and a few others stood a cart on its back end and up against the building with the wheels scotched to prevent it from rolling back. They climbed up the cart's shafts and onto the roof, only to discover that the soldiers they had seen, and they were "quite a number," were already prisoners. An American private had surrounded them "all by himself" and captured them, and when Grant and his friends arrived, the lone sentinel was standing guard over them. The private had not bothered to disarm them, so Grant and company took the swords from the officers and the muskets from the soldiers, and the latter they broke by hitting them against the wall before throwing them to the ground.[26]

On the American left, eventual victory came only as a result of artillery and cavalry support. After the infantry withdrew, Duncan's battery unleashed a heavy pounding on Casa Mata, which, along with a renewed attack and the collapse of the Mexican position down the line at Molino del Rey, eventually forced the enemy to abandon the structure. The Second Dragoons provided valuable service on the left flank by keeping Mexican lancers at bay. When the enemy troopers attempted to attack the American flank, General Cadwalader, who commanded the reserves, called his mounted troops forward to block their advance. Twice Edwin Sumner's dragoons charged the lancers and forced them back. On one occasion, when the opposing forces were arrayed against each other and the dragoons were preparing to attack, a lone Mexican lancer rode out from his lines in a way that the Americans interpreted to be an invitation to individual combat. An American sergeant accepted the challenge by riding forward to face his opponent, and when a trumpet sounded, the two men charged each other at full speed. At the last instant, the dragoon veered left, dodged the lance, and, with the swing of his sword, almost decapitated the Mexican. Then with a coolness that drew the admiration of his comrades, the sergeant grabbed the reins of the lancer's horse and took it back with him to his own lines. Moses Barnard of the Voltigeur Regiment witnessed the deadly affair and later described it as a "romantic incident."[27]

By midmorning the battle gradually subsided as the enemy abandoned what had been a powerful defensive position. The determined fight of the enemy soldiers and the near-impregnable nature of their line caught the Americans by surprise. "No one knew or even surmised the strength of the place," wrote Kendall, who thought it a "wonder" that anyone survived the tremendous enemy fire. However, after more than two hours, and after suffering their own rising toll of casualties, the Mexican troops melted away and struck out for the safety of the castle a few hundred yards away. As they filtered away, the grim task of caring for the injured began immediately as ambulances arrived on the field. As the process of collecting the dead and wounded got underway, the Mexicans lobbed a few shells from Chapultepec at the wagons, an act that fostered a certain bitterness among the Americans. About that time, Scott and Trist also arrived, and an officer sarcastically asked the diplomat if he had another peace proposal in his pocket.[28]

The price for this hard-fought victory was high—Worth lost almost 25 percent of his force. Out of a total of 789 casualties, 116 men had been killed, and the result was a melancholy gloom that fell over the army in the aftermath of the battle. Anger, sorrow, and indignation all aptly described soldiers' sentiments, and their emotions were made the more distressing by the painful realization that such carnage might have been avoided if only Scott had not allowed Santa Anna to regain his balance by giving him a nineteen-day grace period after Churubusco. And worse, a search of the buildings revealed some cannon molds, but no cannon and no cannon production. The heavy cost of blood had purchased nothing significant. Pennsylvanian Richard Coulter did not participate in the fight; nevertheless, he asserted that the Battle of Molino del Rey "is condemned by the entire army and reflects anything but credit upon General Scott." It was not just the heavy loss that so disheartened the army—they had suffered heavy losses before. Rather, it was the fact that they gained so little from it. Ethan Allen Hitchcock called the battle "a sad mistake." It was the second bad decision that Scott had made in less than three weeks.[29]

Yet according to Lieutenant Grant, the army could have achieved real success on this day. He believed that the Americans could have pursued the retreating Mexicans to the castle and beyond without additional loss of life. The enemy guns from the castle could not have fired on them without hitting their own men. Recalling the battle in his *Memoirs*, he asserted that "It is always . . . in order to follow a retreating foe." Grant, that Civil War general who, according to historian Russell F. Weigley, ushered into the later war a strategy of annihilation, found Scott's deliberate approach technically sound but fraught with moderation. Thomas Barclay believed that during the entire campaign Scott had displayed a want of aggressiveness, especially during his long stay in Puebla. "How much bloodshed would have been spared had Gen. Scott only had a little more of the go-ahead Napoleon spirit about him."[30]

After the battle, Ralph Kirkham returned to the place where he last had seen his best friend, William Burwell, during the charge. He found him near the spot where he had gone down and discovered the grisly results of his mutilation. Burwell's dog, a pointer, was lying next to him, licking his face, but the animal had also been shot and died within a few minutes. Kirkham picked up a lock of his companion's hair that had been severed by the blow of the lance, then had his body removed and buried beside other officers in the unit. Meanwhile, General Scott ordered Casa Mata destroyed, and Lieutenant William Armstrong of the Second Artillery was engaged in the task when the resulting explosion killed him. That night, Kirkham wrote a detailed account of the day's events in his journal. Then he sat down to pen a letter to his wife, making sure to spare her the gory details of the battle. "I cannot give any particulars," he wrote, but he did acknowledge that they had attacked with inadequate information about the enemy position and as a result had lost many of their best men. Before closing his correspondence, he wrote, "I feel very lonely tonight, I assure you, with my roommate and companion dead, and I sit here alone."[31]

CHAPTER TWELVE

God Is a Yankee

The Capture of Chapultepec

But usually one side is more strongly motivated, which tends
to affect its behavior: the offensive element will dominate, and
usually maintain its continuity of action.
—Carl von Clausewitz

The Americans were no closer to capturing Mexico City after the Molino del Rey battle than they had been before it, and the same question about how to advance on the city remained. Inadequate reconnaissance on August 20 and inadequate intelligence on September 8 had resulted in the two costliest engagements of the campaign, so Scott spent the next three days carefully gathering information about the enemy defenses. Six roads approached the city: two from the west and four from the south. All were raised and exposed causeways, which made for a treacherous approach. Before entering the capital, each road passed through a *garita*, or fortified gate, consisting of a strong block house, and these structures anchored the defenses that ringed the city. Two of the roads intersected at the Belén *garita* near the southwest corner of the town, one running from the Chapultepec castle to the west and the other running from the little village of Piedad to the south. The other causeway on the west side terminated at the San Cosme *garita* and was accessible from the castle by traveling north then turning due east to the city gate. The other roads on the south side all lay east of the Piedad causeway, each approximately a thousand yards from the next. One ran into the Niño Perdido *garita;* the next, the Acapulco Road, ran into the San Antonio *garita;* and the final road passed through the La Viga *garita* before entering the city's southeast corner.

Choosing the best route for his final approach to the city constituted Scott's immediate dilemma, and engineers Zealous Tower, Isaac Stevens, Robert E. Lee, and P. G. T. Beauregard conducted exhaustive reconnaissance in gathering information to help Scott make his decision. On Thursday, September 9, and the two days that followed, Scott renewed his interest in the southern causeways, and he even accompanied Lee in a close inspection of the southern gates on at least one occasion. By this time, it was familiar terrain for Beauregard and others who had been reconnoitering the area since before the Battle of Molino del Rey, and their inspections revealed growing enemy strength along the causeways and around the *garitas*. Around the San Antonio gate, the Mexicans had constructed fieldworks with six guns in embrasure. Additional fieldworks, trenches, and guns connecting the *garitas* of Niño Perdido, San Antonio, and La Viga were under construction, with hundreds of laborers engaged in the various projects. The layout of the works allowed them to command all of the southern approaches. The dangerous work of the engineers did not end when the sun went down. They conducted numerous missions at night, when they could creep closer to the enemy's position, and on one such occasion, Beauregard, accompanied by a small escort and a Mexican guide, attempted to get into the city and examine the defenses from the inside. The effort, however, failed when the guide panicked in the face of a Mexican sentry.[1]

Scott ordered Bennet Riley's brigade of Twiggs's division up to Piedad to cover the engineers while they worked and to present a strong military presence around the southern causeways. On September 9, Riley ordered Lieutenant D. H. Hill's company forward to the Niño Perdido causeway, and while there, Hill observed for himself the "immense force" and impressive fieldworks clustered around the *garitas* and connecting the roads. Later, Riley ordered the company to return to the regiment, and as it prepared to do so, one of General Gideon Pillow's staff officers arrived and instructed Hill to hold his position until another company arrived to relieve him. Hill had no knowledge of the brigade being placed under Pillow's authority, so rather than obey "an ignorant puppy," the lieutenant opted to do as his veteran brigade commander had instructed. On this occasion, Hill revealed his utter contempt for the Tennessee general, and his actions probably conveyed the feelings of many other regular officers. Having already referred to Pillow in his diary as "an ass" and "a pitiful fool," he simply refused to obey the order. When the Tennessean found out, he confronted Hill and in "harsh and insulting language" reprimanded the lieutenant, but Hill cut him off by shaking his sword in his face and demanding that Pillow not speak to him in such a tone. Pillow then arrested him, although he later released him at Riley's request and "retracted the offensive language."[2] Such was the resentment of the young professional officers for someone who owed his rank to political connections.

By Saturday, September 11, Scott decided "to avoid that net work of obstacles" on the southern approach to the city, and he called a conference to discuss options. Lee, Beauregard, and Tower were out on a reconnaissance mission when they were summoned at 10:00 A.M. to report to the church in Piedad, and when they arrived there, the principal parties were gathered:

Generals Cadwalader, Pierce, Pillow, Quitman, Shields, Twiggs, and Bennet Riley, recently promoted to brigadier general. Worth and Persifor Smith were on duty elsewhere and did not attend. The engineers were also present, as was Nicholas Trist and members of Scott's staff. Scott began the meeting by stating the obvious. The previous two battles had been costly; therefore, it was imperative that the upcoming attack be made where there was the least risk of casualties and the greatest chance of success. He went on to give his views on the advantages and disadvantages of attacks from both the south and west before expressing his opinion in favor of the latter. Although the Chapultepec castle, perched atop a steep hill, posed an ominous threat to attackers, if captured, Scott pointed out, it could serve as a safe place to lodge U.S. troops and a base for future assaults if necessary. The castle might even surrender without an assault but after an effective bombardment, and once the castle fell, he opined that the city might capitulate. In addition, the ground on the west side of the city was harder and more conducive for artillery and troop maneuvers. Although Scott did not say so, one wonders if, in his mind, a decision for a southern approach would make the attack on Molino del Rey seem all the more irrelevant.

Having voiced his preference, the commanding general opened the floor for other opinions. Gideon Pillow was the first to speak. In a lengthy monologue, he persuasively argued for an attack from the south so as to avoid the castle defenses. Then when Quitman requested to hear from the engineers, four of them, including Lee, spoke in agreement with Pillow's views. So Quitman, followed by Shields, Cadwalader, and Pierce also came out for the southern approach, but Twiggs sided with the commanding general. Riley, a veteran of the War of 1812 who was in his thirty-fourth year of army service, then asked the engineers which approach would require less time and labor in constructing batteries. When they responded the western, he pointedly said, "Well, I go in for less work and more fighting." At this point of the discussion, Trist and Colonel Hitchcock began to prod Lieutenant Beauregard to speak his mind. Beauregard had been surprised to hear his fellow engineers argue for an attack up the southern causeways, a course that he regarded as a mistake in judgment, but not wanting to oppose his friends publicly, he had resolved to remain silent. As Trist and Hitchcock urged and Beauregard demurred, their whispering from across the room attracted Scott's attention. Looking right at the lieutenant, Scott demanded, "You, young man, in that corner, what have you to say on the subject?"

Beauregard then launched into the most forceful argument offered by anyone present. He explained to the generals that he had been engaged in close reconnaissance of the southern defenses for the past four days and he could attest to the steady and impressive buildup on that side. The open terrain, irrigation ditches, and soft ground all made for a dangerous approach. Furthermore, a flank attack was impossible, and Beauregard pointed out that such maneuvers had been the cornerstone of American tactics thus far in the campaign. Taking all things into consideration, he asserted that to attack from the south would be fraught with more difficulties than the assault on Churubusco. After explaining that Santa Anna anticipated an attack from the south, he reminded them of the maxim, "never do what your enemy expects and wishes you to do." When Beauregard finished, the room fell silent. Scott then asked for further comments, and Pierce spoke up, changing his mind in favor of a western approach. More silence. Then Scott rose from his chair and firmly stated, "Gentlemen, we will attack by the Western gates!"[3]

Everyone understood that Chapultepec was the key to victory. The castle, which sat atop a two-hundred-foot-high rocky hill, had been built in the previous century by a Spanish viceroy, but since 1841, it housed the military college of Mexico. The stone walled complex formed a rectangle three quarters of a mile long and a quarter of a mile wide. On the western extreme of the grounds and about a thousand yards from the castle stood the buildings of Molino del Rey. Near the mill, the ground was flat but broken by numerous irrigation ditches that kept it drained. Proceeding east from the mill and toward the castle one encountered a marshy bog where the muddy ground provided an impediment for advancing infantry, and beyond that stood a grove of large cypress trees thick enough to provide cover for both attackers or defenders. From there, the ground sloped sharply up to the western face of the castle—a difficult climb, yet not as severe as the precipice that bounded the other three sides. Attackers ascending this incline would first encounter a redan—an angled field fortification shaped like two sides of a triangle designed to provide defenders with protection from the front and both flanks. Farther up the hill was a minefield and beyond that a ten-foot-deep fosse—a ditch or moat designed to impede the advance of infantry—that was in musket range of the castle above. Finally, a parapet wall surrounded the castle itself. The incline was steeper south of the castle, but a road cut into the side of the hill led to the summit. In the elbow of this road, the Mexicans had constructed a circular redoubt, inside of which they had mounted a field gun with entrenchments extended on both sides. Across the northern edge of the Chapultepec grounds ran an old aqueduct, but its arches had been filled in with bricks and mortar, making it a solid wall, and the vertical rock face on that side, as well as to the east, made an attack from those directions impossible.

To the Americans, the castle appeared as a fortress with its infantry trenches, sandbag redans, and ten cannon, but appearances can deceive. Because the Mexicans lacked the time and material to convert the academy

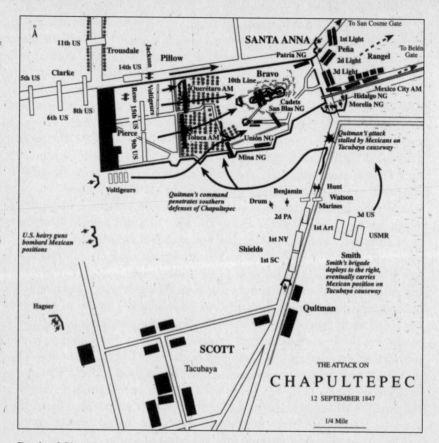

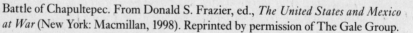

Battle of Chapultepec. From Donald S. Frazier, ed., *The United States and Mexico at War* (New York: Macmillan, 1998). Reprinted by permission of The Gale Group.

grounds into a real bastion, its defenses were actually inadequate and incomplete. Santa Anna remained fixed on defending the southern approach to the city, and consequently Major General Nicolás Bravo commanded no more than nine hundred men on the Chapultepec grounds—less than half the number needed to repel an attack. Furthermore, its worst feature was its isolated location two miles southwest of the city, and the same raised causeways that made it difficult for the Americans to approach the city also made it hazardous for Mexicans to come to the castle's aid. Scott hoped that an all-day bombardment on September 12 would induce the castle garrison to surrender thus negating the need for an assault.[4]

Scott's plan called for a feint against the southern *garitas* on September 12, coupled with the bombardment of the castle. Then, if necessary, he would

attack the Chapultepec complex. Scott hoped that Santa Anna would inter-
pret movements around Chapultepec as a diversion from a southern attack.
Before dismissing the generals from the conference, he ordered Quitman
and Pillow to march their divisions to Piedad that afternoon and join Riley's
brigade, which was already there. He wanted a troop buildup there before
sunset so that the Mexicans could see the Americans massing to the south.
Then around midnight, Quitman and Pillow were to move their men west
to Tacubaya, where Worth's division was stationed. Scott ordered Twiggs to
remain in Piedad with Riley's brigade to carry out the demonstration along
the Niño Perdido causeway next day and to move his other brigade under
Persifor Smith up from San Angel to Mixcoac. While he shuffled his troops
under cover of darkness, Scott also wanted batteries constructed and ready
to fire on the castle next morning.[5]

All night (September 11–12), the Americans prepared their gun emplacements. Lee, along with Captain Benjamin Huger of the Ordnance Department, supervised the artillery preparations. It was the first night of a
forty-eight-hour stretch that Lee would go without sleep. Captain Simon H.
Drum commanded a battery of three guns, a howitzer and two 16-pounders,
that he placed in a concealed position along the road just north of Tacubaya
and a thousand yards from Chapultepec. A two-gun battery consisting of a
howitzer and a 24-pounder under Lieutenant Peter V. Hagner rested to the
west and also just above Tacubaya. These five guns opened on the castle Sunday morning and kept up a steady fire all day. Several hours after sunrise, two
additional batteries with three guns total and located just south of Molino
del Rey joined in the bombardment. Not only did the cannonade pound the
castle, but occasional well-placed canister prevented the enemy soldiers clustered in the western suburbs of the city from reinforcing Bravo's force. Scott
listened to the bombardment all day from his Tacubaya headquarters, and he
waited in vain for news of the garrison's surrender.[6]

Meanwhile, south of the capital, Riley's brigade orchestrated a day-long
demonstration as if it intended to advance up the causeways. Two batteries of
small-caliber field guns under Captains Francis Taylor and Edward Steptoe
fired at the city's southern defenses from the Belén and Niño Perdido causeways. In addition, that morning, some of Riley's brigade advanced as if in
preparation for an attack toward the Niño Perdido gate, and he ordered the
Fourth Artillery up the causeway to disperse some Mexican infantry. They
remained within range of the enemy's guns for some time before rejoining
the regiment and withdrawing toward Piedad. In his report of the operation,
Scott characterized this movement as effective in holding Mexican troops
in their defensive posture on the south side. However, because the entire
brigade never deployed and showed itself on the causeway, the ever-critical

D. H. Hill thought the feint was inadequate and of too short a duration to be effective.[7]

In the afternoon, an anxious Scott summoned Captain Lee to his headquarters to report on the day's bombardment. Lee arrived with Tower and Beauregard to find the commanding general in an irritable mood. Scott, contemplating a night attack, needed information about the effects of the day's bombardment, and he was angry that Lee had not reported to him sooner. When Scott questioned them about the prospect of attacking the castle that evening, the engineers expressed skepticism about their ability to be ready, and Lee tactfully argued the merits of a daylight attack the next morning. But Scott's fear concerned the possibility that Santa Anna might send additional troops to reinforce Chapultepec during the night, and he wanted to attack when the enemy was most vulnerable. However, as Scott calmed down, he began to agree with Lee's recommendation, and at dusk, he ordered the guns to cease fire and called a conference of his division commanders.[8]

At 8:00 P.M., Lee returned to Scott's headquarters, where the generals had gathered for final instructions. During the conference, Pillow, in an incredible breach of etiquette, audaciously proposed his own plan for the next morning's attack. The commanding general listened to Pillow's "peculiar plan" in "polite and patient amazement," then, "with an exactitude not to be misunderstood," he laid out his plan and issued orders to each of his subordinates. Riley's brigade would remain at Piedad to cover the army's right flank and once again demonstrate against the southern causeways. Meanwhile, the artillery would resume a brisk fire on the castle, followed by a two-pronged infantry assault. Pillow would attack up the western slope from Molino del Rey with Worth's division in support, and Quitman would attack up the Tacubaya Road from the south, with Smith's brigade from Twiggs's division in support. And because Scott did not trust Pillow and lacked complete confidence in Quitman's volunteers, he instructed the supporting units (regulars) to supply 250 volunteers to spearhead each attacking column. Worth was to furnish 250 men to lead Pillow's charge, and Twiggs was to furnish 250 men to attack at the head of Quitman's division. These storming parties would carry ladders with them as they advanced, and their perilous task was to breach the enemy's defenses by scaling the outer walls and clearing a way for the rest of the troops. These spearhead attacks, "the forlorn hope," were unenviable tasks certain to result in heavy casualties, but promises of promotions resulted in no shortage of volunteers to fill their ranks.[9] Scott had formulated his plan to ensure that every division would have troops in the fight, which in turn would safeguard against disgruntled generals who were prone to complain about their unit's role.

Most of the generals left the conference depressed, except, of course, Quitman, who had begged Scott on previous occasions for an opportunity to fight. He now had his chance, and he would make the most of it. Pillow was displeased with the plan and concerned about the outcome. Worth believed that the attack would fail. Even Scott expressed apprehension to his most trusted staff officer, Colonel Hitchcock. Feelings among the troops were no better. The bloody but fruitless victory at Molino del Rey just four days earlier had a significant psychological effect on the army. A hard fight at the southern gates would at least gain them entry into the city, but the prospects of assaulting an impregnable hilltop bastion that, if captured, would still leave them two miles outside their objective was not an appealing thought. Scott, however, believed that the castle defenses were weaker than those along the southern causeways, and he certainly understood that the approach to Chapultepec offered more cover for attacking troops than did elevated roads. Besides, he still hoped that a Mexican capitulation would render an attack on the city unnecessary. Nevertheless, all of the troops knew that the assault would require great sacrifice, and so the attack order cast a "deep depression" over the army. Lieutenant Hill, who had volunteered for one of the storming parties, thought that the situation "now looked dark and gloomy in the extreme." Scott's decision shook the army's confidence in his leadership.[10]

There was consternation on the Mexican side as well. General Bravo's nine hundred defenders were made up of some veteran units but mostly of ill-trained national guardsmen, along with artillerymen and forty-six cadets who refused to leave when the college was evacuated. Bravo thought it imperative that he defend the woods west of the castle, but he needed more men. He requested that Santa Anna send him reinforcements, and he got a battalion, which he posted in the grove. However, the display of American infantry south of the city on September 12 convinced Santa Anna that Scott's main thrust would come from that direction. So not only did he refuse to send additional troops to Chapultepec that evening, but he also recalled the battalion that he had previously sent. Santa Anna and Bravo met during the night before the American attack, and the Mexican commander urged that Bravo abandon the grove and concentrate his forces on the hill and castle. However, Bravo was adamant, and after a lengthy discussion, Santa Anna committed to send more men before dawn. Bravo left their meeting thinking that he would be reinforced, but Santa Anna never sent the promised aid. Sagging morale and desertion was a significant problem among the Mexican troops.[11]

Throughout the night, engineers repaired damaged platforms and cannon in preparation for the morning's artillery barrage, and Lee, up for a second straight night, refused to sleep. In accord with Scott's instructions, and to assuage his concern over reinforcements reaching the castle, Quitman sent a detachment of some fifty men to perform the dangerous task of establishing an advance picket on the Belén causeway. While posted there, they became engaged in a "brisk skirmish" with Mexican troops, whom Quitman assumed to be the van of a larger body of infantry that he suspected would try to pass from the city to the castle. To meet this threat, Quitman sent Lieutenant George Andrews and a single piece of artillery to join the detachment, and on arriving at the road, Andrews used his gun to "rake the road with several discharges of canister." No enemy soldiers passed along the road that night.[12]

At 5:30 A.M., Scott gave the order, and the batteries opened on the castle again. As the sun came up, Pillow and Quitman prepared their units. Near Molino del Rey, Pillow organized his men into three attacking columns, and he attached himself to the center group, which was composed of four companies of the Voltigeurs, the Ninth and Fifteenth Regiments, along with Lieutenant Jesse L. Reno's mountain howitzers. Captain Lee would go in with the center column and help direct the way. Their line of attack was straight across the marshy bog, through the grove of trees, and up the west slope of the hill. To their right, Pillow placed four more companies of Voltigeurs under Lieutenant Colonel Joseph E. Johnston and Captain Samuel McKenzie's storming party. Their mission was to advance along the outside of the southern outer wall, force their way through an opening in the wall, and attack the castle from the southwest. On Pillow's left, his fellow Tennessean and future governor of the state, Colonel William Trousdale, would follow the aqueduct forward with the Eleventh and Fourteenth Regiments supported by a section of guns under Lieutenant Thomas Jackson. Pillow ordered Trousdale to get into position to cut off a Mexican retreat north.[13]

Quitman prepared his force along the road that led north out of Tacubaya. His collection of units was composed of the Pennsylvania, South Carolina, and New York volunteer regiments, the storming party from Twiggs's division under command of Captain Silas Casey, another group of 120 volunteers designated as stormers and commanded by Major Levi Twiggs, a contingent of forty marines under Captain John G. Reynolds, and Persifor Smith's brigade, which had arrived that morning from Mixcoac. Four field guns, one each commanded by Captain Drum and Lieutenant Calvin Benjamin and two under Lieutenant Henry J. Hunt, would follow Quitman's column into the fight, their position and targets governed by circumstances. Including Riley's brigade in Piedad, the American fighting force totaled about 7,200 men, and their opponent, huddled behind their defensive works around Chapultepec and the city, numbered perhaps 15,000.[14]

At 8 o'clock, the guns ceased their pounding, and the silence served as Scott's prearranged signal for the infantry assault to begin. Pillow's three columns advanced from the mill simultaneously. In the center, inside the walls of the compound, the four Voltigeur companies led the way, with the Ninth and Fifteenth (Pierce's brigade) close behind deployed for battle. Outside the southern wall, Johnston led the other Voltigeur companies and McKenzie's storming party as they rushed the gate in the center of the wall, which the Mexicans had blocked with a sandbag redan. They seized the redan, forced their way into the compound, and plunged through the edge of the woods before charging up the hill and capturing the circular redoubt and entrenchments. In their fighting on the southwest side of the castle, Johnston's men "virtually annihilated" the Mexican San Blas Battalion. There they took cover, and soon Pillow's force arrived and linked with Johnston's left.

But Pillow's center column had encountered more difficulties than had Johnston's men. It had pushed through the open ground, then became bogged down in the mud and tall grass, while Reno's howitzers fired shells over their heads into the Mexican defenses. As Pillow, on horseback, led his men into the cypress grove, they drove the enemy from their lodgment in the woods, which Bravo had correctly believed required more men to defend. As the Americans worked their way through the huge cypress trees, the enemy on the hill above depressed their artillery and began to fire canister and grape into the trees, splintering the limbs and causing confusion among the men. Units had already become intermingled as they emerged on the east side of the woods, and there near the base of the hill, a ricocheting ball of grapeshot hit Pillow at the top of his left foot, breaking his ankle. Lee, who was nearby, instructed some men to carry him out of the line of fire, and they placed him behind a large tree. From there, Pillow instructed a staff officer to go to the rear and call Worth's supporting division forward with "great haste"; then he turned command over to Cadwalader. Pillow's men started up the hill amid rumors that their general had been killed, and soon they linked on their right with Johnston's Voltigeurs.[15]

Colonel Trueman B. Ransom, trying to urge his regiment on up the hill and into the face of the castle's western defenses, stood waving his sword and shouted, "Forward, the Ninth!" Instantly, a musket ball struck him in the forehead and he fell dead. Despite seeing their commander shot down, they charged ahead anyway but were met with a hail of musketry. Some made it as far as the fosse and took cover there while the rest of the Ninth and the other units found shelter as best they could farther down the hill. Now pinned down, they discovered that the scaling ladders had not made it to the front. Without the ladders to get them over the wall that surrounded the castle, there was no point in pushing up the hill. They simply remained in place for at least fifteen minutes, exchanging musket fire with the enemy.[16]

While stuck in their scattered position on the lower half of the hill, they made another unsettling discovery. Some of the men noticed on the hillside around them small mounds of dirt. Perhaps they were buried soldiers from the previous day's bombardment? No, they were mines. This realization came as Cadwalader, Captain Joseph Hooker, and the rest of Pillow's staff were moving among the men trying to keep them steady. Unknown to the Americans at the time, the Mexican engineer, Manuel Aleman, whose job it was to detonate the mines at the appropriate moment, had deserted his post. Quickly the Americans located and cut most of the canvas powder trains that were necessary to ignite the explosives and thus avoided a potential disaster.[17]

Meanwhile, Trousdale's column advanced east on the Anzures causeway that ran along the outside of the north wall. After going only a short distance, a Mexican battery at the northeast corner of the rectangular compound opened fire, as did infantry shooting from the north face of the castle above. James Elderkin, who was engaged on the Anzures causeway and who later fought in the Civil War, remembered years later that Chapultepec was "the hottest engagement I ever experienced." At one point the musket balls were flying so thick that he felt the urge to put his hands up to protect his face. Lieutenant Thomas Jackson led two 6-pound field pieces up the road in support of the infantry, and as soon as the enemy opened fire, all twelve of the horses pulling his guns were killed or disabled, and one of the guns was damaged so badly that it was no longer serviceable. Unable to go any farther, Jackson tried to unlimber the other gun on the spot, but incessant enemy fire caused his artillerymen to scramble for cover behind boulders and shrubs on the side of the road. Jackson remained alone in the road, trying to position the gun amid animal carcasses that blocked the road, when former West Point classmate, Lieutenant George H. Gordon of the cavalry, rode by. "Well, Old Jack, it seems to me you are in a bad way!" Gordon chided. "Pears I am," Jackson responded.[18]

Jackson cooly walked along the road with musket balls kicking up dirt all around him as he exhorted his men to help him with the gun. "There is no danger," he shouted, later recalling that it was the only lie he ever told. "See? I am not hit!" No sooner had that sentence left his lips than a cannonball hit between his feet and bounced through his legs. His cajoling finally brought one sergeant up out of the ditch, and the two men struggled with the gun until they had it ready to return fire. The two of them repeatedly loaded and fired their small-caliber piece until Jackson's superior, Captain John B. Magruder, arrived. Reaching the point in the road where Jackson was working his gun, Magruder's horse was shot from under him, but he dusted himself off and, with the help of a few other men, dragged the damaged gun up alongside the other. Until reinforcements arrived, Jackson remained in the road, aiming and firing his guns. Once he was ordered to fall back, but he refused. Later, when someone asked him why he had not retreated in the face of such overpowering enemy fire, he responded that "it would have been no disgrace to have died there, but to have failed to gain my point it would."[19]

As these events were unfolding in Pillow's command west of the castle, all the while, Quitman was advancing from the south. At the signal to attack, he sent Smith's brigade off to the right to cover his flank as the remainder of his column pushed straight up the causeway. Deep ditches paralleled the road on both sides, making it difficult to cross over to the flat and relatively dry meadows that extended on both the right and left. Other ditches running perpendicular made it difficult to navigate the fields, so the men kept to the road even after they came under fire from Mexican infantry standing on risers behind the outer wall. The deadly musketry took its toll on Quitman's men, but they pressed on toward the southeast corner of the compound. Upon turning a slight curve in the road, a battery of five enemy guns, posted where the Tacubaya and Belén causeways intersected, opened fire from two hundred yards. The excellent Morelia Battalion of national guardsmen, commanded by Brigadier General Andrés Terrés, lined the intersection just east of the Chapultepec compound in support of the battery. To Private George W. Hartman, it seemed as if "thousands of muskets" were firing on them. Captain Casey fell seriously wounded and Major Twiggs was killed, shot through the chest. Now under intense fire from two directions—front and left oblique—the Americans scrambled for cover in the ditches and a few adobe huts on the side of the road.[20]

Despite efforts to push forward, Quitman's attack quickly stalled. A few members of the storming party tried to move off the road and lead a flank attack on the guns, but when they looked back, no one had followed, so they retraced their steps. Among them were Lieutenants Hill and Barnard Bee, both members of the storming party. Before the assault, they had discussed how their actions on this day would bring them notice back home, but this was not what they had in mind. Some of the officers tried in vain to get the marines to assist in another effort to charge the guns, and according to one source, their commander, Captain Reynolds, was sitting in the ditch, refusing to budge. Quitman pulled his men back about fifty yards to some shelter that was offered by the bend in the road, but he knew he could not stay there motionless. He instructed Shields to take the three volunteer regiments to the left, cross the corner of the meadow between the road and the compound, and try to penetrate the fifteen-foot-high outer wall. As they climbed out of the ditch and struck off across the low ground, some of the New Yorkers had a laugh at the marines' expense, yelling, "why don't you come along?"[21]

It was three hundred yards from the road to the south wall, and all of it across the Mexican front. The volunteers took heavy fire from behind the wall, and as a consequence their casualties mounted as they scrambled through the tall grass, a cornfield, and half a dozen irrigation ditches. Shields, having recovered from his near-fatal Cerro Gordo wound, was hit in the arm but refused to leave the field. Captain Abram Van O'Linda was killed at the head of his company of New Yorkers, and Lieutenant Colonel Charles Baxter, that regiment's commander, fell mortally wounded. A bullet struck A. J. Bates in the thigh, but it was not serious, so he pressed on. Within minutes, he was hit in the other thigh and he dropped to the ground unable to go further. Others went down after being hit multiple times by musket balls. Lieutenant Colonel John W. Geary of the Pennsylvania regiment was also wounded during the attack. However, two Pennsylvania volunteers accused Geary of cowardice for twice abandoning his men during the day's fighting. The unsubstantiated charge appeared to be politically motivated, for Geary was promoted to colonel after the battle and went on to serve with distinction as a general in the Union army.[22]

Upon reaching the shelter of the wall, the volunteers caught their breath for several minutes and tried to form their companies. Then the Pennsylvanians and New Yorkers moved to the left and began to pour through the redan that Johnston's Voltigeurs had opened just minutes earlier. Meanwhile, the South Carolinians found a break in the wall caused by the bombardment and used their bayonets to chisel it wide enough for a man to squeeze through, and in two places the volunteers began swarming into the Chapultepec compound. They ran to the foot of the hill, and in some cases officers, in the confusion, gave conflicting orders to move up the hill in this direction or that. But many of the men just ran straight up without hearing or caring about orders, and as they advanced from the southwest, they found the Voltigeurs and deployed to the right, thus giving the Americans a continual line of attackers from the west face of the castle curving around to the south face.[23]

The progress of both Quitman's and Pillow's columns had been slow and uncertain, but at this point, the situation began to change decidedly in favor of the Americans. Exact timing is difficult to approximate in a battle, but after what must have been about fifteen or twenty minutes stalled on the western slope, the scaling ladders arrived. Colonel Newman Clarke's crack brigade of regulars from Worth's division arrived too, giving the other units the momentum to push up the steepest part of the hill. Now in a concerted and concentric manner the mingled units of Pillow's and Quitman's commands began to close in on the castle at the summit. At the ten-foot-deep

Storming the walls of Chapultepec. Courtesy of Special Collections Division, University of Texas at Arlington Libraries.

fosse, some of the men tossed ladders in, jumped after them, and leaned them on the opposite side to climb out, while others laid the ladders across from lip to lip and using them as bridges, walked on the rungs to the other side, oblivious to their friends in the ditch below, who carried their muskets with bayonets pointed upward. As they pushed on to the final parapet, the Mexicans continued their heavy fire into the advancing lines. Leading the way for Clarke's Eighth Infantry was Lieutenant James Longstreet carrying an American flag. He was hit in the leg, and as he staggered to the ground, Lieutenant George Pickett grabbed the standard and continued to the top. Upon reaching the final wall, dozens of ladders went up and the bravest, or perhaps the most reckless, began to climb. Moses Barnard of the Voltigeurs was the first to plant a flag atop the Mexican works. A severe struggle for control of the parapet ensued, and in such situations, the bayonet, or perhaps the butt of a musket, was the weapon of choice. For several minutes the close combat raged until gradually the U.S. troops won the contest and began to pour over the wall. The defenders scattered across the terrace that surrounded the castle as Americans surged in greater numbers over the wall, across the grounds, and into the castle itself. Soon there was no delineation between the intermingled Americans and Mexicans.[24]

On the east side of the castle, Americans depressed some captured guns and began to fire down at the enemy stronghold at the north end of the Tacubaya causeway. This was just the assistance that Quitman needed. He organized the men left under his command and mounted another attack on the battery that had caused his column so much trouble an hour earlier. This time his men swept into the works, motivated by what Quitman called "desperate valor," and engaged the enemy in a hand-to-hand struggle that forced the Mexicans to give up their guns and retreat. Among Quitman's storming party was D. H. Hill, who, along with his comrades, turned left, entered the compound from the east, and started up the road that led to the summit. When Hill looked up, he saw the Stars and Stripes already flying from the top of the castle. But the fighting was not over; the Mexicans continued to resist in isolated pockets as they tried to escape.[25]

Hill penned in his diary what he saw when he reached the top. "The havoc among the Mexicans was now horrible in the extreme. Pent up between two fires they had but one way to escape and all crowded toward it like a flock of sheep." What Hill then described was an ugly attempt to exact revenge for the slaughter of American wounded at Molino del Rey. "I saw dozens hanging from the walls and creeping through holes made for the passage of water and whilst in this position were shot down without making the least resistance." All the while, American soldiers shouted, "give no quarter to the treacherous scoundrels." Israel Uncapher of the Second Pennsylvania recorded in his diary that he and half a dozen others "ran along the parapet and fired at the yellow devils as they ran." Several dozen teenage boys, *niños heroicos*, "heroic children," all cadets at the military college, had remained at the castle to help defend it. Six of them died late in the battle, jumping to their deaths from the castle walls, one clutching a Mexican flag. Today, these young cadets are honored inside the castle with a ceiling mural depicting one of them plunging to his death. Inside the castle, American soldiers broke down doors to find rooms filled with Mexicans pleading for mercy. Another Pennsylvanian, Richard Coulter, remembered that "some officers were taken prisoners, but few others were taken alive."[26]

To the north on the Anzures causeway, the Americans were also making progress. Early in the battle, Scott, unaware that Pillow had requested aid from Worth's division, had ordered Worth to move his troops east along that road to be in position to block both retreating and reinforcing enemy troops moving along the roads between Chapultepec and the city. Worth had dispatched Clarke's brigade to assist Pillow; then, in compliance with Scott's order, he sent his other brigade, Garland's, to reinforce troops struggling on the causeway. Worth followed Garland's brigade and ordered an attack on the Mexican position at the northeast corner, which broke through at about the same time that Quitman's men routed the enemy two hundred yards to the south. It was now about 9:30, and the fighting on the castle plateau began to die down as officers regained control of their men. Most of the Mexicans who had not been killed or captured were snaking their way down the steep rock face and retreating toward the city. General Bravo surrendered to Lieutenant Charles B. Brower of the New York regiment, handing the subaltern his diamond-studded sword.[27]

Two miles away, at Mixcoac, thirty more casualties occurred the instant the American flag went up over the castle. They were among the condemned deserters of the San Patricio Battalion. The other twenty whose death sentences had been upheld had been hanged in the previous three days, and Scott had assigned the forty-seven-year-old Colonel William Harney the task of carrying out the final thirty sentences. Harney was a martinet who used harsh punishment on his own men and was remembered for frequently hanging Indians in the Seminole War; his men feared him as much as they respected him. He hated foreigners, and any who got into trouble in his unit could expect rough treatment, usually bucking and gagging or hanging by the thumbs. He was just the sort for this grisly task. Scott had tolerated his insubordination at the beginning of the campaign, and as a result, he had benefitted from his bold and daring combat leadership. He was Scott's kind of soldier, but not his kind of man.

The prisoners had their hands and feet tied, and they stood in wagons beneath the gallows with nooses around their necks. In the distance beyond the village of Tacubaya stood the castle, perched atop its rocky platform high above the valley floor. Harney had decreed that the hangings would occur as soon as the American flag went up over the castle walls. At 6:30 A.M., with the preattack bombardment thundering in the distance, Harney rode over to the gallows where the condemned already had been standing for over an hour. He counted only twenty-nine prisoners and asked, "Where is the thirtieth?" The surgeon who was there to pronounce them dead at the appropriate time informed the colonel that the last man was Francis O'Conner, who had lost both legs in the Churubusco battle and was in the hospital near death. "Bring the damned son of a bitch out!" Harney shouted. "My order is to hang thirty, and, by God, I'll do it!" Several minutes later, litter bearers arrived with an unconscious O'Conner. They tossed him into the wagon, leaned him up against the driver's seat, and put a rope around his neck. Then Harney read General Order No. 283, which proclaimed their sentence.

For the next three hours, they all watched the castle in the distance, trying to see through the smoke that enshrouded the hill. After a while one of the prisoners, hoping that the Mexicans would successfully defend their hilltop bastion, yelled to Harney, "If we won't be hung until your dirty old flag flies from the castle, we will live to eat the goose that will fatten on the grass of your own grave, Colonel." But Harney acted as if he did not hear the man. Later, when another one made a derisive comment aimed at Harney, the colonel dismounted, climbed up into that man's wagon, and hit him in the mouth with the hilt of his saber, knocking out some of his teeth. Finally, at 9:30, while peering through his brass telescope, Harney saw the Stars and Stripes go up, and he ordered the teamsters to pull the wagons forward, thus leaving the deserters to dangle to their death.[28]

From Mexico City, Santa Anna and other officers had been watching the battle and the castle. He thought of sending reinforcements but hesitated until it was too late, still fearing an attack from the south. In the span of just a few minutes, he watched the Americans swarm over the walls of the castle, saw the Mexican tricolor lowered down the flagstaff and the Stars and Stripes go up, and saw, too, the remains of the Chapultepec defenders streaming in his direction. "I believe if we were to plant our batteries in Hell the damned Yankees would take them from us," he reportedly exclaimed. A subordinate officer nearby simply hung his head and muttered, "God is a Yankee."[29]

CHAPTER THIRTEEN

A Devil of a Time

Belén and San Cosme *Garitas*

When these deeds become known, our Country will be astonished,
but I regret to say with weeping.
—John W. Geary, Second Pennsylvania Volunteers

The bloody contest for Chapultepec ended after about an hour and a half, but it was only a lull in the battle. Some of the most intense fighting of the day lay ahead at the gates of the city. The castle acted as a magnet that morning, attracting the high-ranking officers of the army who wanted to see the prize up close. Pillow had some soldiers carry him up the hill in a blanket, or as one soldier called it, a "Buffalo robe," and while there, he listened to Cadwalader harangue the division with a patriotic speech from one of the castle's balconies. At one point, Pillow asked Sergeant Thomas Barclay, who stood nearby, what unit he was with. He was from the Second Pennsylvania, a part of Quitman's division that four months earlier had been part of Pillow's brigade. Remembering the aspersions that Pillow had cast on the unit after Cerro Gordo, Barclay boldly responded, "this is the 2nd Pa. Regt., the men who you said waved at Cerro Gordo." Pillow's pleasant disposition immediately turned to anger, and he shot back, "I think you have a damn sight of impudence for a sergeant."[1]

At the eastern base of the hill, Quitman gave instructions for his men to resupply their ammunition and form around the aqueduct on the Belén causeway in preparation to push on to the city. Then he ascended to the top to collect the rest of his division. Once at the castle, he stood on a parapet to examine the road leading into the city. Like the Anzures causeway that skirted the north wall of Chapultepec, it had an arched aqueduct running down the middle, but unlike that of Anzures, its arches had not been filled in with masonry. Its support columns were eight feet wide, and through the arches, one could pass from one side of the road to the other. Groups of retreating Mexican troops were still visible moving east along the road, and at the far end behind breastworks and redoubts, Quitman saw a large cluster of enemy soldiers around the Belén *garita*. That was his objective. He intended to pry the city open at the southwest gate, and he was in a hurry. Probably fearing that he would receive a halt order from the commanding general at any moment, he intended to push toward the city and out of Scott's reach as soon as possible. Scott had shunned an aggressive pursuit after Cerro Gordo and had refused to march on the capital after Churubusco, and now Quitman intended to press the American advantage all the way into what he perceived to be the ultimate objective. In addition, Quitman probably surmised, or at least hoped, that this would be the last battle of the war, and having been kept in the shadows throughout the campaign, he desperately wanted to seize this opportunity to distinguish himself. Before leaving the summit, his aides quickly gathered Shields's brigade, instructing them to collect on the road below, while he conferred with Pillow, convincing him to release his division to join Quitman's in an advance.[2]

A short time after Quitman left, Scott arrived with his staff. He and Hitchcock had been watching the battle from a housetop in Tacubaya, and when the general had seen the American flag go up, he mounted his horse and rode to the castle as quickly as possible. As he rode onto the summit, his men cheered and gathered around him, and he, in turn, lavished praise on all present. Then an officer brought General Bravo to Scott, and the two generals had a brief and cordial conversation. Next, Scott turned to Lieutenant George Davis, one of Quitman's aides, and asked the whereabouts of the division commander. When Davis told him that Quitman was massing his division for an advance on the Belén *garita*, a testy Scott asked, "Is it General Quitman's intention to advance without orders?" The question put Davis in a predicament. He did not answer—could not answer. What would he say, yes in defiance or no in dishonesty? His silence, however, sufficiently served as an answer. So Scott instructed Major Edmund Kirby to go to Quitman and order him to fall back to Chapultepec, which is precisely what the division commander had feared.[3]

Not only was Quitman acting without orders, but he was also thwarting Scott's plans. The Chapultepec victory represented yet another successful application of the sword, and Scott may have intended to halt and hold the castle until he could ascertain Mexican intentions. To have done so would have been consistent with his previous statements and actions. Once again, he had placed the city in "imminent danger of capture," which he had stated as a requirement for conquering a peace, and once again he had taken "a strong position from the enemy" and had done so "in view of the city." Now it was time to await the Mexican response. Conventional wisdom assumes that the city was Scott's primary objective on September 13 and that he intended to press on to the western gates, but with his old friend Worth in the vanguard. Perhaps. However, Scott's strategy of moderation would have dictated that he pause first to see if the city would capitulate without a fight. How long he might have halted operations, if at all, is impossible to know—a day, maybe only a few hours. If an assault on the city became necessary, he indeed meant to bestow that honor on Worth, and he already knew how he intended to approach the city. He would feint at the Belén *garita* with Quitman's division and send Worth's division to assault the San Cosme *garita*, the weakest gate of the city's west side. Quitman's rashness, however, threatened to put the day's events out of the commanding general's control, but again, this was just such a possibility that Scott had predicted in his Puebla letter. He wrote that after defeating the enemy or seizing a strong position, he would give the city officials a chance to surrender, "if he could restrain the enthusiasm of his troops." Seeing that he could not, he issued orders designed to have his tactical plans catch up with the facts of the situation. So he instructed Worth to collect his division, follow the Anzures causeway's dogleg to the north, and proceed two miles to the San Cosme causeway, then east to the San Cosme *garita*. The commanding general intended to throw every available unit in that direction while he continued to try to turn Quitman's advance into a mere diversion.[4]

Perhaps the best evidence suggesting that Scott did not intend to move immediately on the city lies in the fact that he attacked Chapultepec in the first place. It was a fortified position much like El Peñon to the east, and like El Peñon, it could have been bypassed or turned by a circuitous route and thus rendered useless. According to Ulysses S. Grant, whose *Memoirs* benefitted from four decades of reflection and the keen eye of the most famous commanding general of the Civil War, the castle could have been easily avoided. Scott could have reached his objective without ever coming under fire from the Chapultepec guns. By swinging around west of Molino del Rey, then north, the army could have gained the San Cosme causeway a mile and a half farther west and approached the *garita* in the same manner as Worth, with the entire route out of the castle's range. Furthermore, Grant contended, the Belén *garita* could have been approached from Piedad and remained outside the range of the castle's artillery. This kind of turning movement to avoid the strength of the castle fortification would have been entirely consistent with Scott's previous tactics and with his desire to preserve the lives of his men. Therefore, in hindsight, Grant proclaimed the attack on the castle to be "wholly unnecessary."[5] But that assumes that the city was Scott's objective when it most likely was not. History can never know precisely what was in Scott's mind, and in his reports of the battle, he certainly made it seem as if the attack on the *garitas* was a seamless continuation of the morning's action, but it is not farfetched to assume that Quitman's impetuosity altered what could have been a different ending to the campaign.

It took time for Worth to organize his column, replenish his ammunition, and fill in a trench across the road. The Mexicans had dug the trench across the front of their battery at the northeast corner of the castle compound to impede an infantry assault on their guns, but now it served the additional function of retarding the American pursuit. A similar trench across the Tacubaya Road protected the five-gun battery at the southwest corner, but while Quitman had gone to the top of the Chapultepec hill to gather his men, General Persifor Smith had supervised the task of filling it in with broken pieces of the outer wall. While Worth's men waited for the road to be repaired, they watched as two American civilians on horseback—"army followers," as one observer called them—rode over to some bushes about two hundred yards from the road. Hidden there were two Mexican soldiers, likely wounded and unable to keep up with their retreating unit, who got on their knees to plead for mercy. But the Americans drew their pistols and shot each man repeatedly. The U.S. soldiers watching from the road let out a "loud murmur of disapprobation at this atrociously savage act," and one even fired his musket at the two men. When they returned to the road where the soldiers were gathered, "they received a shower of curses and epithets, showing how much their infamous conduct was detested."[6] The disapproval of this kind of behavior presents a stark contrast to the actions of American soldiers who gave no quarter a short time earlier on the castle grounds. Those men, however, were largely volunteers from James Shields's brigade and relatively new recruits of Franklin Pierce's brigade—the types of soldiers notorious for undisciplined behavior. The ones down below on the Anzures causeway were the disciplined veterans of Worth's division of regulars.

The morning was slipping away by the time Worth's column turned left and started away from the castle. Worth had superseded Trousdale, who originally commanded that portion of the Chapultepec assault force. Now augmented by Sumner's dragoons, another light battalion, and batteries commanded by Duncan and Magruder, Worth pushed north in full view of the city on his right. But Quitman had a head start and a shorter distance to cover, and his column had already encountered resistance from a two-gun battery halfway up the Belén causeway. The Rifle Regiment led Quitman's column, but it had to take cover inside the archways when Mexicans began to rake the road with canister. Supporting their cannon was a redan to the right filled with infantrymen who began to pour musket fire into Quitman's troops. At the front of the column, Beauregard was hit in the thigh and had his shoulder grazed. Captain Drum brought his guns forward and returned fire as the Rifles advanced from arch to arch. An hour later, the Rifles had closed the distance enough to charge the battery and drive the Mexicans back to the Belén *garita*.[7]

When Major Kirby arrived with Scott's directive to stop, the first of several such messages that Scott sent to his division commander that day, Quitman ignored it. He was determined to be the first one inside the city, and, unwilling to allow orders to dampen his zeal, Quitman pressed on into the teeth of the heavily fortified gate. Santa Anna arrived at the gate to personally direct the defense and had brought with him more artillery and infantry. As Quitman advanced, he faced not only artillery and musket fire from the gate's blockhouse, but also the oblique fire from a battery on the Piedad causeway. Thus, as the forenoon turned to afternoon, Quitman found himself in a situation similar to the one he had been in that morning on the Tacubaya Road. In addition Santa Anna had posted guns along a promenade that ran north from the Belén *garita* and extended along the entire western edge of the city. They, too, opened fire on his advancing troops, forcing them to again seek shelter within the archways. The marshy ground prohibited any approach other than straight up the road. Fortunately, the width of the columns provided enough space to conceal about a half dozen men, and in this fashion, the Rifles, now intermingled with men of the South Carolina Regiment, moved from arch to arch, gradually nearing the gate. When the fire from the Piedad causeway became "very annoying," to use Quitman's descriptive understatement, Drum fired a few rounds of canister in that direction, which dispersed the Mexican gunners.[8]

Already wounded twice while on the causeway, Beauregard met more misfortune as the Americans inched closer to the *garita*—although perhaps "good fortune" is a more appropriate characterization. At one point while he, Quitman, Shields, and Smith tried to talk over the noise of battle, a shell struck the top of the arch they were standing under, sending debris down on them. Only moments later, grapeshot from the *garita* struck him; one slammed into his saber and did no harm, but the other hit him in the side, knocking him down. Stunned and with the breath knocked out of him, a friend gave him a drink of whiskey to resuscitate him. He unbuttoned his coat and found that the ball had hit right where he kept his gloves and eyeglasses. They had stopped the bullet's momentum, resulting in only a bruise.[9]

Quitman's casualties mounted, but his men kept working their way through the arches while Drum's artillery, firing from both sides of the aqueduct, provided support. Some time during their slow advance, Quitman and Beauregard left the causeway and attempted to survey the adjoining marshes when they both fell into a water-filled canal and the general lost one of his boots. At a little after 1:00 P.M., the rate of Mexican fire began to slacken as a result of two developments. First, they ran low on ammunition, and second, rumors that more Americans were advancing along the southern causeways induced some of their infantry to fall back to the city. With the gate now but a short dash away, Quitman took a weapon from a wounded rifleman, fired his last round, and tied a red silk handkerchief to the barrel. Waving it over his head, he yelled for the men to follow him into the works. The Rifles and Palmettos rushed to the gate and began to pour over the parapets, ending all Mexican resistance in that citadel. Israel Uncapher thought it was "the most bloody & hardest contested battle which has been fought in Mexico."[10]

It was 1:20 when the Belén *garita* fell, four hours since the capture of Chapultepec. But this proved to be only a lull. If the Americans thought that capturing the outer gate would gain them entry into the capital, they were soon disappointed. The gate stood three hundred yards from the city proper and from the Ciudadela at the city's edge. The Ciudadela, a converted tobacco factory, housed the garrison that was permanently stationed at Mexico City, and it presented another imposing obstacle blocking Quitman's ultimate triumph. The unfortified east side of the *garita* offered minimal protection for the American troops once inside, thus exposing them to fire from the city. The Belén defenders had withdrawn to the Ciudadela, and they soon resumed firing from there. Santa Anna had left earlier to go up to the San Cosme *garita* to prepare it for Worth's arrival, but now he hastened back to the Ciudadela with more men and artillery as the fight between the two strongholds intensified.[11]

When Drum ran out of ammunition, he and his battery mates abandoned their guns and turned a captured 8-pounder around to continue firing. According to one volunteer, "Drum displayed the most coolness & daring of any man I saw. He worked at the gun & leveled it every time himself while his men were falling fast around him." Quitman later referred to the artilleryman's "iron nerve" when recounting his division's action on the causeway. Within an hour, Drum was mortally wounded and his battery decimated: both of his lieutenants wounded, one of them, Lieutenant Calvin Benjamin, mortally, one sergeant killed, and all the other noncommissioned officers save one wounded. The lone uninjured sergeant became the battery commander. A Mexican cannonball took off both of Drum's legs, but he lived until after nightfall. "There has been no greater slaughter in any one company during the whole war," wrote D. H. Hill, also of Drum's Fourth Artillery. Hill also thought that Drum's company was "cut all to pieces" because "the raw levies which supported it behaved most cowardly."[12] It is unclear to which units Hill referred. He was always critical of the volunteers, and all three volunteer regiments were with Quitman on the Belén causeway that afternoon. However, the general indicated in his battle report that the volunteer regiments, especially the Palmettos, were in the thick of the fight with the Rifle Regiment. Perhaps he meant the Ninth Regiment of Pierce's brigade, which had been authorized and raised earlier that year and had joined the army at Puebla only five weeks earlier. They were truly "raw levies." In fact, all of Pierce's regiments fell into that category, but apparently only the Ninth accompanied Quitman up the road, and it is conspicuously absent from the general's battle report except for one passing reference.

With his situation becoming increasingly desperate in midafternoon, Quitman sent his aide, Lieutenant Davis, to find Scott and request artillery, ammunition, and artillerymen. The commanding general was on the San Cosme causeway, following closely behind Worth's column. When Davis located him and delivered Quitman's request, an irritated Scott responded that Quitman might as well "call on me for field-marshals." By rushing toward the Belén *garita*, Quitman had advanced into the strongest part of the city's western defenses, which is precisely why Scott wanted the main effort to be directed against the San Cosme gate. "Those views I repeatedly, in the course of the day communicated to Major General Quitman," wrote Scott five days later. But Quitman was out of his reach—in fact had temporarily removed himself from his superior's control, and standing in front of Scott was one of that general's aides. So to take out his frustrations, Scott proceeded to lecture the subaltern about Quitman being out of position and about his having advanced too far up the causeway. Furthermore, he had no available troops to send him, so Quitman would have to make do with what he had.[13]

Before the afternoon ended, the Mexicans attempted several sorties from the Ciudadela in an effort to push the Americans out of the *garita*, but each time, the muskets of Quitman's intermingled units beat them back. To minimize some of the enemy fire from the promenade, now directly on his flank, Quitman sent two companies from the Second Pennsylvania to a sandbag redoubt a hundred yards to the left of the *garita* with instructions to return a brisk fire in that direction. Quitman held his position in and around the *garita* until dark, when he hoped to bring up more artillery. After dark, the Mexicans ceased firing, thus providing the respite that the Americans needed to resupply, stack sandbags, and prepare gun emplacements for another push against the Ciudadela citadel the next morning.[14]

Meanwhile, to the northwest, Worth had spent much of the day trying to catch up in the race to the city gates. That morning after the Mexican units began to break and peel away from their positions in and around Chapultepec and while chaos and disorganization continued to reign around the castle, Hill and Barnard Bee gathered the remnants of their storming party and entered the Anzures causeway well ahead of Worth's division. They were soon joined by Thomas Jackson, who had mounted his broken guns on wagon limbers. With fewer than fifty men, this brave assortment left the bulk of the army behind and started up the road, pressing large numbers of enemy troops ahead of them. Like the Belén causeway, this road was divided down the middle by a large aqueduct with open arches, so when the Mexicans turned to resist the pursuit, the Americans found cover behind the columns. Much of the way up the road, the two sides fought a running battle, with Jackson periodically stopping to unlimber his guns and fire a few rounds. At one point, Magruder arrived and expressed concern about this small contingent being so far ahead of the rest of the army and the prospects of losing the cannon as a result. However, they persuaded him to allow them to go a little farther, and having done so, General Anastasio Torrejón formed 1,500 lancers on the road and charged the intrepid little band. Jackson cooly positioned his guns on each side of the aqueduct, and as he remembered later, "I opened on them," and with each shot "we cut lanes through them." Perhaps Bee's "stonewall" description, which he applied to Jackson fourteen years later, was merely the expression of an opinion formed in Mexico. After beating back the lancers, Hill, Jackson, and company decided to wait until the rest of Worth's division arrived before continuing.[15]

Hill's and Bee's presence on the Anzures causeway provides an example of how disorganized some of the American units had become. They, along with others in their group, were assigned to Twiggs's division but had been attached to Quitman's for the early morning assault. Now here they were a mile ahead of Worth's division, heading in a different direction from Quitman's force. No matter which approach to the capital the soldiers took or which unit they found themselves with, they were generally swept forward by the momentum of a running battle, and they all hoped that the road they were on would culminate in the city—and with peace.

By early afternoon, Worth's main column had caught up with Hill's improvised vanguard, and the whole pressed on toward the San Cosme causeway with a contingent of troops from John Garland's brigade now leading the way. At the point where the Anzures and San Cosme roads met, the Mexican resistance stiffened with the aid of a one-gun battery in the intersection pointing south. Because the intersection was in the outer suburbs of the city, the Americans were already encountering houses sprinkled along the road. Not only did the Mexicans plant a cannon in the road, but also infantry lined the roofs of nearby houses. In the new lead unit was Ulysses S. Grant of the Fourth Infantry, and he ascertained that the gun could be flanked by using as protection a rock wall that bounded a house at the intersection's southwest corner. Leading a dozen men and staying behind the wall, he crept around the house and formed his troops in the San Cosme Road west of the intersection and only a few yards away from the Mexican artillerists. The sight of the Americans on their flank caused them to immediately run toward the city, and so did their comrades on the rooftops.[16]

It was near the intersection where Scott overtook Worth's column. The commanding general had left Chapultepec late in the morning with his staff and also with Captain Lee. Since the fall of the castle, Lee already had reconnoitered Worth's entire line of advance to the suburbs, although there is little information about what he did and where he was. He was slightly wounded in the process but did not seek medical attention. He had reported back to Scott at Chapultepec and was engaged in escorting him up to Worth's position when he "could no longer keep my saddle." In other words, he passed out. He had been up for fifty-six hours without sleep and his body simply shut down. Friends took him to a safe place to recover and rest, but he was back in the saddle delivering orders before dawn the next morning.[17] Scott pressed on and observed Worth's operations for some time in the suburbs before returning to the castle late in the afternoon. It was sometime while he was on the road that Lieutenant Davis arrived bearing Quitman's request for artillery and reinforcements.

Turning right at the intersection, Worth's men began to make their final approach to the San Cosme *garita*. Houses now lined both sides of the road, and increasingly Mexican troops fired at them from windows and roofs, making a slow and cautious advance. By the late afternoon, they were within three hundred yards of the *garita* and completely stalled. This lightly defended and vulnerable gate had been remarkably transformed since the castle had fallen that morning. The Mexicans had hastily constructed a redoubt, filled in the near arches of the aqueduct with sandbags, and added three cannon to the gate's defenses. Santa Anna gathered additional troops as reinforcements and personally directed some of the day's preparations. The cannon from the gate raked the road with canister, and hundreds of Mexican infantry packed the rooftops, spraying the road with musketry. The scattered resistance that had annoyed Worth's advance throughout the late morning and early afternoon now turned into a storm of lead that completely halted his progress. By this time Quitman's men had been in the Belén *garita* dueling with the Ciudadela for close to two hours, but it would take the remainder of the afternoon and house-to-house street fighting for Worth to reach the San Cosme *garita*.[18]

While reconnoitering south of the road, Grant found a church ideally situated and with a bell tower that appeared tall enough to permit some shells to be lobbed into the *garita*. Upon returning to the main road, he secured a mountain howitzer and enough men to work it, and after they disassembled it, they struck out. Along the way, they had to cross several ten-foot-wide ditches that were chest deep with water. When they finally reached the church, Grant knocked on the door until a priest answered. The clergyman was polite but he refused them entrance, whereupon Grant, in broken Spanish, "explained to him that he might save property by opening the door, and he certainly would save himself from becoming a prisoner." At length Grant convinced him that "I intended to go in whether he consented or not. He began to see his duty in the same light that I did, and opened the door." They reassembled the howitzer in the belfry and proceeded to fire round after round into the *garita* from a little over two hundred yards. Their shots "created great confusion" among the enemy, Grant remembered years later, and he wondered why at such a close range and with no supporting infantry the Mexicans did not send a body of troops to the church to attack them.[19]

Meanwhile on the main road, Worth had ordered soldiers into the houses with pickaxes and crowbars to work their way up the street, going through rather than around the houses. In this manner Worth hoped to gain the north flank of the *garita*. When he saw the effects of Grant's howitzer shots and discovered their place of origin, he instructed Lieutenant John C. Pemberton, the future Confederate commander at Vicksburg, to go to the church, find the officer in charge, and bring him back. When Grant reported to Worth, the general was so pleased with Grant's enterprise that he ordered a captain of the Voltigeurs to go back with Grant and take another howitzer to place alongside the first. Grant did not take time to explain to the general that there was no room in the belfry for a second gun. He returned to the church with the other gun, but did not use it. A similarly ingenious placement of a howitzer on the north side of the road by Lieutenant Raphael Semmes also proved effective.[20]

The sun was rapidly descending in the western sky when the San Cosme *garita* finally fell. The Mexican defenders had fought bravely all afternoon, sending a constant hail of bullets down the road. They had inflicted casualties but had also taken their share, among them Brigadier General Joaquín Rangel, who had been badly wounded while directing the defense. The end came when American soldiers appeared on the roof of a three-story house thirty yards away from the redoubt that commanded the causeway. They were marines and members of the sapper group that for several hours had been methodically cutting their way through the houses on the north side of the road. Their proximity and elevation allowed them to fire a volley right into the works, scattering many of the defenders. To seize their advantage, the marines went back down the stairs, rushed out the door of the building, and stormed right into the redoubt. As they jumped over the works, they ran headlong into a flood of Worth's soldiers, who had also rushed the position and were pouring in from the street. The remaining Mexicans fled, giving Worth possession of the *garita* and its surrounding defenses. As darkness approached, the front of Worth's unorganized column marched into the western edge of the city near the large Alameda park, but he went no further. His men spent that night in houses close to the San Cosme gate, and the day's activities ended with Captain Benjamin Huger aiming a 10-inch mortar toward the National Palace in the center of town and firing five rounds.[21]

Around the San Cosme and Belén *garitas,* exhausted American soldiers rested and prepared their minds and bodies for more heavy fighting the next morning. Having captured both fortified gates, they were now knocking on the door of Mexico City, but at sunrise, they knew that they would have to break through that door and engage the enemy in a house-to-house street fight in order to claim control of the city. Back at the base of Chapultepec where the two western approaches to the city diverged, Scott oversaw the collection of supplies, hastened forward stragglers and various detachments to their respective units, and "sent to Quitman, additional siege guns, ammunition, [and] intrenching tools." At the Belén gate, as soon as it was dark and the fighting died down, Quitman's staff officers, Mansfield Lovell and George Davis, went to work directing soldiers in the construction of fortifications, and Beauregard oversaw the placement of a battery. Quitman's primary obstacle at first light would be the Ciudadela, and his preparations were designed to provide defensive protection from its guns as well as offensive firepower to reduce that stronghold.[22]

Late in the evening, Quitman instructed Davis to go to the rear and bring ammunition forward. Davis went all the way back to Mixcoac, four miles to the south. There he procured two wagons of ammunition, but the drivers were reluctant—frightened about the danger of going that far forward. Davis insisted that they go, and their sense of duty compelled them to comply. One of the drivers, however, had a change of heart along the way and drove his wagon off the road in an attempt to overturn and disable it, but the shoulder was shallow and the wagon remained upright. Davis galloped forward just as the driver was attempting to dismount and flee, and, pointing his pistol at the man's head, Davis threatened to blow his brains out if he did not get back in the driver's seat. The lieutenant delivered the ammunition to the Belén gate in the middle of the night and in time for it to be distributed before sunrise.[23]

As it turned out, Quitman did not need the ammunition. In compliance with the wishes of political leaders to save the city from destruction, Santa Anna collected his disheartened troops, about 12,000 of them, and at 1:00 A.M. marched north to Guadalupe Hidalgo. At about 4:00 A.M., a messenger from the city council arrived at Scott's headquarters, informing him of the army's evacuation and offering terms to surrender Mexico City into his hands. Scott would accept no terms, but he gave one of his own. He demanded an immediate "contribution" of $150,000 to help pay the expenses of the American occupation. Although he demanded the unconditional surrender of the capital, he assured the emissary that they would receive fair treatment from his troops. Unaware of these developments, Quitman was surprised at dawn to see a white flag emerge from the Ciudadela and approach his line. The bearer informed him that the Mexican troops were gone and that the citadel was open to his men. Suspicious of a trap, Quitman agreed to Lovell's and Beauregard's request that they be allowed to go to the Ciudadela to investigate. There they encountered a Mexican officer who asked them to sign a receipt for the fortress, to which Beauregard responded that American troops give "receipts with the points of our swords!" Immediately Quitman ordered his men to arms, and there was great scurrying about as they formed on the road. Still anxious to be the first general in the city, he wasted no time in marching his dirty troops in their battle-stained uniforms straight for the National Palace located in the Grand Plaza. Civilians lined the sidewalks and rooftops and peered through windows, staring in angry amazement as Quitman, still wearing only one boot, led his soldiers, some limping, some wounded, and all ragged and tired, through the streets. At 7:00 A.M., a marine lieutenant raised the American flag over the palace as the men gave a loud hurrah. They were in Mexico City at last. One member of the division, Hachaliah Brown, later wrote to his family about lost friends and about his amazement at having "come off without a scratch" in the fight to capture the city. "Had a devil of a time to get here," he wrote.[24]

Scott, meanwhile, had put on his splendid uniform, left his headquarters before daylight, and ridden with his staff north to the San Cosme *garita*. He entered the city and met General Worth at the Alameda at about 6:00 A.M. Then, in keeping with Scott's penchant for flair, the troops were organized into a procession for the general's formal entry into the city. Harney's dragoons led the way, followed by the commanding general and his staff, with Worth's infantry bringing up the rear. "A brilliant cavalcade," one soldier called it. Historian Douglas Southall Freeman wrote that "Napoleon himself could not have set the stage more theatrically." Lieutenant D. H. Hill marched into the city in Worth's column, and he recorded that the "houses were all open and the balconies crowded. The people gazed at us as at wild animals," but Hill detected no signs of "enmity." Quitman was expecting Scott, and he had his men at attention in the plaza when the clatter of many hoofs announced the commanding general's arrival. Scott entered the plaza at the northwest corner, and Quitman's men lined the western side of the square facing east. Harney's musicians played "Yankee Doodle" as Scott's bay slowly cantered along the front of Quitman's lines. When he saw the flag of the Mounted Rifles, he reportedly uttered what would become the regimental motto: "Brave Rifles! Veterans! You have been baptized in fire and blood and have come out steel." As he reached a point opposite the National Palace, he turned left and rode over to the magnificent facade. In front of the

General Winfield Scott and staff entering the plaza of Mexico City on the morning of September 14, 1847. Courtesy of the Library of Congress.

palace, Scott dismounted, named Quitman the civil and military governor of the city, and walked into the Halls of the Montezumas.[25]

It was 8:00 A.M. when Scott rode into the grand plaza, exactly twenty-four hours after the beginning of the assault on Chapultepec. His presence in the heart of the enemy capital marked the end of a brilliant six-month campaign and crowned his career with remarkable achievement. It was, however, a bloody twenty-four hours. American killed numbered 130, and adding the 703 wounded and 29 missing, losses totaled 862. Mexican losses totaled about 3,000, with over 800 of that number being captured. Since marching into the Valley of Mexico, the American army had suffered 2,703 casualties, 383 of them deaths, in what had essentially been four days of fighting.[26]

Taking possession of the city brought on a few spasms of residual resistance. As the men dispersed from the plaza, they received fire from several rooftops and windows. After surviving all the battles of the campaign, John Garland was the first wounded when a musket ball hit him in the thigh. Others were wounded, some mortally. Thus began three days of sporadic street fighting perpetrated by a coalition of deserters from the Mexican army, looters, and many of the estimated 30,000 convicts that the city's priests had released from jails and prisons. Some of the fighting was simply the typical manifestations of lawless thuggery that occurs in the absence of authority.

Indeed, as Quitman reported, when his men marched into the plaza that morning, the "palace [was] already crowded with Mexican thieves and robbers" and had to be cleared by a battalion of marines. In other areas of the city, looting had already given rise to chaos. However, there were hundreds of Mexicans engaged in the shooting, and the clergy, who had instructed the placement of many of the Mexican snipers and opened the church towers to them, orchestrated much of the uprising. An emboldened citizenry, many of whom took heart in the renegade actions of the deserters and convicts, joined in the resistance as crowds of angry residents took to the streets to threaten the foreign occupiers. All classes of Mexican men and women participated in the opposition. Their weapons were not only muskets but also paving stones thrown from upper stories.[27]

To restore order and quell the resistance, Scott resorted to harsh tactics, or as Quitman called it, "rigorous measures." He sent a message to the mayor threatening to "sack the city" if the shooting continued, to which the mayor responded, "This is all the work of those cursed friars!" Scott also authorized his artillery to open fire on any house from which sniper fire originated, and once the offending house was battered by cannon, it was ransacked by infantry. According to Hill, it was "adopted as a rule to rifle every house from which there came a shot and to kill every armed Mexican found in the streets." The Americans also fired into the angry crowds to clear the streets. As Hachaliah Brown wrote to his family: "I have the death of about 150 poor wretches on my conscience, having been compelled to fire on a large mob assembled in one of [the] streets where my 24 pound howitzer was planted." Robert E. Lee characterized the Mexican sniping as annoying and called their shots "desultory" or erratic, but he contended that "after killing some 500 of the mob & deserters . . . who had not courage to fight us lawfully, the thing was put a stop to." In the process, however, some of the U.S. troops interpreted Scott's stern recourse as "unbridled license" to do as they pleased, and they did. Tuesday, September 14, turned into a shameful display of uncontrolled marauding. Hill became outraged at the actions of some of the men. "Many of them were perfectly frantic with the lust of blood and plunder. In order to sack rich houses many soldiers pretended that they heard firing from them." In several cases, they threw men from housetops and shot women who handed loaded guns to those in the streets. And "in some instances," recalled Brown, "*bullets* passed thro Reverand gowns." For Hill, it was "a day of bloodshed and brutality such as I trust never to see again," and he believed that "its horrors will never be forgotten in Mexico."[28] It has not.

That night, sharpshooters and riflemen took positions in church belfries, in domes, and on rooftops, and the next day, they reportedly killed about fifty armed Mexicans who showed themselves. On September 15 and 16, order gradually returned.[29] The capital remained a dangerous place for isolated or wayward soldiers, and the army took the usual measures of caution consistent with the occupation of hostile territory. As soldiers settled into their new duties, the army began what turned out to be a protracted occupation of central Mexico while they waited for the slow wheels of peace to turn. Conquering a peace, however, took longer than Scott anticipated with the Mexicans—and proved to be altogether impossible within his own army.

CHAPTER FOURTEEN

The Preoccupations of the Occupation

*Strange and almost incredible seems our victory. . . . History will
no doubt speak of our achievement as more glorious than that of
Cortes. I am truly thankful that I took part in the most glorious
battles. . . . Strange is our position at present. We are in the
enemy's Capital and yet all communication with our front and rear
is cut off so that we may almost be said to be besieged in the very
center of the Mexican power.*
—Daniel Harvey Hill, Fourth Artillery

Gideon Pillow called the Battle of Chapultepec "one of the most brilliant fields
known to the American Arms." Hachaliah Brown said that "Chapultepec was
a brilliant 'coup de main' the prettiest affair of the campaign." George Kendall had difficulty believing that the small army had actually made it to Mexico
City. It "seems like a dream. . . . Yet here in Mexico we are, & masters."
"Strange and almost incredible seems our victory," thought Daniel Harvey
Hill when he considered that a Mexican army 17,000 strong gave up its capital
to a force of 7,000. However, maintaining the tranquility of a city with a population of almost 200,000 would prove more challenging. Scott established
martial law and took the unusual step of levying a $150,000 contribution on
the city to defray the occupation costs. While the commanding general res-
urrected the elements of his pacification plan—strict discipline, payment for
food and supplies, and respect for religious and property rights—Quitman,
as military governor, reinstated the city's civil authorities, who helped restore
order among the populace. Excepting the occasional abuses perpetrated by
the worst elements of the army, behavior improved markedly as discipline
was reasserted after the outrages of September 14. Within days, stores reopened and business returned to a semblance of normality.[1]

Having failed at the outset of the occupation to arouse a general uprising
against the Americans, the priests tried again on the first Sunday, September 19, to create ill will among the citizenry. They intended to keep all of the
churches closed in the hopes of arousing the "fanatical prejudices" of the
masses against the army. That morning, Quitman noticed that no church

bells were ringing to signal the coming of Sunday mass, and he and Lieutenant George Davis went to consult with Scott. An American flag flew over
every church in the city to signify the army's protection and the guarantee of
religious freedom, but the priests hoped that by keeping the churches closed,
the populace would assume that the Americans were responsible and that the
flags represented a war against Catholicism. Quickly surmising the priests'
intentions, Quitman ordered the clergy to immediately open their churches
and ring their bells or else both protection and flags would be removed. The
threat worked, and another attempt to turn the people against the Americans
failed.[2]

In the early days of the occupation, caring for the wounded was a top
priority. Scott ordered that those wounded in previous battles and left in
Tacubaya be brought to the capital. Those too seriously injured to ride in
shaky wagons were carried the four miles on litters, "hard work but cheerfully performed." General James Shields, who received an arm wound in the
assault on the castle, did not leave the field to seek medical attention until that
night after the fight at the gate. But he made the triumphant entry into the
city the next morning with the rest of the army, although he did so in a carriage. Doctors dressed James Longstreet's thigh wound, but it healed slowly.
One unfortunate soldier, shot in the head on the morning of September 13,
received no medical attention because doctors assumed his wound was fatal.
It was, but the poor man lingered in agony for five days before dying. Barna
Upton of the Third Infantry regretted joining the army, and in a letter to his
family, he admitted that he had "learned a lesson that will prevent me from
roving about as I have done." Upton languished for a month after receiving a
wound on September 13. He died on October 15, but his family did not learn
of his fate until seven months later, when they received a letter from one of
Upton's friends. Having served with Upton on every battlefield from Palo
Alto on the Rio Grande to Mexico City, William Fogg assured the family
that "a better soldier never served his country or died for it." Robert E. Lee
remembered with remorse the deaths of Simon Drum and Calvin Benjamin,
"noble fellows" who fought "like lions" and were both killed at the Belén gate.
In a letter, Lee, after serious expressions of sorrow, flippantly quipped that
his friend "Joe Johnston is fat ruddy & hearty. I think a little lead, properly
taken is good for a man," referring to Johnston's full recovery from his Cerro
Gordo wounds. He went on to assure his correspondent, "I am truly thankful
however that I escaped all internal doses."[3]

Soldiers continued to die from wounds received at Churubusco and Molino del Rey, and coupled with the injured from the most recent fighting, the
hospitals contained more than two thousand men. Units were depleted. Lieutenant John Sedgwick of the Second Artillery left Puebla with fifty-four men

in his company and entered the capital with twenty-seven. After the capture of Mexico City, many officers applied for leave to go home, but the army's officer ranks had become so depleted by casualties that Scott denied all requests for leave, logically concluding that he could not spare the good officers and he would not reward the bad ones. Lieutenant Ralph Kirkham wrote his wife informing her not to expect him home any time soon, because Scott would not even grant leaves to wounded officers unless they had a doctor's certificate. A few days after the fall of the capital, Kirkham went to a hospital to visit Colonel James McIntosh and Lieutenant Rudolph Ernst, both destined to die of wounds received at Molino del Rey. He later reported to his wife, "I could not bear the sight of the wounded. . . . No one but an eyewitness can imagine the sight of a hospital after an action." He went on to describe "trunks without limbs" and people with such mangled bodies that they were unrecognizable, yet they continued to live. Kirkham, a New England Episcopalian, did what most men of faith do under such trying circumstances. His journal contains his expression of thanks to "my Heavenly Father for having brought me unharmed out of this terrible battle" and a renewed commitment to live a worthy life: "May I by my future conduct express my thankfulness more than I can by words."[4]

Others died during the occupation even though they had escaped injury in battle. William Adee, Third Infantry, wrote to his father in October informing him that he had been sick with diarrhea but was optimistic about his recovery. He gave his family no indication that his illness was serious; however, he had promised in an earlier letter to "provide the means to Inform you" if anything happened to him. Sergeant Charles F. McBride turned out to be the means by which Samuel Adee learned of his son's death. Writing "to offer a stranger's condolence," McBride informed the family that William had contracted dysentery in Veracruz in the spring and never recovered. He had participated in battles, even the fighting around Mexico City, but "he whom death had shunned on the field of battle . . . was reserved to die in his bed, the victim of a protracted and painful disease." He died on October 30, two weeks after his last letter home. Along with a lock of the son's hair, McBride sent the father assurances that William had "died as he lived, a man."[5]

After a slow convalescence in the hospital, Longstreet was fortunate to be moved to the home of the wealthy Escandones family. In general, however, Americans, healthy or infirm, were forbidden to stay in private homes. Most units were housed in public buildings. The Pennsylvanians found quarters in a university, then in a large warehouse. Part of Twiggs's division was housed in a building that had been used by the Mexican army. Members of D. H. Hill's unit quickly became displeased with their accommodations in the National Palace, which Hill referred to as the "filthiest place I have ever seen" and an "immense pile." He and his companions were dismayed at the degree of filth in the city. Hachaliah Brown was among the few lucky soldiers who gained permission to stay in a private residence, and he wrote a letter home bragging of the luxuries he enjoyed. "I wash in porcelain & *urinate* in a *silver* pot-d-chamber."[6]

As the men settled into their lodgings, Scott contemplated his next move. Not knowing how long it would take to secure a treaty and understanding the need to spread out the cost of the occupation, he proposed seizing other cities in central Mexico. That, however, would take more troops, which were, in fact, already en route from Veracruz. As he had been promising for months, Secretary of War William L. Marcy continued to search for additional troops to augment Scott's numbers, and the administration increased its efforts when President Polk learned that Scott had voluntarily cut his own supply lines. The president understood that the army's isolated situation in the interior of Mexico was critical, and he was anxious that communication with the coast be restored. To that end, he sent all available men to Veracruz, either from new, untrained regiments being raised in the States or from veteran volunteer units borrowed from Taylor's army. They arrived in Veracruz piecemeal and wholly unprepared for combat, and commanders assembled them into columns as quickly as possible and rushed them forward. Indeed, as Scott's army marched into Mexico City, one column had already left Veracruz, marching west as troops continued to arrive on the coast.

Among the new troops traveling to Mexico in late summer was a member of the 1847 West Point class named Ambrose Powell (A. P.) Hill. The twenty-one-year-old Virginian was getting to Mexico a year late. He had entered the academy in 1842, but during the summer furlough after his second year, probably while in New York City, he had contracted gonorrhea. The effects of the disease incapacitated him that fall and winter to the point that he had to repeat his third year at the academy. Consequently, when his former roommate, George McClellan, and the rest of his original classmates graduated in 1846 and headed for the theater of war, Hill still had a year of school to complete. His health improved and he finished fifteenth in his class before receiving orders to report to the First Artillery Regiment in Mexico. His gonorrhea was never cured, and its painful effects continued to reappear over the years until it became chronic and debilitating. Eventually it was not the disease that killed him but the musket ball of a Union corporal near Petersburg, Virginia, in 1865, where Hill was serving as a lieutenant general in the Confederate army. But in 1847, the young lieutenant traveled to Mexico with high hopes. He left New Orleans on a steamer that collided with another vessel on the first day out, forcing it to return to the city for two days of repair work. On the way to Veracruz, Hill was fascinated at his first sight of flying fish. He was equally impressed with the "extreme beauty of the panorama" when he arrived at the port city, but he quickly formed a negative opinion of its inhabitants.[7]

By the time Hill arrived at Veracruz, a thousand troops had already departed for Mexico City. The column, commanded by Major Folliott T. Lally, had started inland back on August 6, but it quickly ran into trouble in the guerrilla-infested country between the coast and Jalapa. After being attacked by at least 1,200 Mexicans under Padre Caledonia de Jarauta on August 10, the beleaguered column waited two days at the National Bridge for reinforcements that never got through from Veracruz. Lally's men had to fight their way the remaining forty miles to Jalapa, and by the time they arrived on August 20, they had suffered ninety-two casualties. Lally's experience is an indication of the wisdom of Scott's decision to cut off his communication with the coast. Had he tried to keep supplies and troops moving from Veracruz to the interior, guerrillas would have constituted a serious enough threat to siphon off needed men and matériel. Lally's situation finally improved in late September when Brigadier General Joseph Lane's force of 1,700 men and more than 150 wagons overtook his column west of Jalapa. Lane was an Indiana politician who had received a commission as a colonel of volunteers in 1846 and had fought admirably at the Battle of Buena Vista. When he received orders from Washington transferring his brigade from Zachary Taylor's army, he hurried to Veracruz, then got his bulky column moving inland on September 19. His presence in Veracruz coincided with that of Hill, who was assigned to a contingent of six hundred infantry and cavalry that had left the coast two days behind Lane's column.[8]

Lane skirmished with a guerrilla force, killing seven of them before moving on to the National Bridge. He remained there for four days, then moved through Cerro Gordo to Jalapa. The ground around Cerro Gordo remained littered with cannonballs, spiked cannon, and other artifacts of the battle. Hill traveled with Louisiana volunteers, and he recorded that on their second day out, some of the volunteers burned a hacienda that they thought was Santa Anna's—"wantoness entirely uncalled for and unjustifiable." The road from Veracruz to National Bridge bore evidence that an army had passed through: strewn about were clothing, worn-out shoes, broken wheels, canteens, and knapsacks. In some places the debris lay more thickly than in others, indicating spots where wagon trains had been attacked and cut off by guerrillas. The surrounding terrain, with its thick chaparral and natural defensive positions, was the most "favorable country for ambuscades, surprises, etc." that Hill had ever seen. And when he saw that most of the ranches along the road had been destroyed by passing American troops, he understood why many of the inhabitants turned into guerrillas, "ready to murder the first straggler." These troops, two hundred miles away from the theater commander, neither knew nor cared about the restrictions that pacification dictated. Besides, this was guerrilla warfare, and the rules were different. But alas, the partisan activities of the Mexicans proved inadequate to stop the passage of American troops, and Hill concluded that "they have not the courage to avail themselves of [opportunities] . . . and allow the country to be overrun by a handful of invaders." Many of the houses that Hill saw along the road were thatched buildings made of straw and poles. "They are very respectable chicken coops and thats the way I account for the people being so chicken hearted," he wrote.[9]

When Hill's column got to within four miles of the National Bridge, one of their wagons broke down. Hill had been in command of fifty mounted volunteers who made up the rear guard, and they were ordered to stay behind with the wagon while the rest of the troops marched beyond the bridge and set up camp. Then they would send back help. It was about 7:00 P.M., and the fact that they were in guerrilla-infested country made Hill and company nervous. Hill dismounted his men and instructed them in setting up a defensive position. For three or four hours, all went well; the volunteers were diligent and followed Hill's directives. However, after the passage of time had lessened their sense of danger, they began to grumble about being left behind, and they increasingly discussed riding on to reunite with the rest of the men, in violation of their orders. By midnight, some of them started readying their mounts to leave, and Hill knew that he had to do something. His appearance alone should have been sufficient to keep the men in line. He wore a sombrero, "flaming red flannel shirt," red-trimmed boots, and an "immense pair of Mexican spurs." Even more impressive was the arsenal that he had strapped to his body: a pair of pistols in holsters at each side, two more stuck in his belt, a butcher knife, and his officer's saber. "I was as villianous a looking rascal as ever there was," Hill thought. Without saying a word, Hill mounted his horse, walked it over to a position blocking the road, and turned to face the men. Still silent, he loosened the fastening of his saber and unholstered two of his pistols. There he sat with pistol in each hand quietly, staring at the men and they staring back at him. "[W]e thus passed half an hour, it seemed to me an age, interchanging compliments with our eyes, they afraid to advance expecting the first man to be shot, and I the Lord knows what I intended to do. I expect that I was as much frightened as the men, but force of discipline led me to do what I did." While thus engaged, horses and wagons returned to carry them back to camp.[10]

At their bivouac near the bridge, they received a message from General Lane instructing them to join him at Jalapa as soon as possible. Lane had discovered that the isolated American outpost at Puebla was under siege, and he wanted to gather his men, overtake Lally's column, and rush to the scene of action. Scott had left 2,200 men in Puebla in early August under the capable leadership of Lieutenant Colonel Thomas Childs, a West Point graduate with over thirty years of military experience. Childs's garrison consisted of one company from each of the Second Artillery, Fourth Artillery, and the Third Dragoons, and six companies from the First Pennsylvania Volunteers. Along with a handful from the spy company, Childs commanded a total of about four hundred able-bodied men. But the remainder of the garrison, 1,800, consisted of the sick and wounded, who were too incapacitated to continue with the main army. Puebla was really a detached and isolated hospital facility, but its continued possession by the Americans made it a vital anchor on Scott's otherwise abandoned line of communication. Many of the men left behind were disgruntled that their orders required that they stay behind with the convalescent soldiers, but Scott had predicted that they would be attacked. The Puebla troops soon discovered that he was correct.[11]

Since Scott's departure, Childs had been dealing with escalating problems from a Mexican force of four thousand under the partisan leader General Joaquín Rea. On August 26, partisans captured several hundred animals from the mule pen, and an ad hoc collection of thirty-two teamsters, army followers, and soldiers took off after them. But it was a trap, and twenty-four of them were killed or captured in an ambush not far from the city. Then on September 5, Rea made the remarkable request that his men be allowed to occupy a portion of Puebla to protect the inhabitants from guerrillas bands, and he assured Childs that he would be bound to the terms of the armistice that was in force at that time in Mexico City. Childs refused. By the eleventh, sporadic musket fire between the opposing sides erupted, and on the night of the thirteenth and fourteenth, as Santa Anna evacuated the capital, Rea infiltrated parts of the city and drove away many of the cattle and sheep, thus beginning the month-long siege of Puebla.[12]

Childs concentrated his men in three strongholds. One was in the northeast quadrant of the city, near one of the main plazas where he established his headquarters. It consisted of the Cathedral de San José, which served as the primary hospital for the sick and wounded; across the street was a two-story government building made of stone and suitable for defense. The other two American positions were on the city's northeastern edge at Fort Loretto and Guadalupe Heights. When the Mexicans took control of portions of the city, they punished the residents who had cooperated with the Americans. Girls who had been too friendly to the occupiers had their heads shaved or in some cases their ears cut off. By the sixteenth, Rea had surrounded the city and barricaded streets around the American positions. When Childs refused his surrender demand, Rea began repeated attacks on the strongholds, especially targeting the Plaza de San José. The Mexicans launched repeated attacks over the next week, forcing the outnumbered defenders to remain under arms around the clock. Within days of the fall of Mexico City, bulletins began to circulate among the Pueblans announcing the defeat of Scott's army and calling on the citizens to rise up and crush the Yankees.

Santa Anna arrived on September 22 with additional troops and with a determination to continue the war by seizing Puebla and trapping Scott in the capital. For a second time, Childs refused to surrender, and he countered Santa Anna's arrival by putting a musket in the hands of every able-bodied convalescent soldier. For several days, Mexicans kept up fire at the American positions around the clock as they gradually tightened their grip around the city. The outnumbered Americans fought tenaciously to hold onto their positions, and as their food supply dwindled, their situation became increasingly desperate. During the siege, Lieutenant Theodore Laidley's actions were typical of the able-bodied American troops: he rarely slept, never disrobed, and ate very little. He manned his artillery most of the time and only occasionally napped next to his gun. In the first week of October, the beleaguered and hungry Americans held onto their pockets of the city, hoping that aid would arrive.[13]

Lane was still in Veracruz when the siege started, but his march inland proved fortuitous. By the time he collected all the available troops and incorporated Lally's men, he had a force that numbered over three thousand. When Santa Anna learned of Lane's approach, he took most of Rea's siege force and marched east to set a trap for him. He posted his men in Huamantla thirty miles from Puebla and waited for an opportunity to surprise Lane's force in a mountain pass. However, Lane discovered Santa Anna's presence and diverted his troops to Huamantla, where on October 9, the advance elements of his column under Captain Samuel Walker fought a street battle with a much larger force of Mexican lancers. Hemmed in on all sides, Walker's men held on until the main column arrived to drive the enemy away, but Walker was killed in the battle. In retaliation for the loss of Walker and a dozen other men, Lane allowed his men to plunder the town. They broke into houses and shops, took whatever they wanted, raped the women, and killed the men. It was a drunken orgy of violence and destruction that appalled young Lieutenant Hill. "Twas then I saw and felt how perfectly unmanageable were volunteers and how much harm they did," he remembered.[14]

Three days later, on October 12, Lane's force reached Puebla. As they approached, some of the Mexican troops melted away, but others stayed, requiring a brisk street-to-street fight to drive them out. Much of the hostile fire came from rooftops and windows. Some of the residents were happy to have the siege raised, but others joined in the fight when Lane's men entered the Puebla streets. As Hill's unit marched into town, two men and a woman stepped out onto a balcony with *escopetas* and pistols in hand. From their appearance, one an old man and the other two in their twenties or thirties, Hill assumed them to be a father and two children. All three of them raised their weapons and fired at the Americans, but before they could duck back into the house, they were killed by return fire. After clearing the city of hostile troops, Lane's men repeated their shameful pillaging as if it was a right earned by victory. After the battle, they commenced "plundering without restraint," and one disheartened American simply commented, "This is disgraceful." However, most of the men saw nothing wrong with it, as even some of the volunteers of Childs's garrison joined in. "Some made out very well," remembered Jacob Oswandel, who took only "a splendid gentleman's shawl," which he kept as "a great relic" of his war experience. Next morning drunken soldiers continued to stagger through the streets, some in priest's robes and others in women's clothes.[15]

Lieutenant Hill, apparently easily taken by the fairer sex, frequently referred to Mexican women in his letters home. On the day the siege was lifted, Hill was searching a house for enemy soldiers, and when he opened the door to one room, he found several women hiding. One of them he described as "the most glorious vision ever beheld. And such eyes! . . . My heart melted before their glance like snow before the rays of the noonday Sun. . . . I felt like kneeling at her feet and yielding myself a prisoner of war to the all potent power of beauty." Hill finished his search with the young lady at his side and later made other visits to the house. "'Tis needless to say that I have used all endeavours to cultivate my acquaintance with this fair segnorita." However, he believed that the "most angelic" women he had seen were back in Jalapa. He recalled that the effect of the ladies of that town "on one's nerves is magical, almost causing a fit of delirium," and he quickly concluded that Mexican women have the "sweetest eyes in the world." Despite his praise of—or lust for—Mexican women, he formed a low opinion of Pueblans in general, referring to them as "scoundrels" and "assassins." Murders of lone American soldiers who walked the streets at night were commonplace.[16]

When Lane lifted the siege of Puebla, the greatest threat to Scott's security in Mexico City also ended. The little garrison that desperately held on to Puebla against all odds fought as gallantly as the troops under Scott's immediate command, but their role has been largely forgotten. During the month-long siege, American casualties totaled seventy-three. As historian Richard Bruce Winders asserts, Colonel Childs's stubborn band "held the key to Scott's survival . . . [and] prevented the American army in Mexico City from being stranded."[17]

These events in the towns and on the road between Mexico City and Ve-racruz signaled a different kind of war. The troops and supplies that began to move inland in August and September were the Americans' first attempt to travel through these guerrilla-infested areas since Scott severed his ties to the coast in July. The number of partisans, already numerous in early sum-mer, had grown, and their ability and determination to resist the invaders increased in kind. Now with his army firmly lodged in Mexico City, Scott intended to use the roads again, and regularly, as he reopened his line of communication to his base at Veracruz. With more troops arriving, he could now afford to do what his limited numbers prohibited earlier, which was to garrison towns along the way. Not only that, but he also established fortified posts, especially in areas where guerrilla activity was most prevalent. Begin-ning in mid-October and over the following weeks, the commanding general positioned some of his new units at places like Perote and Rio Frio, and he sent additional troops to Puebla. He also authorized the establishment of sev-eral strong points between Jalapa and Veracruz, two of them at the National Bridge and San Juan. Each location had at least 500 to 750 men, and some had more. From each strong point, troops began to sally forth looking for guerrilla units in a nineteenth-century version of search and destroy, and as illustrated by the actions of Lane's men, the guerrilla war that waged along the roads was harsh and ruthless. Technically American troops were still required to respect the property of unoffending Mexicans, but with a wink and a nod, officers sometimes looked the other way as atrocities occurred. Of course, the heavy hand of war freely and fairly came down on guerrillas and those who cooperated with them.[18]

Several weeks after the occupation of the capital, Scott issued a harsh or-der designed to facilitate the passage of troops and supplies along the roads. Because American troops needed the use of roads "infested" with "atrocious bands" of partisans who "under instructions from the late Mexican authori-ties, continue to violate every rule of warfare observed by civilized nations," Scott ordered that "no quarter will be given to known murderers or robbers, whether guerillas or rancheros, and whether serving under (obsolete) com-missions or not." In his *Memoirs*, Scott responded to critics of this tough pol-icy by noting that "in Mexico, . . . the outlaws, denounced in the order, never made a prisoner, but invariably put to death every accidental American strag-gler, wounded or sick man, that fell into their hands." He pointed out that such a response to guerrilla activity is "a universal right of war." The move-ment of troops and trains increased during the fall as travel became safer, and by February, John Meginess proclaimed, with some exaggeration, that the guerrilla bands between the capital and the coast had been dispersed.[19]

An incident involving Manuel Dominguez's spy company illustrates that despite the depredations that accompanied the unconventional war, the Mexicans knew that as a rule, the Americans adhered to the rules of warfare. Three months after the fall of Mexico City, the spy company was engaged in the countryside tracking down the remnants of the Mexican regular army, and after one skirmish, they captured several of the enemy. When Dominguez ordered the prisoners bayoneted, an American officer stepped in and stopped them, although he was roughed up by Dominguez's men in the process. Members of the spy company had to content themselves with taking jewelry, horses, and other valuables. Next day the American officer had departed, and Dominguez once again threatened to execute his captives, but he ceased when the enemy soldiers reminded him that the Americans would punish him if he carried out his unlawful intention.[20]

The guerrilla war, fostered by the government, supported by many of the priests, and fed by a sizable portion of the population, remained a concern throughout the Mexico City campaign. Now in the postcampaign occupation phase, it became even more so, even if it never posed a significant threat to the army's operations. While the partisans had the ability to hamper, and on rare occasions stop, the flow of supplies, the antiguerrilla activities authorized by Scott and executed by Joseph Lane, Jack Hays, and others kept the roads open, thus preventing the bulk of the army from leaving a predominantly conventional posture. One study indicates that by the end of November, the troop buildup in central Mexico had brought the strength of American forces to over 24,000, with perhaps as much as 25 percent of that number engaged in some form of counterguerrilla activity.[21] That indicates that the partisan activity, although fragmented and unorganized, constituted a force to reckon with. This aspect of the war cannot be brushed aside as insignificant. However, the fact that fully three-fourths of Scott's army remained engaged in non-guerrilla-related activities demonstrates that he was not forced to change his strategy or abandon his conventional tactics. In other words, the guerrilla war was a constant nuisance, but only that.

The guerrilla war never accomplished what some Mexicans hoped it would, in part because it never attracted the support of enough of the citizenry to deny the American army the sustenance it needed in a foreign land. The primary reason for the ineffectiveness of these guerrilla bands was that they lacked coordination. The local leaders tended to act out of local or regional interests, and ultimately they possessed only enough strength to harass. Also, the partisans were often viewed as mere robbers who did not differentiate between Mexicans and Americans, and therefore they could not garner universal support from their countrymen. As late as February 1848, one U.S. soldier reported that the extant guerrilla bands "are roaming about robbing and plundering whoever they meet, making no distinction between their own countrymen or the Americans." Indeed, during the occupation, some of the American soldiers viewed the protection of Mexican lives and property as one of their major roles. In November, six weeks after the fall of Mexico City, a large number of Mexicans wishing to travel to Veracruz requested that they be allowed to avail themselves of the protection of U.S. troops by traveling with a train that was scheduled to leave for the coast. Daniel Harvey Hill thought that "such a sight was never witnessed before, of a people voluntarily placing themselves under the protection of their enemies, so as to be saved from being pillaged by their own troops." He noted that while the guerrillas "have done us but little injury," they have nevertheless been "a terrible scourge to the Mexicans, robbing, pillaging and committing disorders of every kind." In the same month, another soldier who was part of the counterguerrilla force stationed at the National Bridge, wrote, "I could not avoid thinking, how unhappy must be conditions of a country, where a foreign force was demanded to protect citizens against each other."[22]

With the roads open and the administration in Washington working hard to get more troops into the theater of operations, reinforcements arrived in Mexico monthly. In December, General Robert Patterson and a body of troops reached Mexico City, and traveling with his column was the Frenchman M. Le Marquis de Radepont. He arrived with a letter of introduction from the secretary of war and a note from the French minister to the United States attesting to Radepont's character and explaining that he was from the French army come to observe the American army and to "safeguard the rights of French citizens" in Mexico. Scott granted the necessary permission, but Radepont's mission was not as benign as he led the Americans to believe. One of his primary concerns in Mexico was to advance French interests (and block U.S. intentions) in the construction of a railroad across the Isthmus of Tehuantepec. He was alarmed at U.S. expansion and believed that the Americans were a menace. He wanted France in particular and Europe in general to wake up to American designs and stop its expansion before it controlled the entire Caribbean. Radepont remained in Mexico after the American army departed and spent the next few years cultivating friends among Mexican political and financial elites. His goal was to recreate Mexico in a way that made it appear that the Mexican people were choosing monarchy over democracy, and to that end, he helped plan and orchestrate the French intervention in Mexico in 1862, wherein the French emperor Napoleon III tried to install Maximilian as the ruling monarch of Mexico.[23]

Radepont's deceptive intentions were not as apparent in 1847 as were the immediate concerns of the occupation. Mexico remained a dangerous place for American soldiers. In the capital, the usual precautions were in place—a portion of each regiment under arms and on guard at all times, no soldier permitted to walk the streets alone and unarmed—but as time passed, discipline became lax, and soldiers increasingly disobeyed orders. Even after Scott issued a warning of a potential plot by the clerics to instigate an uprising in the city in late September, some men did not take even the most logical precautions. As a result, murders of lone American soldiers was a nightly occurrence. Newcomers to the country like A. P. Hill and Henry Heth quickly formed a negative impression of Mexicans. Heth assumed that Mexicans wore blankets wrapped around them so as to conceal what they had stolen: "Mexico," he wrote, "is a nation of blanketed thieves." Hill referred to them as "thieves and murderers" who are "constantly annoying us by assassinations." Even armed soldiers on sentry duty were not immune from attack. One day a Mexican tried to lasso a guard and drag him away. He succeeded in getting the rope around him, but before he could gallop away, the lassoed American somehow managed to shoot the Mexican dead.[24]

Liquor, or the search for it, often led to careless or dangerous behavior. One or two soldiers isolated in a bar or brothel often created a tempting opportunity that Mexican ruffians could not resist. Lieutenant D. H. Hill lamented that there were "miserable creatures" in the army who "would rush into Hell itself for a bottle of liquor." Israel Uncapher recorded in his diary that there was plenty of liquor on hand and that drinking put the men in a "comfortable" state and made for "a fine jollification." Lieutenant John S. Devlin of the marines was court-martialed for repeated drunkenness in and around Mexico City in late September. Captain John Lowe confessed to his wife that he drank one or two glasses of beer a day, but for medicinal purposes only. He hoped that his wife would understand that he was only human. He went on to tell her that he had visited with an old acquaintance from Ohio, Ulysses Grant, who, he reported, had changed in some respects. Before cautioning his wife not to spread the word back home, he explained that Grant had grown a long beard, put on weight, and drank to excess. Although the frequency of Americans found in a state of intoxication surprised some Mexican officials, the condition and its accompanying rowdiness were attributable to a relatively small number of soldiers. And when such actions led to lawlessness, stiff punishment and even executions resulted.[25]

Lieutenant John Sedgwick noted a difference in the drinking habits of Mexicans and Americans, and he even interpreted the rowdiness of drunken Americans as an indication of a sort of virtue. Such drunken behavior, according to Sedgwick's logic, indicates a special energy and intellect, and in a letter to his sister, he revealed not only stereotypical racial views but anti-Semitism as well. He thought Mexicans were generally more temperate, and when drunk, "you will see them slip off without noise, while if one of our soldiers gets drunk it takes half a dozen sober ones to get him home. It requires something to rouse a man's faculties and his energy," he wrote. "We are the greatest go-ahead people in the world, and we beat the Jews in getting drunk."[26]

If drinking was the leading preoccupation among the troops, romance ran a close second. Soon after the capital's occupation, it became common to see Mexican women on the arms of American soldiers, a fact that the young men of the city resented. Captain Joseph Hooker possessed the kind of manners and personality that made him popular with the ladies and won him the nickname "El Capitan Hermoso," the beautiful captain. Robert Anderson thought that young women from wealthy families were particularly flirtatious, "ogling their lovers and brandishing their charms. These young ladies are pretty, very pretty with languishing black eyes." Lieutenant Ambrose Burnside developed a relationship with a girl named Annita from Tacubaya. "I made love to Annita, went to see her several times," he told his friend Lieutenant Henry Heth. When she saw Burnside kissing another girl, Annita attacked her and "pulled out enough hair from that girl's head to have stuffed a pillow." Next she pulled a knife on Burnside, but he ran to safety. Be careful "about having anything to do with these Mexican girls," Burnside warned Heth; "they are she-devils, the most jealous beings on earth."[27]

Perhaps the most accomplished seducer among the young West Point graduates was the tall and handsome Winfield Scott Hancock, "a magnificent specimen of youthful beauty," according to Heth. Hancock's biographer wrote that his reputation as a ladies' man was well deserved. Heth and Hancock, along with Lew Armistead, were fast friends, and in Mexico City, Heth learned to stick close to Hancock. The women were interested in Hancock, and he often received invitations to social events, and, to Heth's delight, so too did associates who were close at hand when the invitations were extended. At one such event, Hancock met Isabella Garcia, a beautiful and wealthy girl who possessed the added benefit of being fluent in English. According to the lieutenant who shared his experience with Heth, he charmed her by taking her hand and squeezing it gently while asking if he could be her sweetheart. "I kissed her and told her that I had never loved before." To which Heth responded, "How could you have told such a story? I know you have said the same thing to half a dozen girls in the city of Mexico and God knows how many in the States." Hancock defended himself by reminding Heth that "all is fair in love and war."[28]

While many of the young lower-grade officers sought the attention of the ladies, others of all ranks courted the favor of the public back home. The most unflattering aspect of the officer corps in the weeks after the capture of the capital was the contention that arose over competition for credit. Many of the officers wanted to share in the recognition, deserved or not, for the victorious conclusion of the campaign. Immediately after the capture of the capital, Scott did not reprimand Quitman for his insubordination—it would have seemed foolish in the face of such a success. He did, however, suspect that Quitman would try to claim undue credit, and he immediately acted to undermine such an effort in the first letter that he wrote to the War Department after settling into the city. He assured the secretary that Mexico City "was not taken by any one or two corps, but by the talent, the science, the gallantry, the prowess of this entire army. In the glorious conquest, *all* had contributed." Quitman, however, thought that he should have received more credit for "pressing on this bold and vigorous attack upon the city of Mexico," and that the fight at the Belén *garita* should be considered a separate battle rather than simply a continuation of the Chapultepec fight. His interpretation of events would make him not just a prominent participant in one aspect of a big battle, but the leading figure in a separate engagement.[29]

Others were displeased about the amount of praise they received in Scott's battle report. Pierre G. T. Beauregard rightfully felt slighted. After repeatedly conducting extensive and dangerous reconnaissance along the southern approaches to the capital and almost single-handedly swaying the weight of support away from a southern attack to a western attack at the September 11 war council, the lieutenant received only passing mention in the commanding general's report. He was disappointed and came to blame Scott for the unfair oversight. Meanwhile, some of the Pennsylvania volunteers were upset because despite leading the way up the hill during the Chapultepec charge, the New York and South Carolina units received more accolades in the after-action reports. Lieutenant James Coulter attributed the slight to guilt by association stemming from what he believed to be cowardice displayed by the regiment's lieutenant colonel, John W. Geary.[30]

Another complaint regarding the volunteers was not by them but about them. It had been a source of discontent throughout the campaign and resurfaced during the occupation. Regulars contended that the volunteers received too much, and often unwarranted, credit after the battles. After reading the commanding general's report of engagements around the capital, D. H. Hill asserted that the regulars "have been very much mortified at it." He believed Scott, hoping to win favor with the public back home, "lavished praise most profusely on raw levies and Volunteers who he knew did not merit it." Theodore Laidley complained in a letter home about the bogus praise that the press bestowed on the volunteers. "The newspapers create phoney heroes by crediting volunteers for things they did not do, and thus no wonder the people back home think so highly of them." But, Laidley continued, the public never hears the rest of the story, "How they rob houses, steal, sack churches, ruin families, plunder and pillage. . . . The outrages they have committed, here, will never be known by people of the U.S." Robert E. Lee thought that within the army in general, it had been "so much more easy to make heroes on paper than in the field." He maintained that for each true hero one meets, there are twenty paper heroes. These "fine fellows are too precious of persons so dear to their countrymen to expose them to the view of the enemy, but when the battle is *won*, they accomplish with the tongue all that they would have done with the sword, had it not been dangerous so to do." Hill had penned in his diary much earlier that he wished the army could be "rid of these paper heroes."[31]

The most unseemly episode during the occupation phase resulted from several issues that coalesced in the fall of 1847, beginning as a rumbling disagreement and culminating in an eruption of venom and hostility that became the preoccupation of the entire army. What started as a silly effort by Gideon Pillow to claim undue credit for the victories around Mexico City mushroomed into a vitriolic battle over much more than that and involved several of the army's top officers and the president. This imbroglio ultimately pitted Scott against Pillow, Worth, Polk, and artillery officer James Duncan, and while much of the army's rank and file sided with the commanding general, they all recognized that he sank to an unbecoming level of pettiness while confronting his opponents. Finally, the embarrassing and highly publicized series of events beginning in October led to a controversial climax when President Polk dismissed Scott from command of the army.

It started when Scott took issue with some of the statements in Pillow's official reports of the engagements around the Pedregal on August 19 and 20 and at Chapultepec on September 13. On October 2, Scott communicated to Pillow some tactfully worded suggestions that he correct the following inaccuracies in his reports before the documents were forwarded to the War Department. First, in his account of the fighting around Padierna, Pillow claimed that before Scott even arrived on the battlefield, he had issued orders to subordinates regarding the movement of their troops. Scott reminded Pillow that he had actually only forwarded the order at Scott's behest. In his report of the Battle of Chapultepec, Pillow wrote that at the outset of the battle, "I ordered all the batteries silenced and the command to advance," and later "Having carried Chapultepec, and being unable to proceed with my command, I ordered it forward under Generals Quitman and Worth." In both instances, Pillow referred to orders actually given by Scott, and furthermore the commanding general reminded Pillow that after receiving his wound, he actually relinquished command of his division. Pillow wrote his accounts in a fashion that left the impression that he was the one in charge of events and responsible for issuing the orders to the various elements of the army. These were irritants, but there was one other statement that troubled Scott. In his report of the earlier engagement, Pillow had commended the commanding general for his role in the battle. Scott thanked Pillow for the "handsome" compliment but thought it entirely inappropriate for a subordinate officer to write such a commendation about a senior officer. "If the right of a junior to praise be admitted, it would carry with it the correlative right of the junior to censure the senior." Scott concluded that because such praise "appears in an official paper," it is "impossible for the senior to forward it."[32] Pillow's effort to bestow praise on Scott, no doubt given with the best of motives, was more that a breach of military etiquette; it revealed a condescending attitude.

In his brief response, Pillow showered Scott with praise and gratitude and tried to assure him of his pure motives. It too was a tactfully written letter, but what seemed to bother him most was the last sentence of Scott's letter wherein the commanding general had asserted, "There are other inaccuracies . . . which have, or may be, silently corrected" in the final report sent to Washington. Pillow was clearly troubled by the suggestion that his account might be altered. He indicated a willingness to correct inaccuracies, although he admitted to none and twice referred to the portions of his reports that were "deemed" incorrect. He then requested an opportunity to talk about the discrepancies, and because his wound prevented him from visiting Scott, he asked that Scott visit him.[33] It was another act of condescension, even if unintended, and thereafter their syrupy, mutually complimentary correspondence changed tone to a more direct and impatient style.

Scott was too busy with army matters to visit Pillow, so he wrote another letter, this one brief, in which he elaborated on the "other inaccuracies" that Pillow had asked about. Essentially there were two: Pillow inappropriately asserted that in attacking the Mexican rear at Padierna at dawn on August 20, General Smith and Colonel Riley were executing the exact plan that Pillow had outlined for them and that Pillow inaccurately claimed credit for proposing his late morning march around the Pedregal to attack San Antonio in rear. "That part of your report . . . is unjust to me, and seems, without intending it, I am sure, to make you control the operations of the whole army, including my own views and acts." Pillow corrected all of the discrepancies except the one regarding Smith and Riley and so informed Scott on October 3. He continued to insist that the flank attack at Padierna was of his design and a result of his orders, and he politely but firmly requested that his account be retained as the official version. In all other areas, he wrote, "I have altered my report. . . . In deference to your understanding of the facts." Thus in his wording Pillow made it clear that he disagreed with Scott but would subordinate his reports to Scott's wishes. An irritated Scott briefly responded the next day that the "discrepancies between your memory and mine, respecting those operations, are so many and so material, that I regret that you have made any alteration in either report at my suggestion." In other words, Scott wished that he had left the issue alone and simply allowed time to sort out the truth. He then suggested that their correspondence on the matter end.[34]

The question of discrepancies evidently did not retard Pillow's determination to portray himself in a flattering light. Later that month, he informed his wife that she was married to the "Hero of Chapultepec," a title "I have won . . . by the *glorious charge upon that powerful fortification.* It was *daring & glorious . . . unequalled* in the history of the American arms." Also, when Pillow learned that the Englishman James Walker, who was attached to Worth's division as an interpreter, was painting a scene of the Battle of Chapultepec that featured Quitman's attack, he offered the artist $100 to change the picture so that it highlighted his division instead. When that failed, he commissioned Walker to paint a second picture portraying the battle as he wanted. As one officer suggested, some men are born to fame, some have it foisted upon them, but others are intent on acquiring it by whatever means possible.[35]

Concurrent with this issue was another one associated with Pillow. It stemmed from the actions of two of his staff officers who, after the fall of the Chapultepec castle, had placed two captured howitzers in Pillow's personal baggage wagon, presumably as souvenirs. Pillow claimed to have had no knowledge of their actions at the time and stated that when he found out about it, he ordered the officers to remove the guns from his wagon and return them. They failed to do so, and Pillow forgot about the incident for three weeks. When, on October 9, Scott discovered the chain of events, he blamed Pillow for the missing guns. Pillow may well have been innocent, but most people thought that a guilty Pillow, once caught, had tried to shift the blame to his two young staff officers. By this time, his relationship with Scott was badly strained and his reputation within the army, never good, was irretrievably stained. So Pillow asked for a court of inquiry to clear his name. The court met in the last week of October with Worth presiding, and on November 2, it exonerated Pillow from blame in taking the howitzers but found that, in fact, his subordinates did inform him that they had not removed them from the wagon as ordered. Before his inquiry had concluded, Pillow wrote an angry letter to President Polk to inform him of the bribery scheme that Scott and Trist had contemplated while in Puebla. He wrote other letters to Polk and also directly to Secretary Marcy criticizing his commanding general.[36]

Meanwhile, Pillow's battle reports were not the only manifestations of self-adoration that the general produced, nor were they the most fantastic products of his inflated imagination. Unknown to Scott in early October, Pillow had already written or at least assisted in the writing of a lengthy and lofty account of the action at Padierna and Churubusco, which was published in newspapers back home in the form of a letter signed by "Leonidas." New Orleans newspapers first published the Leonidas letter on September 10 and 17; then it made its way to Mexico City, where the English-language newspaper, the *American Star*, reprinted it. These articles, like his reports, had Pillow in charge of the army and overseeing its movements, issuing orders and later simply informing the commanding general, who, in this version, was not present. Indeed, according to Leonidas, "Gen. Pillow was in command of all the forces engaged, except Gen. Worth's division." The letter paints a picture of "gloom" during the third week of August as the army moved around the south of Lake Chalco, and in this desperate situation, Scott called on Pillow to rescue the army from its predicament. This he did with his brilliant battle at Padierna. Leonidas compared Pillow to Napoleon and asserted that Pillow's "plan of battle, and the disposition of his forces, were most judicious and successful. *He evinced on this, as he has done on other occasions, that masterly military genius and profound knowledge of the science of war, which has astonished so much the mere martinets of the profession.*" Later, Leonidas summarized, "The victory was most brilliant and complete. Nothing could have been better planned than this battle."[37]

Despite the pseudonym, most of the army's rank and file immediately assumed that Pillow and Leonidas were one and the same. If Pillow was not the actual author, most believed that he had supplied the words for the one who was. The letter created quite a stir among the officers, many of whom wondered how he could have so skillfully orchestrated the decisive flank attack at Padierna while he slept comfortably at San Agustin four miles away, and by some accounts did not arrive on the battlefield the next morning until it was over. Moreover, a few officers claimed to have heard Pillow exclaim that he wanted to have nothing to do with the battle and had "washed his hands of the whole business." Lieutenant A. P. Hill wrote, "I saw that some fool, supposed to be the gentleman himself, endeavoured to give Pillow the credit and glory of the whole affair." Leonidas not only gave credit where it was not due, but he did so in a way that many found comical.[38] This helps to explain Pillow's obstinance in not wanting to change his battle report in early October. Aware of Leonidas's panegyric account, which had already appeared back home but was as yet unknown in Mexico, Pillow obviously wanted the official battle reports to agree with, not contradict, that version.

Soon another letter surfaced over the name "Veritas," which had also appeared in papers back home. It praised General William Worth for convincing Scott to take the road around Lake Chalco in the approach to Mexico City. This road, once believed impassable, had caused Scott some hesitation for several days in August, and it was to assess this route that Scott had

SELF-INFLATING PILLOW.

Caricature of Gideon Pillow's attempt to exaggerate his role in the campaign. The Nathaniel and Bucky Hughes Collection, courtesy of Lupton Library, University of Tennessee at Chattanooga.

sent out numerous officers to reconnoiter. At Scott's request, Worth had sent Colonel James Duncan on one such mission, and the colonel reported the road useable. So had others. But the Veritas account gave the impression that Worth had saved Scott from a grave mistake by convincing him to march south of Chalco. The letters were "romantic . . . and unique productions" that had a net result of "abusing Genl. Scott." Winslow Sanderson of the Mounted Rifles, who had only heard rumors of the contents of the letters, believed that they represented an attempt to "puff Him," referring to Worth.[39]

Scott had had enough, so two days after seeing the Veritas letter, he issued General Order No. 349, reminding his officers that it was a violation of army regulations to write accounts of military operations for publication. In it, he referred to the "scandalous letters" and the "false credit" they gave to certain officers. Without mentioning names, he made it clear that he believed that the heroes of the letters wrote them or caused them to be written, and he condemned their "despicable self-puffings and malignant exclusions of others." Because Worth was the hero of the Veritas letter, he correctly assumed that Scott's thinly veiled accusation was aimed at him, so he fired off an angry letter to Scott demanding to know if the order alluded to him. When Scott did not give a direct answer, Worth went over his head on November 16, as Pillow had done less than three weeks earlier, and wrote directly to Washington to complain of Scott's "malicious and gross injustice." In the letter, he also charged Scott with conduct "unbecoming an officer and a gentleman" and forwarded a copy to the commanding general. By the last half of November, Scott was furious, and when he learned that both Pillow and Worth had broken the chain of command and appealed to the administration in language both disrespectful and insubordinate, Scott had them arrested. The controversy broadened when Lieutenant Colonel Duncan publicly admitted to writing the Veritas letter. Scott then arrested him also.[40]

When the president became involved, the controversy broadened still further. In December, he received Pillow's letter informing him of the bribery scheme and Pillow's dishonest account of his own role in the episode. He explained to the president that he had at first gone along with the scheme but only reluctantly, then on reflection changed his mind and vigorously opposed it. Polk was outraged. At a cabinet meeting on December 11, he condemned the proposed action and raised the subject of removing Scott from command. A week later, the president and cabinet again discussed the issue and determined to conduct an official investigation when they gathered more information. Then on December 30, Polk read a letter from Pillow informing him of his, Worth's, and Duncan's arrest, and he concluded that the entire problem stemmed from Scott's "vanity and tyrannical temper . . . & his want of prudence and common sense."[41] He was partially correct, for Scott was vain and he carefully sought to protect his share of the glory.

However, Scott did have cause to take action against his subordinates, if only he had not overreacted. A mild reprimand or a stern reminder regarding army regulations would have sufficed, and then Scott could have let history take care of the proper distribution of praise. Polk thought that there was no need "to make so serious an affair" out of the Leonidas and Veritas letters. In this he was correct, but he was incorrect in his belief that Scott's general order caused the trouble. Scott did indeed turn the episode into a more serious offense than it warranted, and in so doing, he looked petty and vindictive, thereby damaging his reputation with the army and giving the administration the ammunition it needed to justify his recall. The opinionated D. H. Hill, who despised Pillow and respected Scott, recorded the following sentiments in his diary: "Genl. Scott has lowered himself very much in the Army by his jealousy of the reputation of his subalterns. He is in many respects a very small man." Captain James Mason of the engineers thought that Scott had "injured himself, the service, and military reputation generally, by his absurd order & ridiculous letters," and through his actions he had shown how "silly" a famous general can be.[42]

In Washington, the president and his advisors had discussed their troubled army several times in the latter weeks of 1847. Polk was most indignant about the effort to bribe Santa Anna into a peace settlement, and he directed Buchanan and Marcy to write to the various actors in the plot requesting details. Most were reluctant to divulge incriminating information, and Scott flatly responded that the meeting in which it was discussed was confidential. With multiple controversies swirling around the army's high command, Polk decided in early January to call a court of inquiry to investigate Scott's actions, his charges against Pillow and Duncan, and Worth's charges against the commanding general. He sent instructions to that effect, as well as an order that Scott release Pillow, Worth, and Duncan from arrest. And as a final insult, Polk dismissed Scott from command because of "the present state of things in the Army," and in his place, he appointed the veteran Major General William O. Butler to replace him at the head of the army.

In an act that characterized the shabby treatment the administration had afforded Scott all along, the general first learned that he was to be replaced and put before a court from newspaper accounts and letters received from home by other officers. Somewhat sarcastically, Scott wrote to Marcy that he had learned of these developments through "slips of newspapers and letters from Washington." "I learn," he continued, "that the President has determined to place me before a court, for daring to enforce necessary discipline in this army against certain of its high officers!" The general concluded his one-paragraph note with, "Perhaps, after trial, I may be permitted to return to the United States. My poor services with this most gallant army are at length to be requited as I have long been led to expect they would be." [43]

Butler assumed command on February 19, but the court of inquiry did not begin until the next month. Even before knowing that Polk would authorize the investigation, Pillow seemed to suspect that such would happen. In a letter to his wife in late November, he was optimistic and looking forward to the opportunity afforded by a clash with Scott. "He has violated . . . my principle of justice in regard to myself & I feel very confident of *flooring him*." Then in a reference to Scott's embarrassing letter-writing episode with the administration eighteen months earlier, Pillow wrote, "I will blow him higher & kill him deader than did the '*hasty plate of soup*' letter or '*the fire in front & fire in rear*.' . . . The whole affair . . . will prove ultimately great to *my advantage*." Later in the letter, he suggested that the general public would be shocked when it compared "my brilliant success" with Scott's infamy. Such a comparison "will show a degree of *malignity* in Scott, as *black* and *atrocious* as ever *disgraced* a fiend." [44]

The court opened its proceedings in the National Palace on March 16. Scott, in his opening statement, summarized his version of the events that brought about the investigation. After drawing up charges and requesting a court-martial of three of his subordinate officers, this "inquiry is the result. I am stricken down from my high command; one of the arrested generals is pre-acquitted and rewarded," and the rest of the parties, the guilty and innocent alike, are "all thrown before you, to scramble for justice as we may." Because some of the officers needed for witnesses had already departed Mexico for home, Scott could not adequately prosecute his charges against Pillow. He wanted to drop the charges against the Tennessean, but Pillow, sensing his advantage, would not permit it. The court provided a perfect platform for Pillow to excel. Acting in his own defense, Pillow demonstrated that in crossing over from military operations to legal proceedings, he now was in his element. In the former he was a mere pretender, but in the latter, he was knowledgeable and experienced, and he scored points interviewing witnesses. Having brought in all of the principal parties who were still in Mexico to testify, the court adjourned on April 22 to reconvene in the United States.[45]

The entire episode created "in the Army a feeling of unmitigated condemnation." In a letter, Robert E. Lee wrote that Scott had been sacrificed for Pillow's gain, and he hoped that "Worth & Pillow may be held up in the light they deserve." In another letter, he wrote that if "the whole truth is known, Genl S. can suffer no injury." Theodore Laidley expressed his opinion that Pillow "will be killed as dead in the states as he is in the army" because blatant "falsehood can too easily be proved on him." Presidential politics was at the root of the whole affair, thought Laidley, and Scott's recall was "the greatest misfortune that could possibly happen to the Army." Everyone knew Scott's history of vanity, pettiness, and injudicious letter writing, but those weaknesses notwithstanding, the soldiers believed in their commanding general and trusted his leadership. Most of them believed that "there is no one of the Generals that can at all compare with him." Before the court convened, Laidley had heard someone remark that "Genl Scott's little finger is more of a general than all the other generals put together." Daniel Harvey Hill offered another critical and somewhat colorful appraisal of Scott's predicament. It resulted from "the intrigues of that arch-scoundrel Pillow. He has very great influence with our weak, childish President." Hill had a low opinion of all officers who attained rank or status as a result of Polk's assignment, and that attitude extended to the new army commander. "Maj. Genl. Butler is a creature of Mr. Polk's appointment and of course a fool." But Hill saved his harshest criticism for Pillow. "That an idiot monkey could cause the greatest Captain of the age to be disgraced upon the very theatre of his glory will not be credited by posterity." Lieutenant Romeyn B. Ayres, a West Point graduate and future veteran of many Civil War battlefields, penned in his diary the following summation: "the General who had fought his way, and led the army triumphantly through every difficulty, to the city of Mexico, and taken the enemy's capital, was suspended from the command, and brought before a court of inquiry, upon charges preferred by a subordinate, who was himself under charges for unmilitary conduct!!! A most anomolous affair!"[46]

The day after the court adjourned, Scott left for Veracruz. As he departed his headquarters, members of the guard unit stationed there, the Rifle Regiment, shed tears as they presented arms. Then Scott mounted a carriage that poignantly symbolized the degree to which he had fallen: the carriage was drawn by mules and serviced by a disabled soldier. But his stature had not fallen with the rank and file of the army. Although he had requested to leave Mexico City quietly, a crowd of soldiers were gathered in the plaza to say farewell. About thirty officers came with their horses and rode with him out of the city until Scott asked that they go back. Before leaving, they all insisted on shaking his hand and saying a personal good-bye. One lieutenant, Theodore Laidley, noted that Scott was returning home from his "noble, meritorious and brilliant achievements" not the recipient of praise, but with "all the disgrace that it was possible to heap on him." Within nine days, he arrived in Veracruz and boarded a steamer for the States.[47]

The court reconvened on June 5 in Frederick, Maryland. Scott had stood before an inquiry in that town a dozen years earlier when Polk's mentor, President Andrew Jackson, attempted to censor Scott for his failed operations against the Seminole Indians. And coincidentally while the 1836 proceedings were underway, Santa Anna traveled through Frederick. The 1848 inquiry ended anticlimactically. Scott had withdrawn his charges against Worth and Duncan, so the legal battle had become something of a showdown between Scott and Pillow. After another month of testimony, the court could not prove that any money exchanged hands in an attempt to bribe Mexican officials, and it determined that the much-discussed scheme had not influenced military operations. Historian K. Jack Bauer's account suggests that the hearings took on the tone of "an inquisition" more than of a legal inquiry. The results were highly satisfactory to Pillow, who was pleased with his "most triumphant vindication," as he put it. The court found that he had indeed tried to claim "a larger degree of participation" in the flank attack at Padierna than he deserved, but otherwise it exonerated him.[48] After Polk decided to drop the matter, the court disbanded on July 6, but its purpose had been served. Scott was out of command and out of favor; the Whig general had been put in his place and rendered politically impotent. From the beginning to the end of Winfield Scott's role in the Mexican War, he came full circle, beginning in 1846 and ending in 1848 with embarrassment at the hands of the president.

Epilogue

*The maximum use of force is in no way incompatible with the
simultaneous use of the intellect.*
—Carl von Clausewitz

The efforts to win a peace settlement almost became lost in the preoccupations that commanded the army's attention in the months after the capture of Mexico City. President Polk's relationship with his chief diplomat became as stormy as the one with his chief general. In September and October 1847, Polk became increasingly displeased with Nicholas Trist, and in his anger, Polk was prone to spitefulness. In his frustration over the continuation of the war, which he mostly attributed to the obstinacy of the Mexican government, Polk had decided to expand his territorial demands as an indemnity. Although Polk was not quite an advocate of the "All Mexico" movement that many Americans had come to embrace, he nevertheless thought that the United States should be compensated for the prolonged conflict and that Mexico should pay for its recalcitrance. Then he learned of the failed two-week armistice and of Trist's willingness to entertain Mexican proposals that Polk deemed entirely inappropriate. With his peace requirements changing and his distrust for Trist growing, Polk decided in October to order the diplomat home. "Mr. Trist had exceeded his instructions," thought the president, and he must return to Washington at once. By the time Polk's recall order arrived in Mexico on November 16, a new Mexican government was in place and serious peace negotiations appeared imminent. General Pedro María Anaya, a moderate, assumed the presidency and promptly appointed Manuel Peña y Peña as foreign minister. Peña was distraught over the prospects of Trist's departure and the stalemate that such would render to the peace process.[1]

The Englishman Edward Thornton had been working behind the scenes to bring both sides together, but Trist's unforeseen recall provided a sudden incentive for them to act. From the Mexican perspective, it seemed to indicate that Washington was not as desperate for a peace treaty as previously assumed, which, if true, meant the loss of a bargaining advantage at the negotiating table. By recalling Trist, Polk may have unwittingly produced a sense of urgency on the part of the Mexicans. Also disturbing was the suspicion that perhaps a new peace commissioner would bring a new and more extensive set of demands from the United States. For his part, Trist wanted to stay and finish the job, and with a moderate government in place the prospect for a treaty improved. Thus the diplomat decided to disobey his instructions to return to Washington. He committed to stay in Mexico until he had a treaty in hand, and he so notified the administration in an insubordinate sixty-five-page letter on December 6. He justified his actions by explaining that the authorities in Washington did not know the state of affairs and that an opportunity for a speedy peace was at hand, which needed to be seized, not lost. The president was indignant when Trist's dispatch arrived in Washington. It was "arrogant, impudent, and very insulting to his Government, and even personally offensive," Polk recorded in his diary. The angry president could do nothing but wait and fume.[2]

Trist's insubordination may have been partially motivated by his knowledge of Polk's shifting territorial demands, and the fear that the president might even succumb to the "All Mexico" temptation. Trist opposed the incorporation of most or all of Mexico because he believed it would be dangerous to the free institutions of the United States and would also infect the nation with "the virus of Spanish corruption." It was a contagious attitude that afflicted not only politicians back home but also soldiers in the army. Robert Anderson agreed with Trist's sentiments regarding the rampant corruption that "underminded every sentiment of morality," but he believed that the remedy was in forcing North American institutions on Mexico. In a letter home, he wrote, "We are bound to take from her one third of her territory and it would be better for her that we took it all. This people is totally incapable of self government." Another soldier named Cantey (probably James Cantey from South Carolina) asserted his opinion about Mexico: "we ought to have it, there is no finer country upon the face of the Western Hemisphere." Then he went on to describe a primary motivation for land acquisition that many Southerners shared. This country has "a climate & soil perfectly adapted to all the products which employ the labour of slaves." And what about the Mexican people? According to this correspondent, "the same fate will await them that happen to the Indian tribes of our own frontier. They will naturally vanish from civilization."[3] This extreme view, however, was the articulation of a disease more deadly than the so-called Spanish virus that Trist feared, and one that was not cured until the Civil War.

When the negotiations finally began in earnest in early January, they progressed quickly, and Trist's patience coupled with firmness resulted in the Treaty of Guadalupe Hidalgo, which the negotiators signed on February 2. In it, Mexico agreed to cede California and New Mexico to the United States, along with acquiescence in the Rio Grande boundary line in return for $15 million. In all, the treaty turned over to the United States over 529,000 square miles, and after adding the cost of the war and the veterans' pensions, the price per acre came to forty-eight cents. The treaty essentially met all of Polk's demands from the previous year, and despite his displeasure, he had no political alternative but to accept its terms. By ignoring the president's orders and seeing the negotiations through to completion, Trist avoided a delay of unpredictable length, and perhaps even prevented a prolonged quagmire.[4] Of course, by the time Trist affixed his name to the treaty, his fate, like that of Scott's, had been determined. The president saw to it that both the diplomat and the general, who together orchestrated the successful conclusion of the war, would be publicly disgraced.

The men who fought in Scott's gallant little army thought that the Mexico City Campaign would be remembered as one of the greatest military operations of American history. Lieutenant Thomas Williams thought that he had just participated in "the great event—the epoch—of the 19th century," and Lieutenant William M. Gardner thought that the army's accomplishment would "astound the world." They also believed that Scott had won for himself exalted status "among the world's great captains." The campaign indeed warranted the lofty accolades that its participants predicted, as did Scott's generalship, but alas, the real epoch of the nineteenth century came a decade and a half later. The magnitude of the Civil War overshadowed everything that came before it and raised up new heroes who easily eclipsed those of the antebellum period, even though the new icons were often former protégés of the ones they surpassed. Writing almost a half century later, James Longstreet, a soldier in both wars, still considered Scott to be "that consummate strategist, tactician, and organizer."[5]

The campaign embodied elements that were both backward and forward looking. The architect of the operation was a studied practitioner of old-school methods. His proficiency in eighteenth-century warfare made it natural for him to devise a strategy in Mexico that was conventional and that emphasized maneuver and holding geographic locations. In battle, he administered several crushing blows with the sword, followed by an extension of the olive branch. Rather than seek to annihilate the Mexican army, Scott's strategy of moderation called for defeating the enemy in battle and seizing key cities, which is precisely what British General William Howe had in mind when he captured New York and Philadelphia during the American Revolution. Scott's plan would take him ever deeper into Mexico, thus adding ever-increasing pressure on its government to treat for peace, and at every step, Scott gave his opponent time to consider the consequences of continued resistance. Before leaving Puebla, he drew in his garrisons and cut his lines back to the coast, which eliminated his greatest vulnerability while giving his army optimal strength for the last leg of the journey. By magnifying his limited numbers, he maximized the threat to the capital. Furthermore, while still in Puebla, he clearly stated what he would do when he arrived in the Valley of Mexico: defeat the enemy and take a strategic point near the city, then await a peace overture from the government.

In addition to his efforts to defeat rather than destroy the enemy army, he sought to limit the impact on unoffending civilians whenever possible. To accomplish this, he devised a pacification plan that was ahead of its time. He foresaw all of the potential dilemmas that an invading army would face and crafted policies to deal with them. Scott was the first American general to invoke martial law while commanding an army on foreign soil. In so doing, he set a precedent that others have followed: the right of a commander to establish military government. It "worked like a charm," Scott recalled in his *Memoirs*. Indeed, he was convinced that without invoking martial law, his army "could not have . . . reached the capital." Unlike Zachary Taylor, who made no effort to set up a form of government or administration in northern Mexico, Scott showed remarkable foresight and efficiency in finding a way to provide both order and security as his army marched through a hostile country. Strict discipline, respect for property, reverence to religion, purchase of supplies, and like measures collectively represented an organized effort to appease the Mexican population and prevent a guerrilla uprising. It did not completely prevent a resort to partisan warfare, but Scott's efforts did preclude it from reaching a level that could threaten his army's security. In short, he fought a limited war. In what could be considered an oxymoron, one might say that he fought a civilized war, or as Scott himself put it, "I carried on war as a Christian, and not as a fiend!" Longstreet referred to Scott as "an example worthy of eternal emulation" because while marching through Mexico, "he was as strict in the requirement of order and protection for non-combatants as he could have been in marching through his own civil communities. The result was speedy peace, respect from all people, admiration and affection from many."[6]

Longstreet's summation is noteworthy, although one might take exception to his reference to a "speedy peace." Scott's willingness to halt operations after major victories to gauge Mexican intentions indicated his understanding of the political nature of warfare; however, it probably prolonged the war by at least a few weeks. Some of his delays were understandable and even unavoidable, but the two-week armistice was a nod too heavily in favor of politics over military action. It was a kind gesture abused by a dishonest foe. It was

Clausewitz who said that in war, "the mistakes which come from kindness are the very worst."[7] His hesitation after Churubusco did what hesitancy usually does; it gave the enemy hope.

The Mexican War was a major formative factor for many of the army's young officers. For one thing, it widened the gap of distrust between professionals and volunteers. Several of the army's professional officers played crucial roles by using their skill as engineers and scouts to help Scott position the army and orchestrate the campaign. The talents of scores of West Point graduates like Robert E. Lee and Pierre G. T. Beauregard were on full display on more than one battlefield, and the knowledge acquired at West Point proved a valuable asset to the army. At a dinner hosted by Scott at his Mexico City headquarters in December 1847, the army commander made sure that the numerous political generals in attendance, those who owed their commissions to presidential favor, understood the value of professional military training. In a voice that all could hear, Scott raised his glass and toasted the "Military Academy—without it we could never have reached the Capital of Mexico." All present heartily agreed, but as one academy graduate speculated, those same volunteer generals will be the first to "abuse the Old Regular Army and the graduates of West Point" when they return to the States.[8]

The young officers also learned from their commanding general. Scott's proficiency in fighting a limited war of maneuver and in the use of flank attacks to surprise his opponent made a lasting impression on many of the future generals. Numerous flank attacks in the Civil War conjure images of Cerro Gordo and Padierna or the march around Lake Chalco. From George B. McClellan's attempt to replicate Scott's campaign on the peninsula in 1862 to Ulysses S. Grant's decision to cut his line of communication at Vicksburg, to Robert E. Lee's numerous flank attacks in 1862 and 1863, Scott's influence is evident. If one were to take a transparency image of the troop movements at Cerro Gordo and invert it, one would find a nearly exact duplicate of the Confederate movements at Chancellorsville. Lee was the most astute pupil of the tactical lessons of the Mexico classroom, and when he became the commander of the Army of Northern Virginia, he, like Scott, benefitted from the advantages that accrue from offensive warfare. Even in their orders regarding the treatment of civilians, Civil War generals like Lee in Pennsylvania and Don Carlos Buell in Tennessee demonstrated that they had learned the lessons of 1847.

An important lesson that both Grant and Lee learned in Mexico was the advantage held by the commander who successfully seizes the initiative. After he became the commanding general of all the Union armies in 1864, Grant succeeded because he took the initiative away from his opponent and dictated the course of the war—something Lee had been doing for the previous two years. Grant's predecessors in Union high command had often merely reacted to what the enemy did—reacted to whatever situation Lee forced on them. That changed in 1864. Grant witnessed in Mexico the benefits that redound to an enterprising general who takes the initiative and forces the enemy into a reactionary role. He also knew what other Union generals obviously did not: that winning the war would require an ongoing, sustained campaign, not merely a single battle. However, unlike Scott, and unlike previous Union commanders who remained fixed in a limited war mind-set, Grant instinctively understood that in total war, capturing a position (Richmond) would not suffice. To win the war, Grant had to destroy the enemy army.

The Civil War and its heroes became the defining moment of the nineteenth century. It emerged as the great watershed event of American history, affecting things that followed for years. In the process, it completely overshadowed the accomplishments of Winfield Scott's gallant little army in Mexico. Historian James I. Robertson offered this succinct but glowing summary of the Mexico City Campaign: "Never had an American general accomplished more, with fewer men, and with less support from his government. The Scott campaign in Mexico had been brilliant."[9] Despite prejudices, lapses of discipline, and other shortcomings, the army and the general had indeed performed brilliantly.

Distances from Veracruz to Mexico City in Quarter-Mile
Increments, Compiled by Captain William H. Shover, Third
Artillery

Site	Miles to Next Point	Miles from Veracruz
To Vergara	3	3
Rio Medio	2.25	5.25
Santa Fe	3	8.25
San Juan	7	15.25
Puente de Las Vegas	10	25.25
Puente Nacional	5.5	30.75
Plan del Río	10.5	41.25
Encero	13.5	54.75
Jalapa	8.75	63.5
La Banderilla	5.25	68.75
San Miguel	3.5	72.25
La Hoya	4.5	76.75
Las Vigas	6.25	83
Cruz Blanca	5.25	88.25
Perote	8.25	96.5
Tepe Algualco	18.5	115
Ogo de Agua	20.75	135.75
Nopaluca	8.5	144.25
El Pinal	7	151.25
Acajeti	6.5	157.75
Amozoque	8	165.75
Puebla	10.5	176.25
San Martin	22.75	199
Rio Frio	18	217
Venta de Cordova	10.5	227.5
Ayotla	9	236
El Peñon	8.5	244.5
Mexico City	7.5	252

Source: Reproduced from William Preston, *Journal In Mexico*,
Beinecke Library, Yale University, New Haven, Conn.

Appendix 2

Officers in Winfield Scott's Army upon Its Departure from Puebla

Name and Unit	Remarks
General in Chief and Staff	
Maj. Gen. Winfield Scott	Commanding the Army
Lt. Col. Ethan A. Hitchcock	Acting Inspector General
Capt. Henry L. Scott	A.D.C. and Chief Adjutant Generals Dept.
1st Lt. Thomas Williams	A.D.C.
Bvt. 1st Lt. George W. Lay	Military Secretary
2nd Lt. Schuyler Hamilton	A.D.C., wounded near Mira Flores, Aug. 12
Maj. J. P. Gaines	Volunteer A.D.C.
Engineer Corps	
Maj. John L. Smith	Chief Engineer
Capt. Robert E. Lee	Wounded at Chapultepec, Sep. 13
Capt. James L. Mason	Severely wounded at Molino del Rey, Sep. 8
Lt. P.G.T. Beauregard	Wounded at Belén Gate, Sep. 13
Lt. Isaac J. Stevens	Wounded at San Cosme, Sep. 13
Lt. Zealous B. Tower	Wounded at Chapultepec, Sep. 13
Lt. Gustavus W. Smith	
Lt. John G. Foster	Wounded at Molino del Rey, Sep. 8
Ordnance Department	
Capt. Benjamin Huger	Chief of Ordnance Dept.
1st Lt. P. V. Hagner	
2nd Lt. C. P. Stone	
Topographical Engineer	
Maj. William Turnbull	Chief Topographical Engineer served with Gen. in Chief
Capt. G. McClellan	Served with Twiggs's division
2nd Lt. George Thom	
Bvt. 2nd Lt. E.L.F. Hardcastle	Served with Worth's division
Quartermasters Department	
Capt. J. R. Irwin	Chief Quartermasters Dept. Serving with Gen. in Chief
Capt. A. C. Myers	Quartermaster (Gen. Worth's division)
Capt. Robert Allen	Quartermaster (Gen. Twiggs's division)
Capt. H. C. Wayne	Assistant to Chief Quartermaster
Capt. J. McKinstry	Commanded a company of volunteers at Churubusco

Name and Unit	Remarks
Capt. G.W.F. Wood	Quartermaster (Harney's Brigade)
Capt. J. Daniels	Quartermaster (Gen. Quitman's division)
Capt. O'Hara	Quartermaster (Gen. Pillow's division)
Capt. S. McGowan	

Subsistence Department

Capt. J. B. Grayson	Chief Subsistence Dept. Serving with Gen. in Chief
Capt. T. P. Randle	

Pay Department

Maj. E. Kirby	Chief Pay Dept. Serving with Gen. in Chief
Maj. A. Van Buren	
Maj. A. W. Burns	
Maj. A. G. Bennett	

Medical Department

Surg. Gen. Thomas Lawson	Served with Gen. in Chief
Surg. B. F. Harney	
Surg. R. S. Satterlee	Chief Surgeon Gen. Worth's division
Surg. C. S. Tripler	Chief Surgeon Gen. Twiggs's division
Surg. B. Randall	Attached to 7th Infantry
Surg. J.J.B. Wright	Medical Purveyor
Surg. J. M. Cuyler	Attached to 4th Artillery
Asst. Surg. A. F. Suter	Attached to Rifle Regiment
Asst. Surg. J. Simpson	Attached to 6th Infantry
Asst. Surg. D. C. DeLeon	Attached to 8th Infantry
Asst. Surg. H. H. Steiner	Attached to 1st Artillery
Asst. Surg. J. Simons	Attached to 4th Infantry
Asst. Surg. J. K. Barnes	Attached to Cavalry
Asst. Surg. L. H. Holden	Attached to 3rd Artillery
Asst. Surg. C. C. Keeney	Attached to 3rd Infantry
Asst. Surg. J. F. Head	Attached to Taylor's Battery
Asst. Surg. J. F. Hammond	Attached to 2nd Infantry
Asst. Surg. J. M. Steiner	Attached to Magruder's Battery
Asst. Surg. C. P. Deyerle	Attached to 2nd Artillery
Asst. Surg. E. Swift	Attached to 1st Dragoons
Surg. J. M. Tyler	Attached to Voltigeurs
Surg. McMillan	Attached 2nd Pennsylvania Volunteers
Surg. C. J. Clark	Attached to South Carolina Volunteers
Surg. W. B. Halstead	Attached to New York Volunteers
Asst. Surg. R. Hagan	Attached to 14th Infantry
Asst. Surg. H. L. Wheaton	Attached to Pillow's division
Surg. R. Ritchie	Attached to Pillow's division
Surg. J. Barry	Attached to Pillow's division
Surg. Edwards	Attached to Marine Corp
Surg. L. W. Jordan	Attached to 14th Infantry
Surg. R. McSherry	Attached to Marine Corp
Surg. Roberts	Attached to 5th Infantry

Appendix 2, *continued*

Name and Unit	Remarks
Cavalry Brigade	
Col. William S. Harney, 2nd Dragoons	Commanding Cavalry
1st Lieut. Wm. Steele, 2nd Dragoons	Acting Assistant Adjutant General
2nd Lieut. Julian May, Mounted Rifles	Aide-de-Camp
1st Dragoons	
Capt. P. Kearny Jr.	Comding 1st Dragoons, wounded at San Antonio Gate, Aug. 20
1st Lieut. R. S. Ewell	
2nd Lieut. Orren Chapman	
2nd Lieut. L. Graham, 10th Infantry	Attached to Co. F, 1st Dragoons, wounded at San Antonio Gate, Aug. 20
2nd Dragoons	
Maj. Edwin V. Sumner	Commanding
Capt. George A. H. Blake	
Capt. Croghan Ker	Severely wounded at Molino del Rey, Sep. 8
Capt. S. B. Thornton	Killed at San Antonio, Aug. 13
Capt. W. J. Hardee	
Capt. H. W. Merrill	
Capt. H. H. Sibley	
2nd Lieut. R. H. Anderson	
2nd Lieut. J. Y. Bicknell	
2nd Lieut. J. M. Hawes	
2nd Lieut. T. F. Castor	
2nd Lieut. Arthur D. Tree	Wounded at El Molino del Rey, Sep. 8
2nd Lieut. James Oakes	
2nd Lieut. W. D. Smith	
3rd Dragoons	
Lieut. Col. Thomas P. Moore	Commanding
Capt. E. B. Gaither	
Capt. A. M. Duperu	
Capt. A. T. McReynolds	Wounded at San Antonio Gate, Aug. 20
1st Lieut. George J. Adde	
1st Lieut. J. A. Divver	
1st Lieut. George E. Maney	
1st Lieut. J. T. Brown	
2nd Lt. J.C.D. Williams	Wounded at Molino del Rey, Sep. 8
2nd Lt. W. C. Wagley	
2nd Lieut. Francis Henry	
2nd Leut. W. Merrihew	
2nd Lieut. William Blood	
2nd Lieut. W. G. Mosely	

Name and Unit	Remarks

Mounted Riflemen
Capt. Charles F. Ruff
1st Lt. John G. Walker
2nd Lt. George H. Gordon

1st Division (Regulars)
Garland's and Clarke's Brigades

B'vt Maj. Gen. William J. Worth	Commanding Division
B'vt Capt. W. W. Mackall	Assist. Adjutant General
B'vt Capt. J. C. Pemberton, 4th Artillery	Aide-de-Camp
B'vt. 1st Lt. L. B. Wood, 8th Infantry	Aide-de-Camp
Maj. Borland, Ark. Vol.	Volunteer Aide-de-Camp
Lt. R. Semmes, U.S.N.	Volunteer Aide-de-Camp

Garland's Brigade

Lt. Col. John Garland, 4nd Infantry	Commanding Brigade
B'vt. Capt. W. A. Nichols, 2nd Artillery	Acting Asst. Adjutant General
2nd Lt. Hermann Thorn, 3rd Dragoons	Aide-de-Camp. Wounded at Molino del Rey

2nd Artillery

Maj. P. H. Galt	Commanded 2nd Artillery, Aug. 19–20; sick, Sep. 8, 12, 13, 14
Capt. S. Mackenzie	Commanded 2nd Artillery, Sep. 8, 12; commanded storming party from 1st Div. on Sep. 13
Capt. & Bvt Lt. Col. C. F. Smith	Commanded Light Infantry Batln. Aug. 19–20 and Sep. 12–14
Capt. & Bvt. Lt. Col. J. Duncan	Commanded Battery on Aug. 19–20; commanded the Artillery at Molino del Rey and battery on Sep. 12–14
Capt. H. Brooks	Commanded 2nd Artillery on Sep. 13
1st Lt. M. L. Shackelford	Mortally wounded at Molino del Rey, Sep. 8
1st Lt. C. B. Daniels	Mortally wounded at Molino del Rey, Sep. 8
1st Lt. L. G. Arnold	Wounded at Churubusco, Aug. 20
1st Lt. F. Woodbridge	Acting Regimental Quartermaster
1st Lt. J. Sedgwick	
1st Lt. A. Elzey	With Light Battalion
1st Lt. Wm. B. Blair	Asst. Commissary of Subsistence
1st Lt. Henry J. Hunt	With Col. Duncan's Battery, commanding section
1st Lt. William Hays	With Col. Duncan's Battery, commanding section
1st Lt. William Armstrong	Killed at Molino del Rey, Sep. 8
1st. Lt. H. A. Allen	
1st Lt. S. S. Anderson	Acting Adjutant on Aug. 19–20 and Sep. 8
1st Lt. John J. Peck	With Col. Smith's Light Infantry Battalion

Appendix 2, *continued*

Name and Unit	Remarks
2nd Lt. H. F. Clarke	With Col. Duncan's Battery
2nd Lt. M.D.L. Simpson	With stormers from 1st Division
3rd Artillery	
Lt. Col. F. S. Belton	
Capt. Martin Burke	
B'vt. Maj. R.D.A. Wade	Wounded at Churubusco, Aug. 20
Capt. Robert Anderson	Wounded at Molino del Rey, Sep. 8
Capt. E. J. Steptoe	Commanded light battery, with Quitman's division
1st Lt. & Adjt. Wm. Austine	
1st Lt. Henry B. Judd	Steptoe's Battery
B'vt. Capt. George W. Ayers	Killed at Molino del Rey, Sep. 8
1st Lt. R. W. Johnston	
1st Lt. H. Brown	Steptoe's battery
1st Lt. Francis J. Thomas	Steptoe's battery
2nd Lt. Joseph J. Farry	Killed at Molino del Rey, Sep. 8
2nd Lt. Louis D. Welch	
2nd Lt. George P. Andrews	
2nd Lt. Hamilton L. Shields	
2nd Lt. John H. Lendrum	
4th Infantry	
Maj. Francis Lee	Commanding Regiment
Br'vt. Maj. R. C. Buchanan	Acting Major of the regiment
1st Lt. Henry Prince	Severely wounded at Molino del Rey, Sep. 8
1st Lt. John H. Gore	
1st Lt. Sidney Smith	Mortally wounded in the City of Mexico, Sep. 14
1st Lt. G. O. Haller	With stormers from 1st Div., Sep. 8
1st Lt. Jenks Beaman	Guarding train at San Agustin, Aug. 19–20
2nd Lt. U. S. Grant	
2nd Lt. Henry M. Judah	
2nd Lt. A. B. Lincoln	Wounded at Molino del Rey, Sep. 8
2nd Lt. T. J. Montgomery	
2nd Lt. A. P. Rodgers	Killed in the assault on Chapultepec, Sep. 13
2nd Lt. D. F. Jones	
2nd Lt. M. Maloney	With stormers at Molino del Rey, Acting Adjutant, Sep. 12–14
2nd Lt. T. R. McConnell	With stormers from 1st Div. In the assault upon Chapultepec
2nd Lt. Edmund Russell	
Clarke's Brigade	
Col. Newman S. Clarke, 6th Infantry	Commanding Brigade
2nd Lt. R. W. Kirkham, 6th Infantry	Acting Assistant Adjutant General

Name and Unit	Remarks
2nd Lt. W. T. Burwell, 5th Infantry	A.D.C. Killed at Molino del Rey, Sep. 8

Fifth Infantry

Name and Unit	Remarks
B'vt. Col. J. S. McIntosh	Commanding Regiment at San Antonio; Commanding 2nd Brig., 1st Div., at Churubusco, and Molina del Rey; mortally wounded at Molino del Rey, Sep. 8
Bvt. Lt. Col. Martin Scott	Killed at Molino del Rey, Sep. 8
Capt. M. E. Merrill	Killed at Molino del Rey, Sep. 8
Capt. E. K. Smith	Commanded the Light Battalion at Molino del Rey; mortally wounded at El Molino del Rey, Sep. 8
Capt. William Chapman	Commanded the regiment at Molino after the death of Lt. Col. Scott, commanded the regiment on Sep. 12–14
Capt. Daniel Ruggles	
Capt. Daniel H. Mc'Phail	
1st Lt. N. B. Rossell	
1st Lt. S. H. Fowler	
1st Lt. P. Lugenbeel	Adjutant; slightly wounded
1st Lt. M. Rosecrants	Sick on Sep. 8, 12–14
1st Lt. C. S. Hamilton	Severely wounded at Molino del Rey, Sep. 8
2nd Lt. F. T. Dent	Severely wounded at Molino del Rey, Sep. 8
2nd Lt. E. B. Strong	Killed at Molino del Rey, Sep. 8
2nd Lt. J. P. Smith	Killed at the assault of Chapultepec, Sep. 13
2nd Lt. P. Farrelly	With Col. Smith's Infantry Battalion; severely wounded at Churubusco, Aug. 20

6th Infantry

Name and Unit	Remarks
Major B.L.E. Bonneville	Commanding
Capt. William Hoffman	
Capt. A. Cady	Wounded at Molino del Rey, Sep. 8
Capt. T. L. Alexander	
Capt. J.B.S. Todd	
Capt. W.H.T. Walker	Wounded severely at Molino del Rey, Sep. 8
Capt. C. S. Lovell	
1st Lt. E. Johnson	
1st Lt. T. Hendrickson	Severely wounded at Churubusco, Aug. 20
1st Lt. L. A. Armistead	Wounded at Chapultepec, Sep. 13
1st Lt. George Wetmore	
1st Lt. John D. Bacon	Mortally wounded at Churubusco, Aug. 20
1st Lt. A. Morrow	Transferred from the 9th to the 6th Infantry after Aug. 20
2nd Lt. A. D. Nelson	
2nd Lt. R. F. Ernst	Mortally wounded at Molino del Rey, Sep. 8
2nd Lt. R. W. Kirkham	Acting Asst. Adjt. Gen 2nd Brigade
2nd Lt. E. Howe	
2nd Lt. S. B. Buckner	
2nd Lt. W. S. Hancock	

Appendix 2, *continued*

Name and Unit	Remarks
8th Infantry	
Major C. A. Waite	Wounded at Molino del Rey, Sep. 8
Bvt. Major George Wright	Wounded while commanding storming party at Molino del Rey
Capt. & Bvt. Maj. W. R. Montgomery	Wounded at El Molino del Rey, Sep. 8
Capt. R. B. Screven	
Capt. J. V. Bomford	
Capt. I.V.D. Reeve	Serving with Col. Smith's Light Battalion
Capt. C. R. Gates	
Capt. Larkin Smith	Wounded at Molino del Rey, Sep. 8
1st Lt. Joseph Selden	Wounded in the assault on Chapultepec, Sep. 13
1st Lt. J. G. Burbank	Mortally wounded at Molino del Rey, Sep. 8
1st Lt. John Beardsley	Wounded at Molino del Rey, Sep. 8
1st Lt. C. F. Morris	Mortally wounded at Molino del Rey, Sep. 8
1st Lt. J. D. Clark	Wounded at Molino del Rey, Sep. 8
1st Lt. J. Longstreet	Wounded at Chapultepec, Sep. 13
2nd Lt. E. B. Holloway	Wounded at Churubusco, Aug. 20 with Col. Smith's Battalion
2nd Lt. C. G. Merchant	
2nd Lt. George Wainwright	Wounded at Molino del Rey, Sep. 8
2nd Lt. J.G.S. Snelling	Wounded at Molino del Rey, Sep. 8
2nd Lt. T. G. Pitcher	Serving with Col. Smith's Light Battalion
2nd Lt. G. E. Pickett	
2nd Division (Regulars)	
Smith's and Riley's Brigades	
Brig. Gen. David E. Twiggs	Commanding Division
1st Lt. W.T.H. Brooks	Acting Asst. Adj. General
1st Lt. P.W. McDonald	Aide-de-Camp
Smith's Brigade	
Bvt. Brig. Gen. Persifor F. Smith	Commanding Brigade
1st Lt. Earl Van Dorn, 7th Infantry	A.D.C. and Acting Asst. Adj. General
Mounted Riflemen	
Major W. W. Loring	Severely wounded near Belén Gate, Sep. 13
Capt. W. F. Sanderson	
Capt. Henry C. Pope	
Capt. George B. Crittenden	
Capt. John S. Simonson	
Capt. J. B. Backenstoss	
Capt. S. S. Tucker	
Capt. B. S. Roberts	
Capt. Andrew Porter	
1st Lt. M. E. Van Buren	Severely wounded at Contreras, Aug. 20
1st Lt. Llewellyn Jones	Absent from regiment on Aug. 19 and 29 and Sep. 12–14

Name and Unit	Remarks
1st. Lt. Noah Newton	
2nd Lt. George McLane	
2nd Lt. R. M. Morris	
2nd Lt. F. S. K. Russell	Slightly wounded on Sep. 13
2nd Lt. D. M. Frost	Regimental Quartermaster
2nd Lt. John P. Hatch	
2nd Lt. Gordon Granger	
Bvt. 2nd Lt. I. N. Palmer	Wounded near Chapultepec on Sep. 13
Bvt. 2nd Lt. James Stuart	
Bvt. 2nd Lt. Alfred Gibbs	

1st Artillery

Name and Unit	Remarks
Capt. & Bvt. Maj. J. Dimick	Commanding
Capt. George Nauman	
Capt. Francis Taylor	Commanded light battery attached to Twiggs's division
Capt. John H. Winder	
Capt. John B. Magruder	Commanding light battery attached to Pillow's Div.
Capt. E. A. Capron	Killed at Churubusco, Aug. 20
Capt. M. J. Burke	Killed at Churubusco, Aug. 20
Capt. John S. Hatheway	
1st Lt. William H. French	Taylor's battery
1st Lt. J. A. Haskin	Wounded at Chapultepec, Sep. 13, with stormers
1st Lt. H. D. Grafton	Ordnance officer, Twiggs's division
1st Lt. S. K. Dawson	Regimental Quartermaster
1st Lt. J. G. Martin	Wounded at Churubusco, Aug. 20, attached to Taylor's battery
1st Lt. J. M. Brannan	Wounded near Chapultepec, Sep. 13, Adjutant
2nd Lt. Henry Coppee	
2nd Lt. E. C. Boynton	Wounded at Churubusco, Aug. 20, Taylor's Battery
2nd Lt. Thomas J. Jackson	Magruder's Battery
2nd Lt. Truman Seymour	Taylor's Battery
2nd Lt. S. Hoffman	Killed at Churubusco, Aug. 20
2nd Lt. John B. Gibson	
2nd Lt. J. P. Johnston	Killed at Contreras, Aug. 19

3rd Infantry

Name and Unit	Remarks
Capt. E. B. Alexander	Commanding Regiment
Capt. J. Van Horne	
Capt. Lewis S. Craig	Severely wounded at Churubusco, Aug. 20
Capt. J. M. Smith	
Capt. W. H. Gorden	
Capt. Daniel T. Chandler	
Capt. Stephen D. Dobbins	Stormers at Chapultepec
1st Lt. O. L. Sheppard	
1st Lt. W. B. Johns	
1st Lt. D. C. Buell	Severely wounded at Churubusco, Aug. 20, Adjt.

Appendix 2, *continued*

Name and Unit	Remarks
1st Lt. I. B. Richardson	Stormers at Chapultepec
1st Lt. A. W. Bowman	Regimental Quartermaster
2nd Lt. Henry B. Schroeder	
2nd Lt. Barnard E. Bee	Stormers at Chapultepec
2nd Lt. Henry B. Clitz	
2nd Lt. W. H. Wood	
2nd Lt. J. D. Wilkins	
2nd Lt. J.N.G. Whistler	
2nd Lt. Michael O'Sullivan	Resigned shortly after the battle of Churubusco
1st Lt. George Sykes	A.C.S. with the 2nd Division
Riley's Brigade	
Bvt. Col. Bennet Riley, 2nd Infantry	Commanding Brigade
Bvt. Capt. E.R.S. Canby, 2nd Infantry	Asst. Adj. General
1st Lt. Julius Hayden, 2nd Infantry	Aide-de-Camp
4th Artillery	
Major John L. Gardner	Commanding Regiment
Bvt. Major H. Brown	
Capt. S. H. Drum	Killed at the Belén Gate on Sep. 13
Capt. S. C. Ridgely	
1st Lt. John W. Phelps	Regimental Quartermaster
1st Lt. J. P. McCown	
1st Lt. G. W. Getty	
1st Lt. A. P. Howe	Adjutant of the regiment
1st Lt. C. Benjamin	Drum's Battery. Killed at the Belén Gate on Sep. 13
1st Lt. D. H. Hill	Wounded on Sep. 13
1st Lt. F. J. Porter	
2nd Lt. F. Collins	Wounded at Contreras on Aug. 20
2nd Lt. A. L. Magilton	
2nd Lt. G. A. DeRussy	Stormers at Chapultepec
2nd Lt. S. L. Gouveneur	
2nd Infantry	
Capt. T. Morris	Commanding 2nd Infantry
Capt. J.J.B. Kingsbury	
Capt. J. R. Smith	Severely wounded at Churubusco, Aug. 20
Capt. Silas Casey	Severely wounded at Chapultepec, Sep. 13, with stormers
Capt. James W. Penrose	
Capt. H. W. Wessells	Wounded at Contreras, Aug. 19
Capt. James W. Anderson	Wounded at San Geronimo; mortally wounded at Churubusco

Name and Unit	Remarks
1st Lt. C. S. Lovell	Wounded slightly at Churubusco, Aug. 20
1st Lt. D. Davidson	
1st Lt. George C. Westcott	Wounded at Contreras, Aug. 20, with stormers on Sep. 13
1st Lt. B. P. Tilden	Regimental Commissary on Aug. 19–20
1st Lt. N. Lyon	Wounded in the City of Mexico
2nd Lt. J. W. Schureman	Sick on Sep. 8, 12–14
2nd Lt. C. E. Jarvis	
2nd Lt. David R. Jones	Adjutant
2nd Lt. Frederick Steele	With stormers on Sep. 13
2nd Lt. Thomas Easly	Killed at Churubusco, Aug. 20
2nd Lt. Nelson H. Davis	
2nd Lt. Wm. M. Gardner	Severely wounded at Churubusco, Aug. 20

7th Infantry

Lt. Col. J. Plympton	Commanding Regiment
Major H. Bainbridge	
Capt. R. H. Ross	Severely wounded at Contreras, Aug. 20
Capt. G. R. Paul	With stormers
Capt. Charles Hanson	Mortally wounded at Contreras, Aug. 20
Capt. J. C. Henshaw	
1st Lt. Henry Little	Regimental Quartermaster
1st Lt. C. H. Humber	Severely wounded at Churubusco, Aug. 20
1st Lt. Levi Gantt	Killed at Chapultepec, Sep. 13 with stormers
1st Lt. S. B. Hayman	
2nd Lt. F. Gardner	Adjutant
2nd Lt. W. K. VanBokklen	
2nd Lt. Edmund K. Smith	
2nd Lt. W. H. Tyler	
2nd Lt. S. B. Maxey	
2nd Lt. T. Henry	

3rd Division (Regulars)
Pierce's and Cadwalader's Brigades

Maj. Gen. Gideon J. Pillow	Commanding Div., wounded at Chapultepec, Sep. 13
Bv't. Capt. J. Hooker	Asst. Adjutant General
1st Lt. G. W. Rains, 4th Art.	A.D.C.
1st Lt. R. S. Ripley, 2nd Art.	A.D.C.
P'sd. Mid. Rogers, U.S.N.	Vol. A.D.C.

Pierce's Brigade

Brig. Gen. Franklin Pierce	Commanding Brigade
Bvt. Capt. O. F. Winship	Assist. Adj. General
1st Lt. H. Fitzgerald, 6th Inf.	Aide-de-Camp

9th Infantry

Col. T. B. Ransom	Killed near Chapultepec, Sep. 13
Major T. H. Seymour	

Appendix 2, *continued*

Name and Unit	Remarks
Capt. J. S. Pitman	
Capt. E. A. Kimball	
Capt. N. S. Webb	
Capt. A. T. Palmer	Not engaged in any of the actions
Capt. Lorenzo Johnson	Not engaged in any of the actions
Capt. C. N. Bodfish	
Capt. J. W. Thompson	
1st Lt. John S. Slocum	
1st Lt. & Adj. C. J. Sprague	Wounded at Chapultepec, Sep. 13
1st Lt. George Bowers	
1st Lt. J. H. Jackson	
1st Lt. Albert Tracy	
1st Lt. J. M. Hathaway	
2nd Lt. D. H. Cram	Not engaged in any of the actions
2nd Lt. T. P. Pierce	
2nd Lt. N. F. Swett	Not engaged in any of the actions
2nd Lt. T. H. Crosby	
2nd Lt. A. T. Palmer	
2nd Lt. R. C. Drum	Wounded at Churubusco, Aug. 20
2nd Lt. John Glackin	
2nd Lt. Levi Woodhouse	
2nd Lt. H. DeWolfe	Not engaged in any of the actions
2nd Lt. W. A. Newman	Wounded at Churubusco, Aug. 20
2nd Lt. John McNabb	
12th Infantry	
Lt. Col. M. L. Bonham	Wounded on the evening of Sep. 13
Capt. N. B. Holden	
Capt. Allen Wood	
Capt. J. W. Denver	
1st Lt. Charles Taplin	
1st Lt. J.H.H. Felch	
1st Lt. W. B. Giles	
1st Lt. John C. Simkins	
2nd Lt. Henry Almstedt	
2nd Lt. W. A. Linn	
2nd Lt. A. E. Steen	
2nd Lt. J. M. Bronaugh	Acting Adjutant
15th Infantry	
Col. G. W. Morgan	Wounded at Churubusco, Aug. 20
Lt. Col. Joshua Howard	
Major F. D. Mills	Killed near San Antonio Gate, Aug. 20
Major Samuel Woods	
Capt. E. Vandeventer	
Capt. Daniel Chase	
Capt. John A. Jones	

Name and Unit	Remarks
Capt. E. A. King	
Capt. Isaac D. Toll	
Capt. Augustus Quarles	Mortally wounded Churubusco, Aug. 20
Capt. M. Hoagland	
1st Lt. G. W. Bowie	
1st Lt. Thomas H. Freelon	
1st Lt. T. F. Brodhead	On Aug. 19–20 detached as Regimental Quartermaster
1st Lt. D. Upman	Adjutant of Regiment
1st Lt. J. B. Miller	
1st Lt. L. C. Marshall	
1st Lt. A. G. Sutton	
1st Lt. J. B. Goodman	Killed at Churubusco, Aug. 20
2nd Lt. Daniel French	
2nd Lt. Charles Peternell	
2nd Lt. J. W. Wiley	
2nd Lt. H. M. Cady	
2nd Lt. S. E. Beach	On Aug. 19–20, A. C. S. Commissary. On Sep. 8, 12–14, Acting Regimental Quartermaster and Commissary
2nd Lt. F. O. Beckett	
2nd Lt. Thomas B. Tilton	
2nd Lt. W.H.H. Goodloe	Wounded at Churubusco, Aug. 20
2nd Lt. P. S. Titus	
2nd Lt. J. R. Bennett	
Cadwalader's Brigade	
Brig. Gen. George Cadwalader	Commanding Brigade
Bvt. Capt. George Deas	Assistant Adj. General
1st Lt. J. F. Irons	Aide-de-Camp. Mortally wounded at Churubusco, Aug. 20
11th Infantry	
Lt. Col. Wm. Graham	Killed at Molino del Rey, Sep. 8
Major J. F. Hunter	
Capt. Wm. H. Irwin	Wounded at Molino del Rey, Sep. 8
Capt. P. Waddell	
Capt. P. M. Guthrie	
Capt. Arnold Syberg	
1st Lt. J. S. Hedges	Not with his regiment in any of the actions
1st Lt. Thomas F. McCoy	
1st Lt. Daniel S. Lee	Wounded on Aug. 20
1st Lt. John Motz	
1st Lt. C. P. Evans	
1st Lt. B. F. Harley	
2nd Lt. G. C. McClelland	
2nd Lt. A. H. Tippin	
2nd Lt. W. H. Scott	
2nd Lt. R.H.L. Johnston	Killed at Molino del Rey, Sep. 8
2nd Lt. M. Stever	Quartermaster of the regiment

Appendix 2, *continued*

Name and Unit	Remarks

14th Infantry
Col. William Trousdale — Severely wounded at Chapultepec, Sep. 13
Lt. Col. P. O. Hebert
Maj. John H. Savage — Wounded at Molino del Rey, Sep. 8
Maj. John D. Wood
Capt. R. G. Beale
Capt. P. B. Anderson
Capt. E. Bogardus
Capt. Thomas Glenn
Capt. J. M. Scantland
Capt. J. P. Breedlove
Capt. J. W. Perkins
Capt. C. T. Huddlestone
1st Lt. James Blackburn
1st Lt. Thomas Shields
1st Lt. H. B. Kelly
1st Lt. R. Humphreys
1st Lt. Thomas Smith
1st Lt. N. McClannahan
1st Lt. A. J. McAllon
2nd Lt. Richard Steele — Wounded at Chapultepec, Sep. 13
2nd Lt. B. Davis — Serving as ordnance officer, Aug. 19–20, Pillow's division

2nd W. H. Seawell
2nd Lt. R. W. Bedford
2nd Lt. Perrin Watson
2nd Lt. A. J. Isaacs
2nd Lt. A. J. Hudson
2nd Lt. J.C.C. Hays
2nd Lt. S. T. Love

Voltigeurs
Col. T. P. Andrews — Commanding Regiment
Lt. Col. J. E. Johnston
Major G. A. Caldwell
Major G. H. Talcott — Wounded at Molino del Rey, Sep. 8
Capt. A. P. Churchill
Capt. O. E. Edwards
Capt. James D. Blair
Capt. Charles J. Biddle
Capt. John E. Howard
Capt. M. J. Barnard
Capt. J. J. Archer
1st Lt. B. D. Fry
1st Lt. James Tilton
1st Lt. A. H. Cross
1st Lt. H. C. Longnecker

Name and Unit	Remarks

1st Lt. W. S. Walker
2nd Lt. Charles F. Vernon   Resigned
2nd Lt. R. C. Forsyth
2nd Lt. T. D. Cochran
2nd Lt. Robert Swan
2nd Lt. George R. Kiger
2nd Lt. G. S. Kintzing
2nd Lt. Wm. J. Martin
2nd Lt. J. H. Smythe
2nd Lt. James R. May
2nd Lt. Edwin C. Marvin
2nd Lt. Robert H. Archer
2nd Lt. Washington Terrett
2nd Lt. F. H. Larned
2nd Lt. James E. Slaughter

Mountain Howitzer Battery
1st Lt. F. D. Callender   Wounded on Aug. 19
2nd Lt. J. L. Reno   Wounded on Sep. 13

Division of Volunteers
(Shields's Brigade and 2nd Pa. Volunteers)
Major Gen. John A. Quitman   Commanding Division
1st Lt. Mansfield Lovell,
    4th Artillery   A.D.C. & Acting Asst. Adj. General
2nd Lt. C. M. Wilcox, 7th Infantry   A.D.C.

Shields's Brigade
Brig. Gen. James Shields   Commanding Brigade
Bvt. Capt. F. M. Page   Asst. Adj. General
1st Lt. R. P. Hammond   A.D.C.
1st Lt. G.T.M. Davis   Vol. A.D.C.

Marine Corps.
Lt. Col. S. E. Watson
Major Levi Twiggs   Killed near Chapultepec on Sep. 13
Major William Dulany
Capt. J. G. Reynolds
Capt. G. H. Terrett
1st Lt. D. D. Baker
1st Lt. J. S. Devlin   Vol. Aide-de-Camp to Gen. Shields
1st Lt. R. C. Caldwell   Commissary of Pillow's division
1st. Lt. W. L. Young
1st Lt. J. C. Rich
2nd Lt. D. J. Sutherland
2nd Lt. F. Norvell
2nd Lt. J. S. Nicholson
2nd Lt. A. S. Nicholson

Appendix 2, *continued*

Name and Unit	Remarks
2nd Lt. C. G. McCauley	
2nd Lt. Thomos Y. Field	
2nd Lt. E. McDonald Reynolds	
2nd Lt. J. D. Simms	
2nd Lt. C. A. Henderson	
New York Volunteers	
Col. Ward B. Burnett	Wounded at Churubusco, Aug. 20
Lt. Col. Charles Baxter	Mortally wounded at Chapultepec, Sep. 13
Major J. C. Burnham	
Capt. C.H.S. Shaw	Resigned
Capt. James Barclay	
Capt. J. P. Taylor	
Capt. D. P. Hungerford	
Capt. M. Fairchild	
Capt. Sam'l S. Gallagher	
Capt. Charles H. Peirson	Mortally wounded at Chapultepec, Sep. 13
Capt. Van O'Linda	Killed at Chapultepec, Sep. 13
Capt. G. Dykeman	Severely wounded at Churubusco, Aug. 20
Capt. J. F. Hutton	Commissary
1st Lt. R. A. Carter	Adjutant
1st Lt. C. H. Sherwood	Resigned
1st Lt. A. W. Taylor	
1st Lt. C. H. Innis	Wounded at Belén Gate, Sep. 13
1st Lt. C. H. Gallagher	Died at Mixcoac, Sep. 10
1st Lt. George B. Hall	
1st Lt. James Miller	
1st Lt. J. S. McCabe	Wounded at Chapultepec, Sep. 13
2nd Lt. Thomas W. Sweeny	Wounded at Churubusco, Aug. 20
2nd Lt. Charles D. Potter	Wounded at Churubusco, Aug. 20
2nd Lt. Jacob Griffin	
2nd Lt. Addison Farnsworth	
2nd Lt. Mayne Reid	Wounded at Chapultepec, Sep. 13
2nd Lt. C. B. Brower	
2nd Lt. Charles S. Cooper	Wounded at Churubusco, Aug. 20
2nd Lt. J. W. Henry	
2nd Lt. E. Chandler	Mortally wounded at Churubusco, Aug. 20, died Aug. 21
2nd Lt. F. G. Boyle	
2nd Lt. John Rafferty	
2nd Lt. David Scannel	
2nd Lt. J. W. Greenel	
2nd Lt. Malahowsky	Resigned
2nd Lt. W. H. Browne	Not engaged in any of the actions
2nd Lt. Francis Durning	Resigned
2nd Lt. F. E. Pinto	

Name and Unit	Remarks
South Carolina Volunteers	
Col. P. M. Butler	Killed at Churubusco, Aug. 20
Lt. Col. J. P. Dickinson	Mortally wounded at Churubusco, Aug. 20
Maj. A. H. Gladden	Wounded at the Belén Gate, Sep. 13
Capt. F. Sumter	
Capt. R.G.M. Dunovant	
Capt. K. S. Moffat	Wounded at Churubusco, Aug. 20
Capt. J. F. Marshall	
Capt. W. Blanding	
Capt. W. D. Desaussure	
Capt. N. J. Walker	
Capt. J. F. Williams	
Capt. James D. Blanding	
Adj. James Cantey	Wounded at Churubusco, Aug. 20
1st Lt. William B. Stanley	
1st Lt. C.S. Mellet	
1st Lt. J. F. Walker	
1st Lt. W. C. Moragne	
1st Lt. J. B. Moragne	Killed at Belén Gate, Sep. 13
1st Lt. A. Manegault	
1st Lt. J. R. Clark	Mortally wounded at Churubusco, Aug. 20
1st Lt. A. B. O'Bannon	
1st Lt. C. P. Pope	Accidentally wounded, Aug. 20
2nd Lt. T. M. Baker	
2nd Lt. S. Sumter	Wounded at Churubusco, Aug. 20
2nd Lt. W. B. Lilley	
2nd Lt. B.W.D. Culp	
2nd Lt. James W. Cantey	Killed at Chapultepec, Sep. 13
2nd Lt. K. G. Billings	Wounded at Churubusco, Aug. 20
2nd Lt. Joseph Abney	Wounded at Churubusco, Aug. 20
2nd Lt. David Adams	Killed at Churubusco, Aug. 20
2nd Lt. L. F. Robertson	
2nd Lt. Ralph Bell	
2nd Lt. J. R. Davis	
2nd Lt. J. N. Moye	Wounded at Belén Gate, Sep. 13
2nd Lt. J. W. Steen	Wounded at Chapultepec, Sep. 13
2nd Lt. M. R. Clark	
2nd Lt. Charles Kirkland	
2nd Lt. W. R. Williams	Killed at Churubusco, Aug. 20
2nd Lt. J. W. Stewart	Wounded at Belén Gate, Sep. 13
2nd Lt. F. W. Selleck	Died in the City of Mexico, Oct. 3
2nd Pennsylvania Volunteers	
Col. W. B. Roberts	Commanding Regiment
Lt. Col. John W. Geary	
Maj. William Brindle	
Capt. Thomas S. Loeser	
Capt. John Humphries	
Capt. Clarence H. Frick	

Appendix 2. *continued*

Name and Unit	Remarks
Capt. C. Naylor	
Capt. E. C. Williams	
Capt. Robert Porter	
Capt. James Murray	
Capt. James Miller	Wounded
Capt. S. M. Taylor	
Capt. James Caldwell	Wounded, died in September
Adj. J. S. Waterbury	
R.Q.M., E.E.L. Clare	
A.C.S., John G. Geven	
1st Lt. Hiram Wolf	
1st Lt. Alex McKamey	
1st Lt. William Wonders	Died at Mixcoac, Sep. 11
Lt. H.A.M. Filbert	
Lt. Richard McMichael	Appointed Lieutenant, Sep. 9
Lt. Samuell Black	
Lt. Charles H. Heyer	
Lt. James Armstrong	
Lt. James Coulter	Wounded
Lt. Isaac Hare	
Lt. A. L. Tourison	
Lt. D. J. Unger	
Lt. H. A. Hambright	
Lt. William Rankin	
Lt. James Kane	
Lt. Wm. P. Skelly	
Lt. L. W. Smith	
Lt. D. N. Hoffins	
Lt. J. Keeffe	Wounded
2nd Lt. John A. Doyle	
2nd Lt. Charles Bowers	On duty as Assistant Surgeon

SOURCE: Compiled from a booklet by Henry L. Scott entitled *List of Officers Who Marched with the Army under the Command of Major General Winfield Scott, from Puebla upon the City of Mexico* (Mexico: American Star Print, 1848). Copy in Virginia Historical Society, Richmond, Va.

The following men who served in Winfield Scott's army in Mexico later served as generals during the Civil War. This is not intended to be a comprehensive list.

Northern generals—Robert Allen, Lewis G. Arnold, Robert Anderson, Joseph K. Barnes, John M. Brannan, William Brooks, Robert Buchanan, Don Carlos Buell, George Cadwalader, Edward Canby, Silas Casey, Napoleon Jackson Tecumseh Dana, Frederick T. Dent, Gustavus Adolphus DeRussy, John Gray Foster, William French, John W. Geary, George W. Getty, Alfred Gibbs, Charles Gilbert, George H. Gordon, Lawrance Graham, Gordon Granger, Ulysses S. Grant, Charles S. Hamilton, Schuyler Hamilton, Winfield Scott Hancock, William S. Harney, Joseph A. Haskin, John Porter Hatch, William Hays, Charles Heckman, Ethan Allen Hitchcock, Joseph Hooker, Henry J. Hunt, Henry M. Judah, Philip Kearny, Michael K. Lawler, Nathaniel Lyon, Jasper A. Maltby, George McClellan, Justus McKinstry, William R. Montgomery, George W. Morgan, James Scott Negley, William Nelson, Innis N. Palmer, Robert Patterson, Gabriel René Paul, John J. Peck, John W. Phelps, Thomas G. Pitcher, Andrew Porter, Fitz John Porter, Henry Prince, Jesse Lee Reno, Israel Richardson, Benjamin S. Roberts, David A. Russell, John Sedgwick, Truman Seymour, James Shields, Charles Smith, Frederick Steele, Isaac Ingalls Stevens, Charles P. Stone, Edwin V. Sumner, Thomas W. Sweeny, George Sykes, Joseph G. Totten, Zealous B. Tower, Stewart Van Vliet, Thomas Welsh, Henry Wessells, Seth Williams, Thomas Williams, George Wright (78).

Southern generals—James J. Archer, Lewis Armistead, P. G. T. Beauregard, Barnard Bee, Milledge L. Bonham, Simon B. Buckner, James Cantey, Benjamin F. Cheatham, George B. Crittenden, Arnold Elzey, Richard S. Ewell, Daniel Frost, Birkett Fry, Franklin Gardner, William Gardner, John B. Grayson, William Hardee, James Hawes, Daniel Harvey Hill, Paul O. Hebert, Benjamin Huger, Thomas "Stonewall" Jackson, Edward Johnson, Joseph E. Johnston, Davis R. Jones, Robert E. Lee, James Longstreet, William W. Loring, Mansfield Lovell, William W. Mackall, John Magruder, George Maney, Arthur M. Manigault, James Martin, Dabney Maury, Samuel B. Maxey, John P. McCown, Abraham C. Myers, John Pemberton, George Pickett, Gideon Pillow, Roswell Ripley, Daniel Ruggles, Henry H. Sibley, James E. Slaughter, Edmund Kirby Smith, Gustavus W. Smith, William Duncan Smith, William Steele, Alexander Steen, David E. Twiggs, Earl Van Dorn, John G. Walker, William Walker, Henry C. Wayne, Cadmus M. Wilcox, John H. Winder (57).

SOURCE: Compiled primarily from Ezra J. Warner, *Generals in Blue: Lives of the Union Commanders* (Baton Rouge: Louisiana State University Press, 1964); Warner,

Generals in Gray: Lives of the Confederate Commanders (Baton Rouge: Louisiana State University Press, 1959); Henry L. Scott, *List of Officers Who Marched with the Army under the Command of Major General Winfield Scott* (1848), copy at Virginia Historical Society, Richmond, Va.; and Cadmus M. Wilcox, *History of the Mexican War* (Washington: Church News, 1892), appx. C.

Appendix 4

Winfield Scott's General Orders, No. 20, of February 19, 1847, declaring MARTIAL LAW.

1. It is still to be apprehended that many grave offences, not provided for in the Act of Congress "establishing rules and articles for the government of the armies of the United States," approved April 10, 1806, may again be committed-by, or upon, individuals of those armies, in Mexico, pending the existing war between the two Republics. Allusion is here made to offences, any one of which, if committed within the United States or their organized Territories, would, of course, be tried and severely punished by the ordinary or civil courts of the land.

2. Assassination, murder, poisoning, rape, or the attempt to commit either; malicious stabbing or maiming; malicious assault and battery, robbery, theft; the wanton desecration of churches, cemeteries or other religious edifices and fixtures; the interruption of religious ceremonies, and the destruction, except by order of a superior officer, of public or private property; are such offences.

3. The good of the service, the honor of the United States and the interests of humanity, imperiously demand that every crime, enumerated above, should be severely punished.

4. But the written code, as above, commonly called the *rules and articles of war,* does not provide for the punishment of any one of those crimes, even when committed by individuals of the army upon the persons or property of other individuals of the same, except in the very restricted case in the 9th of those articles; nor for like outrages, committed by the same class of individuals, upon the persons or property of a hostile country, except very partially, in the 51st, 52d, and 55th articles; and the same code is absolutely silent as to all injuries which may be inflicted upon individuals of the army, or their property, against the laws of war, by individuals of a hostile country.

5. It is evident that the 99th article, independent of any reference to the restriction in the 87th, is wholly nugatory in reaching any one of those high crimes.

6. For all the offences, therefore, enumerated in the second paragraph above, which may be committed abroad—in, by, or upon the army, a supplemental code is absolutely needed.

7. That unwritten code is Martial Law, as an addition to the written military code, prescribed by Congress in the rules and articles of war, and which unwritten code, all armies, in hostile countries, are forced to adopt—not only for their own safety, but for the protection of the unoffending inhabitants and their property, about the theatres of military operations, against injuries, on the part of the army, contrary to the laws of war.

8. From the same supreme necessity, martial law is hereby declared as a supplemental code in, and about, all cities, towns, camps, posts, hospitals, and other places which may be occupied by any part of the forces of the United States, in Mexico, and in, and about, all columns, escorts, convoys, guards, and detachments, of the said forces, while engaged in prosecuting the existing war in, and against the said republic, and while remaining within the same.

9. Accordingly, every crime, enumerated in paragraph No. 2, above, whether committed—1. By any inhabitant of Mexico, sojourner or traveller therein, upon the person or property of any individual of the United States forces, retainer or follower of the same; 2. By any individual of the said forces, retainer or follower of the same, upon the person or property of any inhabitant of Mexico, sojourner or traveller therein; or 3. By any individual of the said forces, retainer or follower of the same, upon the person or property of any other individual of the said forces, retainer or follower of the same—shall be duly tried and punished under the said supplemental code.

10. For this purpose it is ordered, that all offenders, in the matters aforesaid, shall be promptly seized, confined, and reported for trial, before *military commissions*, to be duly appointed as follows:

11. Every military commission, under this order, will be appointed, governed, and limited, as nearly as practicable, as prescribed by the 65th, 66th, 67th, and 97th, of the said rules and articles of war, and the proceedings of such commissions will be duly recorded, in writing, reviewed, revised, disapproved or approved, and the sentences executed—all, as near as may be, as in the cases of the proceedings and sentences of courts martial, *provided*, that no military commission shall try any case clearly cognizable by any court martial, and *provided*, also, that no sentence of a military commission shall be put in execution against any individual belonging to this army, which may not be, according to the nature and degree of the offence, as established by evidence, in conformity with known punishments, in like cases, in some one of the States of the United States of America.

12. The sale, waste or loss of ammunition, horses, arms, clothing or accoutrements, by soldiers, is punishable under the 37th and 38th articles of war. Any Mexican or resident or traveller, in Mexico, who shall purchase of any American soldier, either horse, horse equipments, arms, ammunition, accoutrements or clothing, shall be tried and severely punished, by a military commission, as above.

13. The administration of justice, both in civil and criminal matters, through the ordinary courts of the country, shall nowhere and in no degree, be interrupted by any officer or soldier of the American forces, except, 1. In cases to which an officer, soldier, agent, servant, or follower of the American army may be a party; and 2. In *political* cases—that is, prosecutions against other individuals on the allegations that they have given friendly information, aid or assistance to the American forces.

14. For the ease and safety of both parties, in all cities and towns occupied by the American army, a Mexican police shall be established and duly harmonized with the military police of the said forces.

15. This splendid capital—its churches and religious worship; its convents and monasteries; its inhabitants and property are, moreover, placed under the special safeguard of the faith and honor of the American army.

16. In consideration of the foregoing protection, a contribution of $150,000 is imposed on this capital, to be paid in four weekly instalments of thirty-seven thousand five hundred dollars ($37,500) each, beginning on Monday next, the 20th instant, and terminating on Monday, the 11th of October.

17. The Ayuntamiento, or corporate authority of the city, is specially charged with the collection and payment of the several instalments.

18. Of the whole contributions to be paid over to this army, twenty thousand dollars shall be appropriated to the purchase of *extra* comforts for the wounded and sick in hospital; ninety thousand dollars ($90,000) to the purchase of blankets and shoes for gratuitous distribution among the rank and file of the army, and forty thousand dollars ($40,000) reserved for other necessary military purposes.

19. This order will be read at the head of every company of the United States' forces, serving in Mexico, and translated into Spanish for the information of Mexicans.

Abbreviations

DRTL	Daughters of the Republic of Texas Library, San Antonio
BLY	Beinecke Library, Yale University, New Haven, Conn.
FHS	Filson Historical Society, Louisville, Ky.
LAC	Latin-American Collection
LC	Library of Congress
LR	Letters Received
NA	National Archives
RG	Record Group
SHC	Southern Historical Collection
SW	Secretary of War
TSLA	Tennessee State Library and Archives, Nashville
UNC	University of North Carolina
USMA	United States Military Academy, West Point, N.Y.
UT	University of Texas, Austin
UTA	University of Texas, Arlington
VHS	Virginia Historical Society, Richmond

Prologue

1. Carl von Clausewitz, *On War,* trans. and ed. Michael Howard and Peter Paret (Princeton. N.J.: Princeton University Press, 1976), 119.

2. Moses Barnard Reminiscences, BLY; Winfield Scott, *Memoirs of Lieut.-General Scott,* 2 vols. (1864; Freeport, N.Y.: Books for Libraries Press, 1970), 2:573.

3. Clark to John (brother), Jan. 19, 1848, N. H. Clark Papers, University of Missouri, Columbia.

4. Gardner to brother, Nov. 23, 1847, William Montgomery Gardner Papers, SHC, UNC.

5. For a thorough discussion of this theme, see Ernest Lee Tuveson, *Redeemer Nation: The Idea of America's Millennial Role* (Chicago: University of Chicago Press, 1968), esp. chap. 4.

6. Clark to John, Jan. 19, 1848, N. H. Clark Papers.

Chapter 1. Veracruz: The Gibraltar of Mexico

1. J. Frost, *The Mexican War and Its Warriors* (New Haven, Conn.: H. Mansfield, 1850), 129–30; Israel Uncapher Mexican War Diary, UTA; Chauncey Forward

Sargent, *Gathering Laurels in Mexico: The Diary of an American Soldier in the Mexican American War,* ed. Ann Brown Janes (Lincoln, Mass.: Cottage Press, 1990), 5; William G. Temple, "Memoir," in Philip Syng Physick Conner, *The Home Squadron under Commodore Connor in the War with Mexico* (Philadelphia: Philip Syng Physick Conner, 1896), 60; "The Siege of Vera Cruz," *Southern Quarterly Review* (Jul. 1851). The landing craft were built in lengths of 35 feet 9 inches, 37 feet 9 inches, and 40 feet to facilitate stacking on board the transports. To illustrate that cost overruns are nothing new to the U.S. military, the amount paid for each boat was quadruple the original contract price. For an excellent treatment of the weapons used in the Mexican War, see Richard Bruce Winders, *Mr. Polk's Army: The American Military Experience in the Mexican War* (College Station: Texas A&M University Press, 1997), chap. 6, esp. 92–97.

2. Daniel Harvey Hill, *A Fighter from Way Back: The Mexican War Diary of Lt. Daniel Harvey Hill, 4th Artillery, USA,* ed. Nathaniel Cheairs Hughes Jr. and Timothy D. Johnson (Kent, Ohio: Kent State University Press, 2002), 73; H. Judge Moore, *Scott's Campaign from the Rendezvous on the Island of Lobos to the Taking of the City* (Charleston: J. B. Nixon, 1849), 6; George B. McClellan, *The Mexican War Diary of General George B. McClellan Diary,* ed. William Stan Myers (New York: DaCapo Press, 1972), 53–54; K. Jack Bauer, *The Mexican War, 1846–1848* (1974; Lincoln: University of Nebraska Press, 1992), 244; Amasa Gleason Clark, *Reminiscences of a Centenarian* (Bandera, Tex.: Amasa Gleason Clark, 1930), 14; K. Jack Bauer, *Surfboats and Horse Marines: U.S. Naval Operations in the Mexican War, 1846–48* (Annapolis: United States Naval Institute, 1969), 78–79. An eyewitness account puts the time of the signal shot at 4:00 P.M., while K. Jack Bauer places the time at 5:30. There seems to be general agreement, however, that the Americans hit the beach at about 5:30. Assuming that to be accurate, and assuming that it could not have taken more than ten to fifteen minutes to row to shore, it seems logical to conclude that the signal gun was fired sometime between 5:00 and 5:30. See Unknown, "Campaigns in Mexico," BLY; Clark, *Reminiscences,* 12; George Turnbull Moore Davis, *Autobiography of the Late Col. Geo T. M. Davis, Captain and Aid-de-Camp Scott's Army of Invasion* (New York: Jenkins and McCowan, 1891), 124. In the nineteenth century, the "Star Spangled Banner," written by Francis Scott Key after watching the shelling of Fort McHenry, was set to the music of an old English drinking song entitled "To Anacreontic in Heaven."

3. Winfield Scott, *Memoirs of Lieut.-General Scott,* 2 vols. (1864; Freeport, N.Y.: Books for Libraries Press, 1970), 2:404.

4. Justin H. Smith, *The War with Mexico,* 2 vols. (New York: Macmillan, 1919), 1:536, n. 2; William A. DePalo Jr., *The Mexican National Army, 1822–1852* (College Station: Texas A&M University Press, 1997), 118; Meade to wife, Jul. 9, 1846, in George Meade, *The Life and Letters of George Gordon Meade,* 2 vols. (New York: Charles Scribner's Sons, 1913), 1:188; Samuel Chase to Conner, Dec. 20, 1846, David Conner Papers, LC; Thomas D. Tennery, *The Mexican War Diary of Thomas D. Tennery,* ed. D. E. Livingston-Little (Norman: University of Oklahoma Press, 1970), 76; Samuel Lauderdale to James Lauderdale, Apr. 2, 1847, Lauderdale Fam-

ily Papers, TSLA; T. H. Towner to Benjamin Towner, Feb. 12, 1847, Benjamin T. Towner Papers, Duke University, Durham, N.C.

5. Bauer, *Mexican War,* 70–71; Smith, *War,* 1:198; David M. Pletcher, *The Diplomacy of Annexation: Texas, Oregon, and the Mexican War* (Columbia: University of Missouri Press, 1973), 398–99, 455; Ivor Debenham Spencer, *The Victor and the Spoils: A Life of William L. Marcy* (Providence: Brown University Press, 1959), 155; James K. Polk, *The Diary of James K. Polk,* ed. Milo Milton Quaife, 4 vols. (Chicago: A. C. McClurg, 1910) 1:408; Eugene Irving McCormac, *James K. Polk: A Political Biography* (Berkeley: University of California Press, 1922), 419; Scott to Marcy, May 21, 1846, Senate Docs., No. 378, 29th Cong., 1st Sess. For an excellent overview of the events leading to the war, see Richard Bruce Winders, *Crisis in the Southwest: The United States, Mexico, and the Struggle over Texas* (Wilmington, Del.: Scholarly Resources, 2002).

6. Polk, *Diary,* 1:415, 419–22, 428; Marcy to Scott, May 25, 1846, and Marcy to Wetmore, Jun. 13 and Jun. 28, 1846, William L. Marcy Papers, LC, Washington D.C.; Scott to Marcy, May 25, 1846, Senate Doc., No. 378, 29th Cong., 1st Exec. Scott to Thomas Ritchie and John Heiss, Jun. 10, 1846, Charles Winslow Elliott Collection, New York Public Library; Scott to Duncan Clinch, Jul. 10, 1846, Robert Anderson Papers, LC; Scott, *Memoirs,* 2:385. Marcy's biographer speculated that the secretary disagreed with Polk's decision to remove Scott from field command but dutifully went along with the president's decision. See Spencer, *The Victor and the Spoils,* 155. Historian Sam W. Haynes has described Polk as a "dogmatic" man who had a "penchant for disingenuousness, if not outright deception." See his study, *James K. Polk and the Expansionist Impulse* (New York: Longman, 1997), 43, 94–95; 71–72, 155.

7. Others would claim credit for the idea to capture Veracruz and use it as a base of operations against Mexico City. However, Scott is known to have discussed the idea with Marcy as early as Jul. 9. In his memoirs, Scott asserted that the idea to launch at attack beginning at Veracruz was "an idea always mine." See Scott, *Memoirs,* 2:404. In September, Polk had ordered the capture of the coastal town of Tampico 250 miles south of the Rio Grande, but its distance from Mexico City and its lack of good roads made it an unfavorable invasion point. See Bauer, *Mexican War,* 233.

8. Winfield Scott, "Vera Cruz & Its Castle," Oct. 27, 1846, LR, RG 107, NA; Scott to War Department, Oct. 27, 1846, House Exec. Doc. No. 60, 30th Cong., 1st Exec.; Irving W. Levinson, *Wars within War: Mexican Guerrillas, Domestic Elites, and the United States of America, 1846–1848* (Forth Worth: Texas Christian University Press, 2005), 18–19. The three states occupied by Taylor's army had 276,512 inhabitants, or less than 4 percent of Mexico's total population.

9. Spencer, *The Victor and the Spoils,* 156, 160–61; Polk, *Diary,* 2:227, 243–45, 247, 275–77, 282, 301–2, 399; Bauer, *Mexican War,* 235. Many Whigs saw the conflict as a war of aggression and condemned it. They condemned Polk for his treatment of Scott. See Michael F. Holt, *The Rise and Fall of the American Whig Party: Jacksonian Politics and the Onset of the Civil War* (New York: Oxford University Press, 1999), 249.

10. Paul Foos, *A Short, Offhand, Killing Affair: Soldiers and Social Conflict during the Mexican-American War* (Chapel Hill: University of North Carolina Press, 2002), 98; Thomas Williams to father, Jan. 12, 1847, Williams Letters, Justin H. Smith Collection, LAC, UT; Scott, *Memoirs*, 2:392–94; Allan Peskin, ed., *Volunteers: The Mexican War Journals of Private Richard Coulter and Sergeant Thomas Barclay, Company E, Second Pennsylvania Infantry* (Kent, Ohio: Kent State University Press, 1991), 127; Haynes, *Polk and the Expansionist Impulse*, 152; Hill, *Fighter from Way Back*, 28, 47; John Lillard to father, Feb. 10, 1847, Lillard Family Papers, FHS; Henry O. Whiteside, "Winfield Scott and the Mexican Occupation: Policy and Practice," *Mid-America* 52 (1970): 103, 105–6.

11. Whiteside, "Winfield Scott," 105–6; "The Special Message," Jan. 2, 1847, John W. James Collection of Mexican War Articles, BLY. For an overview of the lessons that Scott learned from the Napoleonic Wars, see Timothy D. Johnson, *Winfield Scott: The Quest for Military Glory* (Lawrence: University Press of Kansas, 1998), 166–69.

12. Scott to Taylor, Nov. 25, 1846, and Scott to Marcy, Dec. 27, 1846, Marcy Papers, LC; Scott to Taylor, Dec. 20, 1846, House Executive Doc. No. 56, 30th Cong., 1st Exec.; Bauer, *Mexican War*, 238; Holman Hamilton, *Zachary Taylor: Soldier of the Republic* (Hamden, Conn.: Archon Books, 1966), 115, 228–29; Henry S. Lane, "The Mexican War Journal of Henry S. Lane," ed. Graham A. Barringer, *Indiana Magazine of History* 53 (Dec. 1957): 418; Scott to Marcy, Jan. 24, 1847, LR, AGO, RG 94, NA; K. Jack Bauer, *Zachary Taylor: Soldier, Planter, Statesman of the Old Southwest* (Baton Rouge: Louisiana State University Press, 1985), 192–93; Dabney Herdon Maury, *Recollections of a Virginian in the Mexican, Indian, and Civil Wars* (New York: Charles Scribner's Sons, 1894), 29.

13. Scott to Marcy, Jan. 16 and Jan. 27, 1847, Marcy Papers.

14. George Rollie Adams, *General William S. Harney: Prince of Dragoons* (Lincoln: University of Nebraska Press, 2001), 80–85, 88, 91–92; General Orders No. 5, Jan. 28, and General Orders No. 11, Feb. 2, 1847, Justin H. Smith Collection, LAC, UT; Polk, *Diary*, 2:385.

15. George C. Furber, *The Twelve Months Volunteers; or, Journal of a Private, in the Tennessee Regiment of Cavalry, in the Campaign Mexico, 1846–7* (Cincinnati: J. A. & U. P. James, 1848), 403–4; Paul D. Casdorph, *Prince John Magruder: His Life and Campaigns* (New York: John Wiley, 1996), 64; Meade to wife, Jan. 24 and Feb. 26, 1847, Meade, *Life and Letters*, 1:175, 185.

16. General Orders No. 21, Feb. 19, 1847, Smith Collection.

17. Moore, *Scott's Campaign*, 1–2; Sargent, *Gathering Laurels*, 4; John Hammond Moore, ed., "Private Johnson Fights the Mexicans, 1847–1848," *South Carolina Historical Magazine* 67 (Oct. 1966): 204; Kirby Smith to wife, Feb. 28, 1847, in E. Kirby Smith, *To Mexico with Scott: Letters of Captain E. Kirby Smith to His Wife*, ed. Emma Jerome Blackwood (Cambridge, Mass.: Harvard University Press, 1917), 105; Scott to Conner, Feb. 26, 1847, and William Hunt to Conner, Mar. 4, 1847, David Conner Papers, LC; Alfred Hoyt Bill, *Rehearsal for Conflict: The War with Mexico, 1846–1848* (New York: Alfred A. Knopf, 1947), 206; Bauer, *Mexican War*, 240; Smith, *War*, 1:368, 2:18.

18. Bauer, *Surfboats*, 80–82; Unknown, "Campaigns in Mexico," BLY; Raphael Semmes, *Service Afloat and Ashore during the Mexican War* (Cincinnati: Wm. H. Moore, 1851), 128; quote from Lee to Mary Lee, Mar. 13, 1847, George Bolling Lee Papers; Kendall to *Picayune*, Mar. 12, 1847, Kendall Family Papers, UTA; Clark, *Reminiscences*, 15.

19. Thomas L. Alexander Diary, BLY; Peskin, *Volunteers*, 80; Ethan Allen Hitchcock, "Sketches of the Campaign," Ethan Allen Hitchcock Papers, USMA; A. P. Hill quoted in James I. Robertson Jr., *General A. P. Hill: The Story of a Confederate Warrior* (New York: Random House, 1987), 18; Madison Mills Diary, FHS; Hill, *Fighter from Way Back*, 57–61; Ulysses S. Grant, *Personal Memoirs of U. S. Grant*, 2 vols. (New York: Charles L. Webster, 1885), 1:123–24.

20. Gustavus Woodson Smith, *Company "A" Corps of Engineers, USA, 1846–1848, in the Mexican War*, ed. Leonne M. Hudson (Kent, Ohio: Kent State University Press, 2001), 1–18.

21. Lee to Mary, Feb. 22, 1847, Lee Family Papers, VHS; H. J. Moore Mexican War Diary, BLY; Maury, *Recollections*, 29–30; Mills Diary, FHS.

22. Anderson to wife, Mar. 12, 1847, Robert Anderson Papers, LC: Hill, *Fighter from Way Back*, 73.

23. Moses Barnard Reminiscences, BLY.

24. John Sedgwick, *Correspondence of John Sedgwick, Major-General*, comp. Henry D. Sedgwick, 2 vols. (DeVinne Press, 1902), 1:72; Hill, *Fighter from Way Back*, 73–74; Lee to Mary, Mar. 13, 1847, George Bolling Lee Papers; McClellan, *Mexican War Diary*, 54; Smith to wife, Mar. 13, 1847, in Smith, *To Mexico with Scott*, 114–15.

25. Hitchcock, "Sketches," Hitchcock Papers.

26. Navy Department, *Dictionary of American Naval Fighting Ships*, 8 vols. (Washington, D.C.: Naval History Center, 1991), 6:585; Hill, *Fighter from Way Back*, 74; Ripley to mother, Mar. 16, 1847, Roswell Ripley Papers, BLY; Winslow Sanderson to wife, Mar. 31, 1847, Winslow Fuller Sanderson Papers, BLY.

27. Davis, *Autobiography*, 279; William Campbell to David Campbell, Mar. 28, 1847, in William Bowen Campbell, *Mexican War Letters of Col. William Bowen Campbell of Tennessee, Written to Governor David Campbell of Virginia, 1846–1847*, ed. St. George L. Sioussat (reprinted from *Tennessee Historical Magazine*, Jun. 1915), 161.

28. Hill, *Fighter from Way Back*, 74–75; Unknown, "Campaigns in Mexico," BLY; Patterson to Scott, Mar. 14, 1847, LR, AGO, RG 94, NA; Wiley Hale to mother, Feb. 18, 1847, Wiley Pope Hale Papers, TSLA. Hale obviously dated his letter Feb. 18 by mistake; it should have been March.

29. Hill, *Fighter from Way Back*, 74–75; Grant, *Personal Memoirs*, 1:126; Bauer, *Mexican War*, 246; Peskin, *Volunteers*, 45.

30. John Edwards Weems, *To Conquer a Peace: The War between the United States and Mexico* (College Station: Texas A&M University Press, 1974), 331; Moore, *Scott's Campaign*, 12.

31. Scott, *Memoirs*, 2:223–24; Bauer, *Mexican War*, 245–46; Marcy to Scott, Dec. 22, 1847, United States War Department Letters, BLY.

32. Hitchcock, "Sketches," Hitchcock Papers; William Walker to wife, Mar. 13, 1847, William Walker Papers, Duke University; Weems, *To Conquer a Peace*, 332.

33. Peskin, *Volunteers*, 47–48. Private George W. Hartman said that it was the railroad that ran parallel to and near to the Alvarado Road, where Pillow had so dangerously positioned his men. Perhaps he did this in both places. See George W. Hartman, *A Private's Own Journal: Giving an Account of the Battles in Mexico, under Gen'l Scott* (Greencastle: E. Robinson, 1849), 7.

34. Hill, *Fighter from Way Back*, 76–77.

35. E. Kirby Smith, who wrote that he had seen Alburtis's body, also mentioned walking past as the doctors amputated Miller's leg. See his letter quoted in Arthur Howard Noll, *General Kirby-Smith* (Sewanee, Tenn.: University Press at the University of the South, 1907), 49. Although he no doubt saw comrades attending to their wounded friend, Smith was mistaken about the loss of the leg, as are other accounts of this episode. Captain Winslow Sanderson, a member of the same unit, was present when Miller was wounded; in fact, he killed two of the enemy officers in the skirmish. In two letters to his wife, Mar. 31 and May 2, Sanderson reported "Miller will save his leg." See Sanderson Papers.

36. Bauer, *Mexican War*, 246; Uncapher Diary; Francis B. Heitman, *Historical Register and Dictionary of the United States Army*, 2 vols. (1903; Baltimore: Genealogical Publishing, 1994), 1:155; Hill, *Fighter from Way Back*, 76–77; Lee to Mary, Mar. 13, 1847, George Bolling Lee Papers; Uncapher Diary.

37. Lee to Mary, Mar. 13, 1847, George Bolling Lee Papers; McClellan, *Mexican War Diary*, 56–57; Unknown, "Campaigns in Mexico," BLY.

38. Bauer, *Mexican War*, 246; quote from Lee to Mary, Mar. 13, 1847, George Bolling Lee Papers; Robert Anderson, *An Artillery Officer in the Mexican War, 1846–7* (New York: G. P. Putnam's Sons, 1911), 79; Judge Zo. S. Cook, "Mexican War Reminiscences," *Alabama Historical Quarterly* 19 (fall–winter 1957): 441–42; Temple, "Memoir," 64; Scott to Marcy, Mar. 14, 1847, LR SW, RG 107, NA; Joseph Rowe Smith Diary, Joseph Rowe Smith Papers, BLY.

39. McClellan, *Mexican War Diary*, 58.

40. Noll, *General Kirby-Smith*, 49–50; Twiggs to Scott, Mar. 15, 1847, LR, AGO, RG 94, NA; Hill, *Fighter from Way Back*, 76, 79.

41. Scott to Marcy, Mar. 21, 1847, LR SW, RG 107, NA; Bill, *Rehearsal*, 213.

Chapter 2. Veracruz: The Slow, Scientific Process

1. William Campbell to David Campbell, Mar. 20, 1847, in William Bowen Campbell, *Mexican War Letters of Col. William Bowen Campbell of Tennessee, Written to Governor David Campbell of Virginia, 1846–1847*, ed. St. George L. Sioussat (reprinted from *Tennessee Historical Magazine*, Jun. 1915), 159.

2. Scott to Marcy, Mar. 12, 14, and 21, 1847, LR SW, RG 107, NA; Meade to wife, Feb. 24, 1847, in George Meade, *The Life and Letters of George Gordon Meade*, 2 vols. (New York: Charles Scribner's Sons, 1913), 1:184.

3. General Orders No. 53, Mar. 13, 1847, Justin H. Smith Collection, LAC, UT; Joseph Rowe Smith, "Diary," Joseph Rowe Smith Papers, BLY.

4. P. G. T. Beauregard, *With Beauregard in Mexico: The Mexican War Reminiscences of P. G. T. Beauregard,* ed. T. Harry Williams (New York: DaCapo Press, 1969), 26–27.

5. Scott to Marcy, Mar. 18, 1847, LR SW, RG 107, NA; Justin H. Smith, *The War with Mexico,* 2 vols. (New York: Macmillan, 1919), 2:28; Hazard Stevens, *The Life of Isaac Ingalls Stevens,* 2 vols. (New York: Houghton Mifflin, 1900), 1:113; Bradford to Carry, Mar. 27, 1847, Edmund Bradford Papers, BLY; William Montgomery Gardner, *The Siege of Vera Cruz,* photocopy from Gardner's published memoirs, William Montgomery Gardner Papers, SHC, UNC; George B. McClellan, *The Mexican War Diary of General George B. McClellan Diary,* ed. William Stan Myers (New York: DaCapo Press, 1972), 62–63.

6. Daniel Harvey Hill, *A Fighter from Way Back: The Mexican War Diary of Lt. Daniel Harvey Hill, 4th Artillery, USA,* ed. Nathaniel Cheairs Hughes Jr. and Timothy D. Johnson (Kent, Ohio: Kent State University Press, 2002), 200–201, quotes found on 80, 86–87.

7. Gustavus Woodson Smith, *Company "A" Corps of Engineers, USA, 1846–1848, in the Mexican War,* ed. Leonne M. Hudson (Kent, Ohio: Kent State University Press, 2001), 22; McClellan, *Mexican War Diary,* 62–63; Hiram B. Yeager to John C. Yeager, Mar. 20, 1847, Hiram Yeager Papers, DRTL; General Orders No 33, Feb. 25, 1847, Justin H. Smith Collection. So meticulous were Scott's orders that he instructed the work parties to take their muskets with them "loaded and with bayonets fixed." He ordered that they leave cartridge boxes and other equipment in camp but carry two or three extra rounds in their pockets. They were not to stack their muskets, but each man was to place the weapon "three paces behind his work."

8. Unknown, "Campaigns in Mexico," 39, BLY; Sedgwick to father, Apr. 2, 1847, in John Sedgwick, *Correspondence of John Sedgwick, Major-General,* comp. Henry D. Sedgwick, 2 vols. (DeVinne Press, 1902), 1:75; Robert Anderson to wife, Mar. 12, 1847, Robert Anderson Papers, LC; Hill, *Fighter from Way Back,* 82; Smith to wife, Mar. 17, 1847, E. Kirby Smith, *To Mexico with Scott: Letters of Captain E. Kirby Smith to His Wife,* ed. Emma Jerome Blackwood (Cambridge, Mass.: Harvard University Press, 1917), 120.

9. Scott to Conner, Mar. 18, 1847, David Conner Papers, LC; Scott to Marcy, Mar. 25, 1847, LR SW, RG 107, NA; William Austine to cousin, Apr. 1, 1847, William Austine Papers, SHC, UNC; Bradford to Carry, Mar. 27, 1847, Bradford Papers; Robert Anderson, *An Artillery Officer in the Mexican War, 1846–7* (New York: G. P. Putnam's Sons, 1911), 87.

10. Pedro Santoni, *Mexicans at Arms: Puro Federalists and the Politics of War, 1845–1848* (Fort Worth: Texas Christian University Press, 1996), 163, 173–74, 180–87, 190–91; Edward H. Moseley, "The Religious Impact of the American Occupation of Mexico City, 1847–1848," in *Militarists, Merchants, and Missionaries: United States Expansion in Middle America,* ed. Eugene R. Huck and Edward H. Moseley

(Tuscaloosa: University of Alabama Press, 1970), 45; William A. DePalo Jr., *The Mexican National Army, 1822–1852* (College Station: Texas A&M University Press, 1997), 115.

11. Scott to Marcy, Mar. 21, 1847, LR SW, RG 107, NA; Hill, *Fighter from Way Back*, 63; Richard Bruce Winders, *Mr. Polk's Army: The American Military Experience in the Mexican War* (College Station: Texas A&M University Press, 1997), 10; Anderson to wife, Feb. 14, 1847, in *Artillery Officer*, 43.

12. K. Jack Bauer, *The Mexican War, 1846–1848* (1974; Lincoln: University of Nebraska Press, 1992), 247; Hill, *Fighter from Way Back*, 83, 86; S. R. Anderson to A. R. Wynne and George Crockett, Mar. 18, 1847, Wynne Family Papers, TSLA.

13. William Higgins to uncle, Jan. 4, 1848, William Higgins Papers, BLY; Allan Peskin, ed., *Volunteers: The Mexican War Journals of Private Richard Coulter and Sergeant Thomas Barclay, Company E, Second Pennsylvania Infantry* (Kent, Ohio: Kent State University Press, 1991), 49; Hill, *Fighter from Way Back*, 75; John Hammond Moore, ed., "Private Johnson Fights the Mexicans, 1847–1848," *South Carolina Historical Magazine* 67 (Oct. 1966): 207; Thomas Claiborne, "Reminiscences of the Mexican War," 15, Thomas Claiborne Papers, SHC, UNC.

14. Hill, *Fighter from Way Back*, 80–81, 83.

15. Anderson, *Artillery Officer*, 87–88; Scott to Marcy, Mar. 21, 1847, LR SW, RG 107, NA; K. Jack Bauer, *Surfboats and Horse Marines: U.S. Naval Operations in the Mexican War, 1846–48* (Annapolis: United States Naval Institute, 1969), 86–88.

16. Alfred Hoyt Bill, *Rehearsal for Conflict: The War with Mexico, 1846–1848* (New York: Alfred A. Knopf, 1947), 214; Raphael Semmes, *Service Afloat and Ashore during the Mexican War* (Cincinnati: Wm. H. Moore, 1851), 133, 135; William G. Temple, "Memoir," in Philip Syng Physick Conner, *The Home Squadron under Commodore Connor in the War with Mexico* (Philadelphia: Philip Syng Physick Conner, 1896), 69; Chauncey Forward Sargent, *Gathering Laurels in Mexico: The Diary of an American Soldier in the Mexican American War*, ed. Ann Brown Janes (Lincoln, Mass.: Cottage Press, 1990), 7; Moore, "Private Johnson," 208.

17. Thomas D. Tennery, *The Mexican War Diary of Thomas D. Tennery*, ed. D. E. Livingston-Little (Norman: University of Oklahoma Press, 1970), 73; Bauer, *Surfboats*, 90–91; Anderson, *Artillery Officer*, 88.

18. Roswell Ripley to mother, Mar. 16, 1847, Roswell Ripley Papers, BLY; Hiram Yeager to John Yeager, Mar. 20, 1847, Yeager Papers; Scott to Morales and Morales to Scott, Mar. 22, 1847, LR SW, RG 107, NA.

19. Timothy D. Johnson, *Winfield Scott: The Quest for Military Glory* (Lawrence: University Press of Kansas, 1998), 12–13; Francis B. Heitman, *Historical Register and Dictionary of the United States Army*, 2 vols. (1903; Baltimore: Genealogical Publishing, 1994), 1:189.

20. Bankhead to Scott, Mar. 24, 1847, LR, AGO, RG 94, NA; Bauer, *Surfboats*, 89; Navy Department, *Dictionary of American Naval Fighting Ships*, 8 vols. (Washington: Naval History Center, 1991), 5:585; Smith to wife, Mar. 24, 1847, Smith, *To Mexico with Scott*, 123.

21. Stevens Thomson Mason to ?, Mar. 23, 1847, Daniel Family Papers, VHS; McClellan, *Mexican War Diary*, 67–69; Smith to wife, Mar. 24, 1847, Smith, *To Mexico with Scott*, 123; Yeager to Yeager, Mar. 27, 1847, Yeager Papers.

22. Moore, "Private Johnson," 209; Hill, *Fighter from Way Back*, 86; Bill, *Rehearsal*, 223.

23. Hill, *Fighter from Way Back*, 86; Sargent, *Gathering Laurels*, 7; Winfield Scott, *Memoirs of Lieut.-General Scott*, 2 vols. (1864; Freeport, N.Y.: Books for Libraries Press, 1970), 2:426.

24. Yeager to Yeager, Mar. 27, 1847, Yeager Papers. Captain Robert Anderson described the most likely scenario resulting in Vinton's death in *Artillery Officer*, 91. See also Bankhead to Scott, Mar. 24, 1847, LR, AGO, RG 94, NA; Charles Judah and George Winston Smith, *Chronicles of the Gringoes: The U.S. Army in the Mexican War, 1846–1848, Accounts of Eyewitnesses and Combatants* (Albuquerque: University of New Mexico Press, 1968), 175–76, n. 25, 484; Scott, *Memoirs*, 2:429; Bradford to Carry, Mar. 27, 1847, Bradford Papers; Smith to wife, Mar. 24, 1847, Smith, *To Mexico with Scott*, 124; Napoleon Jackson Tecumseh Dana, *Monterrey Is Ours! The Mexican War Letters of Lieutenant Dana, 1845–1847*, ed. Robert H. Ferrell (Lexington: University Press of Kentucky, 1990), 193; Arthur Howard Noll, *General Kirby-Smith* (Sewanee, Tenn.: University Press at the University of the South, 1907), 51–52.

25. Smith to wife, Mar. 24, 1847, Smith, *To Mexico with Scott*, 124–25; Bankhead to Scott, Mar. 24, 1847, and Scott to Marcy, Mar. 24, 1847, LR SW, RG 107, NA; Nathaniel Cheairs Hughes Jr. and Roy P. Stonesifer, *The Life and Wars of Gideon J. Pillow* (Chapel Hill: University of North Carolina Press, 1993), 54.

26. It was probably Lieutenant Benjamin Roberts of the Mounted Rifles, who would later be a veteran of Civil War battles at Cedar Mountain and Bull Run.

27. Unknown, "Campaigns in Mexico," BLY.

28. Semmes, *Service*, 135; Bauer, *Surfboats*, 93; Smith, *Company "A,"* 23; Yeager to Yeager, Mar. 24, 1847, Yeager Papers; Bauer, *Mexican War*, 250; Bankhead to Scott, Mar. 24, 1847, LR SW, RG 107, NA; Beauregard, *With Beauregard in Mexico*, 29–30.

29. Smith, *Company "A,"* 23–24.

30. Hachaliah Brown to Lemuel Brown, Apr. 6, 1847, Lemuel C. Brown Papers, BLY; Bauer, *Mexican War*, 250; Paul D. Olejar, "Rockets in Early American Wars," *Military Affairs* 10 (winter 1946): 17–18, 21–24, 27.

31. William Walker to wife, Mar. 25, 1847, William Henry Talbot Walker Papers, Duke University; Theodore Laidley, *Surrounded by Dangers of All Kinds: The Mexican War Letters of Lieutenant Theodore Laidley*, ed. James M. McCaffrey (Denton: University of North Texas Press, 1997), 50; Bradford to Carry, Apr. 2, 1847, Bradford Papers; E. Kirby Smith to General Joseph W. Brown, May 27, 1847, E. Kirby Smith Papers, BLY.

32. James I. Robertson Jr., *Stonewall Jackson: The Man, the Soldier, the Legend* (New York: Macmillan, 1997), 52–54.

33. Scott to Marcy, Mar. 25, 1847, LR SW, RG 107, NA; Hill, *Fighter from Way Back*, 87.

34. See Irvin W. Levinson, *Wars within War: Mexican Guerrillas, Domestic Elites, and the United States of America, 1846–1848* (Forth Worth: Texas Christian University Press, 2005), 29–30, for a critical assessment of Scott's refusal to stop the bombardment. For support, he cites Scott, *Memoirs*, 2:421, 427. Jose C. Valades called Scott "cruel" in his "punishment" of the citizens of Veracruz in *Breve Historia de la Guerra con los Estados Unidos* (Manuel Gutiérrez Nájera, 1947), 167. Levinson also referenced Scott's role as the commanding officer overseeing the removal of the Cherokee Indians as if to add weight to the assertion that Scott was callous toward civilians. It is a curious reference given Scott's dislike for that duty, which President Martin Van Buren ordered him to fulfill, and considering that he issued orders to the troops involved in the removal to show all "possible kindness" to the Cherokee. His order, dated May 17, 1838, and reprinted in his memoirs, went on to say that if "in the ranks, a despicable individual should be found capable of inflicting a wanton injury or insult on any Cherokee man, woman, or child, it is hereby made the special duty of the nearest good officer or man instantly to interpose, and to seize and consign the guilty wretch to the severest penalty of the laws." This unpleasant and deadly affair came to be known as the Trail of Tears, but the fault cannot be laid at Scott's feet. See his *Memoirs*, 1:320.

35. Meade to wife, Mar. 25, 1847, *Life and Letters*, 1:192–93; Ethan Allen Hitchcock, "Sketches of the Campaign," Ethan Allen Hitchcock Papers, USMA; William Campbell to David Campbell, Feb. 19, 1847, Campbell, *Mexican War Letters*, 153; Scott, *Memoirs*, 2:424.

36. Bankhead to Scott, Mar. 24, 1847, and Scott to Marcy, Mar. 25, 1847, and Perry to Scott, Mar. 25, 1847, LR SW, RG 107, NA; Scott to Stribling, Mar. 25, 1847, Dreer Collection, Historical Society of Pennsylvania, Philadelphia; Bauer, *Surfboats*, 95.

37. Hachaliah Brown to Lemuel Brown, Apr. 6, 1847, Brown Papers; J. Frost, *The Mexican War and Its Warriors* (New Haven, Conn.: H. Mansfield, 1850), 137–38; George C. Furber, *The Twelve Months Volunteers; or, Journal of a Private, in the Tennessee Regiment of Cavalry, in the Campaign Mexico, 1846–7* (Cincinnati: J. A. & U. P. James, 1848), 541–43; Christopher T. Losson, *Tennessee's Forgotten Warriors: Frank Cheatham and His Confederate Division* (Knoxville: University of Tennessee Press, 1989), 15–16; Bauer, *Mexican War*, 251; Hughes and Stonesifer, *Pillow*, 60.

38. Hitchcock to Lizzie, Mar. 27, 1847, Ethan Allen Hitchcock Papers, LC; Albert C. Ramsey, ed. and trans., *The Other Side; or, Notes for the History of the War between Mexico and the United States* (New York: John Wiley, 1850), 186; Bill, *Rehearsal*, 216; Judah and Smith, *Chronicles*, 193; Dana, *Monterrey Is Ours!*, 196–97; Hill, *Fighter from Way Back*, 93–94; Austine to cousin, Apr. 1, 1847, Austine Papers; Anderson, *Artillery Officer*, 104; Smith, *War with Mexico*, 2:32.

39. Lee to Custis Lee, Apr. 11, 1847, Lee Family Papers, VHS; Smith, *War with Mexico*, 2:32–33. In a twist of irony, fifteen years later, it would be Pillow as one of the ranking generals at the besieged Fort Donelson who handed command over to a subordinate in order to avoid the odious task of surrendering to Ulysses S. Grant.

40. Anderson, *Artillery Officer*, 98; Bauer, *Mexican War*, 251–52; DePalo, *Mexican National Army*, 119.

41. Judah and Smith, *Chronicles*, 194; Scott, *Memoirs*, 2:429; Bauer, *Surfboats*, 97; Smith, *War with Mexico*, 2:34, n. 28, 341; Bauer, *Mexican War*, 252; Ramsey, *Other Side*, 195; Lee quoted in Emory M. Thomas, *Robert E. Lee: A Biography* (New York: W. W. Norton, 1995), 123. Casualty figures from José María Roa Barcena, *Recuerdos de la Invasion Norteamericana: 1846–1848* (Mexico City: Editorial Porrúa, 1993), are given in Levinson, *Wars within War*, 29.

42. Thomas Williams to father, Mar. 25, 1847, Williams Letters, Justin H. Smith Collection, LAC, UT.

43. Furber, *Twelve Months*, 559; George Turnbull Moore Davis, *Autobiography of the Late Col. Geo T. M. Davis, Captain and Aid-de-Camp Scott's Army of Invasion* (New York: Jenkins and McCowan, 1891), 129.

44. Ripley to mother, Apr. 3, 1847, Ripley Papers; Israel Uncapher Mexican War Diary, UTA; Kendall to *Picayune*, Apr. 4, 1847, Kendall Family Papers, UTA.

45. Sargent, *Gathering Laurels*, 7; Kendall to *Picayune*, Apr. 4, 1847, Kendall Papers; Furber, *Twelve Months*, 558–59; Bill, *Rehearsal*, 217–18.

Chapter 3. The Army Advances

1. Israel Uncapher Mexican War Diary, UTA; *Niles' National Register*, LXXII, Mar. 27, 1847, 59–64; Bevin Alexander, *How Great Generals Win* (New York: W. W. Norton, 1993), 24; Robert W. Johannsen, *To the Halls of the Montezumas* (1985; New York: Oxford University Press, 1987), 102–3; Charles Judah and George Winston Smith, *Chronicles of the Gringoes: The U.S. Army in the Mexican War, 1846–1848, Accounts of Eyewitnesses and Combatants* (Albuquerque: University of New Mexico Press, 1968), 192–93.

2. Samuel Lauderdale to James Lauderdale, Apr. 2, 1847, Lauderdale Family Papers, TSLA; Smith to Joseph Brown, May 27, 1847, Edmund Kirby Smith Papers, BLY; Barna Upton to brother Elias, Apr. 4, 1847, Barna N. Upton Papers, BLY; John Hammond Moore, ed., "Private Johnson Fights the Mexicans, 1847–1848," *South Carolina Historical Magazine* 67 (Oct. 1966), 209; Hiram B. Yeager to John C. Yeager, Jun. 10, 1847, Hiram B. Yeager Papers, DRTL; Thomas Williams to father, Apr. 5, 1847, Williams Letters, Justin H. Smith Collection, LAC, UT; Jackson quoted in James I. Robertson Jr., *Stonewall Jackson: The Man, the Soldier, the Legend* (New York: Macmillan, 1997), 54–55, 58; William B. Campbell to David Campbell, Apr. 18, 1847, in William Bowen Campbell, *Mexican War Letters of Col. William Bowen Campbell of Tennessee, Written to Governor David Campbell of Virginia, 1846–1847*, ed. St. George L. Sioussat (reprinted from *Tennessee Historical Magazine*, Jun. 1915), 166.

3. Robert Anderson, *An Artillery Officer in the Mexican War, 1846–7* (New York: G. P. Putnam's Sons, 1911), 97, 100–101; Bankhead to Scott, in Unknown, "Campaigns in Mexico," BLY; Hitchcock to Lizzie, Mar. 27, 1847, Ethan Allen Hitchcock Papers, LC.

4. Pillow quoted in Nathaniel Cheairs Hughes Jr. and Roy P. Stonesifer, *The Life and Wars of Gideon J. Pillow* (Chapel Hill: University of North Carolina Press, 1993), 65; Campbell to Campbell, Mar. 29, 1847, in Campbell, *Mexican War Letters*, 161.

5. Robertson, *Stonewall Jackson*, 55; Daniel Harvey Hill, *A Fighter from Way Back: The Mexican War Diary of Lt. Daniel Harvey Hill, 4th Artillery, USA*, ed. Nathaniel Cheairs Hughes Jr. and Timothy D. Johnson (Kent, Ohio: Kent State University Press, 2002), 93; Robert A. Law, "A Letter from Vera Cruz in 1847," *Southwestern Historical Quarterly* 18 (Oct. 1914): 218; Bradford to Carry, Apr. 2, 1847, Edmund Bradford Papers, BLY; Upton to brother, Apr. 4, 1847, Upton Papers; see also Smith, Diary, Joseph Rowe Smith Papers, BLY.

6. Hill, *Fighter from Way Back*, 92–93; Lee to Custis Lee, Apr. 11, 1847, Lee Family Papers, VHS; Arthur Howard Noll, *General Kirby-Smith* (Sewanee, Tenn.: University Press at the University of the South, 1907), 54; Bradford to Carry, Apr. 2, 1847, Bradford Papers; George C. Furber, *The Twelve Months Volunteers; or, Journal of a Private, in the Tennessee Regiment of Cavalry, in the Campaign Mexico, 1846–7* (Cincinnati: J. A. & U. P. James, 1848), 561, 569–70.

7. Thomas D. Tennery, *The Mexican War Diary of Thomas D. Tennery*, ed. D. E. Livingston-Little (Norman: University of Oklahoma Press, 1970), 77; Ripley to mother, Apr. 3, 1847, Roswell Ripley Papers, BLY; Lieutenant Stevens to wife, Apr. 3, 1847, in Hazard Stevens, *The Life of Isaac Ingalls Stevens*, 2 vols. (New York: Houghton Mifflin, 1900), 1:115; Law, "Letter," 217; Anderson, *Artillery Officer*, 112; Kendall to *Picayune*, Apr. 4, 1847, Kendall Family Papers, UTA.

8. Thomas M. Davies Jr., "Assessments during the Mexican War: An Exercise in Futility," *New Mexico Historical Review* 41 (Jul. 1966): 197; K. Jack Bauer, *The Mexican War, 1846–1848* (1974; Lincoln: University of Nebraska Press, 1992), 253; John Edwards Weems, *To Conquer a Peace: The War between the United States and Mexico* (College Station: Texas A&M University Press, 1974), 357; Hill, *Fighter from Way Back*, 89, 91; Anderson, *Artillery Officer*, 81. General Order No. 20 appears in the appendix.

9. Hill, *Fighter from Way Back*, 94; Alfred Hoyt Bill, *Rehearsal for Conflict: The War with Mexico, 1846–1848* (New York: Alfred A. Knopf, 1947), 218–19; George Turnbull Moore Davis, *Autobiography of the Late Col. Geo T. M. Davis, Captain and Aid-de-Camp Scott's Army of Invasion* (New York: Jenkins and McCowan, 1891), 132–36.

10. Timothy D. Johnson, *Winfield Scott: The Quest for Military Glory* (Lawrence: University Press of Kansas, 1998), 179; Davis, *Autobiography*, 136–37.

11. Hill, *Fighter from Way Back*, 94; John Smith Reminiscences, Lothrop Family Papers, BLY.

12. Allan Peskin, ed., *Volunteers: The Mexican War Journals of Private Richard Coulter and Sergeant Thomas Barclay, Company E, Second Pennsylvania Infantry* (Kent, Ohio: Kent State University Press, 1991), 65.

13. Gen. Orders No. 87, Apr. 1, 1847, House Exec. Doc. No. 60, 30th Cong., 1st Exec.; Stevens to wife, Apr. 3, 1847, in Stevens, *Life*, 1:115; Anderson, *Artillery Officer*, 83.

14. Hill, *Fighter from Way Back*, 93–94; Judge Zo. S. Cook, "Mexican War Reminiscences," *Alabama Historical Quarterly* 19 (fall–winter, 1957): 442–43.

15. Henry O. Whiteside, "Winfield Scott and the Mexican Occupation: Policy and Practice," *Mid-America* 52 (1970): 108.

16. Robert E. Lee, *Memoirs of Robert E. Lee, His Military and Personal History,* ed. A. L. Long (Secaucus, N.J.: Blue and Grey Press, 1983), 66–71.

17. Bill, *Rehearsal*, 221; Scott to Marcy, Apr. 5, 1847, LR SW, RG 107, NA; Marcy to Scott, Apr. 30, 1847, United States War Department Letters, BLY.

18. Bauer, *Mexican War*, 260; Mark Crawford, ed., *Encyclopedia of the Mexican-American War* (Santa Barbara, Calif.: ABC-CLIO Publishers, 1999), 9.

19. Jack Allen Meyer, *South Carolina in the Mexican War: A History of the Palmetto Regiment of Volunteers, 1846–1917* (Columbia: South Carolina Department of Archives and History, 1996), 58–59; Robert E. May, *John A. Quitman: Old South Crusader* (1984; Baton Rouge: Louisiana State University Press, 1985), 175; Law, "Letter," 216; Crawford, *Encyclopedia*, 143.

20. Campbell to Campbell, Feb. 19, Mar. 6, and Mar. 20, 1847, in Campbell, *Mexican War Letters,* 153, 157, 159; George Rollie Adams, *General William S. Harney: Prince of Dragoons* (Lincoln: University of Nebraska Press, 2001), 97; Kendall to *Picayune*, Apr. 4, 1847, Kendall Papers; Frederick Cartwright, *Disease and History* (New York: Dorset Press, 1972), 144–50; Raphael Semmes, *Service Afloat and Ashore during the Mexican War* (Cincinnati: Wm. H. Moore, 1851), 113–16.

21. Lee to Mary, Apr. 12, 1847, George Bolling Lee Papers, VHS; Tom Reilly, "Jane McManus Storms: Letters from the Mexican War, 1846–1848," *Southwestern Historical Quarterly* 85 (Jul. 1981): 35; A. Brooke Caruso, *The Mexican Spy Company: United States Covert Operations in Mexico, 1845–1848* (Jefferson, N.C.: McFarland, 1991), 147; Scott to Marcy, Apr. 5, 1847, LR SW, RG 107, NA.

22. A printed copy of Scott's Proclamation is located in the Campbell Family Papers.

23. Smith, Diary, Smith Papers; Upton to brother Elias, Apr. 4, 1847, Upton Papers; William Higgins to uncle, Jan. 4, 1848, William Higgins Papers, BLY; Romeyn B. Ayres, Mexican War Diary, 13, SHC, UNC.

24. Will Lytle to uncle, Dec. 8, 1847, in William Haines Lytle, *For Honor, Glory and Union: The Mexican and Civil War Letters of Brig. Gen. William Haines Lytle,* ed. Ruth C. Carter (Lexington: University Press of Kentucky, 1999), 46; Chauncey Forward Sargent, *Gathering Laurels in Mexico: The Diary of an American Soldier in the Mexican American War,* ed. Ann Brown Janes (Lincoln, Mass.: Cottage Press, 1990), 8; H. Judge Moore, *Scott's Campaign from the Rendezvous on the Island of Lobos to the Taking of the City* (Charleston: J. B. Nixon, 1849), 72–73.

25. Ethan Allen Hitchcock, "Sketches of the Campaign," Ethan Allen Hitchcock Papers, USMA.

26. Davis, *Autobiography*, 123; John Gardner to Colonel Walbach, May 15, 1847, John Lane Gardner Letter, BLY.

27. Weems, *To Conquer a Peace,* 360; Bradford to Carry, Apr. 2, 1847, Bradford Papers.

28. The precise details of this arrangement could not be determined, nor could all of the facts surrounding this episode. Dorich may have actually been the administrator of Mango de Clavo. Robert E. May, *Manifest Destiny's Underworld: Filibustering in Antebellum America* (Chapel Hill: University of North Carolina Press, 2002), 45–46; Robert E. May, "Henry L. Kinney," in Barbara A. Tenenbaum, ed., *Encyclopedia of Latin-American History and Culture*, 5 vols. (New York: Charles Scribner's Sons, 1996), 3:350; George Wilkins Kendall, *Dispatches from the Mexican War*, ed. Lawrence Delbert Cress (Norman: University of Oklahoma Press, 1999), 195, 199; statement of Nicholas Dorich, n.d., House Exec. Doc. No. 60, 30th Cong., 1st Sess.; H. L. Kinney to Henry Wilson, Apr. 29, 1847, Henry Wilson Papers, BLY.

Chapter 4. Cerro Gordo: A Brilliant Affair

1. Richard Bruce Winders, *Crisis in the Southwest: The United States, Mexico, and the Struggle over Texas* (Wilmington, Del.: Scholarly Resources, 2002), xxviii; Robert L. Scheina, *Santa Anna: A Curse upon Mexico* (Washington, D.C.: Brassey's, 2002), 87–90; Daniel Harvey Hill, *A Fighter from Way Back: The Mexican War Diary of Lt. Daniel Harvey Hill, 4th Artillery, USA*, ed. Nathaniel Cheairs Hughes Jr. and Timothy D. Johnson (Kent, Ohio: Kent State University Press, 2002), 185, n. 41; K. Jack Bauer, *The Mexican War, 1846–1848* (1974; Lincoln: University of Nebraska Press, 1992), 260–61; Santa Anna, Apr. 4, 1847, copy in Genaro Garcia Papers, LAC, UT; Albert C. Ramsey, ed. and trans., *The Other Side; or, Notes for the History of the War between Mexico and the United States* (New York: John Wiley, 1850), 199; Barna Upton to brother Elias, Apr. 4, 1847, Barna N. Upton Papers, BLY.

2. Justin H. Smith, *The War with Mexico*, 2 vols. (New York: Macmillan, 1919), 2:46; quotes found in Chauncey Forward Sargent, *Gathering Laurels in Mexico: The Diary of an American Soldier in the Mexican American War*, ed. Ann Brown Janes (Lincoln, Mass.: Cottage Press, 1990), 8; Hill to parents, Oct. 23, 1847, A. P. Hill Papers, VHS; Fitzgerald to Blackburn, Jul. 10, 1847, Blackburn Family Papers, FHS. Neither Hill nor Fitzgerald were with the army in April; both arrived with reinforcements in summer and fall.

3. Smith, *War with Mexico*, 2:40–41.

4. Twiggs's battle report, Apr. 19, 1847, Sen. Exec. Doc. No. 1, 30th Cong., 1st Sess.; quote from Jamie S. Linder and William B. Eigelsbach, eds., "To War with Mexico: A Diary of the Mexican-American War," *Journal of East Tennessee History* 73 (2001): 82.

5. John Edwards Weems, *To Conquer a Peace: The War between the United States and Mexico* (College Station: Texas A&M University Press, 1974), 356; Smith, Diary, Joseph Rowe Smith Papers, BLY.

6. Twiggs's battle report, Apr. 19, 1847, Sen. Exec. Doc. No. 1, 30th Cong., 1st Sess.; Bauer, *Mexican War*, 263; Alfred Hoyt Bill, *Rehearsal for Conflict: The War with Mexico, 1846–1848* (New York: Alfred A. Knopf, 1947), 226; Smith, *War with Mexico*, 2:48; Campbell to Campbell, Apr. 13, 1847, William Bowen Campbell, *Mexican War Letters of Col. William Bowen Campbell of Tennessee, Written to Governor*

David Campbell of Virginia, 1846–1847, ed. St. George L. Sioussat (reprinted from *Tennessee Historical Magazine,* Jun. 1915), 162.

7. Ramsey, *Other Side,* 203; Craig L. Symonds, *Joseph E. Johnston: A Civil War Biography* (New York: W. W. Norton, 1992), 59; Thomas Claiborne, "Reminiscences of the Mexican War," 18, Thomas Claiborne Papers, SHC, UNC; R.E. Lee to Mary Custis Lee, Apr. 18, 1847, George Bolling Lee papers, VHS.

8. Israel Uncapher Mexican War Diary, UTA; Twiggs's battle report, Apr. 19, 1847, Sen. Exec. Doc. No. 1, 30th Cong., 1st Sess.

9. P. G. T. Beauregard, *With Beauregard in Mexico: The Mexican War Reminiscences of P. G. T. Beauregard,* ed. T. Harry Williams (New York: DaCapo Press, 1969), 33–34.

10. Lee to Mary Custis Lee, Apr. 12, 1847, George Bolling Lee Papers; Winfield Scott, *Memoirs of Lieut.-General Scott,* 2 vols. (1864; Freeport, N.Y.: Books for Libraries Press, 1970), 2:432; John Gardner to Colonel Walbach, May 15, 1847, John Lane Gardner Papers, BLY; Scott quoted in Smith, *War with Mexico,* 2:48.

11. Antonio López Santa Anna, *The Eagle: The Autobiography of Santa Anna,* ed. Ann Fears Crawford (Austin, Tex.: Pemberton Press, 1967), 96; Ramsey, *Other Side,* 200; Santa Anna, Apr. 7, 1847, copy from the Cuban National Archives, in Genaro Garcia Papers, LAC, UT.

12. Smith, *War with Mexico,* 2:43–44; Weems, *To Conquer a Peace,* 354–55; Ramsey, *Other Side,* 200; Allan Peskin, ed., *Volunteers: The Mexican War Journals of Private Richard Coulter and Sergeant Thomas Barclay, Company E, Second Pennsylvania Infantry* (Kent, Ohio: Kent State University Press, 1991), 83.

13. Christopher Phillips, *Damned Yankee: The Life of General Nathaniel Lyon* (Columbia: University of Missouri Press, 1990), 51; Paul D. Casdorph, *Prince John Magruder: His Life and Campaigns* (New York: John Wiley, 1996), 69. Some sources do not mention this tower, and there seems to be some disagreement as to whether it actually existed. It did, and its crumbling remains were still there when I visited the site in 1999. It was with reference to this tower that Lieutenant Edmund Kirby Smith, in his correspondence, referred to El Telégrafo as "castle hill." See Smith to Brown, May 27, 1847, Edmund Kirby Smith Papers, BLY.

14. Ramsey, *Other Side,* 201; Smith, *War with Mexico,* 2:44.

15. Beauregard, *With Beauregard in Mexico,* 35–36; T. Harry Williams, *P. G. T. Beauregard* (Baton Rouge: Louisiana State University Press, 1954), 26.

16. John S. D. Eisenhower, *So Far from God: The U.S. War with Mexico, 1846–1848* (1989; New York: Bantam Doubleday Dell, 1990), 277; Nathaniel Cheairs Hughes Jr. and Roy P. Stonesifer, *The Life and Wars of Gideon J. Pillow* (Chapel Hill: University of North Carolina Press, 1993), 67; Thomas Lindsay Diary, UTA.

17. Peskin, *Volunteers,* 74; Sargent, *Gathering Laurels,* 8–9.

18. Jonathan Wade H. Tipton Journal, TSLA; Linder and Eigelsbach, "To War with Mexico," 84–91.

19. Sargent, *Gathering Laurels,* 9; Thomas D. Tennery, *The Mexican War Diary of Thomas D. Tennery,* ed. D. E. Livingston-Little (Norman: University of Oklahoma Press, 1970), 80.

20. Ramsey, *Other Side*, 203–4.

21. George R. Stewart, *John Phoenix, Esq., the Veritable Squibob: A Life of Captain George H. Derby, USA* (New York: Henry Holt, 1937), 49; Hazard Stevens, *The Life of Isaac Ingalls Stevens*, 2 vols. (New York: Houghton Mifflin, 1900), 1:123–24.

22. Beauregard, *With Beauregard in Mexico*, 38; Reminiscence, Palmer Family Papers, VHS; Douglas Southall Freeman, *R. E. Lee: A Biography*, 4 vols. (1934; New York: Charles Scribner's Sons, 1962), 1:239–40.

23. Lee quoted in Smith, *War with Mexico*, 2:49; Stewart, *John Phoenix, Esq.*, 49; J. Frost, *The Mexican War and Its Warriors* (New Haven, Conn.: H. Mansfield, 1850), 145.

24. Bevin Alexander, *How Great Generals Win* (New York: W. W. Norton, 1993), 107; Edmund Kirby Smith to Brown, May 27, 1847, Smith Papers, BLY.

25. Twiggs's battle report, Apr. 19, 1847, Sen. Exec. Doc. No. 1, 30th Cong., 1st Sess.; Ethan Allen Hitchcock, "Sketches of the Campaign," Ethan Allen Hitchcock Papers, USMA; Smith, *War with Mexico*, 2:50.

26. Freeman, *Lee*, 1:242; Smith, *War with Mexico*, 2:50; Francis B. Heitman, *Historical Register and Dictionary of the United States Army*, 2 vols. (1903; Baltimore: Genealogical Publishing, 1994), 1:831.

27. Claiborne, "Reminiscences," 18, Claiborne Papers.

28. Bill, *Rehearsal*, 226; Smith, *War with Mexico*, 2:51.

29. Claiborne, "Reminiscences," 18, Claiborne Papers; Twiggs's battle report, Apr. 19, 1847, and Harney's battle report, Apr. 21, 1847, Sen. Exec. Doc. No. 1, 30th Cong., 1st Sess.; Lee to Mary Custis Lee, Apr. 18, 1847, George Bolling Lee Papers.

30. Stewart, *John Phoenix, Esq.*, 50–51; Claiborne, "Reminiscences," 19, Claiborne Papers.

31. Twiggs quoted in Smith, *War with Mexico*, 2:52; Claiborne, "Reminiscences," 20, Claiborne Papers.

32. Claiborne, "Reminiscences," 8–9, 20, Claiborne Papers; Ezra J. Warner, *Generals in Blue: Lives of the Union Commanders* (Baton Rouge: Louisiana State University Press, 1964), 490.

33. Stewart, *John Phoenix, Esq.*, 50–51; Dabney Herdon Maury, *Recollections of a Virginian in the Mexican, Indian, and Civil Wars* (New York: Charles Scribner's Sons, 1894), 36; Heitman, *Historical Register*, 1:350.

34. Kendall to *Picayune*, Apr. 25, 1847, Kendall Family Papers, UTA.

35. George Turnbull Moore Davis, *Autobiography of the Late Col. Geo T. M. Davis, Captain and Aid-de-Camp Scott's Army of Invasion* (New York: Jenkins and McCowan, 1891), 147–48. Most notably, he commanded one of three contingents of federal troops in the Shenandoah Valley Campaign in 1862 and was out-maneuvered and out-fought by Stonewall Jackson's smaller but faster command. See Warner, *Generals in Blue*, 444.

36. Smith, *War with Mexico*, 2:50, 52; General Orders No. 111, Apr. 17, 1847, printed in Scott, *Memoirs*, 2:433.

37. Gustavus Woodson Smith, *Company "A" Corps of Engineers, USA, 1846–1848, in the Mexican War,* ed. Leonne M. Hudson (Kent, Ohio: Kent State University Press, 2001), 30, 32–33.

38. Ramsey, *Other Side,* 207; Bauer, *Mexican War,* 265; Smith, *Company "A,"* 33.

39. Smith, Diary, Joseph Rowe Smith Papers.

Chapter 5. Cerro Gordo: Tomorrow Will Settle the Affair

1. William Campbell to wife, Apr. 17, 1847, Campbell Family Papers, Duke University; E. Kirby Smith, *To Mexico with Scott: Letters of Captain E. Kirby Smith to His Wife,* ed. Emma Jerome Blackwood (Cambridge, Mass.: Harvard University Press, 1917), 132.

2. Nathaniel Cheairs Hughes Jr. and Roy P. Stonesifer, *The Life and Wars of Gideon J. Pillow* (Chapel Hill: University of North Carolina Press, 1993), 68, 70; Jonathan Wade H. Tipton Journal, TSLA; Campbell to wife, Apr. 18, 1847, Campbell Papers.

3. Hughes and Stonesifer, *Pillow,* 70; George B. McClellan, *The Mexican War Diary of General George B. McClellan,* ed. William Stan Myers (New York: DaCapo Press, 1972) 81.

4. Gustavus Woodson Smith, *Company "A" Corps of Engineers, USA, 1846–1848, in the Mexican War,* ed. Leonne M. Hudson (Kent, Ohio: Kent State University Press, 2001), 33; Justin H. Smith, *The War with Mexico,* 2 vols. (New York: Macmillan, 1919), 2:53.

5. Smith, *War,* 2:53; Hiram B. Yeager to John C. Yeager (brother), Apr. 20, 1847, Hiram B. Yeager Papers, DRTL; K. Jack Bauer, *The Mexican War, 1846–1848* (1974; Lincoln: University of Nebraska Press, 1992), 265; Hiram Wingate to William English, Apr. 27, 1847, Hiram Wingate Papers, FHS; see also Barna Upton to brother Elias, May 16, 1847, Barna N. Upton Papers, BLY; Smith to Brown, May 27, 1847, Joseph Rowe Smith Papers, BLY.

6. Thomas Claiborne, "Reminiscences of the Mexican War," 20–21, Thomas Claiborne Papers, SHC, UNC; Smith, *Company "A,"* 33; George Rollie Adams, *General William S. Harney: Prince of Dragoons* (Lincoln: University of Nebraska Press, 2001), 100.

7. Smith, *Company "A,"* 33–34; Smith, *War,* 2; 54; Harney's battle report, Apr. 21, 1847, Senate Doc. No. 1, 30th Cong., 1st Exec.

8. Smith, *War,* 2:53; Riley's battle report, Apr. 20, 1847, Senate. Doc. No. 1, 30th Cong., 1st Exec.

9. Smith, *Company "A,"* 33; Richard Ewell to mother, Apr. 22, 1847, Richard S. Ewell Papers, VHS. Tom recounted his experience to brother Richard later in the day before he died of his wound. Robert G. Hartje, *Van Dorn: The Life and Times of a Confederate General* (Nashville: Vanderbilt University Press, 1967), 37.

10. Barna Upton to brother Elias, May 16, 1847, Upton Papers; John Sedgwick, *Correspondence of John Sedgwick, Major-General,* comp. Henry D. Sedgwick, 2 vols. (DeVinne Press, 1902), 1:90.

11. Albert C. Ramsey, ed. and trans., *The Other Side; or, Notes for the History of the War between Mexico and the United States* (New York: John Wiley, 1850), 209–10; Claiborne, "Reminiscences," 22, Claiborne Papers. In Vasquez's honor, a stone marker would be erected about halfway up the southwest slope of El Telégrafo. It is still there today.

12. Thomas Jackson Arnold, *Early Life and Letters of General Thomas J. "Stonewall" Jackson* (New York: Fleming H. Revell, 1916), 93; Paul D. Casdorph, *Prince John Magruder: His Life and Campaigns* (New York: John Wiley, 1996), 68; Upton to brother Elias, May 16, 1847, Upton Papers. Most accounts imply that the enemy guns that Magruder turned on the fleeing Mexican soldiers were on top of El Telégrafo, but it is possible that the Mexican battery in question was near the road on the west side of the hill. The Mexican account of the battle, in Ramsey, *Other Side*, 212, referred to this battery as the one turned on the fleeing Mexican soldiers.

13. Thomas D. Tennery, *The Mexican War Diary of Thomas D. Tennery*, ed. D. E. Livingston-Little (Norman: University of Oklahoma Press, 1970), 82; George Turnbull Moore Davis, *Autobiography of the Late Col. Geo T. M. Davis, Captain and Aid-de-Camp Scott's Army of Invasion* (New York: Jenkins and McCowan, 1891), 151; Douglas Southall Freeman, *R. E. Lee: A Biography*, 4 vols. (1934; New York: Charles Scribner's Sons, 1962), 1:245.

14. John S. D. Eisenhower, *So Far from God: The U.S. War with Mexico, 1846–1848* (1989; New York: Bantam Doubleday Dell, 1990), 283.

15. Hughes and Stonesifer, *Pillow*, 70–71; B. G. Ellis, *The Moving Appeal: Mr. McClanahan, Mrs. Dill, and the Civil War's Great Newspaper Run* (Macon, Ga.: Mercer University Press, 2003), 64; Theodore Laidley, *Surrounded by Dangers of All Kinds: The Mexican War Letters of Lieutenant Theodore Laidley*, ed. James M. McCaffrey (Denton: University of North Texas Press, 1997), 69; Ripley to mother, Apr. 23, 1847, and Ripley to sister, May 2, 1847, Roswell Ripley Papers, BLY. Lieutenant Theodore Laidley assisted in firing the howitzer, and he reported that they fired eight rounds in the brief clash.

16. Hughes and Stonesifer, *Pillow*, 70–71; Bauer, *Mexican War*, 267.

17. Hughes and Stonesifer, *Pillow*, 71.

18. Gideon Pillow Supplemental Report, Apr. 29, 1847, Campbell Papers; Allan Peskin, ed., *Volunteers: The Mexican War Journals of Private Richard Coulter and Sergeant Thomas Barclay, Company E, Second Pennsylvania Infantry* (Kent, Ohio: Kent State University Press, 1991), 78; Hughes and Stonesifer, *Pillow*, 71; Tipton Journal, TSLA.

19. Israel Uncapher Mexican War Diary, UTA; George W. Hartman, *A Private's Own Journal: Giving an Account of the Battles in Mexico, under Gen'l Scott* (Greencastle: E. Robinson, 1849), 11; Ellis, *Moving Appeal*, 64; Hughes and Stonesifer, *Pillow*, 72. Pillow's version of the events indicated that two of his regiments were in position when the shooting started. "I had myself placed Col. Haskell's regiment in position for the assault [and] . . . had placed Col. Robert's regiment (the supporting force of Haskell's regiment) in position a short distance in the rear." See his Supplemental Report, Campbell Papers.

20. Hughes and Stonesifer, *Pillow*, 72; McClellan, *Mexican War Diary*, 85–86.

21. Peskin, *Volunteers*, 78; N. D. Smith to James Lauderdale, Apr. 23, 1847, Lauderdale Family Papers, TSLA.

22. Peskin, *Volunteers*, 78; Hughes and Stonesifer, *Pillow*, 72.

23. McClellan, *Mexican War Diary*, 86; Sedgwick to sister, Apr. 30, 1847, Sedgwick, *Correspondence*, 1:86.

24. McClellan, *Mexican War Diary*, 86–87; Smith, *War*, 2:57.

25. Smith, *War*, 2:57; Campbell to wife, Apr. 18, 1847, Campbell Papers; Campbell to Campbell, Apr. 25, 1847, in William Bowen Campbell, *Mexican War Letters of Col. William Bowen Campbell of Tennessee, Written to Governor David Campbell of Virginia, 1846–1847*, ed. St. George L. Sioussat (reprinted from *Tennessee Historical Magazine*, Jun. 1915), 166; Ripley to sister, May 2, 1847, Ripley Papers.

26. William A. DePalo Jr., *The Mexican National Army, 1822–1852* (College Station: Texas A&M University Press, 1997), 124; Jamie S. Linder and William B. Eigelsbach, eds., "To War with Mexico: A Diary of the Mexican-American War," *Journal of East Tennessee History* 73 (2001): 93, 99–100; Tipton Journal, TSLA; Yeager to John C. Yeager, Apr. 20, 1847, Yeager Papers.

27. Yeager to brother, Apr. 20, 1847, Yeager Papers. The Mexican works were commonly referred to as "breastworks," although they fell far short of the breast. They were generally constructed of "timber laid one above another and suported by stakes." Barna Upton to brother, May 16, 1847, Upton Papers.

28. Napoleon Jackson Tecumseh Dana, *Monterrey Is Ours! The Mexican War Letters of Lieutenant Dana, 1845–1847*, ed. Robert H. Ferrell (Lexington: University Press of Kentucky, 1990), 205–6; Claiborne, "Reminiscences," 10, 22, Claiborne Papers; Richard Ewell to mother, Apr. 22, 1847, Ewell Papers.

29. George R. Stewart, *John Phoenix, Esq., the Veritable Squibob: A Life of Captain George H. Derby, USA* (New York: Henry Holt, 1937), 3–4.

30. Ewell to mother, Apr. 22, 1847, Ewell Papers.

31. McClellan, *Mexican War Diary*, 87; J. Frost, *The Mexican War and Its Warriors* (New Haven, Conn.: H. Mansfield, 1850), 149; Lieutenant Stevens to wife, Apr. 18, 1847, in Hazard Stevens, *The Life of Isaac Ingalls Stevens*, 2 vols. (New York: Houghton Mifflin, 1900), 1:127. This source erroneously gives the date of this letter as Apr. 15.

32. I was unable to conclusively identify the doctor, but it may have been Robert McMillan from South Carolina, who is listed as a surgeon of volunteers in summer 1847 in Francis B. Heitman, *Historical Register and Dictionary of the United States Army*, 2 vols. (1903; Baltimore: Genealogical Publishing, 1994), 1:677.

33. Davis, *Autobiography*, 151–53, 155–56.

34. Lee to Mary Lee, Apr. 18, 1847, George Bolling Lee Papers, VHS; Claiborne, "Reminiscences," 22, Claiborne Papers; Christopher Phillips, *Damned Yankee: The Life of General Nathaniel Lyon* (Columbia: University of Missouri Press, 1990), 51; General Orders No. 111, Apr. 17, 1847, in Winfield Scott, *Memoirs of Lieut.-General Scott*, 2 vols. (1864; Freeport, N.Y.: Books for Libraries Press, 1970), 2:435.

35. Scott's battle report, Apr. 19, 1847, Senate Doc. No. 1, 30th Cong., 1st Sess.;

Smith, *War*, 2:58–59; Bauer, *Mexican War*, 268; Alfred Hoyt Bill, *Rehearsal for Conflict: The War with Mexico, 1846–1848* (New York: Alfred A. Knopf, 1947), 229. The captured Mexican generals were José María Jarero, Rómulo Díaz de La Vega, Luis Noriega, Luis Pinzón, and a general named Obando. See Scott's Apr. 19 battle report.

36. Baron Antoine Henry Jomini, *The Art of War*, trans. G. H. Mendell and W. P. Craighill (Philadelphia: J. B. Lippincott, 1862), 220–21; David G. Chandler, *The Military Maxims of Napoleon*, trans. Sir George C. D'Aguilar (1987; Stackpole Books, 1994), 57; Charles Judah and George Winston Smith, *Chronicles of the Gringoes: The U.S. Army in the Mexican War, 1846–1848, Accounts of Eyewitnesses and Combatants* (Albuquerque: University of New Mexico Press, 1968), 216; Benjamin Wingate to William English, Apr. 27, 1847, Wingate Papers.

37. Wingate to English, Apr. 27, 1847, Wingate Papers; Stewart, *John Phoenix, Esq.*, 48; R. E. Lee to Mary, Apr. ?, 1848, Lee Family Papers, VHS; DePalo, *Mexican National Army*, 124; Robert L. Scheina, *Santa Anna: A Curse upon Mexico* (Washington, D.C.: Brassey's, 2002), 64.

38. Lee to Mary, Apr. 18, 1847, George Bolling Lee Papers; Anderson to wife, Apr. 29, May 1, May 29, 1847, printed in Robert Anderson, *An Artillery Officer in the Mexican War, 1846–7* (New York: G. P. Putnam's Sons, 1911), 147, 151, 191.

39. Bevin Alexander, *How Great Generals Win* (New York: W. W. Norton, 1993), 34; Edmund Kirby Smith to Brown, May 27, 1847, Smith Papers, BLY; Yeager to Yeager, Jun. 10, 1847, Yeager Papers; Upton to brother Elias, May 16, 1847, Upton Papers.

40. Peskin, *Volunteers*, 83; Ramsey, *Other Side*, 212–20; Chauncey Forward Sargent, *Gathering Laurels in Mexico: The Diary of an American Soldier in the Mexican American War*, ed. Ann Brown Janes (Lincoln, Mass.: Cottage Press, 1990), 9; Lee to Mary, Apr. 18, 1847, George Bolling Lee Papers; Kendall to *Picayune*, Apr. 25, 1847, Kendall Family Papers, UTA.

41. Lee to sons, Feb. 27, 1847, Lee Family Papers, VHS; Lee to Mary, Apr. 18, 1847, George Bolling Lee Papers; Canice Ciruzzi, "Phoenix Revisited: Another Look at George Horatio Derby," *Journal of San Diego History* 26 (spring 1980): 77–89; Dabney Herdon Maury, *Recollections of a Virginian in the Mexican, Indian, and Civil Wars* (New York: Charles Scribner's Sons, 1894), 38–39; Johnston quoted on 39.

42. Maury, *Recollections*, 44; Ciruzzi, "Phoenix Revisited."

43. Peskin, *Volunteers*, 82–83; Tipton Journal, TSLA; Uncapher Diary, UTA.

44. Richard Ewell to mother, Apr. 22, 1847, Ewell Papers; Sargent, *Gathering Laurels*, 9.

45. Peskin, *Volunteers*, 82; McClellan, *Mexican War Diary*, 91–92; Hitchcock to Wilson, Apr. 19, 1847, Henry Wilson Papers, BLY; Hitchcock to Scott, Apr. 23, 1847, Ethan Allen Hitchcock Papers, LC.

46. Peskin, *Volunteers*, 82; Smith, *War*, 2:58; Scott to Marcy, Apr. 19, 1847, LR, RG 107, NA; Laidley, *Surrounded by Dangers*, 75.

47. Upton to brother Elias, May 16, 1847, Upton Papers.

Chapter 6. Jalapa: Garden of Mexico

1. W. L. Bliss to sister, Apr. 23, 1847, Mexican War Collection, UTA; Jacob Hoffer to parents, May 24, 1847, Jacob Hoffer Letter, BLY; Scott to Taylor, Apr. 24, 1847, Senate Doc. No. 60, 30th Cong., 1st Sess.; Lee to Mary, Apr. 18, 1847, George Bolling Lee Papers, VHS; George B. McClellan, *The Mexican War Diary of General George B. McClellan,* ed. William Stan Myers (New York: DaCapo Press, 1972), 90; Josiah Gorgas quoted in Frank E. Vandiver, *Ploughshares into Swords: Josiah Gorgas and Confederate Ordnance* (Austin: University of Texas Press, 1952), 379–80; Jack Allen Meyer, *South Carolina in the Mexican War: A History of the Palmetto Regiment of Volunteers, 1846–1917* (Columbia: South Carolina Department of Archives and History, 1996), 63; Thomas D. Tennery, *The Mexican War Diary of Thomas D. Tennery,* ed. D. E. Livingston-Little (Norman: University of Oklahoma Press, 1970), 83; George W. Hartman, *A Private's Own Journal: Giving an Account of the Battles in Mexico, under Gen'l Scott* (Greencastle: E. Robinson, 1849), 12.

2. Stevens to wife, May 1, 1847, in Hazard Stevens, *The Life of Isaac Ingalls Stevens,* 2 vols. (New York: Houghton Mifflin, 1900), 1:134; Wingate to English, Apr. 27, 1847, Hiram Wingate Papers, FHS; Hitchcock to Scott, Apr. 23, 1847, Ethan Allen Hitchcock Papers, LC; Kendall to *Picayune,* Apr. 25, 1847, George Kendall Papers, UTA; Allan Peskin, ed., *Volunteers: The Mexican War Journals of Private Richard Coulter and Sergeant Thomas Barclay, Company E, Second Pennsylvania Infantry* (Kent, Ohio: Kent State University Press, 1991), 80. Upon visiting the village of Cerro Gordo in 1999, I discovered that the story persists among the residents that Santa Anna accepted money from the Americans to lose the battle.

3. Pedro Santoni, *Mexicans at Arms: Puro Federalists and the Politics of War, 1845–1848* (Fort Worth: Texas Christian University Press, 1996), 202, 208; Dean B. Mahin, *Olive Branch and Sword: The United States and Mexico, 1845–1848* (Jefferson, N.C.: McFarland, 1997), 95.

4. E. Kirby Smith to wife, May 27, 1847, Edmund Kirby Smith Papers, UTA; Kendall to *Picayune,* May 3, 1847, Kendall Papers; Edward S. Wallace, *General William Jenkins Worth: Monterey's Forgotten Hero* (Dallas: Southern Methodist University Press, 1953), 140; Raphael Semmes, *Service Afloat and Ashore during the Mexican War* (Cincinnati: Wm. H. Moore, 1851), 207–8. Semmes's criticism was a result of a disagreement with Scott during the campaign that would affect his attitude for the rest of his life. This disagreement will be mentioned later in this chapter.

5. Ripley to mother, Mar. 16, 1847, Roswell Ripley Papers, BLY.

6. Anaya was acting as a substitute president until a general election took place on May 15. See Wilfrid Hardy Callcott, *Church and State in Mexico, 1822–1857* (Durham, N.C.: Duke University Press, 1926), 193.

7. Irvin W. Levinson, *Wars within War: Mexican Guerrillas, Domestic Elites, and the United States of America, 1846–1848* (Forth Worth: Texas Christian University Press, 2005), 34–41.

8. Charles Judah and George Winston Smith, *Chronicles of the Gringoes: The U.S. Army in the Mexican War, 1846–1848, Accounts of Eyewitnesses and Combatants*

(Albuquerque: University of New Mexico Press, 1968), 217–18, 297–98; Wingate to English, Apr. 27, 1847, Wingate Papers; Hiram B. Yeager to brother John, Apr. 20, 1847, Hiram B. Yeager Papers, DRTL; W. L. Bliss to sister, Apr. 23, 1847, Mexican War Collection, UTA; Soldiers' accounts are replete with such descriptions of the town. Robert Anderson, *An Artillery Officer in the Mexican War, 1846–7* (New York: G. P. Putnam's Sons, 1911), 143; H. Judge Moore, *Scott's Campaign from the Rendezvous on the Island of Lobos to the Taking of the City* (Charleston: J. B. Nixon, 1849), 69–71; McClellan, *Mexican War Diary*, 91–92; Kendall to *Picayune*, Apr. 25, 1847, Kendall Papers; Lee to Mary, Apr. 22, 1847; George Bolling Lee Papers; Robert A. Law, "A Letter from Vera Cruz in 1847," *Southwestern Historical Quarterly* 18 (Oct. 1914): 216; Theodore Laidley, *Surrounded by Dangers of All Kinds: The Mexican War Letters of Lieutenant Theodore Laidley*, ed. James M. McCaffrey (Denton: University of North Texas Press, 1997), 75.

9. Christopher Phillips, *Damned Yankee: The Life of General Nathaniel Lyon* (Columbia: University of Missouri Press, 1990), 52; Israel Uncapher Mexican War Diary, UTA; Kirkham to wife, May 8, 1847, in Ralph W. Kirkham, *The Mexican War Journal and Letters of Ralph W. Kirkham*, ed. Robert Ryal Miller (College Station: Texas A&M University Press, 1991), 15; McClellan, *Mexican War Diary*, 91; ? to William Grimes, Dec. 14, 1847, William Henry Grimes Papers, Duke University; Carl M. Becker, "John William Lowe: Failure in Inner-Direction," *Ohio History* 73 (spring 1964): 80; Amasa Gleason Clark, *Reminiscences of a Centenarian* (Bandera, Tex.: Printed by Amasa Clark, 1930), 21; Robert W. Johannsen, *To the Halls of the Montezumas* (1985; New York: Oxford University Press, 1987), 169.

10. Stevens, *Life*, 1:130; Moore, *Scott's Campaign*, 69; Scott to Wilson, Apr. 23, 1847, Henry Wilson Papers, BLY.

11. John R. B. Gardinier to Wilson, May 3, 1847, Joseph Daniels to Wilson, Apr. 29, 1847, and J. B. Porter to Wilson, Jun. 5, 1847, Wilson Papers.

12. Tennery, *Mexican War Diary*, 84, 87; Smith, Diary, 8, Joseph Rowe Smith Papers, BLY; Dabney Herdon Maury, *Recollections of a Virginian in the Mexican, Indian, and Civil Wars* (New York: Charles Scribner's Sons, 1894), 40; Scott quoted in Gary Gallagher, "We Are Our Own Trumpeters: Robert E. Lee Describes Winfield Scott's Campaign to Mexico City," *Virginia Magazine of History and Biography* 95 (July 1987): 368, n. 13. Johnston had previously been wounded in Florida during the Seminole War and would later receive another serious wound in the Battle of Fair Oaks in 1862. Perhaps his personal history helps to explain his Civil War generalship.

13. Judah and Smith, *Chronicles*, 345; Meyer, *South Carolina*, 60–61; Peskin, *Volunteers*, 85, 96.

14. Thomas R. Irey, "Soldiering, Suffering, and Dying in the Mexican War," *Journal of the West* 11 (April 1972): 285–86, 290, 298. The case of Amasa Clark from New York provides a contrary example. He volunteered for service in the Mexican War at age twenty-one, became ill at Jalapa, and was confined to a hospital for several weeks. He recovered and lived to be 101 years old. See Clark, *Reminiscences*, 8–9, 20.

15. Jacob Hoffer to parents, May 24, 1847, Jacob Hoffer Letter, BLY; Uncapher Diary, UTA; Peskin, *Volunteers*, 95; Kendall to *Picayune*, Apr. 25, 1847, Kendall Papers.

16. Judah and Smith, *Chronicles*, 221; Anderson, *Artillery Officer*, 145; Uncapher Diary, UTA.

17. William Harrison to brother, Sep. 16, 1847, Allmand Family Letters, BLY; Lieutenant Isaac Stevens of the engineers agreed. See his May 1, 1847, letter to his wife in Stevens, *Life*, 1:134; Daniel Harvey Hill, *A Fighter from Way Back: The Mexican War Diary of Lt. Daniel Harvey Hill, 4th Artillery, USA*, ed. Nathaniel Cheairs Hughes Jr. and Timothy D. Johnson (Kent, Ohio: Kent State University Press, 2002), 30; Lieutenant Theodore Laidley thought it just the opposite: "The higher classes receive us as kindly as they dare, the lower classes, those whom we are doing great service are our bitterest foes." See a May 19, 1847, letter to his father in Laidley, *Surrounded by Dangers*, 88.

18. Peskin, *Volunteers*, 97; Tennery, *Mexican War Diary*, 88; Uncapher Diary, UTA; General Orders No. 127, Apr. 29, 1847, Justin H. Smith Collection, LAC, UT.

19. Joseph Smith to Juliet, Jun. 13, 1847, Joseph Rowe Smith Papers; John Dodd to wife Eliza, Oct. 24, 1847, John Dodd Papers, BLY; Robert Anderson to sister, Feb. 13, 1848, Mexican War Collection, UTA; Lee to John Mackay, Oct. 2, 1847, Robert E. Lee letter, Folios 137–38, VHS; Kirkham, *Mexican War Journal*, 10; Peskin, *Volunteers*, 93; Johannsen, *To the Halls*, 167–68.

20. William Fraser Diary, BLY; Henry S. Lane, "The Mexican War Journal of Henry S. Lane," ed. Graham A. Barringer, *Indiana Magazine of History* 53 (Dec. 1957): 426–27, 430, 432; Marcy to Wetmore, Apr. 22, 1847, Marcy Papers, LC.

21. P. G. T. Beauregard, *With Beauregard in Mexico: The Mexican War Reminiscences of P. G. T. Beauregard*, ed. T. Harry Williams (New York: DaCapo Press, 1969), 30–31; Worth quoted in Wallace, *General William Jenkins Worth*, 127; statement by Riley, no date and Scott to Riley, May 21, 1847, Riley Papers, USMA.

22. Ripley to Marcy, Jun. 25, 1848, and Pillow to Marcy, Jun. 25, 1848, LR SW, RG 107, NA; Otis A. Singletary, *The Mexican War* (Chicago: University of Chicago Press, 1960), 147; Anderson, *Artillery Officer*, 124.

23. Peskin, *Volunteers*, 86–96; Uncapher Diary, UT Arlington; Chauncey Forward Sargent, *Gathering Laurels in Mexico: The Diary of an American Soldier in the Mexican American War*, ed. Ann Brown Janes (Lincoln, Mass.: Cottage Press, 1990), 10; Tennery, *Mexican War Diary*, 82–92.

24. Marcy to Scott, Apr. 30 and May 20, 1847, House Exec. Doc. No. 60, 30th Cong., 1st Sess.; Ethan Allen Hitchcock, "Sketches of the Campaign," Ethan Allen Hitchcock Papers, USMA; Ulysses S. Grant, *Personal Memoirs of U. S. Grant*, 2 vols. (New York: Charles L. Webster, 1885), 1:135; Meyer, *South Carolina*, 65.

25. James K. Polk, *The Diary of James K. Polk*, ed. Milo Milton Quaife, 4 vols. (Chicago: A. C. McClurg, 1910), 2:466–67, 477–78; David M. Pletcher, *The Diplomacy of Annexation: Texas, Oregon, and the Mexican War* (Columbia: University of Missouri Press, 1973), 499–501; Mahin, *Olive Branch*, 91; Wallace Ohrt, *Defiant*

Peacemaker: Nicholas Trist in the Mexican War (College Station: Texas A&M University Press, 1997), 103.

26. Ohrt, *Defiant Peacemaker,* 104.

27. Marcy to Scott, Apr. 14, 1847, House Exec. Doc. No. 60, 30th Cong., 1st Exec.

28. Ohrt, *Defiant Peacemaker,* 110; Scott to Trist, May 7, 1847, House Exec. Doc. No. 60, 30th Cong., 1st Exec.

29. Scott to Marcy, Apr. 5, 1847, House Exec. Doc. No. 60, 30th Cong., 1st Exec.

30. Mahin, *Olive Branch,* 91–93; Trist to Scott, May 9, 1847, Senate Doc. 52, 30th Cong., 1st Exec.

31. Semmes to Scott, May 8, 1847, House Exec. Doc. 60, 30th Cong., 1st Exec.

32. Scott to Marcy, Apr. 28, 1847, and Scott to Worth, Apr. 28, 1847, House Exec. Doc. No. 60, 30th Cong., 1st Exec.

33. Proclamation to the Mexican Nation, May 11, 1847, House Exec. Doc. No. 60, 30th Cong., 1st Sess. Raphael Semmes, no friend of Scott's, asserted that the proclamation had just the opposite of its desired effect. Many Mexicans were insulted by it and increased their resolve to resist the American invasion. See Semmes, *Service,* 211–13.

34. Stevens, *Life,* 1:135; Thompson Narrative, BLY. The First Dragoons went to guard the train that Nicholas Trist was with. Uncapher Diary, UTA.

35. Moore, *Scott's Campaign,* 72; Tennery, *Mexican War Diary,* 85–86; Kirkham, *Mexican War Journal,* 6; Uncapher Diary, UTA; Peskin, *Volunteers,* 105.

36. Kirkham, *Mexican War Journal,* 13; Ripley to mother, Apr. 23, 1847, and Ripley to sister, May 2, 1847, Roswell Ripley Papers, BLY; William Adee to Samuel Adee, Jun. 16, 1847, William F. Adee Papers, BLY; Moses Barnard Reminiscences, BLY; Stevens to wife, May 1, 1847, in Stevens, *Life,* 1:134.

Chapter 7. Puebla: Waiting All Summer

1. Scott to Worth, Apr. 23 and May 6, 1847, Scott to Marcy, Apr. 28, 1847, House Exec. Doc. No. 60, 30th Cong., 1st Exec.

2. Smith, Diary, 10, Joseph Rowe Smith Papers, BYL.

3. Jackson to sister, May 25, 1847, quoted in James I. Robertson Jr., *Stonewall Jackson: The Man, the Soldier, the Legend* (New York: Macmillan, 1997), 91.

4. Thomas R. Irey, "Soldiering, Suffering, and Dying in the Mexican War," *Journal of the West* 11 (Apr. 1972): 291; James Rowe Smith, Diary, James Rowe Smith Papers, BLY; Justin H. Smith, *The War with Mexico,* 2 vols. (New York: Macmillan, 1919), 2:60.

5. Allan Peskin, ed., *Volunteers: The Mexican War Journals of Private Richard Coulter and Sergeant Thomas Barclay, Company E, Second Pennsylvania Infantry* (Kent, Ohio: Kent State University Press, 1991), 115; Madison Mills Diary, FHS; Smith, Diary, Smith Papers; Chauncey Forward Sargent, *Gathering Laurels in Mexico: The Diary of an American Soldier in the Mexican American War,* ed. Ann Brown

Janes (Lincoln, Mass.: Cottage Press, 1990), 12; William P. Chambliss, "Record of Death & Discharges Company 'C' Tennessee Regiment," BLY.

6. J. Frost, *The Mexican War and Its Warriors* (New Haven, Conn.: H. Mansfield, 1850), 154; Lee to Mary, Apr. 22, 1847, George Bolling Lee Papers, VHS; Mark Crawford, ed., *Encyclopedia of the Mexican-American War* (Santa Barbara, Calif.: ABC-CLIO Publishers, 1999), 213; Wilkins to brother, Apr. 24, 1847, John Darragh Wilkins Memorandum and Papers, BLY. The Perote Prison was also known as the Castle of San Carlos. Among the prisoners held in the castle were some of the members of the ill-fated Mier Expedition in 1842. See Richard Bruce Winders, *Crisis in the Southwest: The United States, Mexico, and the Struggle over Texas* (Wilmington, Del.: Scholarly Resources, 2002), 50, 65–68.

7. Robert Anderson, *An Artillery Officer in the Mexican War, 1846–7* (New York: G. P. Putnam's Sons, 1911), 162.

8. John Wilkins, "Army Chronicle," Wilkins Papers; John Hammond Moore, ed., "Private Johnson Fights the Mexicans, 1847–1848," *South Carolina Historical Magazine* 67 (Oct. 1966), 214.

9. K. Jack Bauer, *The Mexican War, 1846–1848* (1974; Lincoln: University of Nebraska Press, 1992), 271.

10. Bauer, *Mexican War*, 271; Smith, *War*, 2:70; Smith to wife, May 13 and 14, 1847; in E. Kirby Smith, *To Mexico with Scott: Letters of Captain E. Kirby Smith to His Wife*, ed. Emma Jerome Blackwood (Cambridge, Mass.: Harvard University Press, 1917), 160–62; Roswell Ripley to mother, May 21 and Jun. 3, 1847, Roswell Ripley Papers, BLY.

11. Ralph W. Kirkham, *The Mexican War Journal and Letters of Ralph W. Kirkham*, ed. Robert Ryal Miller (College Station: Texas A&M University Press, 1991), 17; Robert W. Johannsen, *To the Halls of the Montezumas* (1985; New York: Oxford University Press, 1987), 31; Charles Judah and George Winston Smith, *Chronicles of the Gringoes: The U.S. Army in the Mexican War, 1846–1848, Accounts of Eyewitnesses and Combatants* (Albuquerque: University of New Mexico Press, 1968), 227–28. From Forts Guadalupe and Loreto, Mexican forces repulsed a French army on May 5, 1862, during Napoleon III's ill-fated attempt to take over Mexico. This Mexican victory is the subject of that country's Cinco de Mayo celebration.

12. Smith, *To Mexico with Scott*, 165, 168; Hiram B. Yeager to John C. Yeager, Jun. 10, 1847, Hiram B. Yeager Papers, DRTL. A Virginian in Taylor's army, T. H. Towner, expressed the same bewilderment regarding that army's ability to march through the country unopposed, and his answer exhibited a feeling of racial superiority similar to that felt by many in Scott's army. In a letter home, he wrote, "They are a miserable race, at least those we have met with, possessing all the degrading traits of the Mexican character." To allow so many foreign soldiers and wagons to travel through densely populated areas, thought Towner, "displays a degree of cowardice & a want of patriotism perfectly incomprehensible to the sons of the Old Dominion, and the fact has convinced me . . . that the Anglo-Saxon race possess more of the higher qualities which enable man than any other on the face of the earth." See T. H. Towner to father, Apr. 14, 1847, Benjamin T. Towner Papers, Duke.

13. Peskin, *Volunteers,* 124; Kirkham, *Mexican War Journal,* 33; Fitzgerald to Blackburn, Jul. 10, 1847, Blackburn Family Papers, FHS.

14. Albert Brackett to Charles Brackett, Dec. 12, 1847, Albert G. Brackett Papers, DRTL; Alfred Hoyt Bill, *Rehearsal for Conflict: The War with Mexico, 1846–1848* (New York: Alfred A. Knopf, 1947), 251; William Pierce Diary, UTA; Moore, "Private Johnson," 216.

15. Moore, "Private Johnson," 218; Kirkham, *Mexican War Journal,* 21; Smith, *To Mexico with Scott,* 178–79; Lee to Mary, Nov. 4, 1846, Lee Family Papers, VHS.

16. Theodore to father, Jun. 3, 1847, in Theodore Laidley, *Surrounded by Dangers of All Kinds: The Mexican War Letters of Lieutenant Theodore Laidley,* ed. James M. McCaffrey (Denton: University of North Texas Press, 1997), 92; H. Judge Moore, *Scott's Campaign from the Rendezvous on the Island of Lobos to the Taking of the City* (Charleston: J. B. Nixon, 1849), 116–17; Smith, *To Mexico with Scott,* 160–62, 165–67; Ulysses S. Grant, *Personal Memoirs of U. S. Grant,* 2 vols. (New York: Charles L. Webster, 1885), 1:123; Bill, *Rehearsal,* 245.

17. Kirkham, *Mexican War Journal,* 19; B. S. Roberts Diary, Justin H. Smith Collection, LAC, UT; Smith, *War,* 2:72; Bill, *Rehearsal,* 248; Anderson, *Artillery Officer,* 211–13.

18. Scott to Trist, May 29, 1847, House Exec. Doc. No. 60, 30th Cong., 1st Sess.

19. Dean B. Mahin, *Olive Branch and Sword: The United States and Mexico, 1845–1848* (Jefferson, N.C.: McFarland, 1997), 95; Bauer, *Mexican War,* 284.

20. Marcy to Scott, May 31, 1847, United States War Department Letters, BLY.

21. Scott to Quitman, May 31, 1847, Scott Letter, BLY; Robert E. May, *John A. Quitman: Old South Crusader* (1984; Baton Rouge: Louisiana State University Press, 1985), 181–82.

22. Anderson, *Artillery Officer,* 226; Ethan Allen Hitchcock, "Sketches of the Campaign," Ethan Allen Hitchcock Papers, USMA; Scott to Worth, Jun. 16, 1847, Ethan Allen Hitchcock Papers, LC.

23. Edward S. Wallace, *General William Jenkins Worth: Monterey's Forgotten Hero* (Dallas: Southern Methodist University Press, 1953), 138; Smith, *War,* 2:72; Scott to Worth, Jun. 19 and Jun. 20, 1847, Hitchcock Papers, LC; General Orders No. 186, Jun. 24, 1847, and No. 196, Jun. 30, 1847, in Hitchcock Papers, LC; Hitchcock, "Sketches of the Campaign," Hitchcock Papers, USMA.

24. Wallace, *General William Jenkins Worth,* 137–38; Raphael Semmes, *Service Afloat and Ashore during the Mexican War* (Cincinnati: Wm. H. Moore, 1851), 317–19; George R. Stewart, *John Phoenix, Esq., the Veritable Squibob: A Life of Captain George H. Derby, USA* (New York: Henry Holt, 1937), 47; Hitchcock, "Sketches," Hitchcock Papers.

25. Hitchcock, "Sketches," Hitchcock Papers; Anderson, *Artillery Officer,* 277.

26. Scott to Quitman, May 31, 1847, Scott Letter, Beinecke; Marcy to Scott, Apr. 30 and May 20, 1847, United States War Department Letters, Beinecke; Scott to Marcy, Jun. 4, 1847, House Exec. Doc. No. 60, 30th Cong., 1st Sess.

27. A. Brooke Caruso, *The Mexico Spy Company: United States Covert Operations in Mexico, 1845–1848* (Jefferson, N.C.: McFarland, 1991), 152–53; Robert Ryal Miller, *Shamrock and Sword: The Saint Patrick's Battalion in the U.S.-Mexican War* (Norman: University of Oklahoma Press, 1989), 76; Judah and Smith, *Chronicles of the Gringoes*, 229–32; Bauer, *Mexican War*, 274; Kirkham, *Mexican War Journal*, 39; Daniel Harvey Hill, *A Fighter from Way Back: The Mexican War Diary of Lt. Daniel Harvey Hill, 4th Artillery, USA*, ed. Nathaniel Cheairs Hughes Jr. and Timothy D. Johnson (Kent, Ohio: Kent State University Press, 2002), 106; Edmund Bradford to John Tazewell, Jan. 2, 1848, Edmund Bradford Papers, BLY.

28. Moore, "Private Johnson," 218; Bauer, *Mexican War*, 284; Kirkham, *Mexican War Journal*, 22; Mills Diary, FHS; Israel Uncapher Mexican War Diary, UTA; Moses Barnard Reminiscences, BLY.

29. William Austine to cousin, Jul. 4, 1847, William Austine Papers, SHC, UNC; Hill to friends, Nov. 8, 1847, A. P. Hill Papers, VHS; Albert Nicholson to Thomas Nicholson, Apr. 22, 1848, Albert C. Nicholson Papers, BLY; George C. Furber, *The Twelve Months Volunteers; or, Journal of a Private, in the Tennessee Regiment of Cavalry, in the Campaign Mexico, 1846–7* (Cincinnati: J. A. & U. P. James, 1848), 311, 402–3.

30. Smith, Diary, Joseph Rowe Smith Papers, BLY; Walker to Molly, Jul. 27, 1847, William Henry Talbot Walker Papers, Duke University.

31. Kirkham, *Mexican War Journal*, 18, 27, and 125, n. 2; Lytle to uncle, Dec. 8, 1847, in William Haines Lytle, *For Honor, Glory and Union: The Mexican and Civil War Letters of Brig. Gen. William Haines Lytle*, ed. Ruth C. Carter (Lexington: University Press of Kentucky, 1999), 47–48; Peskin, *Volunteers*, 181.

32. Frederick Zeh, *An Immigrant Soldier in the Mexican War*, trans. William Orr and Robert Ryal Miller (College Station: Texas A&M University Press, 1995), 52; Edward H. Moseley, "The Religious Impact of the American Occupation of Mexico City, 1847–1848," in *Militarists, Merchants, and Missionaries: United States Expansion in Middle America*, ed. Eugene R. Huck and Edward H. Moseley (Tuscaloosa: University of Alabama Press, 1970), 45; Smith, *To Mexico with Scott*, 171–72; Bill, *Rehearsal for Conflict*, 249.

33. Moore, "Private Johnson," 215; Anderson, *Artillery Officer*, 178; Moore, *Scott's Campaign*, 117; Peskin, *Volunteers*, 125–26; Richard Bruce Winders, *Mr. Polk's Army: The American Military Experience in the Mexican War* (College Station: Texas A&M University Press, 1997), 126.

34. Kirkham, *Mexican War Journal*, 31; Johannsen, *To the Halls*, 31, 34–36; Anderson, *Artillery Officer*, 147–48, 176, 185–86. William Austine to cousin, Nov. 1, 1847, Austine Papers. Mexican writer José Mariá Roa Bárcena described General Scott as "noble and kind" and his men as exhibiting "discipline, vigorous and severe among the corps of the line, which even extended to the volunteers, with the exception of some of the detached forces." See Bárcena, "Memories of the North American Invasion," in *The View from Chapultepec: Mexican Writers on the Mexican-American War*, ed. and trans. Cecil Robinson (Tucson: University of Arizona Press, 1989), 49.

35. Hiram B. Yeager to John C. Yeager, Jul. 16, 1847, Yeager Papers; Hill, *Fighter from Way Back*, 152; Kirkham, *Mexican War Journal*, 31; Irvin W. Levinson, *Wars within War: Mexican Guerrillas, Domestic Elites, and the United States of America, 1846–1848* (Forth Worth: Texas Christian University Press, 2005), chap. 3, esp. 51–53.

36. Winders, *Mr. Polk's Army*, 62–63; Peter F. Stevens, *The Rogue's March: John Riley and the St. Patrick's Battalion, 1846–48* (Washington, D.C.: Brassey's, 1999), 48–55, 171–73, 213; John Meginness Manuscript, John Franklin Meginness Papers, UTA.

37. Winders, *Mr. Polk's Army*, 62; Sargent, *Gathering Laurels*, 14; Peskin, *Volunteers*, 88; Otis A. Singletary, *The Mexican War* (Chicago: University of Chicago Press, 1960), 146.

38. Stevens, *Rogue's March*, 222, 226–29; William Austine to cousin, Jul. 4 and Nov. 1, 1847, Austine Papers. Among the inducements offered to Americans to switch sides was land—a certain number of acres for a year of service in the Mexican army and additional acreage for each additional year. For a private those amounts were 200 and 100, for a corporal 300 and 150, a lieutenant 1,200 and 600. See Wilfrid Hardy Callcott, *Church and State in Mexico, 1822–1857* (Durham, N.C.: Duke University Press, 1926), 198.

39. Moore, "Private Johnson," 219; H. Clay to Mr. Levesh, Nov. 26, 1847, Mexican War Collection, UTA.

Chapter 8. Puebla: Between the Devil and the Deep Blue Sea

1. Smith to wife, Jun. 4, 1847, in E. Kirby Smith, *To Mexico with Scott: Letters of Captain E. Kirby Smith to His Wife*, ed. Emma Jerome Blackwood (Cambridge, Mass.: Harvard University Press, 1917), 177.

2. Justin H. Smith, *The War with Mexico*, 2 vols. (New York: Macmillan, 1919), 2:72, 362, n. 61; H. Judge Moore, *Scott's Campaign from the Rendezvous on the Island of Lobos to the Taking of the City* (Charleston: J. B. Nixon, 1849), 118–19; John Hammond Moore, ed., "Private Johnson Fights the Mexicans, 1847–1848," *South Carolina Historical Magazine* 67 (Oct. 1966): 216, 218–19; George B. McClellan, *The Mexican War Diary of General George B. McClellan*, ed. William Stan Myers (New York: DaCapo Press, 1972), 18.

3. Hiram B. Yeager to John C. Yeager, Jul. 16, 1847, Hiram B. Yeager Papers, DRTL; William Austine to cousin, Jul. 4, 1847, William Austine Papers, SHC, UNC; Smith, *War*, 2:75–77, n. 422; K. Jack Bauer, *The Mexican War, 1846–1848* (1974; Lincoln: University of Nebraska Press, 1992), 273; Madison Mills Diary, FHS.

4. Bauer, *Mexican War*, 273; Mills Diary, FHS.

5. Mills Diary, FHS.

6. James K. Polk, *The Diary of James K. Polk*, ed. Milo Milton Quaife, 4 vols. (Chicago: A. C. McClurg, 1910), 3:79, 88–89; Patrick Galt to Alexander Galt, Jun. 24, 1847, Patrick Galt Papers, Swem Library, College of William and Mary, Williamsburg, Va.

7. This often-cited quote is mentioned in Winfield Scott, *Memoirs of Lieut.-General Scott*, 2 vols. (1864; Freeport, N.Y.: Books for Libraries Press, 1970), 2:466, but is difficult to independently corroborate. James W. Pohl, "The Influence of Antoine Henri de Jomini on Winfield Scott's Campaign in the Mexican War," *Southwestern Historical Quarterly* 77 (Jul. 1973): 98.

8. Bauer, *Mexican War*, 273; Allan Peskin, ed., *Volunteers: The Mexican War Journals of Private Richard Coulter and Sergeant Thomas Barclay, Company E, Second Pennsylvania Infantry* (Kent, Ohio: Kent State University Press, 1991), 108; James I. Robertson Jr., *Stonewall Jackson: The Man, the Soldier, the Legend* (New York: Macmillan, 1997), 60; Thomas Claiborne, "Reminiscences of the Mexican War," 27–29, Thomas Claiborne Papers, SHC, UNC; Irvin W. Levinson, *Wars within War: Mexican Guerrillas, Domestic Elites, and the United States of America, 1846–1848* (Forth Worth: Texas Christian University Press, 2005), 42. Estimates of Mexican losses range from nineteen to as many as sixty.

9. George W. Hartman, *A Private's Own Journal: Giving an Account of the Battles in Mexico, under Gen'l Scott* (Greencastle: E. Robinson, 1849), 15; Peskin, *Volunteers*, 110; Chauncey Forward Sargent, *Gathering Laurels in Mexico: The Diary of an American Soldier in the Mexican American War*, ed. Ann Brown Janes (Lincoln, Mass.: Cottage Press, 1990), 12.

10. Nathaniel Cheairs Hughes Jr. and Roy P. Stonesifer, *The Life and Wars of Gideon J. Pillow* (Chapel Hill: University of North Carolina Press, 1993), 74–79.

11. Mills Diary, FHS; James Fitzgerald to William Blackburn, Jun. 14 and Jul. 10, 1847, Blackburn Family Papers, FHS; Raphael Semmes, *Service Afloat and Ashore during the Mexican War* (Cincinnati: Wm. H. Moore, 1851), 314.

12. Dean B. Mahin, *Olive Branch and Sword: The United States and Mexico, 1845–1848* (Jefferson, N.C.: McFarland, 1997), 97, 102–3; "Memorandum," Ethan Allen Hitchcock Papers, LC.

13. Wallace Ohrt, *Defiant Peacemaker: Nicholas Trist in the Mexican War* (College Station: Texas A&M University Press, 1997), 116; Scott quoted in Charles Winslow Elliott, *Winfield Scott: The Soldier and the Man* (New York: Macmillan, 1937), 491; Smith, *War*, 2:130–31; Richard Griswold del Castillo, *The Treaty of Guadalupe Hidalgo: A Legacy of Conflict* (Norman: University of Oklahoma Press, 1990).

14. Del Castillo, *Treaty of Guadalupe Hidalgo*, 27; Henry I. Seaman, *Speech of Mr. Henry I. Seaman of N.Y. on the Mexican War* (Washington, D.C.: J. & G. S. Gideon, Printers, 1847), 4; Carlos E. Castañeda, "Relations of General Scott with Santa Anna," *Hispanic American Historical Review* 29 (Nov. 1949): 462–67.

15. David M. Pletcher, *The Diplomacy of Annexation: Texas, Oregon, and the Mexican War* (Columbia: University of Missouri Press, 1973), 508–9; "Memorandum," Hitchcock Papers.

16. Hughes and Stonesifer, *Pillow*, 80; "Memorandum," Hitchcock Papers; George Turnbull Moore Davis, *Autobiography of the Late Col. Geo T. M. Davis, Captain and Aid-de-Camp Scott's Army of Invasion* (New York: Jenkins and McCowan, 1891), 178–80; Elliott, *Scott*, 497; Bauer, *Mexican War*, 285.

17. Castañeda, "Relations of General Scott," 468–69; Mahin, *Olive Branch*, 104–5.

18. Worth quoted in Edward S. Wallace, *General William Jenkins Worth: Monterey's Forgotten Hero* (Dallas: Southern Methodist University Press, 1953), 140; Alfred Hoyt Bill, *Rehearsal for Conflict: The War with Mexico, 1846–1848* (New York: Alfred A. Knopf, 1947), 262.

19. Martin A. Haynes, *Gen. Scott's Guide in Mexico: A Biographical Sketch of Col. Noah E. Smith* (Lake Village, N.H.: Reprinted from the *Lake Village Times*, 1887), 18–20; *Vindication of the Military Character and Services of General Franklin Pierce* (circular pamphlet reprinted from various newspapers, 1852), 7, copy in BLY.

20. Haynes, *Gen. Scott's Guide*, 20–21.

21. Ralph W. Kirkham, *The Mexican War Journal and Letters of Ralph W. Kirkham*, ed. Robert Ryal Miller (College Station: Texas A&M University Press, 1991), 39–41; Polk, *Diary*, 2:492; Hiram B. Yeager to John C. Yeager, Jun. 10, 1847, Yeager Papers.

22. Marcy to Scott, Apr. 30, 1847, United States War Department Letters, Beinecke; William P. Chambliss, "Record of Death & Discharges Company 'C' Tennessee Regiment," BLY.

23. John Dodd to Eliza, Jan. 10, 1847, John Dodd Papers, BLY; Ripley to mother, Aug. 27 and Dec. 27, 1847, Roswell Ripley Papers, BLY; Austine to cousin, Jul. 4, 1947, William Austine Papers, SHC, UNC; Lee to John Mackay, Oct. 2, 1847, Lee Letter, Folios 137–38, VHS.

24. Bauer, *Mexican War*, 273–74; Guy Carleton to George Gile Littleton, Nov. 23, 1847, Mexican War Collection, UTA; Israel Uncapher Mexican War Diary, UTA.

25. Both Taliaferro quotes found in Levinson, *Wars within War*, 44–45; excerpts of Oct. 27 letter in Benjamin S. Roberts Diary, Justin H. Smith Collection, LAC, UT.

26. Ethan Allen Hitchcock letter, Jan. 23, 1848, Sen. Doc. No. 60, 30th Cong., 1st Sess. Hitchcock is the sole source for this exchange, and he did not identify the contact in Mexico City who sent Scott the note, although he intimated that it was an Englishman.

27. "Memorandum," Hitchcock Papers; Smith, *War*, 2:77; Robert Anderson, *An Artillery Officer in the Mexican War, 1846–7* (New York: G. P. Putnam's Sons, 1911), 276; Pillow quote found in Walter H. Hebert, *Fighting Joe Hooker* (New York: Bobbs-Merrill, 1944), 29; Davis, *Autobiography*, 175.

28. Twiggs quoted in Smith, *War*, 2:93; Bill, *Rehearsal*, 264–65; Scott, *Memoirs*, 2:465; Austine to cousin, Nov. 1, 1847, Austine Papers.

29. Austine to cousin, Nov. 1, 1847, Austine Papers.

30. Major John L. Smith's engineer report, Aug. 27, 1847, RG 94, LR, AGO; Ethan Allen Hitchcock, "Sketches of the Campaign," Hitchcock Papers, USMA; quote found in Hitchcock letter, Jan. 23, 1848, Sen. Exec. Doc. No. 60, 30th Cong., 1st Sess.

31. Kirkham, *Mexican War Journal*, 39.

Chapter 9. Into the Valley of Mexico

1. George Ballentine, *Autobiography of an English Soldier in the United States Army*, ed. William H. Goetzmann (Chicago: Lakeside Press, 1986), 260; Simon Buckner to cousin, Nov. 17, 1847, Simon Bolivar Buckner Papers, FHS; Moses Bar-

nard Reminiscences, BYL; Robert E. May, *John A. Quitman: Old South Crusader* (1984; Baton Rouge: Louisiana State University Press, 1985), 180.

2. Martin A. Haynes, *Gen. Scott's Guide in Mexico: A Biographical Sketch of Col. Noah E. Smith* (Lake Village, N.H.: Reprinted from the *Lake Village Times*, 1887), 21–22; Winfield Scott, *Memoirs of Lieut.-General Scott*, 2 vols. (1864; Freeport, N.Y.: Books for Libraries Press, 1970), 2:467.

3. Benjamin F. Cheatham Diary, Benjamin Franklin Cheatham Papers, TSLA; K. Jack Bauer, *The Mexican War, 1846–1848* (1974; Lincoln: University of Nebraska Press, 1992), 287; John Sedgwick to father, Aug. 23, 1847, in John Sedgwick, *Correspondence of John Sedgwick, Major-General*, comp. Henry D. Sedgwick, 2 vols. (DeVinne Press, 1902), 1:108; Buckner to cousin, Nov. 17, 1847, Buckner Papers; Ballentine, *Autobiography*, 260–61; Daniel Harvey Hill, *A Fighter from Way Back: The Mexican War Diary of Lt. Daniel Harvey Hill, 4th Artillery, USA*, ed. Nathaniel Cheairs Hughes Jr. and Timothy D. Johnson (Kent, Ohio: Kent State University Press, 2002), 106.

4. Barnard Reminiscences, BLY.

5. Ballentine, *Autobiography*, 261; Will Lytle to unknown, Jan. 15, 1848, in William Haines Lytle, *For Honor, Glory and Union: The Mexican and Civil War Letters of Brig. Gen. William Haines Lytle*, ed. Ruth C. Carter (Lexington: University Press of Kentucky, 1999), 52. Lytle rose to the rank of brigadier general in the Union army and was mortally wounded while leading his brigade at the Battle of Chickamauga in September 1863.

6. Haynes, *Gen. Scott's Guide*, 23–24.

7. Ethan Allen Hitchcock, "Sketches of the Campaign," Ethan Allen Hitchcock Papers, USMA; Justin H. Smith, *The War with Mexico*, 2 vols. (New York: Macmillan, 1919), 2:94–96.

8. Robert Anderson, *An Artillery Officer in the Mexican War, 1846–7* (New York: G. P. Putnam's Sons, 1911), 151; Haynes, *Gen. Scott's Guide*, 25.

9. Bauer, *Mexican War*, 290; Raphael Semmes, *Service Afloat and Ashore during the Mexican War* (Cincinnati: Wm. H. Moore, 1851), 352; Douglas Southall Freeman, *R. E. Lee: A Biography*, 4 vols. (1934; New York: Charles Scribner's Sons, 1962), 1:252–53; Ralph W. Kirkham, *The Mexican War Journal and Letters of Ralph W. Kirkham*, ed. Robert Ryal Miller (College Station: Texas A&M University Press, 1991), 81; Joseph Smith, Diary, Joseph Rowe Smith Papers, Beinecke; Smith, *War*, 2:90–91; Cheatham Diary, Cheatham Papers.

10. Smith, Diary, Joseph Rowe Smith Papers; Allan Peskin, ed., *Volunteers: The Mexican War Journals of Private Richard Coulter and Sergeant Thomas Barclay, Company E, Second Pennsylvania Infantry* (Kent, Ohio: Kent State University Press, 1991), 139; Kirkham, *Mexican War Journal*, 44; Albert C. Ramsey, ed. and trans., *The Other Side; or, Notes for the History of the War between Mexico and the United States* (New York: John Wiley, 1850), 241.

11. Kirkham, *Mexican War Journal*, 44.

12. Scott, *Memoirs*, 2:469; Bauer, *Mexican War*, 290; P. G. T. Beauregard, *With Beauregard in Mexico: The Mexican War Reminiscences of P. G. T. Beauregard*, ed.

T. Harry Williams (New York: DaCapo Press, 1969), 43; George Turnbull Moore Davis, *Autobiography of the Late Col. Geo T. M. Davis, Captain and Aid-de-Camp Scott's Army of Invasion* (New York: Jenkins and McCowan, 1891), 193–94.

13. Hitchcock, "Sketches of the Campaign," Hitchcock Papers; Worth to Scott, Aug. 14, 1847, James Duncan Papers, USMA; Semmes, *Service,* 355, 372; Erasmus D. Keyes, *Fifty Years' Observation of Men and Events Civil and Military* (New York: Charles Scribner's Sons, 1884), 154.

14. Barnard Reminiscences, BLY.

15. Gustavus Woodson Smith, *Company "A" Corps of Engineers, USA, 1846–1848, in the Mexican War,* ed. Leonne M. Hudson (Kent, Ohio: Kent State University Press, 2001), 37; Baron Antoine Henry Jomini, *The Art of War,* trans. G. H. Mendell and W. P. Craighill (Philadelphia: J. B. Lippincott, 1862), 227; Peskin, *Volunteers,* 139–40; Davis, *Autobiography,* 194; Barnard Reminiscences, BLY.

16. William Walker to uncle, Sep. 20, 1847, William Walker Letter, BLY.

17. William Austine to cousin, Nov. 1, 1847, William Austine Papers, SHC, UNC; Anderson to wife, Sep. 2, 1847, Robert Anderson Papers, LC; Kirkham, *Mexican War Journal,* 47.

18. Mason's battle report, Aug. 24, 1847; Worth, Battle Report, Aug. 23, 1847; Smith's engineer report, Aug. 27, 1847, RG 94, LR, AGO.

19. Austine to cousin, Nov. 1, 1847, Austine Papers.

20. Peskin, *Volunteers,* 141.

21. Smith's engineer report, Aug. 27, 1847, RG 94, LR, AGO; Philip Kearny to General Mason, Nov. 1, 1849, Philip Kearny Letter, BLY.

22. Bauer, *Mexican War,* 291–92.

23. Ulysses S. Grant, *Personal Memoirs of U. S. Grant,* 2 vols. (New York: Charles L. Webster, 1885), 1:139; Semmes, *Service,* 379.

24. Smith, *War,* 2:103–4; Nathaniel Cheairs Hughes Jr. and Roy P. Stonesifer, *The Life and Wars of Gideon J. Pillow* (Chapel Hill: University of North Carolina Press, 1993), 82–83.

25. General Smith's battle report, Aug. 23, 1847, Smith's engineer report, Aug. 27, 1847, Captain Edmund B. Alexander's battle report, Aug. 24, 1847, RG 94, LR, AGO; Hughes and Stonesifer, *Pillow,* 82–83; Barnard Reminiscences, BLY.

26. W. W. Loring's battle report, Aug. 24, 1847, RG 94, LR, AGO. Loring rose to the rank of major general in the Confederate army, serving in both the eastern and western theaters of the Civil War. He left the country after the war and served in the Egyptian army for several years before returning to the United States in 1879. Ezra J. Warner, *Generals in Gray: Lives of the Confederate Commanders* (Baton Rouge: Louisiana State University Press, 1959), 194.

27. Bauer, *Mexican War,* 293.

28. William Walker to uncle, Sep. 20, 1847, Walker Letter; Barnard Reminiscences, BLY; Walker rose to the rank of general in the Confederate army. In spring 1864, he was captured and had a foot amputated as a result of a wound suffered at Petersburg. Warner, *Generals in Gray,* 324.

29. Isaac I. Stevens, *Campaigns of the Rio Grande and of Mexico* (New York: D. Appleton, 1851), 64. See also Hazard Stevens, *The Life of Isaac Ingalls Stevens*, 2 vols. (New York: Houghton Mifflin, 1900), 1:187. Stevens's version is credible but should be weighed against the fact that his 1851 account was intended to defend Scott from the Worth, Pillow, and Duncan cabal that arose after the campaign ended. See Robert W. Johannsen, *To the Halls of the Montezumas* (1985; New York: Oxford University Press, 1987), 255.

30. James I. Robertson Jr., *Stonewall Jackson: The Man, the Soldier, the Legend* (New York: Macmillan, 1997), 63; Smith's engineer report, Aug. 27, 1847, RG 94, LR, AGO.

31. Guy Carleton to George Gile Littleton, Nov. 23, 1847, Mexican War Collection, UTA; Stephen W. Sears, *George B. McClellan: The Young Napoleon* (New York: Ticknor & Fields, 1988), 22.

32. Freeman, *Lee*, 1:260; Emory M. Thomas, *Robert E. Lee: A Biography* (New York: W. W. Norton, 1995), 131; Persifor Smith's battle report, Aug. 23, 1847, RG 94, LR, AGO; Hill, *Fighter from Way Back*, 111, 112.

33. May, *John A. Quitman*, 184.

34. Barnard Reminiscences, BLY; Walker to uncle, Sep. 20, 1847, Walker Letter.

35. Smith, *War*, 2:105, 108; Walker to uncle, Sep. 20, 1847, Walker Letter; Beauregard, *With Beauregard in Mexico*, 51–52; Persifor Smith's battle report, Aug. 23, 1847, RG 94, LR, AGO. General Smith gathered and took with him to San Geronimo the Engineer Company, First Artillery, Third Infantry, and part of the Mounted Rifles.

36. Persifor Smith's battle report, Aug. 23, 1847, RG 94, LR, AGO; Walker to uncle, Sep. 20, 1847, Walker Letter.

37. Walter H. Hebert, *Fighting Joe Hooker* (New York: Bobbs-Merrill, 1944), 30; James W. Pohl, "The Influence of Antoine Henri de Jomini on Winfield Scott's Campaign in the Mexican War," *Southwestern Historical Quarterly* 77 (Jul. 1973): 101–2; Beauregard, *With Beauregard in Mexico*, 48.

38. Smith, *War*, 2:105–6; Charles Winslow Elliott, *Winfield Scott: The Soldier and the Man* (New York: Macmillan, 1937), 510.

39. Persifor Smith's battle report, Aug. 23, 1847, RG 94, LR, AGO; John Hammond Moore, ed., "Private Johnson Fights the Mexicans, 1847–1848," *South Carolina Historical Magazine* 67 (Oct. 1966): 221; Freeman, *Lee*, 1:263–64.

40. Smith, *War*, 2:106.

41. Hughes and Stonesifer, *Pillow*, 88–89; Stevens, *Life*, 1:179.

42. Letter to father, Aug. 23, 1847, in Sedgwick, *Correspondence*, 1:111; Robertson, *Stonewall Jackson*, 64; John Wilkins to mother, Aug. 24, 1847, John Darragh Wilkins Memorandum and Papers, BLY.

Chapter 10. The Battle of Pedregal

1. Warren Lothrop to Elias Lothrop, n.d., Lothrop Family Papers, BLY; Moses Barnard Mexican War Reminiscences, BLY.

2. General Smith's battle report, Aug. 23, 1847, and Dimick's battle report, Aug. 23, 1847, RG 94, LR, AGO; William Walker to uncle, Sep. 20, 1847, William Walker Letter, BLY.

3. Barnard Reminiscences, BLY; William Walker to uncle, Aug. 20, 1847, Walker Letter; Daniel Harvey Hill, *A Fighter from Way Back: The Mexican War Diary of Lt. Daniel Harvey Hill, 4th Artillery, USA*, ed. Nathaniel Cheairs Hughes Jr. and Timothy D. Johnson (Kent, Ohio: Kent State University Press, 2002), 112; Justin H. Smith, *The War with Mexico*, 2 vols. (New York: Macmillan, 1919), 2:108; Gardner's battle report, RG 94, LR, AGO.

4. General Smith's battle report, Aug. 23, 1847, and Captain Alexander's battle report, Aug. 24, 1847, RG 94, LR, AGO.

5. Smith, *War*, 2:108; Gustavus Woodson Smith, *Company "A" Corps of Engineers, USA, 1846–1848, in the Mexican War*, ed. Leonne M. Hudson (Kent, Ohio: Kent State University Press, 2001), 42; Walker to uncle, Sep. 20, 1847, Walker Letter.

6. General Smith's battle report, Aug. 23, 1847, RG 94, LR, AGO; Smith, *Company "A,"* 42–43; Lothrop to Elias Lothrop, n.d., Lothrop Papers.

7. William Gardner to brother, Oct. 24, 1847, William Montgomery Gardner Papers, SHC, UNC; Walker to uncle, Sep. 20, 1847, Walker Letter; Major William W. Loring's Battle Report, Aug. 24, 1847, RG 94, LR, AGO; Smith, *Company "A,"* 43.

8. Walker to uncle, Sep. 20, 1847, Walker Letter; General James Shields's battle report, Aug. 24, 1847, RG 94, LR, AGO.

9. Hill, *Fighter from Way Back*, 117; Lothrop to Elias Lothrop, n.d., Lothrop Papers, BLY; Unknown to mother, Sep. 1847, Pope-Humphrey Family Papers, FHS.

10. John C. Waugh, *The Class of 1846* (New York: Warner Books, 1994), 111; Ezra J. Warner, *Generals in Gray: Lives of the Confederate Commanders* (Baton Rouge: Louisiana State University Press, 1959), 97–98; Scott's battle report, Aug. 28, 1847, Sen. Exec. Doc. No. 1, 30th Cong., 1st Exec.

11. Smith quoted in Smith, *War*, 2:109; George S. May, ed., "An Iowan in the Mexican War," *Iowa Journal of History* 53 (Apr. 1955): 172.

12. Preston had been orphaned when his father Charles, who was Joe's brother, died fifteen years earlier. Another of Joe's brothers, Beverly, was Preston's legal guardian, and it was to him that Joe wrote. See Craig L. Symonds, *Joseph E. Johnston: A Civil War Biography* (New York: W. W. Norton, 1992), 45, 65–66.

13. Scott's battle report, Aug. 28, 1847, RG 94, LR, AGO; Winfield Scott, *Memoirs of Lieut.-General Scott*, 2 vols. (1864; Freeport, N.Y.: Books for Libraries Press, 1970), 2:482; Riley's battle report, Aug. 24, 1847, RG 94, LR, AGO; K. Jack Bauer, *The Mexican War, 1846–1848* (1974; Lincoln: University of Nebraska Press, 1992), 295.

14. Bauer, *Mexican War*, 295–96; Loring's battle report, Aug. 24, 1847, RG 94, LR, AGO; Departamento De Distrito Federal, *Batalla de Churubusco el 20 de Agosto de 1847* (Colección: Conciencia Civica Nacional, Mexico, 1983), 69.

15. P. G. T. Beauregard, *With Beauregard in Mexico: The Mexican War Reminiscences of P. G. T. Beauregard*, ed. T. Harry Williams (New York: DaCapo Press, 1969), 55–56; Hill, *Fighter from Way Back*, 115.

16. Ripley to mother, Aug. 27, 1847, Roswell Ripley Papers, BLY; Walker to uncle, Sep. 20, 1847, Walker Letter.

17. Hazard Stevens, *The Life of Isaac Ingalls Stevens*, 2 vols. (New York: Houghton Mifflin, 1900), 1:179; John Sedgwick, *Correspondence of John Sedgwick, Major-General*, comp. Henry D. Sedgwick, 2 vols. (DeVinne Press, 1902), 1:100; Wilkins to mother, Aug. 24, 1847, John Darragh Wilkins Memorandum and Papers, BLY; Jackson quoted in James I. Robertson Jr., *Stonewall Jackson: The Man, the Soldier, the Legend* (New York: Macmillan, 1997), 58; Barnard Reminiscences, BLY.

18. Captured letters published in the *American Star*, Oct. 13, 14, and 22, 1847, BLY; Kirby Smith to wife, Aug. 22, 1847, E. Kirby Smith, *To Mexico with Scott: Letters of Captain E. Kirby Smith to His Wife*, ed. Emma Jerome Blackwood (Cambridge, Mass.: Harvard University Press, 1917), 208–9.

19. Scott's battle report, Aug. 28, 1847, RG 94, LR, AGO; Hill, *Fighter from Way Back*, 117; Barnard, Reminiscences, BLY.

20. Smith, *Company "A,"* 44–45.

21. Pillow and Trist quoted in Nathaniel Cheairs Hughes Jr. and Roy P. Stonesifer, *The Life and Wars of Gideon J. Pillow* (Chapel Hill: University of North Carolina Press, 1993), 89–90.

22. Distrito Federal, *Batalla de Churubusco*, 68; Peter F. Stevens, *The Rogue's March: John Riley and the St. Patrick's Battalion, 1846–48* (Washington, D.C.: Brassey's, 1999), 234; Bauer, *Mexican War*, 296.

23. Robert Ryal Miller, *Shamrock and Sword: The Saint Patrick's Battalion in the U.S.-Mexican War* (Norman: University of Oklahoma Press, 1989), 3, 25, 61, 67; Stevens, *Rogue's March*, 91–92, 231, 238.

24. Scott's battle report, Aug. 28, 1847, RG 94, LR, AGO.

25. Francis Taylor's battle report, Aug. 23, 1847, RG 94, LR, AGO; John Wilkins to mother, Aug. 24, 1847, Wilkins Papers; Gustavus Smith's battle report, Aug. 23, 1847, RG 94, LR, AGO.

26. Scott's battle report, Aug. 28, 1847, RG 94, LR, AGO; Worth's battle report, Aug. 23, 1847, RG 94, LR, AGO; Edward S. Wallace, *General William Jenkins Worth: Monterey's Forgotten Hero* (Dallas: Southern Methodist University Press, 1953), 152.

27. Timothy D. Johnson, *Winfield Scott: The Quest for Military Glory* (Lawrence: University Press of Kansas, 1998), 50.

28. Ralph W. Kirkham, *The Mexican War Journal and Letters of Ralph W. Kirkham*, ed. Robert Ryal Miller (College Station: Texas A&M University Press, 1991), 50; Bauer, *Mexican War*, 297.

29. Sedgwick to sister, Aug. 28, 1847, in Sedgwick, *Correspondence*, 1:114; Raphael Semmes, *Service Afloat and Ashore during the Mexican War* (Cincinnati: Wm. H. Moore, 1851), 394–95.

30. Smith, *War*, 2:113–15; Cadawalader's battle report, RG 94, LR, AGO.

31. Christopher Phillips, *Damned Yankee: The Life of General Nathaniel Lyon* (Columbia: University of Missouri Press, 1990), 54; Kirkham, *Mexican War Journal*, 48; Worth's battle report, Aug. 23, 1847, RG 94, LR, AGO; David M. Jordon,

Winfield Scott Hancock: A Soldier's Life (1988; Bloomington: Indiana University Press, 1996), 5, 16; Hughes and Stonesifer, *Pillow*, 91; Cadwalader's battle report, Aug. 22, 1847, RG 94, LR, AGO.

32. Phillips, *Damned Yankee*, 54; Kendall to *Picayune*, Sep. 8, 1847, George Kendall Papers, UTA.

33. Martin A. Haynes, *Gen. Scott's Guide in Mexico: A Biographical Sketch of Col. Noah E. Smith* (Lake Village, N.H.: Reprinted from the *Lake Village Times*, 1887), 30–31.

34. *Vindication of the Military Character and Services of General Franklin Pierce* (circular pamphlet reprinted from various newspapers, 1852), 8, BLY; Haynes, *Gen. Scott's Guide*, 31.

35. Scott's battle report, Aug. 28, 1847, Sen. Exec. Doc. No. 1, 30th Cong., 1st Exec.

36. Douglas Southall Freeman, *R. E. Lee: A Biography*, 4 vols. (1934; New York: Charles Scribner's Sons, 1962), 1:269; *Vindication*, 8, BLY; Shields's battle report, Sen. Exec. Doc. No. 1, 30th Cong., 1st Exec.

37. James Butterfield, "Reminiscences," Justin H. Smith Collection, LAC, UT.

38. Captain Thompson Morris's battle report, Aug. 23, 1847, and Lieutenant Gustavus Smith's battle report, Aug. 23, 1847, RG 94, LR, AGO; Joseph Rowe Smith, Diary, Joseph Rowe Smith Papers, BLY; Wilkins to mother, Aug. 24, 1847, Wilkins Papers; Stevens, *Rogue's March*, 239–40.

39. John Hammond Moore, ed., "Private Johnson Fights the Mexicans, 1847–1848," *South Carolina Historical Magazine* 67 (Oct. 1966): 221.

40. Jeffry D. Wert, *General James Longstreet: The Confederacy's Most Controversial Soldier* (New York: Simon & Schuster, 1993), 44; Lieutenant Thomas Williams to father, Oct. 1, 1847, Thomas Williams Letters in Justin H. Smith Collection, LAC, UTA; Kirkham, *Mexican War Journal*, 48.

41. Bauer, *Mexican War*, 299–300; Stevens, *Rogue's March*, 241–42.

42. James F. Babcock, *Fate of Major Frederick D. Mills Late of the Fifteenth Regiment, U. S. Army* (pamphlet, ca. 1848), BLY; May, "Iowan," 173.

43. Barnard Reminiscences, BLY; Kirkham, *Mexican War Journal*, 50–51; Kearny to General Mason, Nov. 1, 1849, Philip Kearny Letter, BLY.

44. Babcock, *Fate*, BLY; May, "Iowan," 173, n. 8. Mills County, Iowa, was named for Major Mills.

45. Barnard Reminiscences, BLY.

46. Kirkham, *Mexican War Journal*, 49; Barnard Reminiscences, BLY.

47. Semmes, *Service*, 429; Miller, *Shamrock and Sword*, 85–90; Wilkins to mother, Aug. 24, 1847, Wilkins Papers; Stevens, *Rogue's March*, 242; Worth's battle report, Aug. 23, 1847, RG 94, LR. AGO.

48. Bauer, *Mexican War*, 301, 305, n. 38; Robert Anderson, *An Artillery Officer in the Mexican War, 1846–7* (New York: G. P. Putnam's Sons, 1911), 292, 299–300, 326; Colonel James Duncan's battle report, Aug. 22, 1847, RG 94, LR, AGO.

49. Wilkins to mother, Aug. 24, 1847, Wilkins Papers; Ulysses S. Grant, *Personal Memoirs of U. S. Grant*, 2 vols. (New York: Charles L. Webster, 1885), 1:145.

50. Lee to Mary, Aug. 22, 1847, George Bolling Lee Papers, VHS; captured Mexican soldier letter quoted in Kirkham, *Mexican War Journal*, 53; Hill, *Fighter from Way Back*, 119; Grady McWhiney and Perry D. Jamieson, *Attack and Die: Civil War Military Tactics and the Southern Heritage* (Tuscaloosa: University of Alabama Press, 1982), 78–79.

51. Wilkins to mother, Aug. 24, 1847, Wilkins Papers, BLY; Hill, *Fighter from Way Back*, 111.

Chapter 11. Mortification and Mistake

1. William Austine to cousin, Nov. 1, 1847, William Austine Papers, SHC, UNC.

2. Pedro Santoni, *Mexicans at Arms: Puro Federalist and the Politics of War* (Fort Worth: Texas Christian University Press, 1996), 211; Dean B. Mahin, *Olive Branch and Sword: The United States and Mexico, 1845–1848* (Jefferson, N.C.: McFarland, 1997), 113–15; K. Jack Bauer, *The Mexican War, 1846–1848* (1974; Lincoln: University of Nebraska Press, 1992), 307.

3. Winfield Scott, "Vera Cruz & Its Castle," Oct. 27, 1846, LR, RG 107, NA; Ethan Allen Hitchcock letter, Jan. 23, 1848, Sen. Exec. Doc. No. 60, 30th Cong., 1st Sess.

4. David M. Pletcher, *The Diplomacy of Annexation: Texas, Oregon, and the Mexican War* (Columbia: University of Missouri Press, 1973), 513; Thomas Williams to father, Oct. 1, 1847, Justin H. Smith Collection, LAC, UT; Hitchcock to Lizzie, Aug. 24, 1847, Ethan Allen Hitchcock Papers, LC; Daniel Harvey Hill, *A Fighter from Way Back: The Mexican War Diary of Lt. Daniel Harvey Hill, 4th Artillery, USA*, ed. Nathaniel Cheairs Hughes Jr. and Timothy D. Johnson (Kent, Ohio: Kent State University Press, 2002), 116–17; Stevens quote found in Charles Judah and George Winston Smith, *Chronicles of the Gringoes: The U.S. Army in the Mexican War, 1846–1848, Accounts of Eyewitnesses and Combatants* (Albuquerque: University of New Mexico Press, 1968), 249.

5. Hill, *Fighter from Way Back*, 117; Christopher Phillips, *Damned Yankee: The Life of General Nathaniel Lyon* (Columbia: University of Missouri Press, 1990), 55; George Turnbull Moore Davis, *Autobiography of the Late Col. Geo T. M. Davis, Captain and Aid-de-Camp Scott's Army of Invasion* (New York: Jenkins and McCowan, 1891), 207; Ralph W. Kirkham, *The Mexican War Journal and Letters of Ralph W. Kirkham*, ed. Robert Ryal Miller (College Station: Texas A&M University Press, 1991), 55; Edward S. Wallace, *General William Jenkins Worth: Monterey's Forgotten Hero* (Dallas: Southern Methodist University Press, 1953), 157–60; Robert E. May, *John A. Quitman: Old South Crusader* (1984; Baton Rouge: Louisiana State University Press, 1985), 184–85; Nathaniel Cheairs Hughes Jr. and Roy P. Stonesifer, *The Life and Wars of Gideon J. Pillow* (Chapel Hill: University of North Carolina Press, 1993), 95.

6. Martin A. Haynes, *Gen. Scott's Guide in Mexico: A Biographical Sketch of Col. Noah E. Smith* (Lake Village, N.H.: Reprinted from the *Lake Village Times*, 1887), 35–36.

7. Kirkham, *Mexican War Journal*, 54; Hitchcock to Lizzie, Aug. 24, 1847, Hitchcock Papers; Hill, *Fighter from Way Back*, 119; William Austine to cousin, Nov. 1, 1847, Austine Papers.

8. Hill, *Fighter from Way Back*, 115, 119; Kirby Smith to wife, Aug. 22, 1847, in E. Kirby Smith, *To Mexico with Scott: Letters of Captain E. Kirby Smith to His Wife*, ed. Emma Jerome Blackwood (Cambridge, Mass.: Harvard University Press, 1917), 207; George Wilkins Kendall, *The War between the United States and Mexico* (New York: D. Appleton, 1851), 35; Pletcher, *Diplomacy*, 515; Davis, *Autobiography*, 211; Haynes, *Gen. Scott's Guide*, 36–37.

9. Madison Mills Diary, FHS.

10. Buckner to Mary Kingsbury, Sep. 6, 1847, Simon Boliver Buckner Papers, FHS; Kirby Smith to wife, Sep. 2, 1847, in Smith, *To Mexico with Scott*, 213–14; Dwight Anderson and Nancy Scott Anderson, *The Generals: Ulysses S. Grant and Robert E. Lee* (New York: Alfred A. Knopf, 1988), 85.

11. Davis, *Autobiography*, 209–10, 215–16; May, *John A. Quitman*, 183–84.

12. Mahin, *Olive Branch*, 116–18; Wallace Ohrt, *Defiant Peacemaker: Nicholas Trist in the Mexican War* (College Station: Texas A&M University Press, 1997), 131; Richard Bruce Winders, *Crisis in the Southwest: The United States, Mexico, and the Struggle over Texas* (Wilmington, Del.: Scholarly Resources, 2002), 135; Pletcher, *Diplomacy*, 516–19.

13. Robert Ryal Miller, *Shamrock and Sword: The Saint Patrick's Battalion in the U.S.-Mexican War* (Norman: University of Oklahoma Press, 1989), 92–105.

14. Mahin, *Olive Branch*, 118; Kendall, *War*, 35; Robert Anderson, *An Artillery Officer in the Mexican War, 1846–7* (New York: G. P. Putnam's Sons, 1911), 309–10.

15. Ripley to mother, Aug. 27, Roswell Ripley Papers, BLY; John Sedgwick, *Correspondence of John Sedgwick, Major-General*, comp. Henry D. Sedgwick, 2 vols. (DeVinne Press, 1902), 1:120; Phillips, *Damned Yankee*, 55; Kirkham, *Mexican War Journal*, 55; Frederick Wirtzell to Henry Eddy, Oct. 26, 1847, J. T. Hughes Letters, Justin H. Smith Collection, LAC, UT; Moses Barnard Mexican War Reminiscences, BLY; Hill, *Fighter from Way Back*, 121.

16. Anderson, *Artillery Officer*, 310; Beauregard to Major John L. Smith, Sep. 20, 1847, United States Corps of Engineers, Report of a Reconnaissance of the Niño Perdido and San Antonio Gates of Mexico City, BLY.

17. R. E. Lee to John Mackay, Oct. 2, 1847, Robert E. Lee Letter, Folios 137–138, VHS.

18. Hughes and Stonesifer, *Pillow*, 96; Wallace, *General William Jenkins Worth*, 160.

19. Bauer, *Mexican War*, 308–9; Justin H. Smith, *The War with Mexico*, 2 vols. (New York: Macmillan, 1919), 2:140.

20. Smith, *War*, 2:143–44; Bauer, *Mexican War*, 309; Worth's battle report, Sep. 10, 1847, RG 94, LR, AGO, NA.

21. Anderson, *Artillery Officer*, 312; Kirby Smith to General Brown, Oct. 29, 1847, Edmund Kirby Smith Papers, BLY; Smith, *To Mexico with Scott*, 217. *Forlorn*

hope was a military term often used to describe a storming party that is assigned the dangerous assignment of leading an attack. Smith's use of the term here was to convey a sense of desperation over the difficult task that lay ahead.

22. Worth's battle report, Sep. 10, 1847, Wright's battle report, Sep. 10, 1847, RG 94, LR, AGO, NA.

23. McIntosh's battle report, Sep. 10, 1847, RG 94, LR, AGO, NA; Kendall to *Picayune*, Sep. 8, 1847, George Kendall Papers, UTA; Bauer, *Mexican War*, 310; Arthur Howard Noll, *General Kirby-Smith* (Sewanee, Tenn.: University Press at the University of the South, 1907), 57–58; Kirkham, *Mexican War Journal*, 57–58. McIntosh lived until Sep. 26 and was able, with the assistance of staff officers, to submit a battle report.

24. Ethan Allen Hitchcock, "Sketches of the Campaign," Ethan Allen Hitchcock Papers, USMA; Kirkham, *Mexican War Journal*, 57–58; Hill, *Fighter from Way Back*, 122.

25. Smith, *War*, 2:147; Garland's battle report, Sep. 9, 1847, RG 94, LR, AGO, NA; Anderson, *Artillery Officer*, 312.

26. Ulysses S. Grant, *Personal Memoirs of U. S. Grant*, 2 vols. (New York: Charles L. Webster, 1885), 1:152–53.

27. Kendall to *Picayune*, Sep. 8, 1847, Kendall Papers; Bauer, *Mexican War*, 310; Barnard Reminiscences, BLY.

28. Kendall to *Picayune*, Sep. 8, 1847, Kendall Papers.

29. Bauer, *Mexican War*, 310–11; Allan Peskin, ed., *Volunteers: The Mexican War Journals of Private Richard Coulter and Sergeant Thomas Barclay, Company E, Second Pennsylvania Infantry* (Kent, Ohio: Kent State University Press, 1991), 202; George Maney to Thomas Maney, Sep. 21, 1847, John Kimberly Papers, SHC, UNC; Ethan Allen Hitchcock, *Fifty Years in Camp and Field: The Diary of Major General Ethan Allen Hitchcock*, ed. W. A. Croffut (New York: G. P. Putnam's, 1909), 297–99.

30. Grant, *Personal Memoirs*, 1:152; Peskin, *Volunteers*, 185. For Russell Weigley's description of Grant the general, see his *The American Way of War: A History of United States Military Strategy and Policy* (Bloomington: Indiana University Press, 1977), 128–52.

31. Kirkham, *Mexican War Journal*, 58–59.

Chapter 12. God Is a Yankee

1. Scott to Marcy, Sep. 18, 1847, RG 94, LR, AGO, NA; Beauregard to Major John L. Smith, Sep. 20, 1847, United States Corps of Engineers, Report of a Reconnaissance of the Niño Perdido and San Antonio Gates of Mexico City, BLY; T. Harry Williams, *P. G. T. Beauregard* (Baton Rouge: Louisiana State University Press, 1954), 28.

2. Daniel Harvey Hill, *A Fighter from Way Back: The Mexican War Diary of Lt. Daniel Harvey Hill, 4th Artillery, USA*, ed. Nathaniel Cheairs Hughes Jr. and Timothy D. Johnson (Kent, Ohio: Kent State University Press, 2002), 121, 123.

3. The most detailed account of the conference, and the one from which this narrative is drawn, is found in P. G. T. Beauregard, *With Beauregard in Mexico: The Mexican War Reminiscences of P. G. T. Beauregard*, ed. T. Harry Williams (New York: DaCapo Press, 1969), 68–72.

4. William A. DePalo Jr., *The Mexican National Army, 1822–1852* (College Station: Texas A&M University Press, 1997), 73; K. Jack Bauer, *The Mexican War, 1846–1848* (1974; Lincoln: University of Nebraska Press, 1992), 313; Justin H. Smith, *The War with Mexico*, 2 vols. (New York: Macmillan, 1919), 2:149–51.

5. Scott to Marcy, Sep. 18, 1847, RG 94, LR, AGO, NA; Robert E. May, *John A. Quitman: Old South Crusader* (1984; Baton Rouge: Louisiana State University Press, 1985), 189; Smith, *War*, 2:152.

6. Douglas Southall Freeman, *R. E. Lee: A Biography*, 4 vols. (1934; New York: Charles Scribner's Sons, 1962), 1:280–83; Scott to Marcy, Sep. 18, 1847, RG 94, LR, AGO, NA; Smith, *War*, 2:152.

7. Scott to Marcy, Sep. 18, 1847, and Major John L. Gardner's battle report, Sep. 20, 1847, RG 94, LR, AGO, NA; Hill, *Fighter from Way Back*, 124–25.

8. Freeman, *Lee*, 1:279–80.

9. Scott to Marcy, Sep. 18, 1847, and Major John L. Gardner's battle report, Sep. 20, 1847, RG 94, LR, AGO, NA; Nathaniel Cheairs Hughes Jr. and Roy P. Stonesifer, *The Life and Wars of Gideon J. Pillow* (Chapel Hill: University of North Carolina Press, 1993), 98; Hill, *Fighter from Way Back*, 125.

10. Hughes and Stonesifer, *Pillow*, 99; Ethan Allen Hitchcock, *Fifty Years in Camp and Field: The Diary of Major General Ethan Allen Hitchcock*, ed. W. A. Croffut (New York: G. P. Putnam's, 1909), 302; Hill, *Fighter from Way Back*, 125.

11. DePalo, *Mexican National Army*, 137; *American Star*, Sep. 23, 1847, 1.

12. Quitman's battle report, Sep. 29, 1847, RG 94, LR, AGO, NA; Donald E. Houston, "The Role of Artillery in the Mexican War," *Journal of the West* 11 (Apr. 1972): 283.

13. Hughes and Stonesifer, *Pillow*, 99–100. As a Union corps commander, Major General Reno was mortally wounded at South Mountain on Sep. 14, 1862. Reno, Nevada, was named in his honor. See John C. Waugh, *The Class of 1846* (New York: Warner Books, 1994), 529.

14. Bauer, *Mexican War*, 317; Smith, *War*, 2:156.

15. Hughes and Stonesifer, *Pillow*, 100; DePalo, *Mexican National Army*, 137.

16. Major Thomas H. Seymour's battle report, Sep. 21, 1847, RG 94, LR, AGO, NA; Hughes and Stonesifer, *Pillow*, 100–101; Smith, *War*, 2:155–56; Ralph W. Kirkham, *The Mexican War Journal and Letters of Ralph W. Kirkham*, ed. Robert Ryal Miller (College Station: Texas A&M University Press, 1991), 62.

17. *American Star*, Sep. 23, 1847, 1; Smith, *War*, 2:156; Bauer, *Mexican War*, 317; Colonel Timothy Patrick Andrews's battle report, Sep. 17, 1847, RG 94, LR, AGO, NA.

18. James D. Elderkin, *Biographical Sketches and Anecdotes of a Soldier of Three Wars* (Detroit: James D. Elderkin, 1899), 69; James I. Robertson Jr., *Stonewall Jackson: The Man, the Soldier, the Legend* (New York: Macmillan, 1997), 66.

19. Robertson, *Stonewall Jackson*, 67.

20. Scott to Marcy, Sep. 18, 1847, RG 94, LR, AGO, NA; George W. Hartman, *A Private's Own Journal: Giving an Account of the Battles in Mexico, under Gen'l Scott* (Greencastle: E. Robinson, 1849), 19; Bauer, *Mexican War*, 317; May, *John A. Quitman*, 190–91.

21. Hill, *Fighter from Way Back*, 126; John S. Devlin, *The Marine Corps in Mexico: Setting Forth its Conduct as Established by Testimony before a General Court Martial* (Washington: Lemuel Towers, 1852), iv. Regarding the marines' behavior during the assault, Bauer simply states that the marines "did not press their advance aggressively" (*Mexican War*, 317). However, another marine officer, Lieutenant John S. Devlin, was present and would later publish an article in the *Brooklyn Daily Eagle* and after that a pamphlet in which he criticized Reynolds and the other marines for refusing to advance. He also named Major William Dulany as a marine officer who refused to advance. Dulany was later court-martialed for looting a convent, and Devlin was suspended from the service for challenging Reynolds to a duel during a verbal confrontation.

22. Quitman's battle report, Sep. 29, 1847, RG 94, LR, AGO, NA; Chauncey Forward Sargent, *Gathering Laurels in Mexico: The Diary of an American Soldier in the Mexican American War*, ed. Ann Brown Janes (Lincoln, Mass.: Cottage Press, 1990), 17; Israel Uncapher Mexican War Diary, UTA; Allan Peskin, ed., *Volunteers: The Mexican War Journals of Private Richard Coulter and Sergeant Thomas Barclay, Company E, Second Pennsylvania Infantry* (Kent, Ohio: Kent State University Press, 1991), 168, 177–78; John W. Geary's battle report, Sep. 15, 1847, John White Geary Papers, BLY. Geary went on to serve as the first mayor of San Francisco, and after the Civil War, he served as governor of Pennsylvania. Pam M. Geary, *Colonel John W. Geary in the Mexican War and California in '49* (Pacifica, Calif.: Shade Tree Press, 2000), 96–98, 105–10; Ezra J. Warner, *Generals in Blue: Lives of the Union Commanders* (Baton Rouge: Louisiana State University Press, 1964), 169–70.

23. Quitman's battle report, Sep. 29, 1847, RG 94, LR, AGO, NA; Uncapher Diary, UTA; Smith, *War*, 2:157.

24. Hughes and Stonesifer, *Pillow*, 101; Jeffry D. Wert, *General James Longstreet: The Confederacy's Most Controversial Soldier* (New York: Simon & Schuster, 1993), 45. Lieutenant P. G. T. Beauregard thought that Lieutenant Lewis Armistead, Sixth Infantry, was among the first over the wall. Beauregard, *With Beauregard in Mexico*, 81–82.

25. Quitman, battle report, Sep. 29, 1847, RG 94, LR, AGO, NA; Hill, *Fighter from Way Back*, 126.

26. Beauregard, *With Beauregard in Mexico*, 82–84; Hill, *Fighter from Way Back*, 126; Uncapher Diary, UTA; Peter F. Stevens, *The Rogue's March: John Riley and the St. Patrick's Battalion, 1846–48* (Washington, D.C.: Brassey's, 1999), 270, 275; Bauer, *Mexican War*, 316; Peskin, *Volunteers*, 171.

27. Scott to Marcy, Sep. 18, 1847, RG 94, LR, AGO, NA; Smith, *War*, 2:160–61; Bauer, *Mexican War*, 318; Quitman's battle report, Sep. 29, 1847, RG 94, LR, AGO, NA; J. W. Geary Papers, BLY.

28. Stevens, *Rogue's March*, 270–76. All quotes found therein. Harney also whipped and branded eight of the fifteen whose sentences had been reduced.

29. Bauer, *Mexican War*, 318.

Chapter 13. A Devil of a Time

1. Nathaniel Cheairs Hughes Jr. and Roy P. Stonesifer, *The Life and Wars of Gideon J. Pillow* (Chapel Hill: University of North Carolina Press, 1993), 101; Page Memoir, Page Family Papers, VHS; Allan Peskin, ed., *Volunteers: The Mexican War Journals of Private Richard Coulter and Sergeant Thomas Barclay, Company E, Second Pennsylvania Infantry* (Kent, Ohio: Kent State University Press, 1991), 179.

2. Quitman's battle report, Sep. 29, 1847, RG 94, LR, AGO, NA; Robert E. May, *John A. Quitman: Old South Crusader* (1984; Baton Rouge: Louisiana State University Press, 1985), 191; Charles Winslow Elliott, *Winfield Scott: The Soldier and the Man* (New York: Macmillan, 1937), 547. Elliott recorded that Quitman's aides "quietly" gathered the division, which suggests an effort on Quitman's part to keep his intentions secret until he could get well underway.

3. Martin A. Haynes, *Gen. Scott's Guide in Mexico: A Biographical Sketch of Col. Noah E. Smith* (Lake Village, N.H.: Reprinted from the *Lake Village Times*, 1887), 41; George Turnbull Moore Davis, *Autobiography of the Late Col. Geo T. M. Davis, Captain and Aid-de-Camp Scott's Army of Invasion* (New York: Jenkins and McCowan, 1891), 234; Elliott, *Winfield Scott*, 547; Justin H. Smith, *The War with Mexico*, 2 vols. (New York: Macmillan, 1919), 2:161.

4. Scott to Marcy, Sep. 18, 1847, RG 94, LR, AGO, NA. James W. Pohl notes in his article comparing the campaign to Jominian theory that "Scott knew . . . that he must have the capital to end the war." Such was not the case. As Scott stated, he would have accepted a peace without capturing the city. James W. Pohl, "The Influence of Antoine Henri de Jomini on Winfield Scott's Campaign in the Mexican War," *Southwestern Historical Quarterly* 77 (Jul. 1973): 99.

5. Ulysses S. Grant, *Personal Memoirs of U. S. Grant*, 2 vols. (New York: Charles L. Webster, 1885), 1:154.

6. George Ballentine, *Autobiography of an English Soldier in the United States Army*, ed. William H. Goetzmann (Chicago: Lakeside Press, 1986), 301–2.

7. Quitman's battle report, Sep. 29, 1847, RG 94, LR, AGO, NA; T. Harry Williams, *P. G. T. Beauregard* (Baton Rouge: Louisiana State University Press, 1954), 31; Smith, *War*, 2:159.

8. Quitman, battle report, Sep. 29, 1847, RG 94, LR, AGO, NA.

9. Williams, *Beauregard*, 31; P. G. T. Beauregard, *With Beauregard in Mexico: The Mexican War Reminiscences of P. G. T. Beauregard*, ed. T. Harry Williams (New York: DaCapo Press, 1969), 88–89.

10. Quitman, battle report, Sep. 29, 1847, RG 94, LR, AGO, NA; Smith, *War*, 2:159–60; May, *John A. Quitman*, 192.

11. May, *John A. Quitman*, 191–93; Smith, *War*, 2:160.

12. Uncapher Diary, UTA; George W. Hartman, *A Private's Own Journal: Giv-*

ing an Account of the Battles in Mexico, under Gen'l Scott (Greencastle: E. Robinson, 1849), 19; Daniel Harvey Hill, *A Fighter from Way Back: The Mexican War Diary of Lt. Daniel Harvey Hill, 4th Artillery, USA,* ed. Nathaniel Cheairs Hughes Jr. and Timothy D. Johnson (Kent, Ohio: Kent State University Press, 2002), 127; Lee to Mackay, Oct. 4, 1847, in Gary Gallagher, "We Are Our Own Trumpeters: Robert E. Lee Describes Winfield Scott's Campaign to Mexico City," *Virginia Magazine of History and Biography* 95 (Jul. 1987): 372–73. Drum and Lee were classmates at West Point.

13. Davis, *Autobiography,* 234–35; Scott to Marcy, Sep. 18, 1847, RG 94, LR, AGO, NA.

14. Quitman's battle report, Sep. 29, 1847, RG 94, LR, AGO, NA.

15. Hill, *Fighter from Way Back,* 126–27; Frank E. Vandiver, *Mighty Stonewall* (New York: McGraw-Hill, 1957), 39; Jackson quoted in James I. Robertson Jr., *Stonewall Jackson: The Man, the Soldier, the Legend* (New York: Macmillan, 1997), 68.

16. Grant, *Personal Memoirs,* 1:155–56; Ralph W. Kirkham, *The Mexican War Journal and Letters of Ralph W. Kirkham,* ed. Robert Ryal Miller (College Station: Texas A&M University Press, 1991), 62; Isaac I. Stevens, *Campaigns of the Rio Grande and of Mexico* (New York: D. Appleton, 1851), 57.

17. Douglas Southall Freeman, *R. E. Lee: A Biography,* 4 vols. (1934; New York: Charles Scribner's Sons, 1962), 1:283; Emory M. Thomas, *Robert E. Lee: A Biography* (New York: W. W. Norton, 1995), 136.

18. Smith, *War,* 2:161–62.

19. Grant, *Personal Memoirs,* 1:157–58.

20. Kirkham, *Mexican War Journal,* 62; Smith, *War,* 2:162; Grant, *Personal Memoirs,* 1:1587–59.

21. K. Jack Bauer, *The Mexican War, 1846–1848* (1974; Lincoln: University of Nebraska Press, 1992), 320–21; Smith, *War,* 2:162; Kirkham, *Mexican War Journal,* 164.

22. Scott to Marcy, Sep. 18, 1847, and Quitman's battle report, Sep. 29, 1847, RG 94, LR, AGO, NA.

23. Davis, *Autobiography,* 236.

24. Scott to Marcy, Sep. 18, 1847, and Quitman's battle report, Sep. 29, 1847, RG 94, LR, AGO, NA; Beauregard, *With Beauregard in Mexico,* 97–98; Hachaliah Brown to Lemuel Brown, Oct. 31, 1847, Lemuel C. Brown Papers, BLY.

25. Amasa Gleason Clark, *Reminiscences of a Centenarian* (Bandera, Tex.: Printed by Amasa Clark, 1930), 29; Hill, *Fighter from Way Back,* 128; Freeman, *Lee,* 1:284; Elliott, *Winfield Scott,* 551–52; John C. Waugh, *The Class of 1846* (New York: Warner Books, 1994), 124.

26. Scott to Marcy, Sep. 18, 1847, RG 94, LR, AGO, NA. The four days of fighting (Aug. 19 and 20, Sep. 8 and 13) does not include the bombardment of Sep. 12.

27. Hartman, *Private's Own Journal,* 19; Wyatt B. Stapp to Sarah Hane Berry, May 16, 1848, Berry Family Papers, FHS; Bauer, *Mexican War,* 322; Quitman's battle report, Sep. 29, 1847, RG 94, LR, AGO, NA; Davis, *Autobiography,* 241; Smith,

War, 2:167; Alfred Hoyt Bill, *Rehearsal for Conflict: The War with Mexico, 1846–1848* (New York: Alfred A. Knopf, 1947), 301–2; Haynes, *Gen. Scott's Guide,* 44.

28. Haynes, *Gen. Scott's Guide,* 44; Quitman's battle report, Sep. 29, 1847, RG 94, LR, AGO, NA; Chauncey Forward Sargent, *Gathering Laurels in Mexico: The Diary of an American Soldier in the Mexican American War,* ed. Ann Brown Janes (Lincoln, Mass.: Cottage Press, 1990), 16–17; Smith, *War,* 2:167; Hill, *Fighter from Way Back,* 128–29; Brown to Lemuel Brown, Oct. 31, 1847, Brown Papers; Lee to John Mackay, Oct. 2, 1847, Robert E. Lee Letter, Folios 137–38, VHS.

29. Brown to Lemuel Brown, Oct. 31, 1847, Brown Papers; Winslow Sanderson to Dear Sir, Nov. 21, 1847, Winslow Fuller Sanderson Papers, BLY.

Chapter 14. The Preoccupations of the Occupation

1. Pillow to Barnard, Sep. 19, 1847, copy in Moses Barnard Reminiscences, BLY; Hachaliah Brown to Lemuel Brown, Oct. 31, 1847, Lemuel C. Brown Papers, BLY; Kendall to *Picayune,* Oct. 3, 1847, George Kendall Papers, UTA; Daniel Harvey Hill, *A Fighter from Way Back: The Mexican War Diary of Lt. Daniel Harvey Hill, 4th Artillery, USA,* ed. Nathaniel Cheairs Hughes Jr. and Timothy D. Johnson (Kent, Ohio: Kent State University Press, 2002), 129–30; R. E. Lee to John Mackay, Oct. 2, 1847, Robert E. Lee Letter, Folios 137–38, VHS; Allan Peskin, ed., *Volunteers: The Mexican War Journals of Private Richard Coulter and Sergeant Thomas Barclay, Company E, Second Pennsylvania Infantry* (Kent, Ohio: Kent State University Press, 1991), 192.

2. George Turnbull Moore Davis, *Autobiography of the Late Col. Geo T. M. Davis, Captain and Aid-de-Camp Scott's Army of Invasion* (New York: Jenkins and McCowan, 1891), 258–59.

3. Peskin, *Volunteers,* 191; Page Memoir, Page Family Papers, VHS; Jeffry D. Wert, *General James Longstreet: The Confederacy's Most Controversial Soldier* (New York: Simon & Schuster, 1993), 45; Chauncey Forward Sargent, *Gathering Laurels in Mexico: The Diary of an American Soldier in the Mexican American War,* ed. Ann Brown Janes (Lincoln, Mass.: Cottage Press, 1990), 17; Barna Upton to Elias Upton, May 16, 1847, and William W. Fogg to Nehemiah Upton, Apr. 20, 1848, Barna N. Upton Papers, BLY; Lee to John Mackay, Oct. 2, 1847, Robert E. Lee Letter, Folios 137–38, VHS.

4. Sedgwick to father, Oct. 15, 1847, in John Sedgwick, *Correspondence of John Sedgwick, Major-General,* comp. Henry D. Sedgwick, 2 vols. (DeVinne Press, 1902), 1:130; Ralph W. Kirkham, *The Mexican War Journal and Letters of Ralph W. Kirkham,* ed. Robert Ryal Miller (College Station: Texas A&M University Press, 1991), 60, 69, 75–76.

5. William Adee to Samuel Adee, Jun. 16 and Oct. 16, 1847, and McBride to Adee, Nov. 26, 1847, William F. Adee Papers, BLY.

6. Wert, *General James Longstreet,* 45; Amasa Gleason Clark, *Reminiscences of a Centenarian* (Bandera, Tex.: Printed by Amasa Clark, 1930), 31; Hill, *Fighter from Way Back,* 129; Hachaliah Brown to Lemuel Brown, Oct. 31, 1847, Brown Papers.

7. James I. Robertson Jr., *General A. P. Hill: The Story of a Confederate Warrior* (New York: Random House, 1987), 9–15, 318; Hill to brother, Sep. 12, 1847, and Hill to parents, Oct. 23, 1847, Ambrose Powell Hill Papers, VHS.

8. K. Jack Bauer, *The Mexican War, 1846–1848* (1974; Lincoln: University of Nebraska Press, 1992), 330; Justin H. Smith, *The War with Mexico,* 2 vols. (New York: Macmillan, 1919), 2:171–72.

9. Albert Brackett to Charles Brackett, Oct. 29, 1847, Albert G. Brackett Papers, DRTL; Jeremiah Mewhinney to Johnson Mewhinney, Oct. 29, 1847, Mewhinney Family Papers, DRTL; A. P. Hill to parents, Oct. 23, 1847, Hill Papers.

10. Hill to parents, Oct. 23, 1847, Hill Papers, VHS.

11. Richard Bruce Winders, "Puebla's Forgotten Heroes," *Military History of the West* 23 (1993): 8; Theodore to father, Oct. 16, 1847, in Theodore Laidley, *Surrounded by Dangers of All Kinds: The Mexican War Letters of Lieutenant Theodore Laidley,* ed. James M. McCaffrey (Denton: University of North Texas Press, 1997), 107.

12. Childs to Scott, Oct. 13, 1847, LR SW, RG 107, NA; Bauer, *Mexican War,* 328–29; Smith, *War,* 2:171–72, 174.

13. Winders, "Puebla's Forgotten Heroes," 10–14; Madison Mills Diary, FHS; John Dodd to Eliza (wife), Jan. 10, 1848, John Dodd Papers, BLY; Laidley, *Surrounded by Dangers,* 107–15; J. Jacob Oswandel, *Notes of the Mexican War, 1846–47–48* (Philadelphia: J. Jacob Oswandel, 1885), 288–89.

14. Bauer, *Mexican War,* 331; Albert Brackett to Charles Brackett, Oct. 29, 1847, Brackett Papers; A. P. Hill to parents, Oct. 23, 1847, Hill Papers; Jeremiah Mewhinney to Johnson Mewhinney (father), Oct. 29, 1847, Mewhinney Papers; Oswandel, *Notes,* 345.

15. Brackett to Brackett, Oct. 29, 1847, Brackett Papers; A. P. Hill to friends, Nov. 8, 1847, Hill Papers; Mills Diary, FHS.

16. Hill to parents, Oct. 23, 1847, and Hill to friends, Nov. 8, 1847, Hill Papers.

17. Winders, "Puebla's Forgotten Heroes," 23; Oswandel, *Notes,* 359–60.

18. H. Clay to Mr. Levesh, Nov. 26, 1847, Mexican War Collection, UTA; Irvin W. Levinson, *Wars within War: Mexican Guerrillas, Domestic Elites, and the United States of America, 1846–1848* (Forth Worth: Texas Christian University Press, 2005), 61; Will Lytle to unknown, Jan. 15, 1848, in William Haines Lytle, *For Honor, Glory and Union: The Mexican and Civil War Letters of Brig. Gen. William Haines Lytle,* ed. Ruth C. Carter (Lexington: University Press of Kentucky, 1999), 52; Clark to John, Jan. 19, 1848, N. H. Clark Papers, Western Historical Manuscript Collection, University of Missouri.

19. Winfield Scott, *Memoirs of Lieut.-General Scott,* 2 vols. (1864; Freeport, N.Y.: Books for Libraries Press, 1970), 2:574–75; Bauer, *Mexican War,* 332; Meginness Journal, John Franklin Meginess Papers, UTA.

20. Charles Judah and George Winston Smith, *Chronicles of the Gringoes: The U.S. Army in the Mexican War, 1846–1848, Accounts of Eyewitnesses and Combatants* (Albuquerque: University of New Mexico Press, 1968), 232.

21. Levinson, *Wars within War,* 61.

22. Otis A. Singletary, *The Mexican War* (Chicago: University of Chicago Press, 1960), 100; Hill, *Fighter from Way Back*, 139; Meginess Journal, Meginess Papers; H. Clay to Mr. Levesh, Nov. 26, 1847, Mexican War Collection, UTA.

23. Marcy to Scott, May 8, 1847, United States War Department Letters, BLY; Nancy Nichols Barker, *The French Experience in Mexico, 1821–1861: A History of Constant Misunderstanding* (Chapel Hill: University of North Carolina Press, 1979), 151–55, 162, 178; Alfred Jackson Hanna and Kathryn Abbey Hanna, *Napoleon III and Mexico: American Triumph over Monarchy* (Chapel Hill: University of North Carolina Press, 1971), 11–12, 16–17; Michele Cunningham, *Mexico and the Foreign Policy of Napoleon III* (New York: Palgrave Macmillan, 2001), 28.

24. Hill, *Fighter from Way Back*, 131; Peskin, *Volunteers*, 192, 196–97; Henry Heth, *The Memoirs of Henry Heth*, ed. James L. Morrison (Westport, Conn.: Greenwood Press, 1974), 52; Hill to father, Feb. 29, 1848, Hill Papers.

25. Hill, *Fighter from Way Back*, 131–32, 163; Uncapher Mexican War Diary, UTA; Edward H. Moseley, "The Religious Impact of the American Occupation of Mexico City, 1847–1848," in *Militarists, Merchants, and Missionaries: United States Expansion in Middle America*, ed. Eugene R. Huck and Edward H. Moseley (Tuscaloosa: University of Alabama Press, 1970), 41–43; Carl M. Becker, "John William Lowe: Failure in Inner-Direction," *Ohio History* 73 (spring 1964): 80; Sargent, *Gathering Laurels*, 21; Thomas G. Drips to cousin, Jan. 31, 1848, Mexican War Collection, UTA.

26. Sedgwick to sister, Oct. 26, 1847, in Sedgwick, *Correspondence*, 1:136. Sedgwick's reference to "go ahead people" is probably derived from Davy Crockett's famous motto, which became the topic of poems and songs in the early nineteenth century: "Be sure you are right, then go ahead!" See Michael A. Lofaro and Joe Cummings, eds., *Crockett at Two Hundred: New Perspectives on the Man and the Myth* (Knoxville: University of Tennessee Press, 1989), 86–88.

27. Moseley, "Religious Impact," 42; Walter H. Hebert, *Fighting Joe Hooker* (New York: Bobbs-Merrill, 1944), 34; Robert Anderson to sister, Feb. 13, 1848, Mexican War Collection, UTA; Heth, *Memoirs*, 57–58.

28. David M. Jordon, *Winfield Scott Hancock: A Soldier's Life* (1988; Bloomington: Indiana University Press, 1996), 17; Heth, *Memoirs*, 59–60.

29. Scott to Marcy, Sep. 18, 1847, RG 94, LR, AGO, NA; Quitman to George T. M. Davis, Apr. 18, 1856, Quitman Letter, BLY.

30. Bradford to Tazewell, Jan. 2, 1848, Edmund Bradford Papers, BLY; P. G. T. Beauregard, *With Beauregard in Mexico: The Mexican War Reminiscences of P. G. T. Beauregard*, ed. T. Harry Williams (New York: DaCapo Press, 1969), 69–71, 73; Peskin, *Volunteers*, 169–71.

31. Hill, *Fighter from Way Back*, 35, 151; Laidley, *Surrounded by Dangers*, 120; Lee to Mackay, Oct. 2, 1847, Robert E. Lee Letter, Folios 137–38, VHS.

32. Scott to Pillow, Oct. 2, 1847, House Exec. Doc. No. 60, 30th Cong., 1st Exec.

33. Pillow to Scott, Oct. 3, 1847, House Exec. Doc. No. 60, 30th Cong., 1st Exec.

34. Pillow to Scott, Oct. 3, 1847, Scott to Pillow, Oct. 4, 1847, House Exec. Doc. No. 60, 30th Cong., 1st Exec.

35. Nathaniel Cheairs Hughes Jr. and Roy P. Stonesifer, *The Life and Wars of Gideon J. Pillow* (Chapel Hill: University of North Carolina Press, 1993), 104, 106; Davis, *Autobiography*, 263–65.

36. Hughes and Stonesifer, *Pillow*, 109–11.

37. "The Letter of 'Leonidas,'" *New Orleans Picayune*, Sep. 17, 1847. This was the second time the letter was published in a New Orleans paper. The previous week, it appeared in the *New Orleans Delta*. This latter version contained a paragraph not included in the first rendition, which portrayed Pillow as challenging a Mexican officer to one-on-one combat while the battle swirled about them, with the nimble, more skillful Pillow defeating and killing the larger, more muscular Mexican.

38. Hitchcock to Pillow, Nov. 24, 1847, Ethan Allen Hitchcock Papers, LC; William Gardner to sister, Nov. 22, 1847, William Montgomery Gardner Papers, SHC, UNC; A. P. Hill to brother, Sep. 12, 1847, Hill Papers.

39. Hughes and Stonesifer, *Pillow*, 109–10; Raphael Semmes, *Service Afloat and Ashore during the Mexican War* (Cincinnati: Wm. H. Moore, 1851), 358; Charles Winslow Elliott, *Winfield Scott: The Soldier and the Man* (New York: Macmillan, 1937), 568; Winslow Sanderson to Martha, Nov. 25, 1847, Winslow Fuller Sanderson Papers, BLY.

40. General Orders No. 349, Senate Doc. No. 65, 30th Cong., 1st Exec.; Worth to Marcy, Nov. 16, 1847, quoted in Elliott, *Winfield Scott*, 571–73; Scott to Duncan, Nov. 18, 1847, James Duncan Papers, USMA.

41. James K. Polk, *The Diary of James K. Polk*, ed. Milo Milton Quaife, 4 vols. (Chicago: A. C. McClurg, 1910), 3:245–46, 251–52, 266.

42. Polk, *Diary*, 3:267–96; Hill, *Fighter from Way Back*, 145; Mason to Duncan, Mar. 24, 1848, Duncan Papers, USMA.

43. Marcy to Scott, Jan. 13, 1848, United States War Department Letters, BLY; Scott to Marcy, Feb. 9, 1848, in Scott, *Memoirs*, 2:572–73.

44. Pillow to Mary, Nov. 25, 1847, quoted in Hughes and Stonesifer, *Pillow*, 113.

45. "Scott's Address to the Court," Mar. 16, 1848, Senate Doc. No. 65, 30th Cong., 1st Exec.

46. Ethan Allen Hitchcock, *Fifty Years in Camp and Field: The Diary of Major General Ethan Allen Hitchcock*, ed. W. A. Croffut (New York: G. P. Putnam's, 1909), 321; Lee to George Custis, Apr. 8, 1848, and Lee to Mary, Mar. 15, 1848, Lee Family Papers, VHS; Laidley to father, Feb. 11, 1848, in Laidley, *Surrounded by Dangers*, 145; Hill, *Fighter from Way Back*, 151, 171; Romeyn B. Ayres, Mexican War Diary, SHC, UNC; Drips to cousin, Feb. 26, 1848, Mexican War Collection, UTA.

47. Elliott, *Scott*, 585; Laidley to father, May 13, 1848, Laidley, *Surrounded by Dangers*, 159–60.

48. Pillow to Duncan, Jun. 28, 1848, Duncan Papers, USMA; Elliott, *Winfield Scott*, 589; Bauer, *Mexican War*, 373–74. Bauer aptly summarized Scott's treatment on 374: "Despite being the transcendent military figure of the war, his facility for the

inept phrase had provided the opportunity for lesser men to reduce him, temporarily, to their stature."

Epilogue

1. James K. Polk, *The Diary of James K. Polk,* ed. Milo Milton Quaife, 4 vols. (Chicago: A. C. McClurg, 1910), 3:196, 199; K. Jack Bauer, *The Mexican War, 1846–1848* (1974; Lincoln: University of Nebraska Press, 1992), 382.

2. Robert W. Drexler, *Guilty of Making Peace: A Biography of Nicholas P. Trist* (University Press of America, 1991), 115; Wallace Ohrt, *Defiant Peacemaker: Nicholas Trist in the Mexican War* (College Station: Texas A&M University Press, 1997), 137–40; Dean B. Mahin, *Olive Branch and Sword: The United States and Mexico, 1845–1848* (Jefferson, N.C.: McFarland, 1997), 141; Polk, *Diary,* 3:300.

3. Trist quote in Drexler, *Guilty of Making Peace,* 106; Robert Anderson to sister, Feb. 13, 1848, Mexican War Collection, UTA; ? Cantey to John Cantey (cousin), Mar. 6, 1848, John Cantey Papers, Perkins Library, Duke University, Durham, N.C.

4. Bauer, *Mexican War,* 382; Mahin, *Olive Branch,* 186.

5. Williams quoted in Charles Judah and George Winston Smith, *Chronicles of the Gringoes: The U.S. Army in the Mexican War, 1846–1848, Accounts of Eyewitnesses and Combatants* (Albuquerque: University of New Mexico Press, 1968), 418; Gardner to brother, Oct. 24, 1847, William Montgomery Gardner Papers, SHC, UNC; Dabney Herdon Maury, *Recollections of a Virginian in the Mexican, Indian, and Civil Wars* (New York: Charles Scribner's Sons, 1894), 30; James Longstreet, *From Manassas to Appomattox: Memoirs of the Civil War in America,* ed. James I. Robertson (Bloomington: Indiana University Press, 1960), 36–37, 156.

6. Ralph Henry Gabriel. "Notes on Military Government," Box 16, Ralph Henry Gabriel Papers, Stirling Library, Yale University; Winfield Scott, *Memoirs of Lieut.-General Scott,* 2 vols. (1864; Freeport, N.Y.: Books for Libraries Press, 1970), 2:395; General Henry B. Carrington, "Winfield Scott's Visit to Columbus," *Ohio Archaeological and Historical Quarterly* 19 (Jul. 1910): 282; Longstreet, *From Manassas to Appomattox,* 156.

7. Carl von Clausewitz, *On War,* trans. and ed. Michael Howard and Peter Paret (Princeton. N.J.: Princeton University Press, 1976), 75.

8. Daniel Harvey Hill, *A Fighter from Way Back: The Mexican War Diary of Lt. Daniel Harvey Hill, 4th Artillery, USA,* ed. Nathaniel Cheairs Hughes Jr. and Timothy D. Johnson (Kent, Ohio: Kent State University Press, 2002), 147.

9. James I. Robertson Jr., *Stonewall Jackson: The Man, the Soldier, the Legend* (New York: Macmillan, 1997), 69.

Bibliography

Manuscript Collections

Beinecke Library, Yale University, New Haven, Conn.

Allmand Family Letters
William F. Adee Papers
Thomas L. Alexander Diary
Moses Barnard Reminiscences
Beauregard's Reconnaissance Report
Edmund Bradford Papers
Lemuel C. Brown Papers
"Campaigns in Mexico" (author unknown)
William P. Chambliss Papers
John Dodd Papers
William Fraser Diary
John Lane Gardner Letter
J. W. Geary Papers
William Higgins Papers
Jacob Hoffer Letter
John W. James Collection of Mexican War Articles
Philip Kearny Letter
Lothrop Family Papers
Albert C. Nicholson Papers
Roswell Ripley Papers
Winslow Fuller Sanderson Papers
Edmund Kirby Smith Papers
Joseph Rowe Smith Papers
Thompson Narrative
United States War Department Letters
Barna N. Upton Papers
William Walker Letter
John Darragh Wilkins
Henry Wilson Papers

Daughters of the Republic of Texas Library, San Antonio

Albert G. Brackett Papers
Mewhinney Family Papers
Hiram B. Yeager Papers

345

Duke University, Perkins Library, Durham, N.C.

Campbell Family Papers
John Cantey Papers
William Henry Grimes Papers
Benjamin T. Towner Papers
William Henry Talbot Walker Papers

Filson Historical Society. Louisville, Ky.

Berry Family Papers
Blackburn Family Papers
Simon Bolivar Buckner Papers
Lillard Family Papers
Madison Mills Diary
Pope-Humphrey Family Papers
Hiram Wingate Papers

Historical Society of Pennsylvania, Philadelphia

Dreer Collection

Library of Congress, Washington, D.C.

Robert Anderson Papers
David Conner Papers
Ethan Allen Hitchcock Papers
William L. Marcy Papers

New York Public Library

Charles Winslow Elliott Collection

Stirling Library, Yale University, New Haven, Conn.

Ralph Henry Gabriel Papers

Swem Library, College of William and Mary, Williamsburg, Va.

Patrick Galt Papers

Tennessee State Library and Archives, Nashville

Benjamin F. Cheatham Papers
Lauderdale Family Papers
Wiley Pope Hale Papers
Jonathan Wade H. Tipton Journal
Wynne Family Papers

U.S. Military Academy Library, West Point, N.Y.

James Duncan Papers
Ethan Allen Hitchcock Papers

University of Missouri, Library, Columbia

N. H. Clark Papers

University of North Carolina, Library, Southern Historical Collection, Chapel Hill

William Austine Papers
Romeyn B. Ayres Mexican War Diary
Thomas Claiborne Papers
William Montgomery Gardner Papers
John Kimberly Papers

University of Texas at Arlington, Library, Arlington

Kendall Family Papers
Thomas Lindsay Diary
John Franklin Meginess Papers
Mexican War Collection
William Pierce Diary
Israel Uncapher Mexican War Diary

University of Texas, Library, Austin

James Butterfield Reminiscences
Genaro Garcia Papers
J. T. Hughes Letters
Thomas Williams Letters

Virginia Historical Society, Richmond

Richard S. Ewell Papers
Daniel Family Papers
Ambrose Powell Hill Papers
Lee Family Papers
George Bolling Lee Papers
Robert E. Lee letter, Folios 137–138
Page Family Papers
Palmer Family Papers

Government Documents

House Documents. No. 56, 30th Cong., 1st Sess.
House Documents. No. 60, 30th Cong., 1st Sess.
Senate Documents. No. 378, 29th Cong., 1st Sess.
Senate Documents. No. 1, 30th Cong., 1st Sess.
Senate Documents. No. 52, 30th Cong., 1st Sess.
Senate Documents. No. 65, 30th Cong., 1st Sess.
Letters Received by the Office of the Adjutant General, Record Group 94, National
    Archives
Letters Received by the Secretary of War, Record Group 107, National Archives

Newspapers

American Star
New Orleans Picayune
Niles' National Register

Published Works

Primary

Anderson, Robert. *An Artillery Officer in the Mexican War, 1846–7.* New York: G. P. Putnam's Sons, 1911.

Ballentine, George. *Autobiography of an English Soldier in the United States Army.* Edited by William H. Goetzmann. Chicago: Lakeside Press, 1986.

Beauregard, P. G. T. *With Beauregard in Mexico: The Mexican War Reminiscences of P. G. T. Beauregard.* Edited by T. Harry Williams. New York: DaCapo Press, 1969.

Campbell, William Bowen. *Mexican War Letters of Col. William Bowen Campbell of Tennessee, Written to Governor David Campbell of Virginia, 1846–1847.* Edited by St. George L. Sioussat. Reprinted from *Tennessee Historical Magazine,* June 1915.

Chandler, David G. *The Military Maxims of Napoleon.* Translated by Sir George C. D'Aguilar. 1987. Stackpole Books, 1994.

Clark, Amasa Gleason. *Reminiscences of a Centenarian.* Bandera, Tex.: Amasa Gleason Clark, 1930.

Cook, Judge Zo. S. "Mexican War Reminiscences." *Alabama Historical Quarterly* 19 (fall–winter 1957): 435–60.

Cummings, Joe, and Michael A. Lofaro, eds. *Crockett at Two Hundred: New Perspectives on the Man and the Myth.* Knoxville: University of Tennessee Press, 1989.

Dana, Napoleon Jackson Tecumseh. *Monterrey Is Ours! The Mexican War Letters of Lieutenant Dana, 1845–1847.* Edited by Robert H. Ferrell. Lexington: University Press of Kentucky, 1990.

Davis, George Turnbull Moore. *Autobiography of the Late Col. Geo T. M. Davis, Captain and Aid-de-Camp Scott's Army of Invasion.* New York: Jenkins and McCowan, 1891.

Devlin, John S. *The Marine Corps in Mexico: Setting Forth its Conduct as Established by Testimony before a General Court Martial.* Washington: Lemuel Towers, 1852.

Elderkin, James D. *Biographical Sketches and Anecdotes of a Soldier of Three Wars.* Detroit: James D. Elderkin, 1899.

Furber, George C. *The Twelve Months Volunteers; or, Journal of a Private, in the Tennessee Regiment of Cavalry, in the Campaign Mexico, 1846–7.* Cincinnati: J. A. & U. P. James, 1848.

Grant, Ulysses S. *Personal Memoirs of U. S. Grant.* 2 vols. New York: Charles L. Webster, 1885.

Hartman, George W. *A Private's Own Journal: Giving an Account of the Battles in Mexico, under Gen'l Scott.* Greencastle: E. Robinson, 1849.

Heth, Henry. *The Memoirs of Henry Heth.* Edited by James L. Morrison. Westport, Conn.: Greenwood Press, 1974.

Hill, Daniel Harvey. *A Fighter from Way Back: The Mexican War Diary of Lt. Daniel Harvey Hill, 4th Artillery, USA.* Edited by Nathaniel Cheairs Hughes Jr. and Timothy D. Johnson. Kent, Ohio: Kent State University Press, 2002.

Hitchcock, Ethan Allen. *Fifty Years in Camp and Field: The Diary of Major General Ethan Allen Hitchcock.* Edited by W. A. Croffut. New York: G. P. Putnam's, 1909.

Jomini, Baron Antoine Henry. *The Art of War.* Translated by G. H. Mendell and W. P. Craighill. Philadelphia: J. B. Lippincott, 1862.

Judah, Charles, and George Winston Smith. *Chronicles of the Gringoes: The U.S. Army in the Mexican War, 1846–1848, Accounts of Eyewitnesses and Combatants.* Albuquerque: University of New Mexico Press, 1968.

Kendall, George Wilkins. *Dispatches from the Mexican War.* Edited by Lawrence Delbert Cress. Norman: University of Oklahoma Press, 1999.

———. *The War between the United States and Mexico.* New York: D. Appleton, 1851.

Keyes, Erasmus D. *Fifty Years' Observation of Men and Events Civil and Military.* New York: Charles Scribner's Sons, 1884.

Kirkham, Ralph W. *The Mexican War Journal and Letters of Ralph W. Kirkham.* Edited by Robert Ryal Miller. College Station: Texas A&M University Press, 1991.

Laidley, Theodore. *Surrounded by Dangers of All Kinds: The Mexican War Letters of Lieutenant Theodore Laidley.* Edited by James M. McCaffrey. Denton: University of North Texas Press, 1997.

Lane, Henry S. "The Mexican War Journal of Henry S. Lane." Edited by Graham A. Barringer. *Indiana Magazine of History* 53 (Dec. 1957): 383–434.

Law, Robert A. "A Letter from Vera Cruz in 1847." *Southwestern Historical Quarterly* 18 (Oct. 1914): 215–18.

Lee, Robert E. *Memoirs of Robert E. Lee, His Military and Personal History.* Edited by A. L. Long. Secaucus, N.J.: Blue and Grey Press, 1983.

Linder, Jamie S., and William B. Eigelsbach, eds. "To War with Mexico: A Diary of the Mexican-American War." *Journal of East Tennessee History* 73 (2001): 74–100.

Longstreet, James. *From Manassas to Appomattox: Memoirs of the Civil War in America.* Edited by James I. Robertson. Bloomington: Indiana University Press, 1960.

Lytle, William Haines. *For Honor, Glory and Union: The Mexican and Civil War Letters of Brig. Gen. William Haines Lytle.* Edited by Ruth C. Carter. Lexington: University Press of Kentucky, 1999.

Maury, Dabney Herdon. *Recollections of a Virginian in the Mexican, Indian, and Civil Wars.* New York: Charles Scribner's Sons, 1894.

May, George S., ed. "An Iowan in the Mexican War." *Iowa Journal of History* 53 (Apr. 1955): 167–74.

Meade, George. *The Life and Letters of George Gordon Meade.* 2 vols. New York: Charles Scribner's Sons, 1913.

Moore, H. Judge. *Scott's Campaign from the Rendezvous on the Island of Lobos to the Taking of the City.* Charleston: J. B. Nixon, 1849.

Moore, John Hammond, ed. "Private Johnson Fights the Mexicans, 1847–1848." *South Carolina Historical Magazine* 67 (Oct. 1966): 203–28.

Myers, William Stan, ed. *The Mexican War Diary of General George B. McClellan.* New York: DaCapo Press, 1972.

Oswandel, J. Jacob. *Notes of the Mexican War, 1846–47–48.* Philadelphia: J. Jacob Oswandel, 1885.

Peskin, Allan, ed. *Volunteers: The Mexican War Journals of Private Richard Coulter and Sergeant Thomas Barclay, Company E, Second Pennsylvania Infantry.* Kent: Kent State University Press, 1991.

Polk, James K. *The Diary of James K. Polk.* Edited by Milo Milton Quaife. 4 vols. Chicago: A. C. McClurg, 1910.

Robinson, Cecil, ed. and trans. *The View from Chapultepec: Mexican Writers on the Mexican-American War.* Tucson: University of Arizona Press, 1989.

Santa Anna, Antonio López. *The Eagle: The Autobiography of Santa Anna.* Edited by Ann Fears Crawford. Austin, Tex.: Pemberton Press, 1967.

Sargent, Chauncey Forward. *Gathering Laurels in Mexico: The Diary of an American Soldier in the Mexican American War.* Edited by Ann Brown Janes. Lincoln, Mass.: Cottage Press, 1990.

Scott, Winfield. *Memoirs of Lieut.-General Scott.* 2 vols. 1864. Freeport, N.Y.: Books for Libraries Press, 1970.

Seaman, Henry J. *Speech of Mr. Henry I. Seaman of N.Y. on the Mexican War.* Washington, D.C.: J. & G. S. Gideon, Printers, 1847.

Sedgwick, John. *Correspondence of John Sedgwick, Major-General.* Compiled by Henry D. Sedgwick. 2 vols. DeVinne Press, 1902.

Semmes, Raphael. *Service Afloat and Ashore during the Mexican War.* Cincinnati: Wm. H. Moore, 1851.

"The Siege of Vera Cruz." *Southern Quarterly Review* (Jul. 1851).

Smith, E. Kirby. *To Mexico with Scott: Letters of Captain E. Kirby Smith to His Wife.* Edited by Emma Jerome Blackwood. Cambridge, Mass.: Harvard University Press, 1917.

Smith, Gustavus Woodson. *Company "A" Corps of Engineers, USA, 1846–1848, in the Mexican War.* Edited by Leonne M. Hudson. Kent, Ohio: Kent State University Press, 2001.

Stevens, Isaac I. *Campaigns of the Rio Grande and of Mexico.* New York: D. Appleton, 1851.

Tennery, Thomas D. *The Mexican War Diary of Thomas D. Tennery.* Edited by D. E. Livingston-Little. Norman: University of Oklahoma Press, 1970.

Vindication of the Military Character and Services of General Franklin Pierce. Circular pamphlet reprinted from various newspapers, 1852. Copy in Beinecke Library, Yale University.

Zeh, Frederick. *An Immigrant Soldier in the Mexican War.* Translated by William Orr and Robert Ryal Miller. College Station: Texas A&M University Press, 1995.

Secondary

Adams, George Rollie. *General William S. Harney: Prince of Dragoons.* Lincoln: University of Nebraska Press, 2001.

Alexander, Bevin. *How Great Generals Win.* New York: W. W. Norton, 1993.

Anderson, Nancy Scott, and Dwight Anderson. *The Generals: Ulysses S. Grant and Robert E. Lee.* New York: Alfred A. Knopf, 1988.

Arnold, Thomas Jackson. *Early Life and Letters of General Thomas J. "Stonewall" Jackson.* New York: Fleming H. Revell, 1916.

Babcock, James F. *Fate of Major Frederick D. Mills Late of the Fifteenth Regiment, U. S. Army.* Pamphlet, ca. 1848. Copy in Beinecke Library, Yale University.

Barcena, José María Roa. *Recuerdos de la Invasion Norteamericana: 1846–1848.* Mexico City: Editorial Porrúa, 1993.

Barker, Nancy Nichols. *The French Experience in Mexico, 1821–1861: A History of Constant Misunderstanding.* Chapel Hill: University of North Carolina Press, 1979.

Bauer, K. Jack. *The Mexican War, 1846–1848.* 1974. Lincoln: University of Nebraska Press, 1992.

———. *Surfboats and Horse Marines: U.S. Naval Operations in the Mexican War, 1846–48.* Annapolis: United States Naval Institute, 1969.

———. *Zachary Taylor: Soldier, Planter, Statesman of the Old Southwest.* Baton Rouge: Louisiana State University Press, 1985.

Becker, Carl M. "John William Lowe: Failure in Inner-Direction." *Ohio History* 73 (spring 1964): 75–89.

Bill, Alfred Hoyt. *Rehearsal for Conflict: The War with Mexico, 1846–1848.* New York: Alfred A. Knopf, 1947. Reprint ed., New York: Cooper Square Publishers, 1969.

Callcott, Wilfrid Hardy. *Church and State in Mexico, 1822–1857.* Durham, N.C.: Duke University Press, 1926.

Carrington, Henry B. "Winfield Scott's Visit to Columbus." *Ohio Archaeological and Historical Quarterly* 19 (Jul. 1910): 279–92.

Cartwright, Frederick. *Disease and History.* New York: Dorset Press, 1972.

Caruso, A. Brooke. *The Mexican Spy Company: United States Covert Operations in Mexico, 1845–1848.* Jefferson, N.C.: McFarland, 1991.

Casdorph, Paul D. *Prince John Magruder: His Life and Campaigns.* New York: John Wiley, 1996.

Castañeda, Carlos E. "Relations of General Scott with Santa Anna." *The Hispanic American Historical Review* 29 (Nov. 1949): 455–73.

Castillo, Richard Griswold del. *The Treaty of Guadalupe Hidalgo: A Legacy of Conflict.* Norman: University of Oklahoma Press, 1990.

Ciruzzi, Canice. "Phoenix Revisited: Another Look at George Horatio Derby." *Journal of San Diego History* 26 (spring 1980): 77–89.

Clausewitz, Carl von. *On War.* Translated and edited by Michael Howard and Peter Paret. Princeton, N.J.: Princeton University Press, 1976.

Conner, Philip Syng Physick. *The Home Squadron under Commodore Connor in the War with Mexico.* Philadelphia: Philip Syng Physick Conner, 1896.

Crawford, Mark, ed. *Encyclopedia of the Mexican-American War.* Santa Barbara, Calif.: ABC-CLIO Publishers, 1999.

Cunningham, Michele. *Mexico and the Foreign Policy of Napoleon III.* New York: Palgrave Macmillan, 2001.

Davies, Thomas M., Jr., "Assessments during the Mexican War: An Exercise in Futility." *New Mexico Historical Review* 41 (Jul. 1966): 197–216.

DePalo, William A., Jr. *The Mexican National Army, 1822–1852.* College Station: Texas A&M University Press, 1997.

Departamento De Distrito Federal. *Batalla de Churubusco el 20 de Agosto de 1847.* Colección: Conciencia Civica Nacional, Mexico, 1983.

Drexler, Robert W. *Guilty of Making Peace: A Biography of Nicholas P. Trist.* University Press of America, 1991.

Eisenhower, John S. D. *So Far from God: The U.S. War with Mexico, 1846–1848.* 1989. New York: Bantam Doubleday Dell, 1990.

Elliott, Charles Winslow. *Winfield Scott: The Soldier and the Man.* New York: Macmillan, 1937.

Ellis, B. G. *The Moving Appeal: Mr. McClanahan, Mrs. Dill, and the Civil War's Great Newspaper Run.* Macon, Ga.: Mercer University Press, 2003.

Foos, Paul. *A Short, Offhand, Killing Affair: Soldiers and Social Conflict during the Mexican-American War.* Chapel Hill: University of North Carolina Press, 2002.

Frazier, Donald S., ed. *The United States and Mexico at War.* New York: Macmillan, 1998.

Freeman, Douglas Southall. *R. E. Lee: A Biography.* 4 vols. 1934. New York: Charles Scribner's Sons, 1962.

Frost, J. *The Mexican War and Its Warriors.* New Haven, Conn.: H. Mansfield, 1850.

Gallagher, Gary. "We Are Our Own Trumpeters: Robert E. Lee Describes Winfield Scott's Campaign to Mexico City." *Virginia Magazine of History and Biography* 95 (Jul. 1987): 363–75.

Geary, Paul M. *Colonel John W. Geary in the Mexican War and California in '49.* Pacifica, Calif.: Shade Tree Press, 2000.

Hamilton, Holman. *Zachary Taylor: Soldier of the Republic.* Hamden, Conn.: Archon Books, 1966.

Hanna, Alfred Jackson, and Kathryn Abbey Hanna. *Napoleon III and Mexico: American Triumph over Monarchy.* Chapel Hill: University of North Carolina Press, 1971.

Hartje, Robert G. *Van Dorn: The Life and Times of a Confederate General.* Nashville: Vanderbilt University Press, 1967.

Haynes, Martin A. *Gen. Scott's Guide in Mexico: A Biographical Sketch of Col. Noah E. Smith.* Lake Village, N.H.: Reprinted from the *Lake Village Times,* 1887.

Haynes, Sam W. *James K. Polk and the Expansionist Impulse.* New York: Longman, 1997.

Hebert, Walter H. *Fighting Joe Hooker.* New York: Bobbs-Merrill, 1944.

Heitman, Francis B. *Historical Register and Dictionary of the United States Army.* 2 vols. 1903; Baltimore: Genealogical Publishing, 1994.

Holt, Michael F. *The Rise and Fall of the American Whig Party: Jacksonian Politics and the Onset of the Civil War.* New York: Oxford University Press, 1999.

Huck, Eugene R., and Edward H. Moseley, eds. *Militarists, Merchants, and Missionaries: United States Expansion in Middle America.* Tuscaloosa: University of Alabama Press, 1970.

Hughes, Nathaniel Cheairs, Jr., and Roy P. Stonesifer. *The Life and Wars of Gideon J. Pillow.* Chapel Hill: University of North Carolina Press, 1993.

Irey, Thomas R. "Soldiering, Suffering, and Dying in the Mexican War." *Journal of the West* 11 (Apr. 1972): 285–98.

Jamieson, Perry D., and Grady McWhiney. *Attack and Die: Civil War Military Tactics and the Southern Heritage.* Tuscaloosa: University of Alabama Press, 1982.

Johannsen, Robert W. *To the Halls of the Montezumas.* 1985. New York: Oxford University Press, 1987.

Johnson, Timothy D. *Winfield Scott: The Quest for Military Glory.* Lawrence: University Press of Kansas, 1998.

Jordon, David M. *Winfield Scott Hancock: A Soldier's Life.* 1988. Bloomington: Indiana University Press, 1996.

Levinson, Irving W. *Wars within War: Mexican Guerrillas, Domestic Elites, and the United States of America, 1846–1848.* Forth Worth: Texas Christian University Press, 2005.

Losson, Christopher T. *Tennessee's Forgotten Warriors: Frank Cheatham and His Confederate Division.* Knoxville: University of Tennessee Press, 1989.

Mahin, Dean B. *Olive Branch and Sword: The United States and Mexico, 1845–1848.* Jefferson, N.C.: McFarland, 1997.

May, Robert E. *John A. Quitman: Old South Crusader.* 1984. Baton Rouge: Louisiana State University Press, 1985.

———. *Manifest Destiny's Underworld: Filibustering in Antebellum America.* Chapel Hill: University of North Carolina Press, 2002.

McCormac, Eugene Irving. *James K. Polk: A Political Biography.* Berkeley: University of California Press, 1922.

Meyer, Jack Allen. *South Carolina in the Mexican War: A History of the Palmetto Regiment of Volunteers, 1846–1917.* Columbia: South Carolina Department of Archives ad History, 1996.

Miller, Robert Ryal. *Shamrock and Sword: The Saint Patrick's Battalion in the U.S.-Mexican War.* Norman: University of Oklahoma Press, 1989.

Navy Department. *Dictionary of American Naval Fighting Ships*. 8 vols. Washington, D.C.: Naval History Center, 1991– .

Noll, Arthur Howard. *General Kirby-Smith*. Sewanee, Tenn.: University Press at the University of the South, 1907.

Ohrt, Wallace. *Defiant Peacemaker: Nicholas Trist in the Mexican War*. College Station: Texas A&M University Press, 1997.

Olejar, Paul D. "Rockets in Early American Wars." *Military Affairs* 10 (winter 1946): 16–34.

Phillips, Christopher. *Damned Yankee: The Life of General Nathaniel Lyon*. Columbia: University of Missouri Press, 1990.

Pletcher, David M. *The Diplomacy of Annexation: Texas, Oregon, and the Mexican War*. Columbia: University of Missouri Press, 1973.

Pohl, James W. "The Influence of Antoine Henri de Jomini on Winfield Scott's Campaign in the Mexican War." *Southwestern Historical Quarterly* 77 (Jul. 1973): 85–110.

Ramsey, Albert C., ed. and trans. *The Other Side; or, Notes for the History of the War between Mexico and the United States*. New York: John Wiley, 1850.

Reilly, Tom. "Jane McManus Storms: Letters from the Mexican War, 1846–1848." *Southwestern Historical Quarterly* 85 (Jul. 1981): 21–44.

Robertson, James I., Jr. *General A. P. Hill: The Story of a Confederate Warrior*. New York: Random House, 1987.

———. *Stonewall Jackson: The Man, the Soldier, the Legend*. New York: Macmillan, 1997.

Santoni, Pedro. *Mexicans at Arms: Puro Federalists and the Politics of War, 1845–1848*. Fort Worth: Texas Christian University Press, 1996.

Scheina, Robert L. *Santa Anna: A Curse upon Mexico*. Washington, D.C.: Brassey's, 2002.

Sears, Stephen W. *George B. McClellan: The Young Napoleon*. New York: Ticknor & Fields, 1988.

Singletary, Otis A. *The Mexican War*. Chicago: University of Chicago Press, 1960.

Smith, Justin H. *The War with Mexico*. 2 vols. New York: Macmillan, 1919.

Spencer, Ivor Debenham. *The Victor and the Spoils: A Life of William L. Marcy*. Providence: Brown University Press, 1959.

Stevens, Hazard. *The Life of Isaac Ingalls Stevens*. 2 vols. New York: Houghton Mifflin, 1900.

Stevens, Peter F. *The Rogue's March: John Riley and the St. Patrick's Battalion, 1846–48*. Washington, D.C.: Brassey's, 1999.

Stewart, George R. *John Phoenix, Esq., the Veritable Squibob: A Life of Captain George H. Derby, USA*. New York: Henry Holt, 1937.

Symonds, Craig L. *Joseph E. Johnston: A Civil War Biography*. New York: W. W. Norton, 1992.

Tenenbaum, Barbara A., ed. *Encyclopedia of Latin-American History and Culture*. 5 vols. New York: Charles Scribner's Sons, 1996.

Thomas, Emory M. *Robert E. Lee: A Biography*. New York: W. W. Norton, 1995.

Tuveson, Ernest Lee. *Redeemer Nation: The Idea of America's Millennial Role.* Chicago: University of Chicago Press, 1968.

Valades, Jose C. *Breve Historia de la Guerra con los Estados Unidos.* Editorial Patria. Higinio Arias Urzay. Manuel Gutiérrez Nájera, 1947.

Vandiver, Frank E. *Mighty Stonewall.* New York: McGraw-Hill, 1957.

———. *Ploughshares into Swords: Josiah Gorgas and Confederate Ordnance.* Austin: University of Texas Press, 1952.

Wallace, Edward S. *General William Jenkins Worth: Monterey's Forgotten Hero.* Dallas: Southern Methodist University Press, 1953.

Warner, Ezra J. *Generals in Blue: Lives of the Union Commanders.* Baton Rouge: Louisiana State University Press, 1964.

———. *Generals in Gray: Lives of the Confederate Commanders.* Baton Rouge: Louisiana State University Press, 1959.

Waugh, John C. *The Class of 1846.* New York: Warner Books, 1994.

Weems, John Edwards. *To Conquer a Peace: The War between the United States and Mexico.* College Station: Texas A&M University Press, 1974.

Weigley, Russell. *The American Way of War: A History of United States Military Strategy and Policy.* Bloomington: Indiana University Press, 1977.

Wert, Jeffry D. *General James Longstreet: The Confederacy's Most Controversial Soldier.* New York: Simon & Schuster, 1993.

Whiteside, Henry O. "Winfield Scott and the Mexican Occupation: Policy and Practice." *Mid-America* 52 (1970): 102–18.

Williams, T. Harry. *P. G. T. Beauregard.* Baton Rouge: Louisiana State University Press, 1954.

Winders, Richard Bruce. *Crisis in the Southwest: The United States, Mexico, and the Struggle over Texas.* Wilmington, Del.: Scholarly Resources, 2002.

———. *Mr. Polk's Army: The American Military Experience in the Mexican War.* College Station: Texas A&M University Press, 1997.

———. "Puebla's Forgotten Heroes." *Military History of the West* 23 (1993): 1–23.

Adee, Samuel, 244
Adee, William, 244
Alburtis, William, 27
Aleman, Manuel, 220
Alexander, Bevin, 98
Alvarado, 24, 26, 49, 60, 63
American Revolution, 268
Amozoc, 122–23
Anaya, Pedro María, 105, 266
Anderson, Robert, 22, 33, 36, 57, 97, 110, 111, 121, 126, 154, 159, 206, 255, 267
Andrews, George, 218
Antigua, 60
Antigua River, 66
Anton Lizardo, 20, 21
Arizona, 113
Armistead, Lewis A., 185, 337, 255
armistice, 195, 198–202, 248, 269
Armstrong, William, 208
Arroyo, Miguel, 144
attitudes, 6–7, 8, 246–47, 250, 254
    race, 4, 106, 124–25, 146, 254–55, 267, 321
Aulick, John H., 48
Austine, William, 135–36, 138, 146, 149, 159
Ayotla, 154, 157–58
Ayres, George W., 206
Ayres, Romeyn B., 62, 264

Ballentine, George, 152–53
Bankhead, Charles, 126–27, 145, 148, 194
Bankhead, James, 38–39, 40, 111
Baranda, Manual, 135
Barclay, Thomas, 100, 103, 132, 141, 208, 227
Barnard, Moses, 22, 118, 152–53, 171–72, 178, 201, 207, 223

Bates, A. J., 222
Bauer, K. Jack, 6, 69, 93, 265, 298
Baxter, Charles, 222
Beach, Moses, 61, 120
Beauregard, P. G. T., 25, 32–33, 111, 155–57, 210–13, 256, 270
    and Battle of Cerro Gordo, 70, 73–74, 76–77
    and battles around Mexico City, 160, 162, 167, 175, 177, 201, 216, 230–31, 237, 337–38
Bee, Barnard, 87, 221, 233
Belén Garita, 210, 215, 227–33, 237, 243, 256
Benjamin, Calvin, 218, 232, 243
Benton, Thomas Hart, 15–16, 18, 138
Bill, Alfred Hoyt, 69
Black Pass, 120, 140
Bliss, W. L., 102, 105
Bomfield, James V., 188
Bonneville, Benjamin L., 185
Bradford, Edmund, 131
Bravo, Nicolás, 179–80, 183–84, 191, 214–15, 217, 219, 225, 228
Brazos, 17, 18, 19
bribery scheme, 143–44, 170, 259, 262, 265
Brower, Charles B., 225
Brown, Hachaliah, 238, 240, 242, 245
Brydolf, Fabian, 175
Buchanan, James, 14, 113–15, 126–27, 263
Buckner, Simon Bolivar, 152, 185, 199
Buell, Don Carlos, 187, 270
Buena Vista, Battle of, 26, 35, 39, 45, 52, 61, 66, 103, 130, 175, 177, 246
Burnside, Ambrose, 255
Burwell, William T., 205–206, 208
Butler, William O., 263–64

Cadwalader, George, 138–44, 147, 164, 166–68, 172–73, 182, 184–85, 203, 207, 212, 219–20, 227
California, 113
Callender, Franklin, 163, 165
Campbell, William B., 24, 53, 54, 69, 84, 91–92
Canalizo, Valentín, 67, 72
Cantey, James, 267
Carleton, Guy, 165
Casa Mata, 202–205, 207–208
Casey, Silas, 218, 221
Cathedral de San José, 248
Catholic church, 34, 62, 135, 180, 243
  American attitudes toward, 4, 58–59, 110, 132–33
Cerro Gordo, 1, 2, 7, 45, 68–72, 76, 108, 113, 117, 118, 120, 121, 122, 123, 141, 145, 147, 170, 175, 178, 180, 183, 192, 195, 227–28, 243, 246, 270
  Battle of, 79–103, 110, 129, 136
  Casualties, 96–97, 100
Cerro Gordo Pass, 68, 72, 77, 84, 97
Chalco (lake), 153–57, 200, 260–61, 270
Chalco (town), 154, 156
Chambliss, William, P., 146
Chancellorsville, Battle of, 170
Chapultepec, 2, 197, 201–202, 205, 207, 210, 212–13, 215, 228–29, 232–33, 235, 256–57, 259
  Battle of, 7, 218–27, 242
  casualties, 239
  defenses of, 213–14, 217
Cheatham, Benjamin Franklin, 47
Cherokee removal, 306
Childs, Thomas, 109, 120, 198, 248–50
Chippewa, Battle of, 183
Cholula, 131
Churubusco, 179–81, 195, 197, 199, 208, 213, 225, 228, 243, 260, 270
  casualties at, 191–92
  fighting at, 182–90
Ciudadela, 232–33, 238
Civil War, 4, 5, 25, 51, 60, 81, 99, 168, 175, 185, 191–92, 220, 229, 264, 267–68, 270–71, 318, 328

Claiborne, Thomas, 37, 78, 79, 80, 93
Clark, Amasa, 318
Clark, N. H., 4, 7, 8
Clarke, Newman, S., 29, 183–85, 188, 191, 203, 222–23, 225
Clausewitz, Carl von, 3, 270
Collado Beach, 2, 10, 20, 25, 29, 44, 64
Colorado, 113
Congreve, William, 43
Conner, David, 10, 20, 37, 60
Contreras, 160–62, 176, 178, 185
Cordilleras Pass, 151
Cortez, Hernando, 64, 150, 152–53
Coulter, Richard, 36, 100, 108, 208, 224, 256
Coyoacán, 167, 179–80, 182, 186
Crockett, Davy, 342
Cuyler, John, 81

Dana, Napoleon, 93
Daniels, Joseph, 107
Davis, George T., 56, 64, 95, 149, 196, 199, 228, 233, 235, 237, 243
Dawson, Joseph G., 6
Democratic Party, 12, 15–16, 19, 53, 129
DePalo, William A., 6
Derby, George H., 76, 80, 94, 99–100
Devlin, John S., 254, 337
Dimick, Justin, 172–73
disease, 60, 107–108, 112, 122, 136, 137–38, 244–45
  yellow fever, 15, 20, 45, 61, 62, 68, 97, 106, 108, 112, 137
Dodd, John, 110, 146
Dominguez, Manuel, 130, 147, 153, 252
Dorich, Nicholas, 65, 310
Drum, Simon H., 203, 206, 215, 218, 230–32, 243
Duke of Wellington, 140
Dulany, William, 337
Duncan, James, 157, 185, 188, 203, 207, 230, 257, 261–63, 265, 329

Eisenhower, John S. D., 6
Elderkin, James, 220
El Encero, 66, 68, 96, 97

El Pe–on, 154–58, 229

El Telégrafo, 1, 70, 72, 73–74, 77, 80–83, 85–86, 88, 92–94, 97, 100, 102, 111, 311, 314

Ernst, Rudolph, 244

Eurick, William, 2

Ewell, Richard, 37, 85, 95, 100, 160, 190–91

Ewell, Thomas, 37, 85, 86, 93–95, 100

Fair Oaks, Battle of, 318

Farías, Valentín Gómez, 34

First Bull Run, Battle of, 44, 74, 87, 175

Fitzgerald, James, 124

Fogg, William, 243

Foos, Paul, 6

Fort Concepción, 11

Fort Guadalupe, 123, 248

Fort Loreto, 123, 248

Fort Santa Barbara, 11, 42

Fort Santiago, 11

Foster, John, 204

Franklin, battle of, 47

Fraser, William, 110

Frazier, Donald S., xi, 6

Freeman, Douglas Southall, 238

Frost, Daniel, 54

Furber, George, 132

Galt, Patrick, 139

Garcia, Manuel, 65

Gardner, John L., 64, 79, 172, 174–75

Gardner, William, M., 4, 268

Garland, John, 29, 183–85, 203, 206, 225, 234, 239

Geary, John W., 222, 256

Gettysburg, 185

Gordon, George H., 220

Graham, William, 205

Grant, Ulysses, S., 21, 51, 78, 125, 192, 206–208, 229, 234–36, 254, 270–71, 306

Guadalupe Hidalgo, 237
Treaty of, 266–68

guerrillas, 7, 16, 57, 105, 116–18, 120, 131, 134, 138–42, 145, 147–48, 246–48, 251–53, 269

Hagner, Peter V., 83, 215

Hale, William, 43

Hancock, Winfield Scott, 185, 255

Hardee, William, 47, 197

Harney, William S., 18–19, 49, 60, 68, 125–26, 142, 154, 225–26, 238, 338
and Battle of Cerro Gordo, 78, 79–81, 84–87, 92, 95

Harrison, William, 309

Hartman, George, 221, 302

Haskell, William T., 89–91, 314

Haynes, Sam W., 299

Hays, Jack, 252

Henry, Robert Selph, 5

Herrera, Miguel, 48

Heth, Henry, 254–55

Higgins, William, 36

Hill, Ambrose Powell, 21, 67, 245–47, 249–50, 254, 260

Hill, Daniel Harvey, 21, 22, 27, 29, 32–33, 36, 37, 40, 44, 54, 55, 109, 131, 134, 193, 196, 211, 215, 217, 221, 224, 232–33, 238, 240, 242, 244–45, 253–54, 256–57, 262, 264
and fighting at Padierna, 165, 172, 174, 178

Hitchcock, Ethan Allen, 21, 25, 47, 53, 128–29, 143, 148, 196, 208, 212, 217, 228

Hoffer, Jacob, 102

Hooker, Joseph, 139, 149, 220, 255

Howe, William, 268

Huamantla, 249

Huger, Benjamin, 203–204, 215, 237

Hughes, Nathaniel Cheairs, 93

Hunt, Henry J., 218

Hunter, Charles G., 60

Ibarra, Domingo, 127, 142

Isthmus of Tehuantepec, 113, 253

Jackson, Thomas J., 44, 53, 54, 87, 120, 141, 165, 170, 177–78, 218, 220–21, 233–34, 312

Jalapa, 29, 64, 66, 72, 82, 92–93, 96, 98–100, 102, 104, 121, 122, 124, 126,

Jalapa, *continued*
    127, 133, 135, 137, 139–42, 147, 195,
    246–47, 250–51
  occupation of, 105–120, 139–40
Jarauta, Caledonio Domeco, 140–41, 246
Johannsen, Robert W., 6
Johnson, William, 37, 53, 60, 122, 124,
    168
Johnston, Joseph E., 58–59, 69, 99, 107,
    165, 175, 218–19, 222, 243, 318
Johnston, Preston, 107, 165, 175, 330
Jomini, Henri, 96, 140, 158, 338
Judah, Henry Moses, 131

Kearny, Philip, 70, 125, 160, 181, 190–91
Kendall, George W., 20, 50, 81, 98, 103,
    104, 185, 205, 207, 242
Kinney, Henry L., 64–65
Kirby, Edmund, 228, 231
Kirk, Isaac, 56
Kirkham, Ralph, 106, 118, 124, 131, 134,
    145, 150, 159, 183, 189, 191, 205,
    208–209, 244

La Atalaya, 1, 70, 73, 76, 79–85, 94
La Hoya, 120, 140–41
Laidley, Theodore, 43, 125, 249, 256,
    264–65, 314, 319
Lally, Folliott T., 246, 248–49
Landero, José, 48, 121
Lane, Henry S., 110
Lane, Joseph, 246–47, 249–52
Las Vigas, 120, 140–41
Lauderdale, Samuel, 2, 11, 52, 91
Lauderdale, William, 91
La Viga Garita, 210–11
Lay, George Washington, 56
Lee, Robert E., 23, 25, 27–28, 32, 37, 43,
    49, 51, 54, 58–59, 99, 106, 110, 120,
    125, 147, 149, 168, 186–87, 192, 235,
    240, 243, 257, 264, 270
  and approach to Mexico City, 150, 155,
    157, 160–62, 210–12
  and Battle of Cerro Gordo, 76–79, 82–
    83, 85–88, 97
  and Battle of Chapultepec, 215–19

  and fighting at Padierna, 164–66,
    169–70, 175
Lee, Sidney Smith, 42, 49
Leonidas letter, 260, 262
Levinson, Irving W., 6, 306
Lobos Island, 17, 19
Longstreet, James, 188–89, 223, 243–44,
    268–69
Lopez, Rosalie, 56
Lord Lenox, 199
Loring, William W., 163, 173, 328
Lothrop, Warren, 171, 173–74
Lovell, Mansfield, 237–38
Lowe, John, 254
Lyon, Nathaniel, 185, 188, 196, 201
Lytle, William, 132, 153

Macintosh, Ewen, 142
Magruder, John, 19, 51, 87, 163–65, 170,
    175, 220, 230, 234, 314
Malibran, 24, 26
Mango de Clavo, 64–65, 310
Manigault, Arthur, 54
Marcy, William L., 3, 12–14, 18, 19, 26,
    35–36, 59, 101, 110, 111, 113–14,
    127, 130, 146, 196, 245, 259, 263,
    299
Marquis de Radepont, 253
martial law, 17, 19, 55–57, 109–10, 128,
    242, 269
Mason, James L., 155–56, 159, 161–62,
    204, 262
Mason, Stevens, 39, 99–100
Maury, Dabney, 17, 80–81, 98, 107
Maximilian, 253
McBride, Charles F., 244
McCaffrey, James M., 6
McCarty, John, 185
McClellan, George, 19, 21, 23, 25, 28,
    39, 51, 84–85, 90, 92, 95, 106, 137,
    156, 165, 175, 182, 245, 270
McIntosh, James S., 138, 147, 203,
    205–206, 244
McKenzie, Samuel, 218–19
McMillan, Dr., 95, 315
Meade, George G., 19, 30, 45

Medellin, 37, 46
Meginess, John, 251
Merrill, Moses E., 205
Mexicalzingo, 156–57
Mexican units
  Fourth Regular Infantry, 83, 86
  Morelia Battalion, 221
  San Blas Battalion, 219
  Second Light Infantry, 83
  Sixth Infantry, 86
Mexico City, 4, 5, 7, 11, 15, 16, 18, 29,
    34–35, 45, 51, 61, 72, 73, 104–105,
    119, 120, 123, 126–27, 129–33, 139,
    143–45, 148, 152–53, 164, 190, 195,
    197–99, 201, 226, 237, 248–49, 251,
    253, 257, 260, 265–66, 270
  capture of, 238–40
  occupation of, 242–45
  reconnaissance around, 150, 154–57,
    201, 210
Mier Expedition, 141
Mills, Frederick D., 190
Mills, Madison, 21, 138–39, 198
Mixcoac, 197, 200, 215, 218, 225, 237
Molino del Rey, 7, 202, 210–13, 215–18,
    224, 229, 243–44
  Battle of, 203–208
Monterrey, 14, 24, 26, 45, 47, 48, 86, 91,
    130, 167
Morales, Juan, 22, 38, 47, 121
Mora y Villamil, Ignacio, 194
Mount Orizaba, 11

Napoleon, 17, 66, 77, 96, 98, 208, 238,
    260
Napoleon III, 253
National Bridge, 66–68, 117, 138–39,
    146–47, 246–47, 251, 253
National Palace, 237–38, 244, 263
Naval Battery, 37–38, 41–43, 46, 49
Nevada, 113
New Hampshire, 145
New Mexico, 113
Niles' National Register, 52
Ni–o Perdido Garita, 201, 210–11, 215
Nueces River, 200

O'Conner, Francis, 225–26
Ohrt, Wallace, 114, 142
Ojo de Agua, 147
Orizaba (mountain), 11
Orizaba (town), 122
Oswandel, Jacob, 250

Pacheco, José Ramón, 194
Pacification of civilians, 5, 17, 19, 34, 35,
    55–58, 61–62, 108–109, 116, 118–119,
    121–22, 124, 128, 133–34, 140, 242,
    269
Padierna, 160–70, 178, 183, 189, 191, 257,
    260, 265, 270
  casualties, 176
  dawn attack, 171–75
Paso de Ovejas, 138
Patterson, Robert, 21, 26, 27, 46–47, 49,
    63, 70, 74, 110, 111, 253
Pea Ridge, Battle of, 99
Pedregal, 7, 158, 160–64, 166–70, 173,
    176–77, 179, 183, 186, 191–92, 198,
    257–58
Pemberton, John C., 236
Pe–a y Pe–a, Manuel, 266
Peninsula Campaign, 51, 93, 270
Pérez, Francisco, 180
Perote, 29, 98, 106, 115, 119, 120–21, 124,
    127, 137, 140–42, 147, 251
Perote Castle (prison), 121, 321
Perry, Matthew, 37, 38, 39, 46, 53, 60, 115
Picayune (New Orleans), 81, 98, 205
Pickett, George, 223
Piedad, 210–11, 215–16, 218, 229
Pierce, Franklin, 143, 145, 147, 149, 167,
    169–70, 173–75, 186–89, 212–13, 230,
    232–33
Pillow, Gideon J., 24–27, 29, 41, 48, 53,
    113, 141, 143–44, 147, 149, 154, 157,
    170, 176–77, 182–83, 192, 196, 202,
    211–12, 242, 306
  and Battle of Cerro Gordo, 70, 77, 82,
    84–85, 88–93, 111, 314
  and Battle of Chapultepec, 215–22,
    224–25, 227–28
  and fighting at Churubusco, 184

Pillow, Gideon, J., *continued*
and Leonidas affair, 260
and Padierna approach, 162–69
and relations with Winfield Scott, 24, 54,
170, 179, 197, 257–259, 261–65, 329
Plan del Río, 68, 70, 74–76, 78, 82, 84, 99,
102, 107
Plaza de San José, 2, 249
Pohl, James W., 167, 338
Polk, James K., 12–16, 18, 26, 61, 112–14,
127, 138, 139, 141–43, 146, 170, 195,
199–200, 245, 257, 259, 262–63,
265–68, 299
Polkos Rebellion, 34, 61
Popocatépetl, 151
Porter, David D., 39
Puebla, 29, 114, 119–22, 139, 142, 144, 154,
177, 180, 183, 195, 198, 208, 229, 232,
243, 251, 269
occupation of, 123–50
siege of, 2, 247–50
pulque, 131–32
punishment, 56–57, 109–10, 134–36
Pusey, Edward, 59

Quitman, John A., 59–60, 63, 116, 119–23,
127–28, 135, 143–44, 149, 158, 162,
165–66, 168, 176–77, 197, 199, 212,
239–40, 242–43, 256–57, 259
and Battle of Chapultepec, 215–18,
221–22, 224–25
and Belén Garita, 227–35, 237–38

Rangel, Joaquín, 176, 180, 236
Ransom, Trueman B., 219
Rea, Joaquín, 248–49
Regiments (regulars)
Eighth Infantry, 184, 188, 223
Eleventh Infantry, 172, 205, 218
Fifteenth Infantry, 167, 175, 190,
218–19
Fifth Infantry, 84, 123, 184, 188, 204–205
First Artillery, 44, 79, 87, 171, 245, 329
First Dragoons, 117, 125, 160, 181, 190
Fourteenth Infantry, 172, 218
Fourth Artillery, 22, 27, 33, 85–86, 172,
174–75, 177, 196, 215, 232, 248

Fourth Infantry, 131, 234
Mounted Rifles, 27, 79, 82, 97, 99, 125,
140–41, 148, 163–65, 170, 173, 179,
187, 230–32, 238, 261, 265, 329
Ninth Infantry, 218–19, 232–33
Second Artillery, 23, 37, 85, 123, 140,
170, 184, 208, 243, 248
Second Dragoons, 158, 187, 207
Second Infantry, 4, 31, 86, 172, 188, 196
Seventh Infantry, 27, 79, 82, 86, 172–73
Sixth Infantry, 20, 123, 183–85, 189
Third Artillery, 111, 206
Third Dragoons, 248
Third Infantry, 53, 121, 170, 177, 182,
187, 189, 243, 244, 329
Voltigeurs, 69, 163–64, 171–75, 184,
191, 207, 218–19, 222–23, 236
Regiments (volunteers)
Alabama, 25, 112
First Pennsylvania, 19, 20, 77, 84, 89–
91, 93, 112, 248
First Tennessee, 46–47, 77, 84, 89–91,
93, 112
Fourth Illinois, 85, 88
Georgia, 112
Knoxville Dragoons, 75
Louisiana, 19, 246
Mississippi, 19
New York, 19, 25, 85, 88, 112, 171, 174,
188, 218, 222, 225, 256
Second Pennsylvania, 19, 20, 26, 77, 84,
89–92, 93, 112, 120, 218, 222, 224,
227, 233, 244, 256
Second Tennessee, 77, 84, 89–91, 93,
112, 141
South Carolina, 19, 25, 53, 112, 137,
171, 174, 218, 222, 231–32, 256
Third Illinois, 85
Reno, Jesse, 163, 218–19, 336
Reynolds, John G., 218, 221, 337
Richardson, Israel Bush, 170
Riley, Bennet C., 29, 78, 85–87, 111, 163–
64, 166–67, 172–76, 179, 188, 211–12,
215–16, 218, 258
Riley, John, 180, 188–89
Rincón, Manuel, 180, 182
Rio del Plan, 68, 73, 74, 76, 91, 111, 147

Rio Frio, 151, 251
Rio Grande, 17, 18, 113, 127, 130, 158,
    180, 199–200, 243, 268, 299
Río Papaloapán, 59
Ripley, Roswell, 38, 50, 55, 88–89, 93,
    104, 111, 118, 146, 177, 201
Roberson, John, 75
Roberts, Benjamin S., 147–48
Roberts, Lieutenant, 41–42
Robertson, James I., 271
Robles, Manuel, 48, 72, 83
Ruff, Charles F., 147

Saltillo, 130
San Agustin, 157–58, 160, 162, 165, 168–
    70, 176, 180, 186–87, 197, 260
San Angel, 160, 163–64, 166–69, 171,
    174–76, 178–79, 191, 197, 200, 215
San Antonio, 158, 161–62, 167–68, 179–
    81, 258
    fighting at, 176–77, 183–85
San Antonio Garita, 190, 201, 210–11
San Cosme Garita, 210, 229, 232–33, 235–38
Sanderson, Winslow, 261, 302
San Geronimo, 164, 166–71, 174, 176
San Juan de Ulúa, 11, 15, 23–24, 30, 48,
    54–55, 97
San Mateo Convent, 179, 181, 191
San Patricio Battalion, 180, 182, 188–89,
    191, 200, 225
Santa Anna, Antonio López de, 34–35,
    39, 45, 46, 48, 61, 64–67, 102–104,
    108, 116, 120–23, 133, 135, 142–44,
    177–78, 192, 195–98, 201, 208, 213,
    237, 246, 248–49, 263, 265
    and Battle of Cerro Gordo, 72–73, 75–
        77, 79, 83–85, 87–88, 92, 96–98, 110
    and Battle of Chapultepec, 215, 217, 226
    and defense of Mexico City, 150,
        154–56, 160–61, 179–80, 200–201,
        231–32, 235
    and fighting at Churubusco, 186–91
    and fighting west of Pedregal, 166–67,
        169, 171, 174, 176
Sargent, Chauncey, 40, 75
Scheina, Robert L., 6
Scott, Martin, 205

Scott, Winfield, 2, 3, 9, 10, 23, 51, 63, 68,
    70–72, 102, 125, 139, 142, 145–46,
    151–53, 177–79, 190, 193–94, 199,
    208, 211, 233, 235, 237, 243–44, 246,
    250–51, 256, 265, 268–71
    and approach to Mexico City, 153–58,
        161–63, 200, 210, 212–13
    and armistice, 195, 201, 269
    and Battle of Cerro Gordo, 74, 77–78,
        82, 84, 92, 94–97, 100–101, 110
    and Battle of Chapultepec, 214–19,
        224–25
    and campaign strategy, 15, 16–17, 61,
        104, 120, 140–41, 147–50, 180, 195–
        97, 228–29, 251, 268–69, 299
    and court of inquiry, 264–65
    and fighting at Churubusco, 181, 186–
        88, 192
    and fighting at Padierna, 165, 167–69, 176
    at Jalapa, 106–12, 115–21
    and Leonidas letter, 260
    at Mexico City, 238–43
    pacification plan of, 5, 17, 19, 34, 35,
        55–58, 61–62, 108–109, 116, 118–19,
        121–22, 124, 128, 133–34, 140, 242,
        269
    at Puebla, 125, 127–30, 133, 135–36,
        138–40, 323
    and relations with Gideon Pillow, 24, 54,
        170, 179, 197, 202, 257–59, 262–65
    and relations with James K. Polk, 12–
        16, 18–19, 262–63
    and relations with Nicholas Trist, 114–
        16, 126, 142–44
    and relations with William Worth, 64,
        128–30, 257, 261–62
    and relations with Zachary Taylor,
        17–18
    at Veracruz, 25–26, 29, 30, 34–38, 40–
        41, 44–46, 48, 52–53, 55, 303, 306
Seaman, Henry J., 143
Second Bull Run, 191
Sedgwick, John, 92, 170, 177, 184, 243,
    254–55, 342
Semmes, Raphael, 104, 115, 129, 162,
    184, 236
Shenandoah Valley Campaign, 312

Shields, James, 29, 56, 64, 70, 82, 85–88,
    95–96, 98, 107, 143–44, 179, 186–89,
    212, 221–22, 228, 230–31, 243
  and fighting at Padierna, 165, 168, 171,
    174
Shiloh, Battle of, 1, 47
Sierra Madres Mountains, 120
Singletary, Otis, 111
Smith, Edmund Kirby, 27, 28, 34, 39,
    43–44, 49, 52, 54, 77, 84, 98, 104,
    124, 137, 204, 302, 311
Smith, Ephraim Kirby, 84, 204–205
Smith, Gustavus, W., 21, 28, 32–33, 43,
    82–83, 85, 86, 179, 182
Smith, Henry, 132
Smith, James R., 31, 164, 188–89, 191
Smith, John L., 23, 56
Smith, Joseph R., 68–69, 83, 107, 110,
    120, 132, 156
Smith, Justin H., 5, 69, 92, 93, 96, 125, 144
Smith, Noah, E., 145, 151, 153–54, 186
Smith, Persifor F., 29, 42, 78, 110, 115,
    128, 142–43, 163–69, 171–72, 174–75,
    179, 182, 212, 215–16, 218, 230–31,
    258, 329
Southern Historical Society, 99
Star Spangled Banner, 9, 43, 298
Steptoe, Edward, 215
Stevens, Isaac, 32, 55, 57, 76, 95, 102, 118,
    155–56, 159, 164, 169, 177, 180–83,
    196, 210, 329
Stones River, Battle of, 1, 47
Stonesifer, Roy P., 93
Storms, Jane, 61, 120
Sumner, Edwin V., 80, 153, 158, 203, 207,
    230
Swift, Alexander J., 21
Swift, Joseph G., 21

Tacubaya, 180, 194, 197–98, 200, 215, 218,
    225, 228, 243, 255
Talcott, George H., 43, 49, 111
Taliaferro, William B., 147–48
Tampico, 17, 19, 22, 55, 299
Taylor, Francis, 44, 182, 187, 215
Taylor, Zachary, 12, 13, 14, 17–18, 26, 39,

    45, 48, 51–53, 61, 64, 97, 102, 108,
    110, 116, 126, 130, 144, 175, 180, 193,
    195, 245–46, 269
Tennery, Thomas, 107
Ten Regiment Bill, 35, 138
Terrés, Andrés, 221
Texas, 199
Texcoco (lake), 153–55
Thornton, Edward, 127, 142, 148, 266
Thornton, Seth B., 158
Torréjon, Anastasio, 173, 234
Totten, Joseph G., 23, 25, 28, 32–33, 43,
    48, 53, 111
Tower, Zealous B., 69, 74, 84–85, 159,
    172, 210–11, 216
Towner, T. H., 11, 321
Tractarianism (Oxford Movement), 59
Trist, Nicholas P., 112–13, 142, 148, 170,
    179, 194, 196, 199–200, 208, 212, 259,
    266–68
  and relations with Winfield Scott, 114–
    16, 126, 142–44
Tritschler, Martin, 136
Trousdale, William, 218, 220
Turnbull (Englishman), 142
Turnbull, William, 150
Twiggs, David E., 21–22, 27–28, 30, 37,
    41, 62, 63–64, 108, 120, 121, 126,
    128–29, 135, 143–44, 149, 154, 158–
    60, 177, 179, 212, 244
  and Battle of Cerro Gordo, 68–74, 77–
    80, 82–84, 86, 92, 94, 110, 111
  and Battle of Chapultepec, 216, 218
  and fighting at Churubusco, 182–88
  and fighting at Padierna, 163–64, 168–
    70, 176
Twiggs, Levi, 218, 221

Uncapher, Israel, 70, 106, 108, 224, 232,
    254
Upton, Burna, 53, 54, 62, 87, 101, 243
Utah, 113

Valencia, Gabriel, 160–61, 163–64, 166–
    71, 173–76, 178
Van Buren, Abraham, 199

Van Buren, Martin, 306
Vanderlinden, Pedro, 95–96
Van Dorn, Earl, 79, 86, 179
Van O'Linda, Abram, 222
Vásquez, Ciriaco, 1, 83, 86–87, 94
Veracruz, 2, 4, 7, 8, 10, 11, 15, 18, 19, 20,
    72, 77, 82, 97, 104, 105, 106–107, 109,
    112–13, 115–17, 120, 121, 123–24,
    127, 130, 137, 138, 140, 141, 145, 147,
    183, 195, 245–46, 251, 253, 265
  capitulation of, 48–50, 67
  occupation of, 54–61
  siege of, 23–49, 98, 111
Vergara, 28, 29, 30, 36
Veritas, 260–62
Vicksburg, Siege of, 99, 236, 270
Villanueva, José Guiterrez, 48
Vinton, John R., 40–41

Waite, Carlos A., 205
Walker, James, 259
Walker, Molly, 132
Walker, Samuel, 140–41, 249
Walker, William H. T., 26, 43, 132
Walker, William S., 158, 163, 167, 172, 177
Wallace, Edward S., 129
Weigley, Russell F., 208
West Point, 5, 21, 25, 32, 40, 44, 54, 80,
    87, 95, 99, 175, 177, 220, 245, 248,
    255, 264, 270
Whig Party, 12, 16, 53, 91, 129, 265, 299
Wilkins, John D., 121, 170, 177–78, 182,
    188, 192
Williams, Thomas, 49, 268
Wilson, Henry, 101, 106

Winder, John H., 135
Winders, Richard Bruce, 6, 250, 298
Wingate, Benjamin, 85, 97
Worth, William, 20–22, 26, 29, 45–46, 48,
    49, 54–55, 63–64, 72, 102, 106, 119,
    121–22, 149, 154, 156–57, 168–69,
    180, 194, 196, 198–99, 212, 228,
    259–65
  advance on San Cosme Garita, 229–30,
    232–36, 238
  and Battle of Cerro Gordo, 78, 82,
    94, 111
  and Battle of Chapultepec, 215–17, 219,
    222, 225
  and Battle of Molino del Rey, 203, 208
  and fighting at Churubusco, 185, 188–
    89, 191
  and the occupation of Puebla, 123,
    125–26, 128–30, 133
  and relations with Winfield Scott, 64,
    128–30, 144, 257, 261–62, 329
  at San Antonio, 158–59, 162, 170, 176–
    77, 182–84
Wright, George, 203, 205
Wynkoop, Francis M., 89–90, 92, 140
Wyoming, 113

Xochimilco (lake), 153–54, 157–58

Yeager, Hiram, 38, 39, 93, 98, 105, 123,
    138, 146
Yorktown, 51

Zacatepec, 160–63, 167–70